New Perspectives
on the Union War

THE NORTH'S CIVIL WAR
Andrew L. Slap, series editor

New Perspectives on the Union War

Gary W. Gallagher
and Elizabeth R. Varon,
Editors

FORDHAM UNIVERSITY PRESS
NEW YORK   2019

Copyright © 2019 Fordham University Press

All rights reserved. No part of this publication may be reproduced, stored in a retrieval system, or transmitted in any form or by any means—electronic, mechanical, photocopy, recording, or any other—except for brief quotations in printed reviews, without the prior permission of the publisher.

Fordham University Press has no responsibility for the persistence or accuracy of URLs for external or third-party Internet websites referred to in this publication and does not guarantee that any content on such websites is, or will remain, accurate or appropriate.

Fordham University Press also publishes its books in a variety of electronic formats. Some content that appears in print may not be available in electronic books.

Visit us online at www.fordhampress.com.

Library of Congress Cataloging-in-Publication Data available online at https://catalog.loc.gov.

Printed in the United States of America

21 20 19   5 4 3 2 1

First edition

Contents

Introduction
*Gary W. Gallagher and
Elizabeth R. Varon* | 1

Waiting for the Perfect Moment:
Abby Kelley Foster and Stephen
Foster's Union War
Frank J. Cirillo | 9

Elizabeth Keckly's Union War
Tamika Y. Nunley | 39

To Save the Union "in Behalf of
Conservative Men": Horatio Seymour
and the Democratic Vision for War
Jack Furniss | 63

The Union as It Was: Northern
Catholics' Conservative Unionism
William B. Kurtz | 91

"Certain Ill-Considered Phrases":
Edward Bates and the Disunionist
Dangers of Radical Rhetoric
Jesse George-Nichol | 114

"Responsible to One Another
and to God": Why Francis Lieber
Believed the Union War Must
Remain a Just War
D. H. Dilbeck | 143

Building a Union of Banks:
Salmon P. Chase and the Creation
of the National Banking System
Michael T. Caires | 160

"To Transmit and Perpetuate the
Fruits of This Victory": Union
Regimental Histories and the Great
Rebellion in Immediate Retrospect
Peter C. Luebke | 186

Notes 201
Bibliographic Note 241
List of Contributors 245
Index 247

New Perspectives
on the Union War

Introduction

*Gary W. Gallagher and
Elizabeth R. Varon*

"The United States does and must assert its authority wherever it once had power," General William T. Sherman wrote the mayor of Atlanta after capturing that city in September 1864. "Such is the National Feeling," added the general: "This Feeling assumes various shapes, but always comes back to that of *Union*." *New Perspectives on the Union War* explores, at a wide array of points along the political spectrum, the many forms patriotic sentiment took in the loyal states during the Civil War. As a group, the essays in this volume demonstrate that while there was a broad consensus the war was fought, or should be fought, for the cause of the Union, there was bitter disagreement over how to define that cause—a debate not only between political camps but also within them. Among ardent opponents of slavery, those debates concerned means and ends. Defenders of Lincoln saw emancipation as the way to fulfill the unmet promise of the Union, while the president's critics saw emancipation as an end in itself and warfare as an illegitimate means to sustain an unfree Union. In the broad middle of the political spectrum, self-styled moderates focused on the threat the Southern "Slave Power" oligarchy posed to the free-labor republic—to economic development, majority rule, and moral discipline—and debated both which policies and what sort of political tone would bring reunion on the loyal states' terms. Among conservatives, opposition to emancipation and centralization mixed with nostalgia for an imagined past, and debates focused primarily on how to differentiate the Union government from the Lincoln administration and how to support the first while rejecting the second.[1]

The eight essayists in this collection examine disparate elements of the loyal citizenry. Each also engages with the scholarly literature in ways made evident in their notes and in the bibliographical essay that closes this volume. Frank J. Cirillo and Tamika Y. Nunley address the antislavery end of the political spectrum; Jack Furniss and William B. Kurtz the more conservative segments of public opinion; and Jesse George-Nichol, D. H. Dilbeck, Michael T. Caires, and Peter C. Luebke the political center. The essays provide new insights into well-known figures such as Secretary of the Treasury Salmon P. Chase, the political philosopher Francis

Lieber, the African American author/entrepreneur Elizabeth Keckly, the abolitionist Abby Kelley Foster, New York governor Horatio Seymour, and Attorney General Edward Bates. They also offer the perspectives of common soldiers, of the partisan press, of the clergy, and of social reformers. By showing how various interest groups claimed the mantle of moderation and tacked to the center, the essays offer a counterweight to recent scholarship that emphasizes the influence of Radical Republicans and Copperhead Democrats within their respective political parties.

Frank Cirillo leads off by exploring the idealistic, aspirational strain of Northern nationalism that was dominant among reformers. Abolitionists and Radical Republicans answered conservative calls for the "Union as It Was" by envisioning the Union as it might be, purged of slavery and committed to its professed creed of equality. Cirillo demonstrates that these reformers were divided into factions. The vast majority of antislavery immediatists, following the lead of William Lloyd Garrison, embraced the Union war and the chance to cast emancipation as a military necessity and nation-saving measure. But a small and vocal faction led by the formidable husband-and-wife team of Stephen and Abby Kelley Foster insisted that moral ends required moral means and refused to support the Union war until it explicitly became a fight for emancipation. Clinging to the image of abolitionists as uncompromising purists, the Fosters fought against the emerging pro-Lincoln consensus in abolitionism; even after Lincoln issued the Emancipation Proclamation, they cast about for more radical politicians to replace him as the head of the Union war effort. These divisions over wartime means and ends translated into distinct positions on Reconstruction. While those in Garrison's camp celebrated wartime emancipation as the apotheosis of the abolition movement and a mission accomplished, the Fosters regarded the antislavery struggle as unfinished until blacks exercised full citizenship and prejudice itself was uprooted.

Tamika Nunley's essay on Elizabeth Keckly highlights the theme of black leadership in the Union war effort. While Keckly is best known for her role as Mary Todd Lincoln's seamstress and chronicler of the Lincoln White House, Nunley brings to light her wartime political activism on behalf of black refugees and soldiers. Nunley shows how Keckly, through her leadership of the Contraband Relief Association, set in motion a vision for black equality and citizenship. Keckly's social and political organizing—her skillful mobilization of the press, the churches, and indeed of her own celebrity—both addressed the dire material conditions in refugee camps and projected a message of self-determination and independence to the freedpeople of the District of Columbia. Like Cirillo's essay,

Nunley's points up the contingent nature of antislavery gains during the war. Black freedom in Washington, DC, was tenuous, as proslavery whites resisted complying with the 1862 DC abolition act. Keckly and her fellow female activists responded by promoting education and enfranchisement, invoking black men's and women's patriotism as a pillar of a more perfect Union.

Jack Furniss's essay accounts for the political success of the influential Democrat Horatio Seymour, who secured the governorship of New York in 1862. Furniss explains why a significant portion of the electorate was drawn to the Democrats' message in 1862. Seymour appealed to voters, including swing voters such as former Whigs, by trumpeting the legitimacy of partisan opposition in wartime; by calling for a limited, constitutional war of conciliation, to speed restoration of the Union after Northern victory; and by rejecting Republican efforts to label all Democrats as "anti-war" and insisting instead that Northern politics pitted patriotic "conservatives" against disunionist "radicals." In a careful balancing act, Seymour criticized the handling of the war but not the soldiers and generals who fought it—and he sought to claim Lincoln for conservatism by shielding the president from the influence of radicals. Seymour's hope that the war could be won without revolutionary measures against slavery or impeding the constitutional liberties of the North became increasingly chimerical as the war ground on. But, Furniss cautions, we should not project the stridently anti-Lincoln Copperhead rhetoric of 1863–1865 back in time, onto the war's early phases; mainstream Democrats initially tapped into a vast reservoir of national feelings to harness its latent electoral appeal. Seymour's fealty was to a Union that could command the affection and loyalty of conservatives in the North, Border States, and South.

As Will Kurtz's essay reveals, Catholic Americans believed saving the Union also meant preserving the nation's uniquely tolerant laws designed to protect freedom of worship for religious minorities. Some hoped immigrant and Catholic bravery and sacrifice on the battlefield would end the pervasive anti-Catholic nativism that festered despite the laws. Catholics' attachment to the Union led them to resist both the Confederate rebellion and, eventually, the more radical war measures taken by Republicans. As conservatives and Democrats, Catholics strongly resisted attempts to enlarge the purpose of the war, especially on the issue of emancipating Southern slaves. Links between antislavery politics and anti-Catholic nativism in the antebellum North stoked anxieties that Republican attacks on slavery might be followed by assaults on Catholics' and immigrants' civil liberties and citizenship. Kurtz focuses on the leadership of two highly influential men: John Hughes (1797–1864), the Irish American archbishop of New York, and the Bostonian Patrick Donahoe (1811–1901), owner of the *Boston Pilot*, a widely published newspaper. On behalf of Catholic conservatives, these men rallied the faithful with their own distinct pro-war appeals, emphasizing the bravery of Irish Catholic soldiers, the patriotism of the clergy, the need for a united front among Catholics—and the purported dangers posed by Republican abolitionism to the war effort. In their reckoning, emancipation would deepen sectional alienation and divides within the North. Only a return to Democratic conservatism could secure victory and peace.

Jesse George-Nichol shifts attention to Attorney General Edward Bates, elucidating the subtle differences between his brand of conservative Republicanism and President Lincoln's own moderate positions. Both Bates and Lincoln staunchly opposed the extension of slavery and regarded secession as utterly illegitimate and unacceptable. As a conservative, Bates also hoped to subordinate the slavery question and blamed abolitionists and secessionists alike for agitating it, while Lincoln did not think the question could be avoided and considered slaveholders primarily responsible for bringing on the sectional crisis. Bates imagined that his role was to serve as a bulwark, within the Lincoln administration, against extreme abolitionism and to protect the president against a demagogic tendency to resort to divisive language. A Missouri Whig who shared Lincoln's admiration for Henry Clay, Bates urged the president to uphold the distinct political ethos of the western Border States. Supporting a form of conservatism that valued stability, tradition, pragmatism, and compromise, Bates threw himself into the Union war effort and wielded all the powers of his office to defend the Lincoln administration and its war policies. By 1864, however, he was disillusioned. In his mind, the war to preserve the Union and the Constitution had descended into lawlessness; the war to combat Southern radicalism had become instead a crusade of Northern radicalism; and the war for a white, free-labor republic had become a war for a revolutionary, biracial democracy. Bates believed that the "malign influences" of Radical Republicans had confounded his vision of a limited but decisive war.[2]

Building on the theme of limited versus all-encompassing war, D. H. Dilbeck explains why Francis Lieber believed a military effort to save the Union had to remain a justly waged conflict. A Berlin-born jurist and intellectual who immigrated to America in 1827, Lieber argued that if the Union military effort lapsed into indiscriminate violence and barbarity, Federal armies would fail truly to preserve the Union—even if they vanquished Confederate forces on the battlefield. An unjustly prosecuted war would render hollow all the grand claims loyal citizens made about their Union as a beacon of enlightened civilization. For that reason, thought Lieber, Federals could lose their Union not only through Confederate military triumph but also through their own army's immoral conduct. Lieber made it his personal quest to ensure Federal armies waged a just war against the Confederacy, a quest that culminated in April 1863 with the issuance of the Lieber-drafted General Orders No. 100—a primer on the laws of war designed to guide Union military officers and that eventually became known as the Lieber Code. Dilbeck's essay also argues that recent scholarship has failed to convey how many loyal citizens shared Lieber's concerns. Without understanding the degree to which the meaning of Union and the need to wage a just war to save the Union were inseparable, suggests Dilbeck, it is impossible to grasp the character of the Federal military effort.

In the process of fighting to restore the Union, the Civil War generation not only defended their vision of a democratic republic but also redefined economic relationships linking the states, the central government, and the American people. In Michael Caires's essay, Secretary of the Treasury Salmon P. Chase, a prewar Democrat who had been hostile to banks and banking, holds center stage for much of a story that led to the creation of a stable and uniform currency and a system of national banks—both of which demonstrated how the war for Union brought Americans together through new national institutions that in turn transformed the economic lives of millions. For two generations before the war, America's system of state-chartered commercial banks worked against the nation's commercial union by making exchange complicated and expensive. Informed by decades of commentary on the need for a solution to this issue, Chase led the wartime effort to unify the country's banks. In the push to create this new financial system, Republicans in Congress clashed over their conflicting visions of what the Union was and what it might be. This same conversation played out in the popular press as Americans oscillated between fears of centralization and high hopes for the economic prosperity national banks might bring. With the passage of two national bank acts during the war, both these hopes and fears were partially realized as national banks reshaped and promoted economic relationships between regions and increased the federal presence in the national market.

Peter Luebke's essay rounds out the collection with an examination of several dozen regimental histories that appeared immediately after the Civil War. This overlooked genre, as Luebke indicates, reveals a great deal about how soldiers thought of themselves and the broader meaning of the conflict. The regimental histories served as a form of collaborative commemoration, often written by individual authors but drawing on letters, diaries, and other evidence from comrades. Intended audiences included the soldiers and their families, the communities from which the men went into the army as citizen-soldiers, and future historians who would benefit from participants' testimony. Typically noncontroversial in tenor, the regimental histories nonetheless illuminate crucial aspects of the men's view of the conflict. They celebrated the patriotic service of citizens who discharged their military obligation to a nation worth defending and identified preserving the Union as by far the war's most prominent goal and important accomplishment. They blamed slaveholding oligarchs of the South for bringing the cataclysm upon the nation and pronounced emancipation a military tool necessary to suppress the rebellion and prevent future threats to the republic. While some regimental histories celebrated the war as a struggle for African American freedom, the broad consensus in their pages pointed more to an understanding of the war as the shattering of the Slave Power.

Taken together, these essays show a concept of "Union" capacious enough to include a wide range of political agendas.[3] Three core convictions united loyal Americans across the many political fault lines that divided the loyal states. The first was that affection rather than coercion should hold the Union together. Abraham Lincoln famously conjured this "affective theory" of Union in his first inaugural address in 1861. "We are not enemies, but friends," insisted the president: "We must not be enemies. Though passion may have strained, it must not break our bonds of affection. The mystic chords of memory, stretching from every battle-field, and patriot grave, to every heart and hearthstone, all over this broad land, will yet swell the chorus of the Union, when again touched, as surely they will be, by the better angels of our nature." Frederick Douglass gave that theory his own reading in 1863, conjuring a new, just Union. "We are fighting for something incomparably better than the old Union," he stated. "We are fighting for unity; unity of idea, unity of sentiment, unity of object, unity of institutions, in which there shall be no North, no South, no East, no West, no black, no white, but a solidarity of the nation, making every slave free, and every free man a voter."[4]

The second conviction pronounced disunionism a lethal and highly contagious disease. Unionists on the left imagined that a strain of Confederate disunionism afflicted the Copperhead right; Unionists on the right imagined that radical abolitionists harbored destructive impulses and overweening ambitions similar to those evident among Slave Power aristocrats; and Unionists in the mainstream worried that Northerners on the extreme right and left aided, wittingly or unwittingly, the extremists in the South. All agreed that disunionist doctrines and tactics had to be stamped out before Unionism could prevail. Over the course of the war, Radical Republicans and abolitionists were more successful at tarnishing Copperheads with disloyalty than Copperheads were at tarnishing them, in part because the Peace Democrats' argument that the war effort was a failure proved offensive to many Northern civilians and soldiers. In contrast, antislavery advocates, after emancipation was promulgated and black enlistment underway, more often emphasized the military successes of the Lincoln administration and the war effort and thus better avoided the stigma of defeatism. Disdain for the Copperheads became a cohering force among Unionists in the second half of the war. For example, Abial Hall Edwards of the 29th Maine Infantry observed that the two parties contending for supremacy in 1864 were "Unionists & Dis Unionists." "I think as much of a war Democrat as I do of a Lincoln man," he added. Edwards would vote for Lincoln rather than "give up one iota of the victories we have gained to the Rebel hords."[5]

The third shared conviction was that the slavery issue had to be neutralized in order for the Union to achieve stability and fulfill its destiny. How to remove slavery as the principal source of disunion—whether by compromise, reform, or revolution—was the rub. Ironies abound in the way wartime debates over that question evolved. Self-styled conservatives found themselves in the position of arguing, in effect, for wrenching change—namely the *undoing* of the transformations the war wrought, including emancipation, the ascendance of the Republican Party, and the consolidation of the federal government's power. The "Union as It Was" slogan sounded more unrealistic and impractical over time. Political moderates, for their part, found themselves defending as necessary and pragmatic policies that seemed radical at the war's outset—but even as they struggled to establish emancipation they also worked to contain it and to establish new political lines marking off mainstream positions (support for a free-labor economy) from radical ones (support for black suffrage and full citizenship). The sharpest irony is that in order to achieve victory, the Union called upon the military service of immigrants it had marginalized and African Americans it had oppressed. This irony was not lost on immigrant or free black communities in the North, which engaged in complex debates weighing the benefits and obligations of citizenship.[6]

As the essays in this collection suggest, anyone hoping to understand the main currents of political thought, popular sentiment, and ideological friction in the mid–nineteenth century must begin with an acknowledgment of the centrality of Union. As a concept and a shorthand term for the legacy bequeathed to the Civil War generation by their revolutionary forebears, it fired the imagination and inspired actions that, in the end, salvaged the nation and created the possibility of more fully realizing the nation's promise.

We are pleased to thank all the authors in this collection, each of whom has strong ties to the Department of History and to the John L. Nau III Center for Civil War History at the University of Virginia. Each contributor has played a role in fostering a sense of shared investigation in nineteenth-century US history at UVA that has been immensely productive and enjoyable over the past decade and more. More specifically, Will Kurtz, the center's managing director, and Frank Cirillo, who helped coordinate many presentations at the center, proved invaluable. We also thank Andrew Slap, who moved expeditiously in helping us place the project at Fordham University Press. Finally, we acknowledge the unwavering support of John Nau, whose interest and generosity have been remarkable. This book, in significant measure, is an outgrowth of his enthusiasm for Civil War studies at UVA.

Waiting for the Perfect Moment

Abby Kelley Foster and Stephen Foster's Union War

Frank J. Cirillo

As it had done for decades, the abolitionist community of Massachusetts assembled near Framingham to commemorate the Fourth of July in the summer of 1861. In years past, the air at the pastoral grove had been ripe with denunciations of the Union—the American system of government that, under the Constitution, sanctioned chattel slavery. It was at Framingham that the leader of the American Anti-Slavery Society, William Lloyd Garrison, had burned the Constitution seven years earlier to unanimous approval from the attendees. In 1861, however, the wafting winds carried the sounds of cacophony rather than of unison. With the onset of the American Civil War, Garrison and the vast majority of abolitionists had reversed their stances on the Union in order to harness the Union war for emancipationist ends. At Framingham, praise for the Constitution replaced the brimstone—and literal fire—of yore in speech after speech, until a married couple, Stephen and Abby Kelley Foster, proceeded to shatter that pro-war consensus.[1]

Stephen Foster spoke first, expressing his disbelief that his colleagues, including Garrison and the famed orator Wendell Phillips, were "heart and soul in this war." The Union government, Foster declared, "perpetrated the crimes which have disgraced the country for the last seventy-five years." It allowed slavery to continue in four border slave states, returned fugitives, and brooked no talk of emancipation. How, he wondered, did the Union deserve anything other than "obloquy"? It was, in his view, the same "covenant with death and agreement with hell" that Garrison had declared it to be when he had burned the Constitution on that very stage. As a "citizen deeply interested in the honor and welfare of our common country," Foster concluded that he could give "no support or countenance" to the Union as it then stood. Following a heated series of arguments between Stephen and the pro-war speakers, Abby then closed the meeting by sifting through the "confusion of tongues" to validate the Fosters' shared antiwar position.[2]

This essay discusses the Fosters' stand against the Union war. It explores their dissent from the wartime antislavery consensus, as exhibited at Framingham. By doing so, it positions itself in an ongoing historiographical debate over emancipation and Abraham Lincoln's Union war. In recent years, a number of prominent scholars have cast the Union war as an inexorable, virtually inevitable march toward emancipation supported by an antislavery public and soldiery and led by a closet abolitionist—Lincoln. An opposing school has argued instead that the Union war in its early years was prosecuted solely to save the Union, rather than to infringe on the peculiar institution. Lincoln, these studies argue, moved against slavery only when it became politically feasible—and only when it became clear that the Union could not be saved by less drastic means. The Fosters' rejection of the Union war—and their justification that they were acting out of patriotic concern for the national welfare—makes sense only through this second interpretation. Rather than resisting the pull of history toward an evidently inevitable act of emancipation, the Fosters were staying out of a conflict that had nothing to do with ending slavery.[3]

Indeed, not even those reformers who supported the Union war believed that Lincoln would willingly prosecute an antislavery crusade. Lincoln, as the prowar Garrison admitted in his newspaper *The Liberator* in June 1861, intended to "restore the Union" as it was—with slavery intact. He was, a pro-war correspondent later told the *Liberator*, an ill-educated oaf lacking the ability to "foresee the critical position of the nation" and would never end slavery unless spurred to by the "necessity of the hour." As abolitionists clearly understood, emancipation was far from a given at the start of the Civil War.[4]

Why, then, did most abolitionists support the Union war from the start of the conflict—and what made the Fosters different? The answer lies in the idiosyncratic brand of American exceptionalism practiced by abolitionists, here referred to as moral nationalism. As mentioned in antislavery studies, immediatist abolitionists—those reformers who demanded immediate and unconditional emancipation as well as some form of black incorporation into the postemancipation polity—cast their patriotism as support not for the Union as it was but for the Union as it should be. A slaveless and multiracial Union would, as Garrison prophesied in March 1861, have a "future full of richest promise" as a beacon of global democracy that was "one in spirit, in purpose, in glorious freedom." That vision of a more perfect Union shaped the responses of all abolitionists to the Civil War. Those reformers who supported the Union, like Garrison and Phillips, did so in the belief that their intervention could transform an imperfect war into an emancipationist endeavor. They would, their fellow pro-war reformer Moncure Conway declared in the fall of 1861, not "stand back and say, 'I will wait until this is a noble war—a war for humanity.' Let all enter and make it a noble war." Garrison, Conway, Frederick Douglass, and other reformers thus backed the war as moral nationalists, aspiring to overrule Lincoln and create a more perfect Union.[5]

That same engine fueled the Fosters' opposition to the Union war. Though often overlooked in scholarship, the two figures were central to the abolitionist movement. From the 1840s, the pair played key roles in the American Anti-Slavery Society, lecturing and serving in leadership positions. As the Republican Party rose to prominence in the late 1850s and then took the reins of government in 1860, the Fosters became thorns in the side of reformers like Garrison who sought to use the newly ascendant party to achieve moralistic ends. As discussed by their few biographers, the Fosters came to lead a small faction of reformers opposed to any interaction with the Republicans or the Union cause. These scholars have presented the Fosters as unbending pacifists who refused to adapt to changing times or recognize the opportunities presented by the Civil War. This essay argues instead that the Fosters' stance derived from their moral nationalism and, in particular, from the idiosyncratic corollary espoused by their hardline faction: that national regeneration required moral purity. Moralistic ends, in their view, required equally moralistic means. Those activists who employed imperfect methods would adulterate their goals and forfeit their moral objectivity—their abilities, as reformers aloof from the corrupt mainstream, to perceive the true path to national greatness. The antislavery mission would thus fail.[6]

This essay demonstrates how the Fosters' unique interpretation of moral nationalism shaped their response to a national crisis in which antislavery change was far from inevitable. In the buildup to the Civil War, the Fosters assailed the Republicans as sirens that would lure abolitionists away from their radical ideals. The secession crisis brought discord between the pair, as Abby advocated disunion while Stephen encouraged Union coercion. With the onset of war, however, the Fosters united to denounce the conflict. While abolitionists like Conway refused to wait to intervene until the war became "perfect," the Fosters advocated waiting until the Union war was worthy of—and morally safe for—abolitionist support. The Union war as it then stood, they argued, did not fulfill such requirements. Where pro-war reformers saw a war that was imperfect but fixable, the Fosters saw a conflict that seemed unlikely to birth the more perfect Union they desired—one premised on both emancipation and racial equality. An immoral fight in which neither side evinced any sympathy for the slaves, they argued, would not beget such a nation. On the contrary, it would corrupt its antislavery supporters to compromise their own principles. The Fosters thus spent the first years of the war railing against Lincoln and chastising their pro-war colleagues. Though Stephen proved less doctrinaire than Abby in his categorical disdain for the Union war, the two nonetheless effectively led the antiwar opposition within the abolitionist movement.

Though Garrison, Phillips, and other pro-war abolitionists celebrated the Emancipation Proclamation of January 1863 as vindicating their own interpretation of the Union war, the Fosters refused to yield. In their quest for moral Union, the Fosters had long held an expansive view of postemancipation black rights. They envisioned an egalitarian nation bereft of racial prejudice and in which African Americans had attained full political, civil, and social equality. Expedient emancipation, enacted from amoral motivations, would allow racial prejudice to remain intact—and would thus leave the expansive moral Union that the Fosters desired as elusive as ever. Indeed, the move of Garrison and other pro-war reformers toward full-fledged adulation of Lincoln, despite his lack of interest in postemancipation black rights, convinced the Fosters that they had been correct all along. Pro-war reformers had fulfilled the Fosters' grim prophecy, losing sight of their once radical goals. In response, the Fosters shifted their oppositional efforts from the Union war generally to Lincoln specifically. Bending his rules about political noninvolvement to combat pro-war abolitionists' partisanship for Lincoln, Stephen helped found the Cleveland Movement, which sought to defeat the president by championing John C. Frémont as an alternative candidate in the election of 1864. Stephen's turn at political intervention fell short, however, as did his and Abby's attempts to maintain the radicalism of the antislavery movement: Following the victory of the emancipationist Union the following year, Garrison and his followers retired from organized reform. In a conflict where antislavery goals were never inevitable—and never fully achieved—the Fosters waited in vain for the perfect moment to arrive. By exploring the Fosters' wartime actions, this essay opens a window onto the meanings of the Union war for those Northerners who refused to settle for the Union as it was—or as the war made it.

Obscure though they may be in modern historical memory, the Fosters were well-established figures in antislavery reform by the time of the Civil War. Abigail Kelley, born into a modest Quaker family in Massachusetts in 1811, was first drawn to abolitionism at the age of eighteen, upon hearing a lecture by William Lloyd Garrison. Though she had studied to be an educator and spent most of the 1830s teaching at local schools, her "whole soul" gradually became "filled with the subject" of antislavery reform; "it would not leave me in school hours," she would recall years later to her daughter. In 1837, Kelley decided to take up the "divine call" full time, quitting her teaching job in favor of lecturing for the Lynn Anti-Slavery Society, a local affiliate of Garrison's American Anti-Slavery Society. She soon became the fundraising agent for the group, which put her in touch with the national society. From there, Kelley ascended to the national antislavery stage. Her uncompromising positions—she rejected Quakerism by the end of the 1830s for not having a strong enough antislavery stance—won her both fame and infamy, as did her presence as a woman in the public sphere openly advocating for gender equality. Kelley embraced the spotlight—and endured the gendered slings and arrows that women's oratory provoked. She gave her first antislavery speech at a female antislavery convention in Philadelphia in 1838, which was disrupted by rioters enraged at the sight of white women and black men interacting on stage. Upon her election to the business committee of the American Anti-Slavery Society in 1840, a number of outraged male abolitionists abandoned the society to form a more conservative rival organization. Opposition aside, by the 1840s Kelley had become a leading voice for antislavery reform and women's rights.[7]

Kelley would meet her ideological soulmate, Stephen Symonds Foster, the same decade. Foster, born to a devout Congregational family in New Hampshire

Figure 1 Abby Kelley Foster. This lithograph, published in 1846, is based on a daguerreotype taken in Philadelphia.
Source: Library of Congress, Prints and Photographs Division, reproduction no. LC-DIG-pga-13043.

in 1809, had first encountered abolitionism as a student at Dartmouth College. Even as he studied to become a missionary, Foster became increasingly invested in the antislavery cause. After being offered a scholarship by his theological seminary in return for ending his abolitionist advocacy, Foster abandoned his clerical studies and became a lecturer for the New Hampshire Anti-Slavery Society in 1839. The young man soon developed a reputation as a confrontational and unyielding firebrand, known for denouncing the proslavery tendencies of organized religion. It was the militancy of Foster and his close friend Parker Pillsbury, a fellow wayward Congregationalist from New Hampshire who had devoted himself to the moral purist strain of abolitionism, that first drew the attention of Abby Kelley, leading her to travel to their home state in 1841. A courtship between Abby and Stephen ensued, which ended in marriage in 1845 and the birth of their only child, Alla, in 1847.

The Fosters thereby began a partnership that helped shape the antislavery movement in the decades before the Civil War. They served as leading lecturers and committee members of the American Anti-Slavery Society. Together, they traveled to Ohio in 1846 to help revitalize the sagging fortunes of abolitionism there. Along with Pillsbury, they helped create the Western Anti-Slavery Society. The same year, Abby took the fledgling organ of western abolitionism, the *Anti-Slavery Bugle*, under her wing. She recruited an Ohio abolitionist, Benjamin Jones, to edit the struggling newspaper and organized a successful fundraising drive to put it on solid ground. The *Bugle* would reflect her uncompromising views until its dissolution after the start of the Civil War. The Fosters continued their mutually supportive activities in the 1850s, as both spoke at women's rights conventions throughout the decade. By then it had also become apparent that Abby's star was rising within the movement faster than Stephen's. In recognition of her financial skills, she became the lead fundraising agent of the American Anti-Slavery Society in 1854. She also became the general agent, or chief scheduling manager, of the organization three years later. Abby and to a lesser extent Stephen had thus become leading lights within abolitionism before the outbreak of war.[8]

As followers of Garrison and his American Anti-Slavery Society, the Fosters in the 1840s became wholehearted supporters of the organization's platform, known as moral suasion or Garrisonianism. Garrisonians rejected the Constitution as proslavery—an illegitimate charter that made the entire American system of government equally unsuitable. Rather than engage in reform through political involvement, moral suasionists advocated coming out of politics altogether. They aimed to reframe the nation along the moralistic lines of the Declaration of Independence, throwing aside the Constitution. Garrisonians also promoted disunion as an alternative to continued communion with slaveholders, in the hope that a temporary sectional separation would destroy slavery and allow for an eventual reunion on moralistic grounds. In addition, most moral suasionists promulgated the pacifistic doctrine of nonresistance, which discouraged the use of force to resist evil. The Fosters upheld these tenets as faithful moral suasionists throughout the antebellum years.[9]

Moral suasionists comprised one of two competing sects in the wider antebellum abolitionist movement, alongside the group known as political abolitionists. That faction included many African American reformers, such as Frederick Douglass. Douglass, a former protégé of Garrison, came by the 1850s to believe that the Constitution was actually an antislavery document. Though succeeding generations had adulterated its intent, the Constitution, in his view, could serve someday as the basis for an antislavery republic. Douglass thus spurned the Garrisonians in a public rebuke, earning Garrison's lasting enmity. In the 1850s, Douglass and other political abolitionists sought to create radical political parties to foster emancipation through the extant political system. Douglass also pushed back against the moral suasionist doctrines of disunion and nonresistance. Disunion, he argued, would leave slaves at the whims of their masters indefinitely. Nonresistance was also a counterproductive doctrine. Only militant revolts in the South paired with political action in the North, he argued, would overthrow slavery. Throughout the decade leading up to the Civil War, Douglass and other political abolitionists clashed repeatedly with loyal Garrisonians like the Fosters.[10]

Over these years, the Fosters also developed their own, unique brand of moral nationalism: While most reformers viewed emancipation and black citizenship as their paramount objectives, the Fosters also offered top billing to the concept of moral purity. They and the hardline faction they would lead believed that abolitionists had to employ spotless means to achieve emancipationist ends. Anything less would end in disaster. Their fellow antiwar activist Alfred Love explained their position in an 1861 letter. Abolitionism, Love noted, was the "synonym of purity, love, and perfection." Reformers, he argued, had to remain aloof from mainstream society, occupying a "standpoint high above" the base fray. Should they do otherwise—should they become "drift-wood" submerged in the "swelling tide" of the corrupt mainstream—abolitionists would "surrender our strongholds of virtue." Reformers who took shortcuts, employing impure means to facilitate their idealistic ends, would lose their moral objectivity—their ability to guide the nation from on high. Moreover, they would accomplish nothing by doing so. As the antiwar reformer Henry Grew declared the same year, abolitionists could not "do evil" so that "good may come." Immoral means could not beget moral ends. Morally flexible reformers would thereby damage the antislavery mission for no gain.[11]

The Fosters saw political antislavery parties as the basest form of impurity. In the decades before the Civil War, they opposed political organizations that claimed to offer the solution to slavery, such as the Liberty and Free-Soil Parties. The "compromises of the Constitution," Abby explained in 1850, were too great to allow for actual reform from within the political system. All antislavery activism would be "utterly shorn of all strength while bound to it." Antislavery political parties were sirens—false prophets whose only purpose was to prevent genuine antislavery forces from gaining a foothold in the public imagination. True abolitionists thus could not mingle with tainted political parties, appealing though the parties might seem. As Abby told Phillips later in the 1850s, "there can be no middle ground for us while slavery exists." It was this unfaltering belief in moral purity that would shape the Fosters' responses to the Republicans and their Union war.[12]

The rise of the Republican Party in the mid-1850s would lead to an irreparable breach between the Fosters and most moral suasionists. Until that time, the couple had marched in solidarity with the rest of the movement. As the Republicans gained national prominence, however, movement leaders began to reconsider their views of antislavery politics. Phillips, Abby noted in a letter to the famed orator, had begun believing that the "destiny of the anti-slavery pioneers was to fill up the trenches over which politicians might walk" toward moral enlightenment—to lay the groundwork for antislavery parties. Though the Republicans were far from perfect—they opposed the extension of slavery into the western territories rather than slavery itself—these abolitionists saw the party's popularity as a sign that moral suasion was succeeding. Reformers had made possible the national ascendance of a party that would at least chip away at the proslavery political consensus. Most moral suasionists thus became increasingly reluctant to direct their fire at the Republicans. "Was it dangerous to our cause to admit that we had made progress?" asked Garrison at the end of the decade. What was wrong with preferring the Republicans and the modicum of change they would bring to the proslavery Democrats?[13]

The Fosters rejected such a proposition. "I have never before differed" with movement leaders "on any material point," Abby wrote Phillips amid the emergence of the Republicans. While Phillips believed that abolitionists should build bridges for politicians to walk over, Abby argued that reformers should not "lie down and *bid* them walk over." Politicians would be worthy of abolitionist support only when they had walked over the path themselves and attained moral enlightenment, combating slavery in the name of justice. Should abolitionists mingle with politicians who had not yet achieved moral perfection, they would forfeit their own purity. And the Republicans, to the Fosters, were far from perfect. The party, Abby wrote Phillips, was yet another in a long line of morally flawed, political threats to abolitionism. "Those who have any anti-slavery in their souls" should be "utterly disgusted" by the Republicans, she concluded. As an impure antislavery vessel that could only harm the abolitionist crusade, the upstart party deserved only scorn from true reformers.[14]

The Fosters thus acted to defend what they saw as the heart of the antislavery movement—moral purity—from those reformers enamored of Republican pragmatism. Their first public dissents arose at a meeting of the New England Anti-Slavery Convention, an affiliate of the Garrisonian movement, in June 1856. As abolitionist leaders praised Radical Republican politicians like Charles Sumner for speaking out against slavery, Stephen Foster rose to declare that all politicians who "promise[d] support to the Federal Government" were "necessarily tainted" by the ignoble dust of a proslavery political system. "The mission of true anti-slavery," Stephen reiterated, was to separate the morally pure "wheat from the chaff." Abolitionists could not decide now to "accept the chaff *as* wheat." They would imperil the antislavery agenda by doing so.[15]

Writing after the meeting, Abby further explained that the Republican Party was "slaveholding" because it supported the Constitution. All who "stand on its platform" were "indirect slaveholders." Moral relativity had no place in her vision. Republicans, in her view, were functionally as proslavery as the Democrats. No member of the party deserved to be "eulogize[d] as if he were an abolitionist." As Phillips, Garrison, and other abolitionists continued eulogizing the Republicans, however, Abby began fretting in later years that they had become irredeemably "Republicanized." She went as far as to declare at an 1859 meeting that the Republicans were "steadily sucking the very blood from our veins." The Fosters thus persisted in their idiosyncratic beliefs, resisting the growing abolitionist consensus in favor of the Republicans.[16]

The Fosters' uncompromising words drew censure from their colleagues. At the 1859 meeting, Garrison labeled Abby's allusion to Republicans as vampires an "unduly desponding and lugubrious" statement. Garrison's ally Maria Weston Chapman became perhaps their harshest critic. The Fosters and Pillsbury, she told a fellow abolitionist, were "faithful to their own hasty and half formed idea—their own crude conception of duty; but they are not faithful to us." Given the close-knit nature of the small moral suasionist movement, ideological disagreements quickly transformed into personal rifts. Pillsbury, an increasingly frustrated Chapman soon told Phillips, was "far more sensible and right minded than Stephen and Abby." Stephen was even worse than Abby, she observed. The "effort to do one's duty as the wife of such a man," she mocked, would "break down [a] Giantess." The Fosters became shunned outcasts within the Garrisonian movement.[17]

The Fosters' standing within—and fealty to—the movement at large eroded even further in 1859. That year, Abby, the fundraising agent for a society desperately in need of money, requested aid from all available sources, including Republicans. She soon began hearing rumors that Garrison had "emphatically declared" at an antislavery meeting that Kelley had "been fraudulent and obtained money under false pretenses." Abby took offense at the accusation, which struck at the core of her reformist identity—her moral uprightness. When Garrison wrote to smooth things over, explaining that he had indeed criticized her actions but had never mentioned her by name, Abby politely but firmly rebuffed the overture. The *Liberator* editor, she maintained, had to retract his intimation that she was not a "woman of integrity—that I am capable of fraud." Attempting to keep the matter cordial, Abby concluded by noting that she had talked of their correspondence with no one—"not even my husband, from whom I am not wont to withhold any thing."[18]

Garrison, however, exploded in a series of retorts. He declared that Abby had "magnified [a] molehill" to a "mountainous size." Her course of branding the Republicans as the "most dangerous obstacle in our path" was "utterly indefensible." The notion that they were morally comparable to "satanic Democracy" was absurd. Nevertheless, Garrison denied insulting her. Perhaps, he concluded, Abby's misplaced hysteria indicated that she had a "highly excited state of mind." Garrison thus rather cruelly derided the mental health of his erstwhile ally. He also suffocated the Fosters' antislavery influence: That year, Abby complained to Phillips that her and Stephen's "resolutions have ever been smothered" by the "immense personal influence of Mr. Garrison." His "dictatorship" worked to prevent all dissent, as their resolutions were constantly tabled without discussion. By 1859, all "cordial feeling" between the Fosters and their fellow reformers had disappeared, as a reformer wrote Phillips. "It is *war* with them I think." The Fosters were loyal followers no more.[19]

Disillusionment with Garrison sometimes led the Fosters in strange directions. Concurrent with the personal animosities of the late 1850s, Stephen began advocating a new tactic: creating a political party. As a moral suasionist, the New

Hampshire reformer had long opposed political involvement. Political parties, after all, had to pledge allegiance to the proslavery Constitution. As Stephen wrote a fellow reformer, however, the constitutional bulwarks supporting slavery were not weakening under moral suasionist pressure. Indeed, Republicanized Garrisonians now seemed intent on "unit[ing] politically" with proslavery forces, thereby upholding the extant political system. By contrast, the "great national party" that Stephen envisioned would not work within constitutional bounds. Rather, it would attempt to "overthrow the government" through the ballot box, pledging to dismantle the political system upon attaining power. Stephen explained his actions further to Phillips. The "best way to demolish the institutions" that supported slavery, he argued, was to "substitute for these institutions of freedom." Moral suasionist leaders had abandoned that revolutionary platform in favor of working with Republicans. The work of the American Anti-Slavery Society, he confessed, was thus no longer "my work." He would labor "outside of the society," building a righteous party that would enact a revolution through political force. Stephen thus maintained his focus on moral purity even as he adopted unconventional tactics.[20]

Stephen's quixotic political dream met with derision from other abolitionists. Samuel May Jr. offered the plan as an example of the couple's willingness to "take up an adverse position" on "any pretty tolerable pretext." Stephen's idea, May declared, was "incongruous, self-contradictory, and absurd." May even suspected that Abby, though she "always had a very warm and natural sympathy in her husband's persevering labors to advance what he believed true," lacked faith in his plan. May was right in this suspicion: Stephen confessed to Phillips that his "greatest embarrassment in pursuing the course I have marked out for myself is the position and feelings of my wife." Abby, he noted, still attached "undue importance" to cooperation with the American Anti-Slavery Society. She could not abandon her lingering attachment to the institution—or to political abstention. Stephen thus regretted that they could not "see eye to eye in this matter." Despite their disagreement on the issue, Abby defended her husband from accusations of impropriety. Stephen, strange as his ideas seemed, sought to create a "truly anti-slavery party." Abby would continue to defend Stephen even as she remained committed to moral suasion. His experiment culminated in a "Political Anti-Slavery Convention" in September 1860, intended to give form to his idea. After it became apparent that his project was going nowhere, Stephen returned to the American Anti-Slavery Society.[21]

As Stephen's plans faltered, the Republicans and their candidate, Abraham Lincoln, gained traction ahead of the November presidential election. Abby, raising funds in Ohio for the Western Anti-Slavery Society, made clear her position on the election in an October letter. "Those who vote for Lincoln," she noted, "are ashamed to do so in all such places" as had the ethical training to know right from wrong. Though other abolitionists argued that the Republicans were a lesser evil when compared to Democrats, the Fosters refused to choose any evil, lest they compromise their much-cherished moral integrity. Abby, as she admitted to Phillips soon after Lincoln's victory, had "hoped for the success of the Republican party," but she had not done so out of hope for the progress that the Republicans would achieve. Rather, she believed that the Republicans would reveal the true depths of their depravity once in power. The leading moral suasionists, once they had realized that the party was "not to be trusted for any good thing," would see the error of their ways. "We shall hardly need to wait a year," she prophesied, "in order to see Garrison [offer] resolutions as condemnatory of the Republican as of the Democratic Party." The "long quarrel" between the Fosters and the rest of the movement would thus end, and the erstwhile allies would "be all brought together" on an anti-Republican platform. Abby thus anticipated the vindication of her hardline views.[22]

Confident as her prediction was, Abby could not foresee the upheaval that was soon to come. Indeed, reflecting the contingency of the moment, the Fosters had no idea that the election would produce a national crisis. Having lived through an era of political brinksmanship in which Southern threats of disunion coerced Northern politicians into proslavery compromises, the couple expected events to proceed accordingly. "I do not anticipate just yet" a "dissolution of the Union," Abby confided to Phillips in December. Lincoln, she believed, would forge an unholy deal with slaveholders before events reached that stage. Even as she wrote, however, South Carolinians were debating whether to secede from the Union. Their secession later that month sparked a wave that brought seven slaveholding states out of the Union, leading to the creation of the Confederate States of America early the next year.[23]

Secession, though it came as a shock to Abby, produced—at least temporarily—the state of abolitionist accordance for which she had yearned. Not even Garrison could ignore the initiatives issued from the Republican camp during the secession winter, championing reunion through proslavery compromise. Lincoln himself endorsed a constitutional amendment guaranteeing in perpetuity the existence of slavery within its current bounds. Faced with mounting evidence of Republican cowardice, moral suasionists fell back on their longstanding rhetorical support for disunion. Garrisonians had envisioned disunion as a Northern act born of justice, saving the free states from sinful communion with slaveholders. Despite claims that reformers wished to destroy the nation, moral suasionists had seen their plan as an act of moral nationalism. Disunion, in their view, was a temporary measure that would purify both sections. A North no longer beholden to slaveholders could, Garrison argued, "fashion her own institutions and dictate her own policy." Free of demoralizing Southern influence, the section could become the bastion of free-labor morality that it was always meant to be. At the same time, a South shorn of support from federal authorities, who propped up slavery through the Fugitive Slave Law and other provisions, and cotton-craving Northern factories would eventually falter. Slavery would die, and the nation could then reunite on a moral basis. Abolitionists, as Phillips noted, thus advocated disunion as a means to "bring South Carolina back into the Union a free State." Antislavery disunionists saw themselves as patriots, not traitors.[24]

Reformers adapted their disunionist views to the new reality. Secession was markedly different from the abolitionist vision of disunion, precipitated by Southerners to save slavery rather than by Northerners to end it. Abolitionists nonetheless argued during the secession winter of 1860–1861 that separation would produce the same results either way. "If the North, for the sake of freedom will not dissolve the Union," the Foster-supported *Anti-Slavery Bugle* argued, "then let the South do it for the sake of slavery." The South, Abby believed, had sealed its own doom. Abby and other leaders of the Worcester County Anti-Slavery Society contended in a series of February 1861 resolutions that the slaveholding states would now have to "hold up the disgraceful system alone." The "system, deprived of the support it has so long had from the North," would "dwindle and perish." Abby thus rejoiced at the onset of disunion. Most moral suasionists, faced with the likely alternative of compromise, did so as well. Phillips offered perhaps the loudest affirmation when he declared in a January speech, "All hail then, disunion!" At least for the time being, Abby was no longer isolated from the antislavery majority.[25]

Stephen, however, refused to fall in line with the disunionist chorus. Still disillusioned with a movement that had mistreated him and his wife—and, he felt, had led antislavery reform down an errant path—he rejected the Garrisonian consensus yet again. Along with his wife, Stephen had championed the cause of disunion throughout the 1850s. At the same February meeting of the Worcester County Anti-Slavery Society where his wife had joined the majority in upholding disunion, however, he now took "decided ground against disunion." Like his counterparts, Stephen denounced compromise as evil. Disunion, however, was no better. He "did not wish to relinquish the influence he possessed over the condition of the slaves while in the Union with them." Confederates could do as they willed with their slaves, perhaps in perpetuity. The "chance of the slaves for their freedom," he argued, was "much better in the Union, than out of it, in a southern confederacy." Rather than disunion, Stephen thus endorsed Union "coercion against secessionists"—a war through which "slavery could ere long be wiped out." In marked contrast to scholarly emphasis on nonresistance in shaping the behavior of the Fosters, Stephen advocated violent force as an antislavery weapon to purify the nation.[26]

The outbreak of war in April 1861 shifted the battle lines within abolitionism. As calls for compromise faded, replaced with war cries that echoed across the North, most moral suasionists upended their strategies. In part, these abolitionists acted out of fear of a Confederate victory. As Susan B. Anthony admitted at an antislavery meeting, she had to hope for the "triumph of the *less* guilty party" in a zero-sum conflict. More importantly, however, these abolitionists believed in the moral potential of the Union war. "It seems to me," Garrison wrote Phillips soon after the fall of Fort Sumter, "that the war *must*, in effect, be a war of freedom against slavery." However much "crafty politicians" like Lincoln sought to "cover up the issue, it will assert itself." Slavery, after all, powered the Confederate war effort. Emancipation concurrently could become an instrument of war. Most abolitionists came to believe that the public would be receptive to these truths. The unexpected Northern embrace of war—and rejection of compromise with the Slave Power—renewed many reformers' faith in popular progress. In a speech in Boston in late April, Phillips cast the "tread of Massachusetts men marshaled for war" as a pleasant surprise. The people, he argued, were now ripe for moral suasion. It would be the work of abolitionists to seize the opportunity. By joining the war effort, activists could push the Union toward emancipation—and thereby shape an imperfect conflict into a righteous endeavor. They could, a *Liberator* correspondent confirmed, harness the war effort, turning the "rushing torrent into a perennial river of peace and freedom." The majority of reformers thus intervened in the Union war, seeking to perfect it from within.[27]

Once again, the Fosters found themselves outside the antislavery consensus. Whether his late advocacy of coercion had been a heartfelt belief or a contrarian slight of the Garrisonian majority, Stephen now joined Abby in opposing the Union war—and breaking with their pro-war comrades. A number of considerations shaped the decisions of antiwar activists. In part, these reformers despised the notion of a lesser evil. The *Anti-Slavery Bugle*, the Ohio-based newspaper that was, as a western reformer affirmed, a "child" of Abby's "own creation and nursing," addressed the issue in an April article. That the Confederacy was more "avowedly and utterly proslavery" than the Union, editor Benjamin Jones declared, "does not make us any more willing to support the latter than we have been for the last twenty years." As Abby explained further the next year, when "we are ready to accept the less of two sinners, the serpent of compromise has crept into our midst." The Fosters, dedicated to moral purity, deplored in theory the concept of a lesser evil. Abolitionists could not dabble in moral relativity without compromising their own ideals—and the cause—in the process. These hardliners would therefore never choose between evils, even if one were less vile than the other.[28]

To an extent, war itself was an evil to the nonresistant Fosters. They shared the belief of their pacifist ally Alfred Love that it was wrong to seek "devout ends" through "carnal weapons." Important as nonresistance was to the Fosters, however, it has become far more essential to scholarly interpretations of their wartime actions. Scholars have looked no further than the Fosters' pacifistic doctrines to explain their behavior during the crisis of Union. The Fosters, according to such scholars, rejected the Union war because they would not sanction forceful means to resist evil. Their qualms, by implication, lay with the concept of force rather than with the Union war itself. The war could have been a guaranteed vessel for emancipation, the argument goes, and the Fosters still would not have supported it by virtue of its being a war. Such an explanation, however, is insufficient. Many nonresistants came to support the war, including Garrison, who had pioneered the doctrine of nonresistance. The Fosters, however, did not. They opposed the Union war at all costs.[29]

The Fosters' stance derived from their brand of moral nationalism—the rigid worldview that had led them to oppose the Republicans throughout the 1850s as unparalleled threats to the antislavery mission. Now, the Republicans controlled the machinery of government and oversaw a vast war effort. The Fosters thus took issue with the Republican-led Union war specifically, not just with war generally. They aimed their ire at a conflict prosecuted by proslavery Republicans and supported by an equally immoral public. Indeed, despise though they did the notion of a lesser evil, the Foster-led hardliners did not even consider the Union as such. Parker Pillsbury, a close associate of the Fosters, declared that the two contestants were equally deplorable. "At the South," he noted, "we have desperadoes; at the North doughfaces; their only issue a bastard blood of compromises and corruptions." Both sides, after all, maintained protections for the institution of slavery with little public opposition.[30]

The Fosters and their followers thus framed the Union war as a proslavery endeavor unworthy of abolitionist support. Jones, at the helm of the *Anti-Slavery*

Bugle, made his position clear in a spring series of articles. "We are now told" by pro-war reformers, he noted, that the present conflict would, with abolitionist help, "result in the overthrow of slavery. But the abolition of slavery was not the object of the Republican party, nor was it the design of the party leaders." Lincoln aimed solely to maintain the "integrity of the Union." Emancipation was "not authoritatively presented as the present issue." With Republicans controlling the "military machinery" of the government, Jones saw no reason to put his stock in the war effort. He thus could not make sense of the "strange infatuation" that led most reformers to "insist that the war between the proslavery government of the United States and the yet more proslavery government of the Confederate States, is a war between Freedom and Slavery." Jones refused to "aid in upholding a government through whose agency the lifeblood of the slave has been crushed out." The reformer George Bassett noted similarly that he required "some official evidence" that the government had become an "emblem of freedom" before he embraced the war. As the Republicans shunned "any interference with slavery," Bassett found no such proof. For Jones, Bassett, and the Fosters, then, the national path to moral regeneration did not run through a Republican war to preserve the Union. Such a conflict would never create the nation for which they yearned.[31]

The Foster-led faction also doubted Northern moral progress. Northerners who had gone to war to "defend the Constitution," Pillsbury noted, offered "no evidence, or necessary indication, of hostility to slavery." "We are told of the utterings of a Northern conscience," Jones wrote in May. "When we look upon the people," however, "we behold a vast multitude bereft of reason, staggering to and fro as drunken men." Northerners had rallied to war out of jingoistic passion, not a moralistic impetus to destroy slavery. They showed no sign that they would support emancipation, not to mention black citizenship. No groundswell of "Northern conscience" existed. Indeed, Jones experienced popular immorality firsthand: He announced the same month that he was suspending the *Bugle* because "murderous feelings" were "entertained against him." Northerners seemed more interested in attacking antiwar abolitionists than in destroying slavery. To the Foster-led hardline faction, then, the wartime North was the same bastion of proslavery conservatism as ever.[32]

Convinced that a war prosecuted by immoral politicians and fought by immoral citizens could not produce the free, egalitarian Union they envisioned, the Fosters and their allies forswore intervention. While pro-war reformers claimed that they could mold an imperfect war into a moral crusade, antiwar activists advised otherwise. If "we might fight for the Union," the antiwar reformer

B. G. Wright wrote the *Liberator*, then "for God's sake, let it be for an antislavery Union, and not for this cursed covenant with death." If the "friends of the slave are to support the war on the ground of its future antislavery character," Bassett argued in a similar fashion, then let them wait until it "assumes that character." Reformers, in Wright and Bassett's opinions, should not intervene in the Union war as it then stood. Intervention at the current time, which entailed mingling with the imperfect mainstream, would compromise abolitionists and their mission. Reformers, then, had to forestall intervention until the nation had achieved moral enlightenment, fighting to bring justice to the slaves. Until then, activists had to remain morally rigid, objective seers, perched above the impure fray. They would, Jones noted, have to continue to stand aloof from the corrupt mainstream. The work of true abolitionists, Pillsbury explained at a meeting, was not "materially affected by any change whatever in the government, so long as it recognizes slavery as an institution to be promoted." Reformers had to continue to act as gadflies—as agitators working from outside the mainstream to force change.[33]

To an extent that surpassed their antebellum condemnations, the Fosters excoriated their pro-war colleagues over the next two years. From the start of the war, the couple pointed out the flaws in the interventionist policy. At a May meeting of the Worcester County Anti-Slavery Society, the Fosters joined with other speakers to condemn the pro-war position as a "standstill, or waiting policy." Garrison and his followers, they argued, sat in complacency waiting for Lincoln to act, rather than forcing him to do so through outside agitation. Reform, in their view, could not occur from within the war coalition. Stephen went further at the Fourth of July ceremony at Framingham mentioned at the start of this essay. Before Foster's speech, Phillips had delivered an impassioned speech in favor of the Union war. The orator had also endorsed compensated emancipation—a marked departure from the abolitionist refrain of immediate and unconditional emancipation. After offering a resolution declaring the Union to be a proslavery government that would not receive "one cent of his money or one drop of his blood," Stephen attacked his erstwhile friend. While Stephen "still held to the doctrine that righteousness exalteth a nation," Phillips "seemed to have lost his confidence in impartial justice." He had submerged himself in the realm of expediency at the expense of principle. In effect, Stephen implied that Phillips had surrendered his abolitionist credentials. For his own part, Stephen would "never consent to pay the sinner to cease from his sin." The more perfect Union he imagined would not arise through such compromising acts. Unbending justice, in his view, was the only midwife for national redemption.[34]

Stephen's outburst precipitated a heated debate at the celebration. While Abby rose to second the opinions of her husband, Wright moved quickly to table his resolutions. Faced with yet another muzzling of his views, Stephen interrupted the proceedings to declare that the antislavery majority "had been seduced from their allegiance to principle, and had been induced to give their support" to a government that "perpetrated the crimes which have disgraced the country for the last seventy-five years." The Lincoln administration "called [on] the . . . strength and power of the North to put down slave insurrections," instead of to spread freedom. The Republicans were no different from previous proslavery parties. When another reformer proceeded to mock him, Stephen again rose to declare that dissent no longer seemed welcome in the American Anti-Slavery Society. At the conclusion of the meeting, Abby attempted to smooth over the unpleasantness by affirming that all abolitionists "stand together on the platform of the old Anti-Slavery Society." Truisms aside, however, it was only the hardliners who remained on that antipolitical ground. The Framingham meeting had laid bare the very real differences between the Garrisonian majority and the Foster-led minority.[35]

Though Stephen appeared more inflammatory than Abby in public, his wife proved to be the less conciliatory one in private. In August 1861, William Lloyd Garrison Jr., son of the reformer, wrote to Abby seeking a resolution to "painful estrangement" between their families. "To me," Garrison Jr. explained, "it used to seem grand that reformers could differ and discuss and hold opposite opinions, at the same time retaining for each other affection and respect." The lack of both agreement and respect between the Fosters and Garrison made their "separation doubly poignant." Abby replied to Garrison Jr. that the "brand of criminality" his father had bestowed on her destroyed any chance of "social intimacy" between the two longtime reformers. The time of mutual respect between disagreeing colleagues, she sighed, was over. Her "consistency" of principle was met only with "condescension" in meetings. Abby thus refused to let personal niceties interfere with her unyielding mission.[36]

Stephen was more amenable—and less doctrinaire—away from the public eye. He expressed an uncharacteristic burst of optimism in a fall letter to Phillips, perhaps given the August proclamation by the Union general John C. Frémont freeing rebel-held slaves in Missouri as an act of military necessity. Though Lincoln had revoked the proclamation, it nonetheless offered proof that some Northerners were willing to resist slavery. While his fellow hardliners railed against Northern degradation, Stephen now agreed with Phillips's belief that Northern prejudices were "fast dying out." The "public ear" seemed "open to us as never before." Northern moral progress offered an indication that the war did, perhaps, hold antislavery promise after all. Maybe it could eventually bring the nation to the "harbor of liberty, peace, and prosperity." In contrast to his summer screed, Stephen thus petitioned Phillips to lead a "vigorous movement" to "compel a timid and reluctant Administration to proclaim emancipation as the only effectual means of terminating the war." Emancipation as a war measure would be an act of expediency, born out of necessity rather than justice. Stephen bent his rigid stance in light of the potential emancipationist promise of the war. Such willingness to adapt, he charged, did not extend to the Republicans. The administration, the reformer affirmed, seemed "far more careful of the institution of slavery than of the lives of its loyal citizens." To support it would be an act of "indolence and conservatism." Stephen thereby distinguished between the Lincoln administration, which he regarded as irredeemably immoral, and the Union war overall, which could someday earn his support given popular progress.[37]

Stephen strayed from the unyielding position espoused by his wife only for a short time. By the time that the Worcester County Anti-Slavery Society met early the next year, the New Hampshire radical had renounced his opinions regarding the antislavery utility of the war. His change of heart likely derived from the influence of Abby, who had no hope in the conflict. As the entire assembly, including the Fosters, explained at Worcester, the administration was not the only factor holding the Union war back from moral perfection. The Republicans, of course, had an irrefutably "pro-slavery character." But the Northern people were no better. Whatever interest they had in emancipation derived from expediency. Though Stephen had earlier warmed to the notion, he now helped denounce it. Abolitionists, the group announced, demanded "unconditional emancipation as a measure of justice to the slave." The nation had to "repent of and put away her great sin, *because* of her sin," in order to redeem itself. Emancipation "predicated upon the selfish issue of safety to the whites," by contrast, was an imperfect solution that would never lead to the totally free, egalitarian nation that reformers envisioned. The Worcester reformers thus saw "nothing" in the war effort to warrant optimism. The Union war was a false prophet, after all.[38]

Stephen walked back his earlier flexibility even further at the January meeting of the Massachusetts Anti-Slavery Society. In response to a rosy depiction of current events by Garrison, the hardline reformer heaped withering scorn on the government, the public, and pro-war abolitionists as sinners in an unholy Union. As always, Stephen asserted that "there never had been an Administration so thoroughly devoted to slavery as the present." No previous administration had "ever returned so many fugitive slaves" or done "so much to propitiate the Slave Power." Lincoln, however, was not alone in ruling the nation. Indeed, he was the "passive agent of the people of this country," there to "obey the will of his masters." And these masters—the public—were far from perfect. Garrison and other pro-war reformers presented growing public support for expedient military emancipation as an indication of Northern moral progress. It was a mistake, Stephen countered, to overestimate that progress. "If the people wanted freedom," he asked, "why did they not say so, through their representatives?" Stephen, in contrast to pro-war reformers and modern scholars, saw no public mandate for emancipation. Northerners' ears, he now believed, were closed to antislavery voices.[39]

Even a popular groundswell in favor of emancipation, however, would not be enough to save the nation. The original "object of this Society," Stephen reminded his audience, was "not merely to destroy the *form* of slavery, but to destroy" also the "*spirit of oppression*"—the penumbral effects of slavery, such as "bitter and relentless prejudice against color." Until "that spirit was rooted out of the American heart," the work of reformers "would not be done." Northerners had to free the slaves as an act of justice, thereby starting a process that would lead eventually to postemancipation rights for African Americans in an egalitarian nation. Stephen saw nothing to make him believe that Northerners were ready for justice-based emancipation, not to mention black citizenship or social equality. The Union war, absent righteous motivations, was thus a moral dead end. Reformers, in his view, had no sufficient reason for "giving their sanction and support" to it. By doing so, Stephen concluded, they were forsaking their antislavery mission. Abolitionists, he reiterated, had to "keep right themselves," or else they could not "set others right." Any "fault in them was like poison cast into the fountain." Garrison and his followers, by implication, were adulterating antislavery waters through their support for the impure war.[40]

The Fosters fought against their pro-war counterparts throughout 1862. Such sparring brought the couple little joy. Stephen confessed to the British reformer George Thompson that the "wide and growing difference between my old antislavery associates and myself has been to me" a "source of much anxiety." Like Garrison, he yearned for a "war for freedom, justice, and the rights of our common humanity"—one that would "set free both black and white" to create an egalitarian nation. Such a war, however, did not exist. The current conflict was a base contest for "national supremacy" bereft of any moral significance. Those abolitionists who supported the Union were thus abandoning the "clear light of absolute truth and impartial justice" in favor of a "senseless and bewildering patriotism." Reformers who had "stood for so many years with their feet firmly planted on the rock of truth," resisting "every possible temptation," now "faltere[ed] in this hour." They "abdicat[ed] their field of labor" to support an administration "thoroughly subservient to slavery." Referring to his prior travails, Stephen noted that Garrison had refused to endorse his own antislavery political party yet now supported the proslavery Republicans along with immoral measures like compensated emancipation. The reformer mourned the "sad changes" that had compromised the antislavery majority. The unwelcome but necessary duty of remaining on the rock of moral purity, then, would fall to him and his wife.[41]

The Fosters carried out that duty at every antislavery gathering. At a May meeting of the Business Committee of the American Anti-Slavery Society, Stephen offered a resolution lambasting the Lincoln administration for having "in no instance evinced a genuine regard" for African Americans' "rights as citizens." The measure, however, was quickly tabled. The New Hampshire radical tried again at the meeting of the New England Anti-Slavery Convention later that month, affirming that only a Union "established upon the principles of impartial justice"—one grounded in morality, not chauvinism—deserved his support. But the "events of the past year," he explained, had "made no essential change in the spirit" of the government. "The Union means slavery," he declared, "and the war is for that." Lincoln was "as truly a slaveholder as Jefferson Davis." Indeed, the president could not "even contemplate emancipation without colonization" or as anything other than a "derrier [sic] resort"—a desperate war measure rather than an act of justice. The people were no different. Slavery had not "lost a particle of its attractiveness" in the North, Stephen asserted. Taking his hardline stance to its logical conclusion, he declared that he would "neither enlist in the war nor encourage others to enlist." Instead, he would "warn all young men to withhold their support from this government" as it then stood—a borderline treasonous statement.[42]

The pro-war majority was understandably shocked. One reformer found Stephen's inability to understand the "degrees in wrong" between the two sides absurd. Yet the Fosters would not be deterred. The next day, Abby affirmed that the nation was "hopelessly lost." Emancipation, she explained, was far from assured. Even if it did occur, it would emerge "only from a regard to our own safety." Expedient emancipation would not end "hate of the colored race"—the "wickedness" that would "destroy us as a nation." It was, alongside the Union war overall, a dead end in the abolitionist project of national salvation. Rather than support the "practical atheist" Lincoln and a Northern public wedded to "specious" morality, Abby thus advised reformers to return to the "old ground of total abstinence" from corruption. Only by standing on that moral high ground could reformers save the nation. The majority of reformers, however, responded to her plea by exhorting the Union war. Garrison, for example, announced that he "had no pulse that did not beat for Lincoln against Jefferson Davis." All the Fosters could do was interject cries of "Shame on the government!" and "Shame on those who fight for such a Government!" as their resolutions were tabled in favor of pro-war decrees.[43]

As the pro-war and antiwar camps lobbed volleys at each other into the fall, part of the ground on which the latter stood crumbled. Lincoln, increasingly desperate to defeat a resilient Confederacy, announced his support for expedient emancipation in the Emancipation Proclamation. The proclamation, decreeing the freedom of slaves in rebel-held territory, went into effect in January 1863. The Fosters had long argued both that the war would likely not end in emancipation and that military emancipation, even if it did occur, would not produce the more perfect Union that reformers desired. Correct as they had been in asserting the contingency of emancipation, events had now forced Lincoln to act. Could the Fosters stand firm in their uncompromising stances now that emancipation had become a Union war aim?

Rather than abandon their crusade for moral purity, the Fosters shifted their tactics in the wake of the Emancipation Proclamation. As reformers like Douglass were quick to point out, the decree was limited in many respects: It was bereft of moralistic language, it exempted the slave states that had remained in the Union as well as Union-occupied areas of the Confederacy, it depended on military advances for its execution, and, as an executive order, it lacked permanence. Unlike the pro-war Douglass, the Fosters redeveloped their overall views of the Union war around the flawed proclamation. Instead of denouncing the war as proslavery, they now cast it as imperfectly antislavery. The Emancipation Proclamation, they asserted, was a half-measure—an amoral gesture unlikely to spur the Fosters' goals of total emancipation and egalitarian brotherhood. While other reformers praised Lincoln at the June 1863 New England Anti-Slavery Convention, Stephen proclaimed that the "Government stands just where it always stood." It moved against slavery as a war measure rather than as a moral obligation. Its antislavery agenda was thus half-hearted and insufficient. "We oppose slavery," Stephen emphasized in reference to the exemptions of the decree, "not the slavery of 4,000,000 only." A "million men yet remain in slavery, the Administration keep them there and the Courts rule the Fugitive Slave Law to be the law of the land." Referring to the temporary nature of the order, Foster pointed out that Democrats would ban "discussion of anti-slavery ideas," not to mention roll back the proclamation, should they seize power. Realizing the potential for slavery to persist, Stephen thus refused to see freedom as inevitable. A precarious proclamation supported by an untrustworthy president did not entail total emancipation.[44]

Stephen also lacked confidence in the prospects for postemancipation black rights, such as citizenship and social equality. Referencing the recent parade of the 54th Massachusetts Volunteer Infantry Regiment, the African American military unit commanded by Robert Gould Shaw, through Boston, the reformer noted that "too much importance" was attached to the "waving of handkerchiefs" by civilians toward the passing troops. The "very people who waved," he asserted, "would refuse to take the hand of a negro, or admit him into their pew." Bostonians, in his view, were happy to let African Americans die for the Union cause but would never accept them as societal equals. "In point of principle," he concluded, "not one inch of progress has been made in this community." A Union war that did not guarantee total emancipation and that elided entirely other black rights was still imperfect—and thus still undeserving of antislavery support. The "danger to our cause was never greater than now," Stephen reiterated. Abolitionists could not yet surrender their aloofness.[45]

The Fosters continued throughout 1863 to reject the rosy picture painted by their fellow reformers. While Garrison lectured his antiwar counterparts on the "folly [of] neutrality" at their annual Fourth of July celebration, Stephen maintained that "we have a controversy with Abraham Lincoln as well as with Jefferson Davis, until he proclaim liberty throughout the land, unto all the inhabitants thereof." An even larger confrontation loomed ahead of the thirtieth-anniversary celebration of the American Anti-Slavery Society in late 1863. The leading Garrisonians intended the event as a jubilee, commemorating antislavery victories in a spirit of triumph. These pro-war reformers anticipated that their counterparts would have a contrarian attitude. Whether "Stephen or Abby Foster will be with us, I do not know," Garrison noted to a fellow organizer. He feared that any moral purists present would be in a "morbid state of mind relative to the Administration and the Rebellion, and would be more inclined to criminate the former than to denounce the latter." Garrison hoped that he could keep that morose dissent to a minimum.[46]

The pro-war faction portrayed its endeavor as a success, despite the presence of the Fosters. The meeting "was the era of good feeling—everybody joyous," the reformer Sarah Pugh recalled. "Even Stephen and Abby Kelley Foster caught the infection of the hour and went home happier than they came." Indeed, in deference to the significance of the anniversary, Stephen had begun his speech by noting the "great pleasure" he took in commemorating their shared efforts against slavery. However, he soon pivoted toward unhappier topics. "We have become over confident in regard to the success of the movement," he proclaimed. The majority believed that "this war is the end of slavery, that we have already given it its death-blow." He added: "we have no reason to be very confident." Lincoln "has set free a portion of the slaves—he has abolished slavery nowhere." Given that Lincoln was an amoral politician unwilling to ensure a just, total emancipation, Stephen denounced abolitionist confidence in the Union war as misplaced. "I would not trust anybody's liberty in the hands of such a government," he affirmed. "Never," until the government initiated a righteous crusade that "dooms slavery to everlasting perdition," would he "lay off [his] armor." If "you are tired of fighting, if you are weary," Stephen mocked his colleagues, "lay off yours." He, however, would not remove "one particle of my armor until the last fetter is broken." Should the conflict become a war for freedom, Stephen would "go down to Carolina and face the rebel armies" himself. He did not, however, anticipate making such travel plans.[47]

Abby seconded her husband's stance. "We should not be too confident" regarding signs of antislavery progress like popular support for military emancipation, she affirmed. "I do not believe in instantaneous conversion." The "bloodthirsty mob[s]" attacking reformers for decades could not have turned overnight into abolitionist acolytes. "I do not willingly stand here to bring scorn or hatred" upon the populace, Abby lamented. She spoke because Northerners acted "not from the highest but from the lowest motives"—base desires for their safety. Such were "not motives upon which we can rely, and which should make us jubilant." Northern moral progress, in her view, was specious. "Military necessity" would not a more perfect Union make. Should the "rebels lay down their arms today," Northerners would "kill for them the fatted calf" of freedom as soon as possible. Abolitionists had still to engage in "incessant labor," agitating from the moral high ground to bring Northerners from selfishness to righteousness. Only then would Northerners support national regeneration along free and egalitarian lines. Talk of antislavery progress—and, by implication, the idea that the "mission of the Anti-Slavery Society is finished"—was premature. Reformers, in her view, had nothing yet to celebrate.[48]

A chorus of pro-war reformers attempted to rebut the Fosters' speeches. Oliver Johnson, for example, attacked the Fosters' prized concept of moral purity. If emancipation required the people to be "brought up to the standard of absolute justice and righteousness," he asserted, then he would expect slaves to "grind in the prison-house for centuries." A good cause could triumph through "various and mixed motives" just as well as through morally pure ones. The work of antislavery reform, these pro-war advocates emphasized, was nearly done after all. A defiant Stephen responded at the end of the gathering that he was not "living in a cloud," as implied by his coadjutors. He was merely standing upon the original platform of the American Anti-Slavery Society, refusing to brook impurities. "I will continue as I ever have done," he concluded, even if he had to do so leading the "minority, defending the weak point." Despite concerted opposition, the Fosters thus refused to concede what they viewed as a struggle for the soul of abolitionism.[49]

The debates within the antislavery movement over the Union war took on a new cast as the presidential election of 1864 approached. By 1864, pro-war reformers' jubilant attitudes toward the Union war had translated into support for the status quo—and for Lincoln. Garrison, for example, waxed eloquent in a *Liberator* article about how the "cause of the oppressed in our land has been steadily growing brighter and brighter." The reformer played down remaining problems, noting that "full justice for the oppressed" could not "be obtained at a single bound." Rather than focus on these long-term goals, Garrison instead chose to celebrate the antislavery progress that had been made. He reiterated at the January meeting of the Massachusetts Anti-Slavery Society that events had fulfilled the "most sanguine predictions and expectations of the Abolitionists." Taking stock of the triumphs of the past three years, Garrison declared that he had changed his opinion of Abraham Lincoln. In an unprecedented endorsement, the moral suasionist leader declared that, in his judgment, the reelection of Lincoln "would be the safest and wisest course." Garrison thereby became a wholesale supporter of the president.[50]

Garrison's words were, to the Fosters, signs of his corruption. The hardline reformers had warned their pro-war counterparts that engagement with the adulterated mainstream would compromise their moral objectivity. Now, the man who had once burned the Constitution in a pledge of unyielding agitation was voicing his complacency with the state of events and engaging in blatant politicking. By flouting the ideal of moral purity, he had lost his ethical compass. Stephen tried to rescue his erstwhile leader from the errant path at the January meeting. The New Hampshire reformer offered a resolution that "we can consent to no settlement of our present national troubles which fails to recognize the manhood of the negro." Abolitionists "demand for [African Americans] an equal share with the white race" in the nation, according to the principles of "justice and democratic equality." Liberty and equality, Stephen reminded Garrison, had always been inseparable goals for abolitionists. Garrison, however, had separated them. He expressed satisfaction with—and explicitly endorsed—a president who showed no interest in postemancipation black rights. Lincoln denied black troops equal pay and offered a lenient plan for Reconstruction without mention of black political, social, or economic rights. Indeed, even the president's commitment to total liberty was questionable. Lincoln, Stephen affirmed, kept "a million of slaves in bondage." He was the "embodiment of the Dred Scott decision," who "sought to save the Union, and save slavery at the same time." Slavery persisted in the Border States because of him. Stephen thus expressed his surprise that Garrison should "nominate for President" such a man. Garrison had thereby betrayed his antislavery mission.[51]

In order to counter Garrison and his increasing advocacy of Lincoln's reelection, the Fosters dedicated their efforts to defeating the president. An antislavery struggle over the Union war became, in effect, a referendum on Lincoln. Hardline reformers welcomed a new ally in this endeavor: Phillips, who had become disillusioned with the Union war's lack of progress on black rights. The powerful orator had inveighed against Lincoln at the Massachusetts Anti-Slavery Society meeting. The Fosters rejoiced at his defection from the Garrisonian majority. "The radicals have breathed more freely since your speech," Stephen wrote Phillips in February. "Stephen expressed himself [too] cooly [sic]," Abby added. "My joy exceeds all expression." Not all pro-war reformers had succumbed to the temptations of the mainstream after all.[52]

Alongside Phillips, the Fosters tried at every meeting to impugn Lincoln. At the May meeting of the American Anti-Slavery Society, Stephen resolved that the current administration partook in a "deeper infamy than any of its predecessors." Lincoln had the ability under the "war power" to "pronounce the doom of slavery" yet chose not to do so. On the contrary, "more fugitives have been returned to slavery" under Lincoln than under his predecessors. "The fact is indisputable," Stephen asserted. "And yet, strange to say, Mr. Garrison is advocating the reelection of Mr. Lincoln to the Presidency!" At the New England Anti-Slavery Convention later that month, Abby announced that Lincoln "preferred to shed the blood of loyal white men, rather than to free the slaves of the Border States." Abolitionists had to judge leaders by the "claims of principle and righteousness," and by those standards, Lincoln was a resounding failure. Stephen reiterated that the president "confessedly has no sympathy with our cause of immediate emancipation and full justice." He was thus "opposed to re-instating Mr. Lincoln." While Lincoln aimed to end the rebellion, abolitionists should not desire the rebellion to "end till the black is the political equal of the white." To ensure those goals—to create their more perfect Union—Stephen had tried to "push the present administration to a higher level." Having failed to do so, he now found it necessary to "prepare to have it succeeded by a better." The Fosters thus yearned for a president compatible with antislavery interests.[53]

Consumed by disdain for Lincoln, whom he saw as an intransigent obstacle to the abolitionist mission, Stephen turned to a previously anathema tactic: politicking. The Fosters had long maligned those reformers who delved into politics as traitors to the antislavery movement and its preeminent precept of moral purity. Now, as most reformers lined up to support Lincoln's reelection, Stephen cast about for a way to save what remained of the abolitionist mission from self-destruction. The only viable solution, he decided, was to try to engineer the president's defeat. In order to save abolitionism from political corruption, he too would, temporarily, descend into the muck. In May, Stephen joined a newspaper call for a convention opposing Lincoln in Cleveland later that month. This "People's Committee," of which he was a part, wished to support a presidential candidate who would halt the "destructive wave" seeking to engulf the "liberty and dignity of the nation." While Stephen had previously tried to form his own abolitionist political party before the election of 1860, the so-called Cleveland Movement that he helped create was a different animal altogether. The movement drew in antipolitical Garrisonians like Pillsbury alongside Radical Republicans like the Missouri politician B. Gratz Brown. Rather than a quixotic, morally pure party, it was a diverse coalition that aimed to achieve victory. In order to save the Union from continued moral decay under Lincoln, Stephen thus became a bona fide political operative.[54]

The movement soon settled on a preferred candidate: John C. Frémont, the emancipationist general. Alongside Pillsbury and Phillips, Stephen advocated Frémont's election and even served as a delegate to and committee organizer for the nominating convention in Cleveland. Almost immediately, he realized the folly of pursuing moral perfection through politics. In order to gain widespread support, the other convention organizers reached out to a faction of Democrats. This unholy alliance of anti-Lincoln Radical Republicans and conservative Democrats nominated Frémont for president and War Democrat John C. Cochrane for vice president. Moreover, the platform produced by the convention included a resolution that "the rebellion has destroyed Slavery." Though the resolution went on to call for a constitutional amendment to secure "to all men absolute equality before the law," it was clear to the abolitionists in attendance that their envisioned radical platform had been diluted. Stephen, the *Liberator* later reported, had "combated the heresy" of proclaiming slavery dead in vain. Even the platform's concession to equality limited itself to the law, rather than to the social equality that hardline reformers desired. Witnessing their opponents participating in a compromising affair, pro-Lincoln abolitionists pounced. Stephen, the antislavery *New York Independent* declared, "charged upon the Government the guilt of holding one million slaves in bonds" while also "unit[ing] in putting forth a statement that slavery is already dead!" By doing so, he had brought "lamentable discredit" on himself. Faced with smug accusations of his own hypocrisy, Stephen backed away from public involvement in the movement. His political experiment had failed.[55]

With Lincoln's reelection, the Garrisonian leaders fell in line with the goals of the administration. Lincoln supported the passage of the Thirteenth Amendment, which ended slavery, as he prosecuted the end of the Civil War. As the victory of an emancipationist Union loomed in early 1865, Garrison and his followers declared that the work of reform was done. The "rebellion is washed, and slavery along with it," Garrison wrote his wife in April. Slavery was "annihilated beyond any hope of resurrection." As a result, he asserted, the "American Anti-Slavery Society may reasonably conclude that its specific mission is ended." The Fosters disagreed. Though Lincoln had enacted one of their goals, total emancipation, he left their other objective, postemancipation black rights, unfulfilled. The Fosters viewed the Thirteenth Amendment as an incomplete, imperfect, and insufficient half-measure that offered nothing in the way of justice to the former slaves. Abolitionists, Abby affirmed at the January meeting of the Massachusetts Anti-Slavery Society, demanded constitutional recognition of "every man as free and equal, under the law" as part of "any reconstruction in a rebel State." The current amendment, as Stephen asserted at another antislavery meeting, was a "deceitful device, and a proslavery measure." Jefferson Davis, he declared, would "sooner recognize the manhood and equality of the negro than Lincoln." By supporting a half-hearted amendment that fell far short of abolitionist goals as a triumph of "Anti-Slavery progress," Garrison had thus "forsaken and betrayed the cause." Abolitionists, in their view, had work left to do to achieve a more perfect Union. Settling for anything less than moral perfection was treasonous.[56]

Reformers' disagreements over the endpoint of abolitionism came to a head at the May 1865 meeting of the American Anti-Slavery Society. Garrison, as the society's president, declared its work accomplished. "Have we not consummated our great object?" he asked. Though Lincoln had been assassinated, Garrison felt that the emancipationist achievements of the Union war were inviolable. The moral suasionist leader accordingly moved to disband the organization. When the society voted against his proposition, he announced his resignation from the movement. The Fosters led the dissent against his actions. Abolitionists, Abby argued, still had to "secure the proper, legal guarantees of the black man's rights."

They could do so only through a "deep and radical regeneration" of public sentiment through moral suasion—the longstanding practice of the society. Reformers, Stephen reiterated, had sworn to fight "until the last fetter shall be broken, and [their] object shall be completely and perfectly achieved." The Declaration of Sentiments of the American Anti-Slavery Society, he reminded his audience, had called for both the abolition of slavery and the "elevation of the colored people to an equality with the whites, and to full enjoyment of all their social, civil and political rights and privileges." Was "that work done?" he asked. "Is there not a bitter prejudice existing throughout the whole country today, that puts its heel upon the negro?" Only after reformers had "imprint[ed] the law of justice upon the American heart," so that "there will be no negro cars, there will be no disfranchisement of men on account of color, no hooting after black men when they walk arm in arm with white men," could the society disband. Until then, it would have to continue the struggle against the penumbral effects of slavery. By advocating otherwise, Garrison, shorn of his morally rigid principles since he joined the war effort, had succumbed fully to corruption.[57]

The American Anti-Slavery Society, sans Garrison, would persevere for five years after the end of the Civil War under the leadership of Phillips. As newly appointed Executive Committee members, the Fosters continued working to complete the antislavery struggle. They sought to achieve the missing pieces of their more perfect Union, such as postemancipation black rights. In defiance of the inexorable—and completed—march to emancipation depicted by Garrison and modern scholars, the couple even doubted whether total emancipation had been secured. Referring to the presidential Reconstruction policies of Andrew Johnson, Stephen predicted in July 1865 that a resurgent South would soon be able to "re-enslave the blacks." Nothing was a given where imperfect politicians were involved. Retired activists mocked the Fosters for their troubles. The incessant attitude of the Fosters in "distrusting the future," the British reformer Mary Estlin confessed, was "very incomprehensible." If the "Fosters choose to wear the old clothes" of the society, Garrison's ally Oliver Johnson sneered, "let them. It will be the old story over again of the ass in the lion's skin." Moreover, as Abby wrote in 1869, the "position of many of our old co-workers, who have left us in the ground, has had the effect very much to cripple our resources and cramp our operations." Nevertheless, the Fosters carried on to forge a Union better than the imperfect nation the war had created.[58]

The Fosters' unyielding struggle for justice sheds light on the nature of the Union war. Had the Republican-led war been an inexorable march to emancipation, buoyed by an antislavery public, the couple would not have hesitated to support it. An antislavery endeavor that required no compromising of reformist principles would have received their endorsement, rather than their scorn. Instead, however, the Fosters viewed the Union war as a proslavery enterprise that, when it eventually managed to achieve certain antislavery measures, did so only in a half-hearted manner. Neither Lincoln nor Northerners in general were trustworthy allies in the fight for national moral regeneration. Never, not even after the Emancipation Proclamation of 1863 and the Thirteenth Amendment of 1865, did the Fosters rest secure in the belief that emancipation was total and inviolable. Postemancipation black rights had even bleaker prospects. The Fosters' overwhelmingly pessimistic stance perhaps underestimated the achievements of the Union war and Reconstruction. Total emancipation and constitutional—though ultimately nominal—guarantees of black citizenship and suffrage emerged from the Civil War era. Nevertheless, the Fosters offer a sobering check on our understanding of the racial intentions and transformations of the Union war. To their dying days, Abby and Stephen believed their mission unaccomplished. Their perfect moment never arrived.

Elizabeth Keckly's Union War

Tamika Y. Nunley

What would a formerly enslaved woman have to say about the critical transformations that took place during the American Civil War? In the 2012 film *Lincoln*, Steven Spielberg depicts a bustling White House, with black and white men and women moving in and out of the president's home and tending to the daily business and tasks of the Executive Mansion. One black woman in particular makes a modest appearance in this account of Lincoln's presidency during the Civil War. Audiences might place her as one of the many black servants that worked in the White House, but some would recognize her as none other than Elizabeth Keckly: seamstress and confidante in the Lincoln household and leading activist among free African Americans in Washington, DC.[1]

In 1868, Elizabeth Keckly stirred controversy across the nation when she published her memoir, *Behind the Scenes: or Thirty Years a Slave and Four Years in the White House*. Keckly offered a telling reminiscence of her life as a slave and the intimate role she played in the Lincoln household. Some speculated that Keckly didn't write her memoir and that instead the Civil War–era journalist Jane Grey Swisshelm had authored *Behind the Scenes*.[2] As Kate Masur shows in *They Knew Lincoln*, African Americans in Washington engaged in their own traditions of oral history and memory.[3] Such efforts worked toward preserving Keckly's legacy and accomplishments. Furthermore, a perusal of Keckly's correspondence with her contemporaries and her editorials reinforce her intellectual ability to write her own memoir.

While Keckly is in many respects an exceptional figure, she is also representative of the many black activists who led critical efforts "behind the scenes" of America's most transformative war. Indeed, as Stephen Kantrowitz argues, "The struggle among the states about the question of free black citizenship—a struggle the 'colored citizens' provoked—would play a critical role in causing the Civil War."[4] These "colored citizens" of the antebellum era tirelessly organized on behalf of refugees and soldiers in the nation's capital and demonstrated an unwavering commitment to the Union war despite countless efforts to exclude them. The connections Keckly made between her experiences as a slave and her activism as a free woman illuminate our understandings of what the Union war meant to many African Americans.

Keckly recalled her experiences and memories of slavery and freedom to underscore the necessity of black leadership and participation in the Union war effort, which she, along with many women, demonstrated in her work within makeshift encampments that housed refugees in the nation's capital. Keckly worked among contemporary African American leaders such as John F. Cook, an educator and founder of the Social, Civil, and Statistical Association, and Henry McNeal Turner, pastor of Washington's largest African American church during the Civil War, Israel Bethel AME.[5] Turner also served as a chaplain for the Union army. African Americans found in Washington, a locus of political and social mobilization, a place in which to plant their desires for full inclusion within the Union.

Responses to the war involved a large-scale collective effort among enslaved, free, fugitive, and refugee African Americans. An examination of Elizabeth Keckly's story offers an example of one of the many ways the Union war and its outcomes politicized African American communities. Moreover, I argue that the social and political organizing of black women like Keckly culminated in a strategic campaign designed to link the Union war effort directly to justifications for an American commitment to black freedom and equality. In *An Example for All the Land*, Kate Masur argues that the work of black activists in Washington in the era of emancipation represents "upstart claims" to equality, and Kantrowitz shows the breadth of Northern black struggles for equality and citizenship throughout the nineteenth century.[6] An examination of Keckly's activism connects her antebellum and wartime experiences to show her trajectory of claims making "behind the scenes."

This essay provides a new perspective on Keckly by examining her life and political activism within the broader context of the Union war. This aspect of her life has not received sustained attention from scholars but only fleeting consideration; most of the historiography on Keckly focuses on her relationship with her most popular patron, Mary Todd Lincoln.[7] Serious consideration of the life and activism of Elizabeth Keckly shows that an ethos of black political mobilization, rooted in a patriotic commitment to the Union, took shape among leading black women during the Civil War era. Although some had only recently escaped the stronghold of slavery, the black women in Keckly's social milieu nonetheless viewed themselves as the more experienced purveyors of free life than the freed people crossing over into Union lines. Furthermore, the "community" referred to in this essay comprised the circle of people with whom Keckly identified and socialized, namely the black leaders in Washington. Analyzing Keckly's identity within this social and regional context affords one of many angles from which to understand the contributions of black women in wartime Washington. At the heart of the nation, women like Keckly strategically and creatively crafted their support for the Union.

Early Life and Memoir

Exposing the brutality of slavery, autobiographies of former slaves galvanized support for abolition leading up to the war, but Keckly's memoir, along with at least half of the existing slave narratives, was published after the war. G. W. Carleton of New York City published and advertised her story. The book generated substantial attention, but many in the North resented the account particularly for the intimate portrait Keckly painted of life in the White House. Too often dismissed by contemporaries as an opportunistic violation of confidence, the memoir did more damage than good to her reputation. Keckly, however, understood the political implications of her account and wrote as an insider who navigated the worlds of both African Americans and white Americans. Even as Keckly exercised caution in her portrayal of the Lincolns, her memoir conventionally captured a noble president and a troubled first lady. With her account of life in the White House and her own biographical experiences with slavery and freedom, the memoir served as a treatise on nineteenth-century race relations that offended and complicated the sensibilities of both Northern and Southern audiences.

Having brought "truth to the surface," Keckly positioned herself as a revisionist who offered a corrective to problematic assumptions about people of African descent.[8] Buried beneath the controversial reactions to her portrayal of the Lincolns and the complete dismissal of her reputation as a writer by white reviewers, a rich and complex telling of the black experience remains. For this reason, the memoir continues to provide a wealth of insight into the complexities of the Union war experience, particularly among enslaved and free African Americans. Telling her story constituted one of many avenues that she utilized to craft a public persona that countered demeaning characterizations of black women that typically prevailed throughout the nineteenth century. The narrative arc of her autobiography begins with slavery and ends with the aftermath of the Civil War. Her experiences as an enslaved woman, however, set the moral tone of her political project.

In February 1818, Elizabeth Keckly was born in Dinwiddie, Virginia, to Agnes, a slave, and Armistead Burwell, a slaveowner. Keckly resided in the Burwell house and, unlike most slaves, learned to read, write, and sew. At the age of fourteen, she was sent to live with the eldest Burwell son, Robert, and his wife, Margaret, who strongly disliked Keckly and found many opportunities to abuse her. Keckly recounted stories of their attempts to "break her" by repeatedly torturing her with beatings in order to "subdue" her "stubborn pride." Referring to the man instructed to "break her," she states, "With steady hand and practiced eye he would raise the instrument of torture, nerve himself for a blow, and with fearful force the rawhide descended upon the quivering flesh." The beatings left permanent scars imprinted on her body. She recalled, "It cut the skin, raised great welts, and the warm blood trickled down my back." As she remembered the painful memory of brutal violence, Keckly offered, "I can feel the torture now—the terrible, excruciating agony of those moments. I did not scream; I was too proud to let my tormentor know what I was suffering."[9]

Similar accounts of "slave breaking" appear in narratives, most notably the narratives of Solomon Northup and of Frederick Douglass, who became a close friend of Keckly's during the war. The connections that Keckly drew between her painful experiences and her future rise to prominence supported an ongoing discourse for the possibilities of racial uplift. Underscoring the brutality she experienced spoke to her audience, emphasizing the necessity of framing the Union war as a battle to defeat slavery and as the beginning of the path to black citizenship. In the years leading up to the war, however, Keckly and her contemporaries understood all too well that emancipation was not a given but more reflective of the hopes and determination of enslaved and free black people. They knew that if political factions actually reached compromise, slavery could very well remain intact. For Keckly, recollections of the brutality and trauma of slavery reminded America of the imperatives for racial progress. In her narrative, Keckly decidedly exposed the "dark side of slavery," including those aspects most painful to her.[10]

When the Burwells moved to North Carolina, Alexander M. Kirkland, a social acquaintance of the family, repeatedly sexually assaulted Keckly.[11] In her memoir, Keckly at one point stated, "I was regarded as fair-looking for one of my race, and for four years a white man—I spare the world his name—had base designs upon me." She undoubtedly weighed the implications of the disclosure of such violent and intimate matters. She noted, "I do not care to dwell upon this subject, for it is one that is fraught with pain. Suffice it to say, that he persecuted me for four years, and I—I—became a mother."[12] Keckly subsequently gave birth to a son, whom she named George.

In *Incidents in the Life of a Slave Girl*, Harriet Jacobs, Keckly's contemporary and fellow wartime activist, also recounted the painful details of her attempts to escape the harassment and sexual violence of one Dr. Flint. The tension between disclosing past experiences with sexual violence and representing identities that counter stereotypes about black women in autobiography underscores what Darlene Clark Hine refers to as a culture of dissemblance—"the behavior and attitudes of Black women that created the appearance of openness and disclosure but actually shielded the truth of their inner lives and selves from their oppressors."[13] In particular, slaveholders, who utilized black women as sexual and economic commodities, harnessed the sexuality of black women for their own personal profit and pleasure.

Keckly's disclosure of her experiences with sexualized violence underscored the grave cruelty of slavery while also giving testament to her identity as a survivor and the protection of that identity particularly as it shielded her sexuality as her own. Much of the narrative she builds about her early life reveals a delicate balance between communicating the realities of trauma and sexualized violence, even at the risk of readers calling her virtue into question. What is clear is that Keckly maintains full control of how she tells the story of her life. She wields command of her voice as she decides which aspects of her life to emphasize and what meaning is to be assigned to each event—the kind of work outside of the purview of a ghostwriter with no proximity to the experiences of enslaved women.

After Armistead Burwell died in 1842, Keckly was sent to live with Armistead's daughter Anne and her husband, Hugh Garland. In 1847, the Garlands moved to St. Louis, where Keckly managed to create many opportunities for herself through her sewing. Taught by her mother at a young age, Keckly honed her sewing skills, and not long after her move to St. Louis, her dresses were in high demand, particularly among elite white women. In her memoir, Keckly states, "I was fortunate in obtaining work, and in a short time I had acquired something of a reputation as a seamstress and dress-maker. The best ladies in St. Louis were my patrons, and when my reputation was once established I never lacked for orders."[14] In particular, she made dresses for a group of wealthy white women who eventually helped her raise funds to manumit both herself and her son, for a total of $1,200, in November 1855.

Keckly remained in St. Louis until she repaid her patrons for the money used toward her manumission. "The twelve hundred dollars with which I purchased the freedom of myself and son I consented to accept only as a loan. I went to work in earnest, and in a short time paid every cent that was so kindly advanced by my lady patrons of St. Louis."[15] Keckly took immense pride in paying "every cent" required of her freedom, a conviction of principle that reinforced her commitment to self-reliance and the virtue of hard work. She thereafter enrolled her son in classes at Wilberforce University and moved to Baltimore in 1860 in hopes of starting a dressmaking school for young black women.[16] After an unsuccessful stint running the school, she decided to move to Washington, where she made a dress for the wife of Robert E. Lee, an opportunity that opened doors for her to work for the wives of the political elite.

Keckly's memoir highlights the social prominence of the white women who paid for her services, including Mary Anna Custis Lee, Varina Davis, and Margaret McLean. Varina Davis, the wife of then senator Jefferson Davis, hired Keckly to work as her modiste, or fashion designer. Keckly gained an insider's perspective on Southern plans for secession in November 1860. "Almost every night, as I learned from the servants and other members of the family, secret meetings were held at the house." The meetings were held at discreet times, and she noted that during these "very late" hours, "prospects of war were freely discussed in my presence by Mr. and Mrs. Davis and their friends."[17] Scholarship on slavery discusses the ways that slaves and servants listened to conversations among slaveholders, particularly during mounting political conflict. This was not unusual—but Keckly's memoir provides a unique window into such scenes, as she reveals how she reacted to these conversations.

While discussing the possibilities of war, Keckly reported that Varina Davis told her that "the Southern people will not submit to the humiliating demands of the Abolition party; they will fight first." Feigning no deep interest in or knowledge of sectional strife, Keckly asks, "And which do you think will whip?" Any expressed hope or assumption of Southern defeat would have jeopardized this moment of confidence that Mrs. Davis seemed to place in her. Davis retorts, "The South, of course. The South is impulsive, is in earnest, and the Southern soldiers will fight to conquer. The North will yield, when it sees the South is in earnest, rather than engage in a long and bloody war."[18] Davis proposed that Keckly remain with the family, stating, "You had better go South with me; I will take good care of you. Besides, when the war breaks out, the colored people will suffer in the North." Davis forecasted a poor reception of African Americans, arguing that "the Northern people will look upon them as the cause of the war, and I fear, in their exasperation, will be inclined to treat you harshly."[19] Although Keckly was a free woman, Davis's proposition mirrored typical justifications for slavery as a "positive good," deriving from the paternalistic ethos that defended Southerners' presumed guardianship of an inferior race. Keckly, however, had earned her freedom, and dependence on the Davis family did not factor into her professional aspirations.

While working for Davis, Keckly negotiated with her to reserve time to work for other clients. Keckly did the same while sewing for Mrs. Lincoln, always maintaining a separate set of clients to supplement her portfolio. Keckly understood the great demand for her dresses, and, although each high-profile client required much of her attention, she understood as an astute entrepreneur that it was more profitable to maintain additional clients. Her patrons represented a range of political commitments, many of which included the belief that women such as Keckly should be enslaved. Even for the women that remained indifferent to the slavery debate, the general assumption of black racial inferiority prevailed in Washington's elite social circles.

Keckly navigated the polarizing social and political terrain that too often positioned free blacks as a nuisance and slavery as a necessary evil to keep the Union intact. After working tirelessly for clients who eventually represented both the Confederacy and the Union, Keckly obtained a license for a dress salon, which she opened at 388 Twelfth Street in Washington. In this manner, Keckly transitioned from enslaved to free seamstress and highly sought-after designer. She masterfully crafted a professional identity that allowed her to achieve social mobility in Washington and profit from clients with social and political convictions that too often hinged on the exploitation and discrimination of women like her. Keckly's experiences as an enslaved woman, a seamstress to the family of the future president of the Confederacy, and eventually modiste in the Lincoln household politicized her. Her insider's perspective positioned her to develop a stance along a political spectrum that excluded her. Keckly determinedly used her reputation and experiences to leverage her political activism during the Union war.

Keckly and the Contraband Relief Society

A bridge between antebellum antislavery ferment and late-nineteenth-century racial "uplift work," Elizabeth Keckly's activist efforts, and those of her peers, set the stage for the black clubwomen's movement that emerged later in the century.[20] In particular, Keckly's initiatives with the Contraband Relief Association reveal a growing push toward grassroots organizing led by black women in Washington. Her work with the Contraband Relief Association involved not only the collective efforts of women in her community but also occasional collaboration with white patrons such as Mary Todd Lincoln and other wives of Union politicians.

Her account, however, illuminates what the Union War meant to her. Regarding Keckly's narrative, Janaka B. Lewis offers, "It becomes part of the foundation on which she builds her discussion of the turmoil in America during the Civil War with specific references to the plight of black refugees, then freedmen and freedwomen." The experiences of refugees and freedpeople help us understand the broader reach of the war effort. Lewis states further, "Like Jacobs, who describes the Nat Turner revolt and its aftermath in her own household, Keckly uses her own versions of then-current events but writes about them specifically from her perspective; she is part of, not removed from, these histories."[21] White Americans found such traditions of truth telling difficult to ingest, since the testimonies of the enslaved were largely regarded with suspicion.

Until recently, scholars focused on Keckly and her story for the details they furnished about the lives of her white patrons. As Lewis argues, black women like Keckly and Harriet Jacobs developed opinions and insights about historical events with particular attention to how such transformative occurrences affected the millions of African Americans that inhabited and toiled in the country. Keckly and countless others cared deeply about the outcome of the Union war and found ways to rally behind the effort even at the risk of disappointment and even amid the rejection of their stories.

Well before the Confederate attack on Fort Sumter, Keckly pondered the prospect of a civil war between the states and the political gains at stake. She offered, "The Republican party had just emerged from a heated campaign, flushed with victory, and I could not think that the hosts composing the party would quietly yield all they had gained in the Presidential canvass." Fully aware of the Republican Party's commitment to the Union, Keckly at least hoped that a war against the Confederate states would also mean the possibility for emancipation and citizenship. As Keckly determined which side to support, she ultimately placed her bets on the Union. "A show of war from the South, I felt, would lead to actual war in the North; and with the two sections bitterly arrayed against each other, I preferred to cast my lot among the people of the North."[22]

As the Union war commenced, Keckly embraced her role in the effort—that of political activist. The historian Martha S. Jones analyzes the particular ways in which black women interrogated themes of equality and citizenship in the nineteenth century somewhat differently from their white counterparts. Using "public culture" as the frame for collective and communal interpretations and understandings of the issues black men and women confronted, Jones argues that throughout the nineteenth century, particularly during the Civil War era, black women did not limit their political activities to those constructed around gender consciousness and women's issues alone. For Keckly, gender, race, and the experience of slavery critically informed her activism. The historian Elsa Barkley Brown provides a poignant paradigm for understanding black women's political engagement during that time. Examining black women's politics in Richmond, Brown concludes that "focusing on formal disfranchisement obscures women's continued participation in the external political arena," as evidenced by the fact that black women's "exclusion from legal enfranchisement did not prevent [them] from shaping the vote and political decisions."[23]

Indeed, throughout the late 1860s and 1870s, black women actively participated in the political and public sphere, in large part because African Americans embraced a collective identity within their localities. As Brown observes, Southern black women emphasized their own "cultural, economic and political traditions" rather than relying on "arguments for superior female morality or motherhood." A departure from nineteenth-century ideas about women's activism in the domestic spheres, black women envisioned a broader reach into civic participation. Brown argues that "collective autonomy" offered the framework from which "African Americans reconstructed families, developed communal institutions, constructed schools and engaged in formal politics after emancipation."[24] Brown's work indicates that black women did not limit their work to the advancement of women's interests alone; instead, their political agenda engaged their entire community. They understood and navigated the complex array of issues that not only affected them as women but also affected the men and children in their lives.

Additionally, much of black women's political culture, including Keckly's Contraband Relief Association, stemmed from activities based in their churches. Black women viewed the church as not only a religious space but also a political and social institution where activism took root. The historian Evelyn Brooks Higginbotham states, "Black church women were conveyers of culture and vital contributors to the fostering of middle-class ideals and aspirations in the black community." Positioned to do this kind of cultural work, Keckly and her social milieu modeled such ideals. Higginbotham noted that women like her "adhered to a politics of respectability that equated public behavior with individual self-respect and with the advancement of African Americans as a group."[25] This "politics of respectability," by seeking to dismantle the demeaning stereotypes of black people, shows the ways in which the concept of "black womanhood" became politicized among black Baptist women.

Revising this interpretation of respectability to reflect an antebellum context, the cultural historian Erica Ball argues that the aims of the black middle class transcended the "politics of respectability" and instead revealed a personal commitment to shape lives as "living, breathing refutations of the arguments used to justify the institution of slavery and its concomitant racism."[26] While Higginbotham explains how respectability became a tenet of social and political mobilization among black women in the late nineteenth century, Ball's work demonstrates that "to live an antislavery life" was deeply tied to a political commitment to liberation, independence, and self-definition. The scholars Treva Lindsey and Brittney Cooper show later interpretations of respectability and the ways black women reinvented and challenged expressions of respectability.[27] Moreover, just as Keckly navigated elite circles (in both the antebellum era and the late nineteenth century), she also embodied the experiences and commitments of a former enslaved woman. Thus, the trajectory of her life modeled an antislavery nexus between bondage and liberation and the continued work of black freedom and self-definition after emancipation. It is within this cultural, social, and political context that Keckly's activism took root.

For figures like Keckly, black women's political culture during the Union war aspired to strengthen the political and social autonomy of refugees in the form of (but not limited to) fundraising for material resources and instilling the values of self-reliance and education. Moved by the destitute conditions freedmen and -women faced during and after the Civil War, Keckly organized a meeting to create a plan that would ameliorate their condition. Some military and government officials in Union territory employed the term "contraband" in ways that underscored the legality of pieces of wartime legislation such as the Confiscation Acts, but the term also reinforced the idea that the refugees were property and therefore held no rights to the privileges of citizenship.[28] In places such as Washington, DC, many government officials, Democrats, and slaveholders remained averse to the growth of the free black population and looked upon refugees with particular disdain. Local black leaders also took a complicated stance as they rallied to support the growing population of freed people.

As free blacks expressed enthusiasm for the abolishment of slavery, many also viewed themselves as key liaisons that communicated the realities and demands of free life. In her memoir, Keckly observed that, although many of these former slaves had grand hopes and visions of freedom, they found bitter disappointment when they arrived further north to begin their new "free" life. "Often I heard them declare that they would rather go back to slavery in the South, and be with their old masters, than to enjoy the freedom of the North." Invoking her perspective on the effects of slavery, she opined, "I believe they were sincere in these declarations because dependence had become a part of their second nature, and independence brought with it the cares and vexations of poverty."²⁹ This statement is rather ironic given that Keckly went to such great lengths to distance herself from the characterization of "dependence" associated with slavery when she became free.

Self-determination and independence remained the core message conveyed by free blacks to freed people arriving in the nation's capital. Throughout her memoir, Keckly described her efforts to be free as "self-reliance," a term that underscored her worthiness of freedom and her fitness for citizenship. Rather than referring to slavery as the root of dependence, as she did when she assessed the condition of freed people, she looked to slavery as the training ground for self-reliance when recounting her experience as a recently freed slave: "Notwithstanding all the wrongs that slavery heaped upon me, I can bless it for one thing—youth's important lesson of self-reliance."³⁰ Here, Keckly remembers that as a four-year-old slave she was required to tend to the baby of the plantation mistress. With work and responsibility imposed upon her at such a young age, she commented on how she was forced to rely upon her own instincts and develop a work ethic during slavery, thus rejecting the paternalist assumption behind tropes that characterized slaves as lazy and dependent. Black leaders offered commentary shrouded in problematic assumptions about the enslaved with a slight air of condescension even as they set out to generate support for the refugees making the tumultuous journey to Union lines. This complex and often contradictory assessment of the condition of freed people is captured in the naming of the organization Keckly founded—the Contraband Relief Association.

Promoting self-reliance and education, Keckly and the Contraband Relief Association set out to break the culture of "dependence" that they believed suffused the institution of slavery, by responding to their material realities first. The term "contraband" reflected the terminology used by General Benjamin Butler near the beginning of the war when Shepard Mallory, Frank Baker, and James Townsend abandoned Confederate fortifications they were forced to build.³¹ They arrived at Union-occupied Fort Monroe, where Butler refused to return them to their owner, Confederate colonel Charles Mallory, on the grounds that they were prohibited from aiding the rebellion and that they were contraband of war. Even as Butler creatively deployed the property status of these enslaved men to release them from Mallory, the term "contraband" reinforced the legal status of fugitives as confiscated property. Despite the fact that in April 1862 the District of Columbia passed an emancipation act that set in motion the freedom of the enslaved, the term "contraband" persisted throughout the nation's capital during the course of the Civil War, even among free blacks. Thus, as the emancipation process went underway in the Union, the question regarding the status of enslaved persons remained in flux and at times imbued with contradiction. Refugees and fugitives in neighboring slaveholding states placed their bets on arriving on free soil in the District, which ultimately resulted in scores of formerly enslaved women, men, and children taking up residence under dire conditions in Washington. As the Union government worked through the details of the legal and citizenship status of refugees, black organizers stepped in to provide relief for them.

Accordingly, on August 9, 1862, Keckly, along with women from her church, met and agreed to form the CRA, electing Keckly as its first president. An article for the black-owned publication *The Christian Recorder*, titled "Societies in DC for the Benefit of Contraband," described Keckly's visit to Philadelphia to raise funds for the Contraband Relief society. The article noted her extensive involvement in her church and stated that upon "seeing and hearing of the sufferings of the contrabands who are sent to Washington, proposed to some of her lady friends, when returning from church one Sabbath day, the necessity of a contraband relief association." He observed that the CRA "appears to have met with warm approval from friends." Her travel to Northern cities housing notable networks of free blacks underscores the scope of the CRA's reach and the ways that Keckly's reputation preceded her.[32]

The article underscored the connection between social activism and the broader role of leading black women. The resources collected and "the "warm approval" from like-minded friends painted a portrait of "Societies in DC," as reflected in the title of the article. Their style of philanthropic organizing reflected a burgeoning black middle-class sensibility that made activism a central tenet of black people's compatibility with civic virtue and social equality.

Ultimately, the decision to create the Contraband Relief Association blossomed into a widespread effort spanning major cities such as Philadelphia and other areas of Washington. Kate Masur's work examines the black struggle to gain simultaneously political and social equality while also developing independent black institutions.[33] While black Washingtonians demanded equal access to public institutions, transportation, and accommodations, they did not necessarily favor assimilation into white communities. To the contrary, they realized that this might involve the forfeiture of a broad array of institutions, both public and private, that they had worked so hard to build, maintain, and support.

Nonetheless, recognizing the need for political and social equality, Keckly strategically used her celebrity status in elite social circles and in the black press to advance the cause of the Contraband Relief Association. As president of the association, she wrote an article in the *Christian Recorder* to generate awareness about relief efforts on behalf of black families. In that article, she stated, "We have now, in our immediate vicinity, from eight to ten thousand poor men, women and children, in a most distressing and deplorable condition." Appealing to the generosity and self-determination of the wartime community of free African Americans, Keckly explained, "We need for them food, clothing and money. We have now several invalid families of women and children under our care, for whose house-rent, fuel and medical attendance, we are obliged to expend money."[34]

To satisfy these needs, Keckly leveraged the resources of her church membership, appealing to those who might be able to donate. Her article, for instance, noted that the plight of destitute freedmen could be alleviated even within their "immediate vicinity," where thousands lacked access to basic necessities. Clarifying the overall aims of the organization, she further stated, "Our society, 'The Contraband Relief Association,' was formed for the purpose, not only of relieving the wants of those destitute people, but also to sympathize with, and advise them, we have endeavored to carry out this spirit." With regards to what this looked like on the ground, Keckly reports that "We have visited and counseled them, and we have, as far as we have the ability, relieved their wants by giving them food, clothing, and medicine." Without the vital contributions of supporters, Keckly lamented that "much which our hearts longed to do, we have been obliged to leave undone, for want of means."[35]

Through this appeal to potential donors, Keckly not only emphasized their Christian duty to help meet the most basic needs of the freedmen but also to "sympathize with, and advise them." In the process, she alludes to the mantle of leadership she assumed, stressing that her elite black peers possessed the ability to "advise them" in the ways of freedom as those more experienced with such a reality. In this respect, her charge projects the responsibility of relief on the existing free black community, realizing that the needs of freed people would be most effectively met through intraracial collective efforts. However, interracial support also informed the leveraging of resources that characterized her wartime organizing.

An article reporting on the first anniversary of the Contraband Relief Association provides the most telling account of Keckly's influence and of the interracial impact of the organization. The reporter noted the "unusually interesting character" of the event, which included a large group of both black and white men and women in attendance. In their first year of existence, the association raised a total of $885.64, not including the barrels of clothing and donations they received from numerous donors and organizations.[36]

Before the event, Keckly suggested the design of a flag to present to the First District Regiment of Colored Volunteers in their honor, so the women in the association organized a fundraising festival for the flag. The flag, designed by Mr. D. B. Bowser, a black artist from Philadelphia, was adorned on one side with the image of the American eagle and on the other side with the Goddess of Liberty, whose foot was placed on a serpent's head. That side, the reporter states, "is represented in the act of handing a musket to a colored man—her very eyes seem to flash with patriotism; the lips, though dumb, seem to speak the motto above her, 'God and Liberty.'"[37]

Black leaders viewed the enlistment of black soldiers as a critical decision that would undoubtedly affect the outcome of the war. Appointed as a recruiting agent for the 54th Massachusetts Volunteer Infantry Regiment, Frederick Douglass gave a compelling speech in New York that historicized the opportunity before them. He noted in his speech "Men of Color, to Arms!" that "a war undertaken and brazenly carried on for the perpetual enslavement of colored men, calls logically and loudly upon colored men to help to suppress it."[38] He further implored the potential recruits to reflect on earlier accounts of resistance, stating, "Remember Denmark Vesey, of Charleston! Remember Nathaniel Turner of South Hampton! Remember Shields Green, and Cope and all those who followed noble John Brown, and fell as glorious martyrs for the cause of the slave." Douglass too invoked the narrative arc of slavery as a vital lens from which to view racial oppression. "Remember, that, in a contest with oppression, the Almighty has no attribute which can take sides with the oppressor."[39] The Union war, as conceived by many black leaders like Douglass, represented a continuation of a freedom struggle that had begun long before the outbreak of war. Calling upon the legacy of former insurrections, Douglass invited the men in the audience to make history.

At the anniversary celebration, Mr. J. F. Cooke, a black soldier, presented the flag on behalf of the Contraband Relief Association, making references in his speech to the moral significance of the American Revolution and the Civil War in promoting "humanity and civilization" in America.[40] Recognizing the noteworthy presence of the black soldier, he admonished them to not lose hope: "You, America's outcasts, go forth to do battle for your country, with but little positive reliance that your deeds will receive even their just reward. And while you do battle for the noble cause of country, remember that you fight for the still nobler cause, 'God and Liberty.'"[41] It is thus clear that Cooke and the soldiers fighting in the regiment viewed their efforts as part of their duty not only for their country but also for the liberty to which they felt entitled. These remarks were particularly poignant and timely for many in attendance, including Keckly, who had lost her son in 1861, at the Battle of Wilson's Creek, after he enlisted in the Union army as a white soldier.[42]

Keckly and countless others with families enlisted in the Union military remained steadfast in their support for the cause. Even as black leaders worked collaboratively with white officials, they sustained a critique of the how the war should be framed. In a speech delivered in the winter of 1863, Frederick Douglass, a dear friend and contemporary of Keckly's, reinforced the meaning he and others assigned to the war: "What business, then, have we to fight for the old Union? We are not fighting for it. We are fighting for something incomparably better than the old Union." Douglass noted that the Union's current structure proved insufficient for the kind of transformation that made racial equality and national unification a possibility. Looking to the potential of the future Union, Douglass asserted, "We are fighting for unity: unity of object, unity of institutions, in which there shall be no North, no South, no East, no West, no black, no white, but a solidarity of the nation, making every slave free, and every free man a voter."[43] The purpose of the war, according to Douglass, required the removal of inequality as the prerequisite for an authentic Union. For him and many others, Union could not be the operative term until everyone in the country embodied the unity, equality, and access to citizenship that gave the Union its noble and democratic meaning. Douglass would remind himself of the significant opportunity the country faced even as his own sons, Charles and Lewis, fought bravely with the 54th Massachusetts Volunteer Infantry Regiment.

At the commemorative event that Keckly hosted to honor the soldiers fighting for the Union, Mr. Cooke presented the flag to Captain James J. Ferree. The white officer, temporarily in charge of the colored regiment, gave a speech championing the bravery of black soldiers. He lauded their contributions to battles on behalf of American liberty prior to the Civil War despite over two hundred years of oppression, proclaiming, "Ladies of the Contraband Relief Association, we thank you, and permit me to say that the colored brother represented on the beautiful flag you have given us, with a musket in his hands, is the emblem of the salvation of the white race." He added, "The efficiency of colored regiments has been tested at Port Hudson, Milliken's Bend, and yet more recently and more gloriously at Fort Wagner."[44] These remarks—at a time when slavery was teetering but had not fallen and when few individuals would conceptualize the white race as being in need of "salvation"—were radical.

After Ferree received a roaring applause, Colonel Forney, another white officer, was asked to offer remarks. The journalist reported that before the war Forney held his own prejudices against the black race but ultimately had come to the conclusion that "if liberty is to be secured to us, permanent and practical liberty, it must be by the aid of the colored races upon this continent."[45] Forney's presence at the event—and remarks praising the efforts of black soldiers—created quite an impression on those in attendance, who also hoped for a more "permanent and practical" liberty. His remarks particularly resonated with black women and men in attendance, such as Keckly and other prominent black Washingtonians, who worked tirelessly in their advocacy for freedom and equality during the Union war. To receive praise from white officials reaffirmed their aims and objectives.

The tone and quality of the words spoken at the anniversary thus highlighted not only the leadership of Keckly and the collective efforts of black women who painstakingly organized relief efforts but also the platform created by black women's political culture during the Union war. The strategic manner in which Keckly and other elite black women organized independent associations centered on a notion that self-determination and independence, once achieved, entitled them to political and social equality. Other prominent black leaders hosted similar celebrations, such as the reception hosted by George T. Downing in honor of Ulysses S. Grant.[46] White locals, however, would not relent so easily to the idea of blacks' full inclusion into society.

Envisioning a Black Citizenry

Faced with legal hurdles, uncertainty, and white hostilities, black women and men continued to envision a society that included them as citizens. Wartime emancipation policies and the provision in the Emancipation Proclamation permitting the enlistment of black soldiers laid the groundwork for the June 28, 1864, repeal of the Fugitive Slave Act of 1850. This repeal, which broadened the scope of emancipation, was intended to protect black soldiers from reenslavement in loyal slaveholding states within the Union. As the war ignited an exodus of former slaves and their families into the District of Columbia, however, black residents and soldiers became vulnerable to legal conflict. Black soldiers fighting on behalf of the Union, for instance, were not exempt from racial violence or imprisonment. One officer announced that he would "put as many bullets through a nigger recruit as he would through a mad dog."[47] *Leslie's*, moreover, reported that former slaves and other black inhabitants of Washington were unjustly imprisoned. Complaints concerning the criminalization of "respectable" black residents—many of whom had a long history of residence in the city and organized relief for the former slaves that migrated there during the war—appeared in print as well. A reporter for the *Daily National Republican* offered, "I have been called upon repeatedly by colored persons of the most respectable character in this District, and asked if, in organizing the police of the District, we intended to oppress them as a class."[48] These black residents, typically affiliated with churches and uplift organizations, were not shielded from the criminalizing impulses of local police and the violence of angry mobs.

During the summer of 1862, just months after local emancipation and days before the Supplemental Act empowering blacks to testify against whites, one correspondent asked if "there was no law to prevent low rowdies from committing outrages on peaceable colored females when going to or from the house of worship on the Sabbath Day." He reported that local black women, particularly near Alexandria, Virginia, were "subjected to the grossest insults. Sometimes with kicks by these low men." The reporter argued that black people lacked protection under the law not only in Alexandria, the retroceded portion of the region, but also in the District of Columbia, where the Emancipation Act had just passed. Black locals understood that wartime emancipation alone would not ensure freedom. Subject to black codes, members of the antebellum free black population knew all too well the need to protect their fragile legal status.[49]

News accounts noted the mounting frequency with which former slaves arrived to the nation's capital in hopes of escaping bondage, locating family members, or seeking employment. The *Daily National Republican* reported, on June 4, 1863, that 110 "contrabands" had arrived that morning. In total, it was reported that up to forty thousand former slaves had made it to the District as "contrabands," now living in camps and settlements near Freedmen's Village in Arlington and throughout the District in makeshift shanties. Half of the refugees arrived at the camps as families, with each person averaging about forty cents per day in wages. The arrival of former slaves expanded the black population significantly as they found ways to make the capital their home. But they did not arrive to a welcome committee. To the contrary, during deliberations over the Emancipation Act in Washington, local politicians and white citizens persistently disputed the authority of the government to free slaves in the District.[50]

As countless citizens across the country looked to the capital to see how recently freed blacks would be integrated into society after the Emancipation Act of 1862, they witnessed resistance not only from white locals but also from District government officials. The Board of Aldermen and Board of Common Council of the City of Washington compiled a Joint Resolution of Instruction protesting local emancipation. The resolution read: "The sentiment of a large majority of the people of this community is averse to the unqualified abolition of slavery in this district at the present critical Junction in our national affairs." Local officials thus

Figure 2 Black refugees in Freedman's Village, Arlington, Virginia. The photographer highlighted the possibility for education in refugee camps by showing African American adults and children with books.
Source: Library of Congress, Prints and Photographs Division, reproduction no. LC-DIG-ppmsca-34829.

attempted to make a case against black emancipation. By framing the Union war as an event that had little relevance to the status of slaves, whites—particularly Democrats—endeavored to carve out emancipation from the scope of "national" concerns and affairs, suggesting that emancipation represented an unnecessary digression from the war effort and a deviation from accepted social norms.[51]

The legislative battle between Congress and the local board members continued as city officials reminded Congress of their duty as the "constitutional guardians of the interests and rights of the people of this District." In using the term "people," city officials did not include free blacks or refugees. The board members thus requested that Congress provide "proper safe-guards" against the free black population, highlighting the fact that the city was located between two slaveholding states. They warned that, absent safeguards, the city would be transformed "into an asylum for free negroes, a population undesirable in every American community, and which it has been deemed necessary to exclude altogether from some even of the non-Slaveholding States." Despite the fact that even before the war the "hiring out" system of slavery and the growth of the free black population had given the District a moderate reputation for its treatment of blacks, it was nonetheless clear that white locals were displeased with the decision to emancipate local slaves and even more dismayed at the possibility of black equality and citizenship. The emancipation moment consequently exposed white hostilities toward black freedom within Union lines. Nevertheless, freedpeople employed every resource and strategy toward full inclusion.[52]

With no voting rights and wielding no government authority, wartime conditions in the city left black women and men in the District politically constrained. Further, even if black Washingtonians had been granted the right to vote, that gendered right would not have extended to black women like Keckly. This made the freedom of black women even more tenuous. While black women ultimately could not access the voting booth until the twentieth century, they nonetheless understood and navigated the complex array of political issues that affected their communities through alternative avenues for action.[53]

As Keckly's work shows, black women in the District were fully engaged in a local protest tradition in which they served as catalysts for racial advancement. For instance, although black men were the designated signers of a petition protesting their lack of legal representation and voting privileges, black women informed the content of the petition.[54] They served as teachers, fundraisers, organizers, and owners of property in Washington's black community—black women held a stake in debates about equality and citizenship. In December 1865, a statement penned by "the Colored Citizens of the District of Columbia" addressed the political disparities between black and white inhabitants. Specifically, the statement emphasized that while black residents paid "no inconsiderable amount of taxes," with "the proceeds of their labor taken and disposed of without a single voice," and were "intelligent enough to be industrious; to have accumulated property; to build and sustain churches, and institutions of learning," they had no access to political suffrage. No one understood this better than Keckly, a single African American woman who paid taxes, owned her own business, and had organized the CRA.

Even with limited means and often through the collective contributions of African Americans, black women articulated an agenda for uplift in the midst of disenfranchisement. Elizabeth Keckly, along with other female congregants at the Fifteenth Street Presbyterian Church, organized to meet the material needs of freedpeople during the Union war, in order to "alleviate their sufferings, and help them towards a higher plane of civilization." Noting these efforts of black women, who often invited freedpeople into the basements and kitchens of their homes and churches, Henry McNeal Turner, pastor of Washington's Israel AME Church, stated, "It is female assistance which has given impetus to all reforming enterprises, and redeeming deeds." Further, black women educated their children "without the aid of any school-fund," while simultaneously subsidizing through their taxes the education of local white children in the public schools.[55]

Black women such as Harriet Jacobs played a critical role in these education initiatives, serving as teachers and developing strategies for fundraising and curriculum building despite scarce resources. Some of the "redeeming deeds" that Turner referred to included the establishment of sustainable communities, including Freedmen's Village in Alexandria, which was organized and supported by notable black female activists such as Harriet Jacobs and her daughter.[56] At Freedmen's Village, Harriet Jacobs supported the refugees in their transition to freedom and established a school. Freedwomen were required to work in Union camps under harsh conditions, with inadequate food rations and exorbitant rent fees for cramped living spaces. Freedmen's Village was a significant departure from the notorious Camp Barker in Washington and offered a model for sustainable black communities where families built and maintained their own homes and cultivated their own land. Condemning those who "refused to help themselves" and lauding those who worked with "commendable energy," Keckly noted that freedpeople sought sustainable communities having "built themselves cabins, and each family cultivated for itself a small patch of ground."[57]

Residents of Freedmen's Village paid a percentage of rent and raised funds to build a community school. Named after Harriet Jacobs, the construction of the Jacobs School was a tremendous triumph, given the extreme conditions of poverty freedpeople encountered. Keckly remarked, "Whoever visits the Freedmen's Village now in the vicinity of Washington will discover all of these evidences of prosperity and happiness." The organization of a subsistence economy, along with cooperative efforts to build institutions, made the Freedmen's Village an exemplar of the possibilities for freedpeople. Keckly observed, "The schools are objects of much interest. Good teachers, white and colored, are employed, and whole brigades of bright-eyed dusky children are there taught the common branches of education." She noted the intellectual capacity of the children at the school: "These children are studious, and the teachers inform me that their advancement is rapid."[58]

To capture their progress, Jacobs arranged for a photograph to be taken in front of the school. The *Freedman's Record* observed, "It is delightful to see this group of neatly dressed children, of all ages, and with faces of every variety of the African and mixed type, all intelligent, eager, and happy."[59] Northern reformers described school operations as "diligent and efficient," a place of black improvement. Why did Jacobs arrange this photo shoot? Perhaps to demonstrate that despite the circumstances, the former slaves had proven themselves as "worthy citizens" that embodied order, intelligence, and self-determination.[60] These characteristics are problematic in that they suggest a narrow prescription for the just and equal treatment of African Americans. Having understood this, however, Jacobs used this photograph to deploy a visual articulation of the potential for full black inclusion into American society—citizenship.

As the Union war came to a close, the 1865 statement from "Colored Citizens" of the District—which noted that unequal laws hindered progress, industry, and "virtuous citizenship"—thus echoed black female initiatives to prove that the character of the black poor was no different than that of their white counterparts. Indeed, "virtue" was a term commonly deployed by black activist women at the time to validate their personhood and entitlement to equal rights. They were ready to claim what they felt they had earned through their efforts during the Union war. In arguing for equality, the 1865 statement also invoked notions of citizenship and patriotism by emphasizing black military service during the Civil War. Referencing the war effort, the statement reported that black soldiers comprised "three full regiments, over 3,500 enlisted men, while the white citizens out of a population of upwards 60,000 sent only about 1,500 enlisted men for the support of the Union, the Constitution, and the Laws." Just as white locals zealously deployed the Constitution in defense of a white-only citizenry, blacks similarly utilized the Constitution as a political tool, touting its tenets of liberty and justice as evidence that blacks deserved to share the privileges of freedom and citizenship.[61]

At the core, black inhabitants of the District knew that racial inequalities and disparities could not be remedied without political empowerment—that is, the ability to change the laws. With a tone of cautious gratitude, the 1865 statement thus conveyed that while Congress gave black people "a free District, and a free Country," blacks were "still without the political rights enjoyed by every other man" and only "nominally free." The "colored citizens" concluded that "without the right of suffrage, we are without protection, and liable to Combinations of outrage." Two years thereafter, Congress overrode a veto from President Andrew Johnson and granted the franchise to all males over the age of twenty-one, regardless of race.[62]

Black women's collective efforts across class and gender lines left an imprint on wartime and postwar political activism in Washington, DC. Their reform efforts culminated in a significant—albeit ephemeral—political transformation. Whereas the mayor of the District in 1860, James Berret, was a Southern Democrat and supporter of Southern secession, by 1868, black male residents of the

District were exercising the right to vote, and Sayles J. Brown, a Republican and supporter of black civil rights, was elected mayor. In fact, 90 percent of eligible black voters in the District participated in the election as enfranchised citizens.[63] Just one year later, the Board of Police hired Charles C. Tillman and Calvin C. Caruthers, the first black policemen of the District of Columbia.[64] Despite these political gains, however, racial equality was not fully realized in the daily life of most blacks in postwar Washington, and the triumph of political agency in the 1867 city election evaporated into a faint memory eleven years later, when black and white males were disenfranchised. The fact that black women could not vote was an obvious indicator that the contestations over citizenship had hardly reached a firm conclusion. The historian Robert Harrison identifies the Reconstruction era as a moment of biracial democracy that ended in 1874 largely because of the decisions of District policy makers that focused on city planning, infrastructure, and beautification at the expense of social Reconstruction.[65] By the late 1870s, the capital represented a romantic symbol of liberty in black politics, but the reality for black women resembled an all-too-familiar terrain of uncertainty as they persistently worked to shape a life of freedom.

Conclusion

Under the leadership of women like Keckly, African Americans collected resources, raised funds, visited with refugees, and searched for ways to alleviate the dire conditions that freedpeople confronted when they arrived in the national capital—all while navigating the limits of racism and sexism. African Americans, however, did not relent in framing the Union war effort as an opportunity not only to restore the Union and free the enslaved but also to chart a course that allowed for full inclusion and racial equality as a feature of a more perfect Union. Douglass noted, "It is a war for the Union, a war for the Constitution, and a war for Republican Institutions, I admit; but it is logically such a war, only in the sense that the greater includes the lesser." The link between the Constitution and the future of slavery appeared inseparable for Douglass. "Slavery has proved itself the strong element of our national life. In every rebel state it has proved itself stronger than the Union, the Constitution, and Republican Institutions." If the Republicans in power were to preserve the legislative gains set in motion during the war, then, he argued, "this strong element must be bound and cast out of our national life before union, the Constitution, and Republican Institutions can become possible." According to Douglass, emancipation remained uncertain without the power of a constitutional amendment to support it. "An abolition war therefore includes union, Constitution, and Republican Institutions and all else that goes to make up the greatness and glory of our common country."[66] From Douglass's perspective, and that of countless others, the Union war was an abolition war.

Slavery overwhelmed the Union, overshadowed interpretations of the Constitution, and undercut the integrity of the egalitarian impetus of the Republic. Moreover, African Americans and Republicans identified a critical opportunity for emancipation as well as black citizenship regardless of whether government officials initially portrayed the Union war as a war to abolish slavery or to preserve the Union. In 1865, the Rev. Henry Highland Garnet, pastor of the Fifteenth Street Presbyterian Church that Keckly attended throughout the war, was the first African American to give a sermon at the Capitol Building in Washington. As he concluded his remarks, he stated, "If slavery has been destroyed merely from necessity, let every class be enfranchised at the dictation of justice." When everyone possessed the franchise, "then we shall have a Constitution that shall be reverenced by all, rulers who shall be honored and revered, and a Union that shall be sincerely loved by a brave and patriotic people, and which can never be severed."[67] Just days before the ratification of the Thirteenth Amendment, Garnet in his sermon implored the leaders seated attentively in the Capitol to complete the unfinished work of formally recognizing black Americans as citizens.

Not all African American leaders embraced the perspectives of Keckly or of Garnet and Douglass. Colonization remained a possibility that appealed to some free blacks throughout the war.[68] Indeed, Lincoln held on to the possibility of colonization as a response to wartime emancipation. With the influence of black leaders, however, Lincoln eventually veered away from such a project.[69] Still, patriotism and a desire for inclusion within the Union appeared unrealistic and unpalatable to some free blacks who had embraced the wartime moment as an opportunity to settle beyond the boundaries of the nation and possibly migrate to Latin America or Africa. Those who envisioned life within the Union did so while facing the uncertainties of life after the war.

Keckly, Douglass, Jacobs, and Garnet represented a small yet significant set of the leading African American voices that shaped black discourses about the Union war throughout the wartime years and long after the surrender at Appomattox. The Union war presented an opportunity for which black women and men showed up. And while their efforts were frequently met with resistance, they determinedly followed through on the conviction that they should be free and regarded as equal citizens. Keckly and countless others understood that the work of equality remained incomplete. She devoted her life to activism and shared a complex and deeply personal account of her own experiences in slavery, freedom, and later segregation. Keckly offered her view from "behind the scenes" of a time and place marked by the determination to exclude women like her. While not representative of all African Americans, Keckly's story illuminates the complex ways the Union war politicized various communities of free blacks. Keckly and countless others regarded the Union war as a definitive moment in which inclusion appeared within the realm of possibility.

To Save the Union "in Behalf of Conservative Men"

Horatio Seymour and the Democratic Vision for War

Jack Furniss

In the fall elections of 1862, the Democratic Party scored a series of dramatic victories across the Northern states. Indiana, Pennsylvania, Ohio, New York, New Jersey, and Illinois all returned a majority of Democrats in their congressional races. In the single most dramatic outcome, New York—the leading contributor of men, materiel, and money to the war effort—elected Democrat Horatio Seymour as its new governor. All told, the Republican vote declined 16 percent from 1860. Explaining these results, President Lincoln cited the lost ballots of absent soldiers and a backlash against the Preliminary Emancipation Proclamation fomented by hostile and influential newspapers. The New York diarist George Templeton Strong pointed to war weariness and frustration with the Union army's lack of progress, claiming that "two-thirds of those who voted for Seymour" did so to convey to Washington that "my business is stopped, I have got taxes to pay, my wife's third cousin was killed on the Chickahominy, and the war is no nearer the end than it was a year ago. I am disgusted . . . and shall vote for the governor or congressman you disapprove, just to spite you." Historians have generally seen these explanations, all hinging entirely on voters reacting *against* the Republicans, as sufficient assessments of the 1862 canvass. This essay argues, by contrast, that in order to explain Democratic successes we need to appreciate the appeal, in its own right, of the Democratic vision of and for the Union war. We need to understand why people cast their ballots *for* Democrats, not just *against* Republicans. Dissatisfaction with the Lincoln administration is only part of the picture.[1]

The nature of the Democrats' electoral appeal has been obscured by a historiography that has commonly seen Democrats as "obstructionists and racists, who reacted to Republican-inspired policies on the basis of expediency" and who "often flirted with treason." Two influential works of the 1970s, by Jean H. Baker and

Joel H. Silbey, rowed against this tide, stressing the fundamental respectability and loyalty of the party during wartime. Recent studies by Jennifer Weber and Michael Landis have swung the pendulum back. Landis considers the Northern Democratic Party of the 1850s to have been unabashedly proslavery and pro-Southern. Analyzing the war years, Weber's *Copperheads* argues that antiwar sentiment was widespread, profoundly threatening to the nation, and fostered by influential and numerous Peace Democrat politicians. Weber has, in Robert Sandow's words, "reasserted the Republican paradigm of Democratic disloyalty." This essay seeks to change the focus of this historiography by finding a new lens through which to appraise wartime Democrats.[2]

The labels "War Democrat" and "Peace Democrat" are common to virtually all the existing literature but are deliberately absent here. Such monikers uncritically perpetuate the view of the Democratic Party that Republicans propagated. To do so is problematic. First, and crucially, scholars tend to apply these labels to the entire war, when chronologically they only gained meaningful weight from 1863 onward, as my argument will illustrate. In addition, the vast majority of Democrats identified themselves primarily with the overarching cause of the Union rather than committing irrevocably to war or to negotiation. Many of those commonly designated War Democrats argued fiercely that compromise represented an honorable course of action, to be pursued in conjunction with military efforts. Most Peace Democrats never admitted that they would accept anything less than Union as an outcome of negotiations following an armistice. The Republican Party worked hard to conflate loyalty with war and treason with negotiation. As the war dragged on, they added support for emancipation as a requirement of loyalty, an equation they had explicitly rejected in 1861. In hindsight, we may agree with Republican judgments, but amid the bloodletting, many questioned such assertions.

Portrayals of the wartime Democratic Party that center on the extent of their disloyalty make it difficult to comprehend why so many Northern voters supported them in 1862. Even for those voters most disillusioned with the incumbents, they still had to deem the alternative credible and acceptable. For many Northerners, the Democrats offered a substantive vision that they believed held the best chance of realizing their central priority: winning the war and restoring the Union. Focusing on the first two years of the war and the successful election campaign of Horatio Seymour in 1862, this essay will elucidate the concrete components of the vision of the Union war that Democrats articulated, one waged "in behalf of conservative men."[3]

During the 1862 canvass, Horatio Seymour consistently advocated four key positions that formed the foundation blocks of Democratic ideology, identity, and messaging. Most basic was the legitimacy of partisan opposition during wartime, based on a clear differentiation between the administration and the government. Articulated most fervently in the early months of the conflict, but not abandoned thereafter, was a second idea: that compromise was an honorable, traditional, and patriotic course of action. This meant that peace negotiations, as long as they did not involve disunion, were not necessarily viewed as inimical to the war effort. Third, Seymour was a fierce and constant advocate of a strict Jacksonian interpretation of the Constitution, and he specifically enumerated the rights he believed that it guaranteed to both the individual and to the states under a federal system. He viewed measures like the suspension of habeas corpus and emancipation as critically undermining the very liberties that made the Union worth protecting.

Seymour's Unionism represented by far the most important element of his and the Democratic appeal, and it encompassed all the previously mentioned positions. The content of this Unionism will be explored at length, but it focused relentlessly on a conservative war of restoration. The war had to be fought in a limited, constitutional manner to ensure that, after victory, the South could resume its position as the North's equal partner. A war that permanently destroyed Southern society could not be a war for Union. Seymour focused this appeal around his confidence in the fundamental Unionism of the Southern masses. This belief, however wishful, was common to Republican understandings of the Slave Power conspiracy. Embracing a war fought to relieve and strengthen Southern Unionists might easily appeal across party lines. Inherently, this also offered a prescription for Reconstruction—namely, there would be no Reconstruction, only restoration and reunion with loyal Southerners.

In terms of tactics, Democrats had to find the means to convince the electorate that they genuinely supported the war while earnestly criticizing its handling. At a time when a patriotic people viewed partisan behavior with great skepticism, they recast the political divide as conservative against radical, not Democrat against Republican. To drive the point home, men like Seymour proclaimed that their victory would actually strengthen the hand of the president. Despite his recent issuance of the Preliminary Emancipation Proclamation, many Democrats and a considerable number of Republicans saw Lincoln as a conservative at heart, locked in a bitter struggle with the radicals within his own party. Seymour claimed that Democratic success would answer the president's "private prayers" by "shaking off those radical influences by which it has heretofore been annoyed and embarrassed." Democrats, for both political and constitutional reasons, were much happier focusing their attacks on men like Horace Greeley, Charles Sumner, Wendell Phillips, or Salmon Chase than against President Lincoln. This approach helped Seymour motivate the Democratic base and reach out to the swing voters of the Civil War, many of whom self-identified as "conservatives."[4]

The Conservative Middle

Many who self-identified as conservative voted Democratic, but by no means all. Similarly, not all Democrats were generally considered conservatives. Those conservatives most electorally available tended to be former adherents of some, or all, of the Whig, Free Soil, American, or Constitutional Union parties. These voters often held the balance of power, particularly in the Lower North and Midwest. During the previous decade, they had been cast adrift by the utter breakdown of the Whig Party and the repeated traumas of the Democratic Party.

The chaos in party organization during the 1850s had done more than break up organizations and affiliations—it had blended and confused traditional principles and beliefs. The Democratic Party had taken on positions previously associated with Northern Whigs. Men like Stephen Douglas embraced the nationalistic economic improvement agenda of the Whig Party while also taking up the compromise mantle of Henry Clay. In cozying up to the urban financial class, Democrats seemed to abandon some of the anti-elite, frontier everyman message that Andrew Jackson embodied. Republicans attempted to work this formerly Democratic soil with an antislavery message tailored to free white laborers looking to move west. All of this is to say that part of why the Democratic vision of the Union war could appeal beyond the confines of its party base is that the ideology it espoused had shifted. It had moved onto territory that appealed to voters who had themselves been ideologically orphaned. This helps explain, for instance, how Ethan Rafuse's recent biography of George McClellan successfully roots McClellan's positions as a Democrat in the Whig beliefs and culture in which he grew up. While policy considerations leaned particular conservatives to one party or another, the biggest uniting factor for this voting bloc was also the most amorphous—their temperament.[5]

As recent work by historians such as Adam I. P. Smith and Matthew Mason has shown, conservatives coalesced around rhetoric and policy that gravitated toward the national political center, encapsulating moderation and condemning extremes. Some held antislavery views, but all considered the maintenance of the

Union and the Constitution as their most hallowed principles. Conservative in personality and politics, they insisted that change should happen gradually and constitutionally. They believed the American political system to be rooted in the principles of order, conciliation, and compromise, all serving as bulwarks against fanaticism. Whatever partisan allegiances had brought them to 1860, these men believed in the greatness of America in its current form and abhorred all those—be they abolitionist or secessionist—who, they believed, schemed to destroy it under the pretense of perfecting it.[6]

William E. Gienapp argued convincingly some years ago that Republican success in 1860 hinged on the party's ability to bring many conservatives, aligned to Fillmore and the American Party in 1856, into their fold. Republicans feared that the Democratic successes in 1862 peeled off a substantial number of these voters. This is, undoubtedly, what Salmon P. Chase had in mind when he wrote to Benjamin F. Butler after the elections, stating: "The party which now opposes the National Government is not in any just sense the Democratic party and ought not to be so called. It is simply the opposition, in which old Whigs, know-nothings, and Democrats unite to expel the Republicans from power." At the very least, many contemporaries believed this interpretation. Such voters joined the Democratic masses because they embraced a conservative vision for the Union war.[7]

On the stump in 1862, Horatio Seymour spoke to four particular conservative constituencies. Democrats held no hope of reaching out to those in the Republican Party that they classed variously as "radical," "ultra," "extreme," or, most pejoratively, "Black Republican" or "Abolition Disunionist." These labels connoted those voters and candidates holding the most fervently antislavery or anti-Southern agendas. But there were men in the Republican coalition they believed could be converted, those Seymour called his "Republican friends." Conservative Republicans tended to be old-line Whigs for whom, as Eric Foner has written, "devotion to the Union was the cornerstone of their political outlook ... Daniel Webster and Henry Clay were the conservatives' ideal statesmen." Many were mildly antislavery but infuriated by abolitionists and fire-eaters alike. Generally nationalistic in outlook, they resented the South primarily for blocking economic measures like a higher tariff, a homestead bill, and internal improvements that they believed essential to the nation's prosperity.[8]

Conservative Whigs who had remained unattached to either major party represented the Democrats' best hope for additional votes. Although long opposed to the tenets of Jacksonian democracy, when they looked at Republicans they remembered Clay's injunction against the Whig Party becoming a "contemptible abolition party ... utterly subversive of the Constitution and the Union." Sectional compromise and the rule of law represented sacred principles, and many backed the Constitutional Union Party in 1860. As one such voter explained, Seymour needed to reach out to "tens of thousands of voters who were to be found in every town in the state who had belonged to the 'American party,' together with Old line Whigs in great numbers who had never been connected with either the Democratic or Republican parties."[9]

The third group that Seymour addressed consisted of Democrats who had sided with the administration only with the outbreak of war, deeming partisan opposition unacceptable when the nation's fate hung in the balance. Daniel S. Dickinson, a longtime New York Hardshell and Hunker Democrat who backed Breckinridge in 1860, quickly became one of the most effective stump speakers against his former party. Many of these men would never return to the Democrats. But no one knew this at the time, and many Democrats hoped that they could be reunited with the main body of the party. John White Geary, a fervent Democrat in 1860 and elected Republican governor of Pennsylvania in 1867, showed that many administration Democrats hoped for a glorious return to their former banner. In 1864, when welcoming Lincoln's imminent reelection, Geary nonetheless prophesied longingly that "the day is not far distant when the true & pure democracy with 'full eyed truth' will come forth unfettered & purified, into eternal youth like a Phoenix from the fire . . . then and then only will her gallant sons return to the fold, and democracy shall be like truth." Men such as Geary moved to support the administration early in the war, when Lincoln articulated a decidedly limited war, one he hoped would not descend into a "remorseless revolutionary struggle." As the war became more all-encompassing, many former Democrats expressed unease at the administration. Some returned to the Democrats, although many, having made their new bed, continued to sleep in it.[10]

The regular party faithful represented the final group that had to turn out in droves to secure success for Seymour and the Democrats in 1862. The organizational machine that Democrats since Van Buren had built up was formidable and resilient. As Richard Bensel has suggested, Democrats could turn out large numbers of "ordinary men" who "handed in a party ticket in return for a shot of whisky, a pair of boots, or a small amount of money." But, as Jean Baker has most lucidly illustrated, the party had also built up an enormously powerful and substantive heritage as a party steeped in American nationalism and representative of the broad mass of "the People." The Democrats tarred with elitism first the Federalists, then the Whigs and Republicans, convincing many to become "Democrats because they were democrats." The policies and rhetoric of the Seymour campaign offered much red meat to this base. By 1862, however, this core

Democratic constituency did not represent a sufficient bloc to win elections. To succeed, the party had to sway a portion of the non-Democratic conservative vote. The Democratic vision of the Union war would help bring together a viable, if fleeting, conservative coalition.[11]

It is impossible to establish exactly the proportion of non-Democratic conservatives who voted in 1862. But it seems clear that Democratic gains involved conversions and were not merely the result of high turnout. This essay follows scholars such as Adam I. P. Smith and Mark E. Neely, who argue that "party identities and alignments were fluid not fixed." Analysis by Michael Holt is highly suggestive, showing that only 58 percent of congressional races in 1862 were Republican versus Democrat, falling to 19.6 percent in 1863; by 1864, a semblance of realignment had stabilized, with 83 percent of races being Union versus Democrat. These percentages demonstrate the remarkable growth of Union parties, the war's most electorally successful organizations. Forming at the state level from 1861 and culminating in Lincoln's National Union Party of 1864, Union parties' great strength came from capturing conservative swing voters. Although in a few states Democrats formed the majority within Union parties and succeeded in peeling off conservative Republicans to join them, most iterations of Union parties brought Republicans together with wavering Democrats and unaffiliated conservatives. Setting aside controversial questions of policy, these movements forged new political alliances premised on the most widespread and deeply held allegiance within the nation. Although Seymour retained the Democratic label, he utilized many tactics similar to those of Union parties in order to take advantage of the weak partisan affiliation of many voters during the war.[12]

Even more than statistics, the anecdotal evidence from newspapers, diaries, and letters makes clear that people understood themselves to be in an era of bewildering flux in party allegiances, labels, and positions, with no certainty over what political landscape would emerge from the maelstrom of war. Scholarship in political science on "affective intelligence" and the role of emotions in voting also suggests that traditional party allegiance weakens significantly in times of crisis, when heightened anxiety prompts voters to reconsider candidates and platforms. Such evidence all helps us grasp the circumstances that created a significant number of swing voters within the 1862 electorate.[13]

While Seymour serves here not as biographical subject but as conduit to understand the Democratic appeal, it is still necessary to provide a brief sketch of his political past. By the time of his nomination, in 1862, Seymour, aged fifty-two, had already spent thirty years in New York Democratic politics. Within the byzantine politics of New York, Seymour stood first with the more conservative

Hunker Democrats rather than the antislavery Barnburners who defected in 1848 to back former president Martin Van Buren's Free Soil Party. Seymour then stood with the "soft-shell" Democrats who welcomed the Free Soil renegades back into the party after the Compromise of 1850. In 1852, the reunited party elected him for his first term as governor. When Seymour narrowly failed to secure reelection in 1854, his defeat was blamed on the national administration's support of the Kansas-Nebraska Bill and on Seymour's own veto of a temperance bill that he deemed unconstitutional. His term also saw him approve further canal expansion and expenditure.[14] While Democrats generally opposed internal improvements, Seymour's desire for subsidized growth typified many New York Hunker Democrats, who tended to a "Whiggish economic outlook." Seymour's beliefs also benefited his private interests, represented in a lifelong business partnership and friendship with the New York Republican Hiram Barney, with whom he invested in the Fox and Wisconsin Improvement Company, aiming to ease river transport between the Mississippi and the Great Lakes.[15]

On the slavery question, Seymour's Northern-leaning but moderate positions helped supporters envisage him as a possible national candidate in the late 1850s. Seymour endorsed popular sovereignty and supported Stephen Douglas twice for the presidency. In 1856, he declared that in the North slavery was "repugnant to our sentiments," but he mostly avoided such stark rhetoric and ardently defended the rights of Southern states to self-government. Seymour regularly chided antislavery agitation because he believed that history clearly favored the North. Slavery had been legal in all the colonies but now there existed a majority of free states. The North had exceeded the South in growth and productivity. The Democrats were a "Let Alone party," while the Republicans were a "Meddling Party." Left alone, the Union, and especially the North, had thrived. Summing up his speeches in this period, Seymour's biographer Stewart Mitchell avers that Seymour repeatedly expressed the common conservative hope that "abolitionists and slave-holders would not destroy the whole country with their mutual suspicion and hatred." The outbreak of war could be seen to validate these fears, but it also represented a profound failure of moderates to bridge the nation's divides.[16]

The political and military dynamics of the first year and a half of the war provide vital context for understanding the resurgence of appeals to conservatism and the resonance of the Democratic message in the fall of 1862. The secession crisis saw most Democrats come down on the side of Senator John Crittenden's compromise proposals, willing to grant further concessions to the South. Many Republicans, most significantly President Lincoln, refused to budge from their 1860 platform's absolute commitment to the nonextension of slavery. But partisan lines were not rigid, and to many at the time, there seemed, as Russell McClintock puts it, "the genuine possibility that the turmoil of party realignment would resume—or more accurately, continue." This was nowhere more true than in New York, where leading Republicans—Secretary of State Seward, Governor Edwin Morgan, and party boss Thurlow Weed—all joined Seymour in advocating further attempts at compromise and flexibility toward Southern demands. The uncertainty ended abruptly with the firing on Fort Sumter, which produced a remarkable coalescing of sentiment. Democrats and Republicans shared a resounding patriotism and enlisted together to put down rebellion and save the nation. Nonetheless, the question remained of what political and military objectives could bolster this shared sense of purpose.[17]

While Crittenden's peace proposals failed to bring national unity, the Kentuckian still managed to foster a form of political and military harmony across the states that remained in the Union. The Crittenden-Johnson Resolution of July 1861, passed almost unanimously after the disastrous Battle of Bull Run, exemplified Democratic hopes for a war waged for no "purpose of conquest or subjugation" and only to "defend and maintain the supremacy of the Constitution and to preserve the Union, with all the dignity, equality, and rights of the several States unimpaired." Such a pledge corresponded exactly with the war many people initially expected: one of a limited number of set-piece battles between uniformed armies. Beyond that, the resolution served as a statement of beliefs as much as a practical guide for action. While congressional radicals immediately opposed this limited articulation of the war's aims and methods, it nonetheless served as the official administration position. Moreover, many Democrats and conservative Republicans believed that Lincoln himself fully supported Crittenden's attempt to ensure a constitutional war for Union and only Union.[18]

Democrats realized they could offer little political opposition while the Crittenden-Johnson Resolution represented the nation's stated military objective. As a result, the fall elections of 1861 saw some Democrats break ranks to join Republicans in various fusion Union movements. This produced a series of resounding victories over Democrats who maintained their regular organization and offered half-hearted opposition. In New York, Democratic breakaways joined Republicans in a "People's Convention" that placed Daniel Dickinson at its head, running for attorney general, with four Democrats, four Republicans, and one American below him on the ticket. The conservative Republican Thurlow Weed drafted resolutions that offered robust support for the war while condemning both abolition and secession. Dickinson made clear that "It is not Lincoln and the Republicans we are sustaining. They have nothing to do with it. It is the government of our fathers, worth just as much as if it was administered by Andrew Jackson." The People's Ticket secured majorities of over one hundred thousand, more than double Lincoln's margin in 1860 and ten times what Seymour would garner in 1862. As an indication of the size of the non-Republican section of this vote, for one office—that of canal commissioner—the Republicans refused to accept the People's candidate and ran their own nominee in a three-way race. This race split the "People's" vote and produced the only regular Democratic victory. The Democratic nominee, Wright, triumphed with 198,385, compared to 179,691 for the Republican and 105,721 for the People's candidate. This result shows that non-Republicans made up over a third of the popular support for the People's Union movement.[19]

While overtly a disaster for Democrats, the 1861 election nonetheless had a silver lining. The number of Democratic votes had dropped by over 120,000, approximately 40 percent, from Douglas's total in 1860. Taking into account the much lower turnout, the Democratic share of the vote dropped from 46.5 percent to 38.5 percent. The party's unwillingness to oppose seriously the administration left few compelling reasons for voters to prefer them. But it also served to demonstrate their loyalty. Even Horace Greeley's *Tribune*, ever looking for Democratic traitors, would judge after the 1861 elections that within the Democratic Party "nine-tenths of it is probably strenuous in the determination that the constitutional authority of the government shall be maintained and enforced." A series of events in the following year would present Seymour opportunities to formulate an alternative to Republicans while adhering to the loyalty the party had established.[20]

Radicals in Congress worked quickly to influence the course of the war. By the time the election season of 1862 approached, the Crittenden-Johnson Resolution had been overturned, the Committee on the Conduct of the War established, two Confiscation Acts passed, and slavery abolished in the District of Columbia and the Federal Territories. In September 1862, the president added the Preliminary Emancipation Proclamation to this list and, two days later, suspended the writ of habeas corpus throughout the North. All of these events lent credence to the notion that the radicals had taken control of the Republican Party and the administration. Hints of conscription in the summer of 1862 added more than a tinge of radicalism to the administration's war measures: The national government had never before forced men into federal service.

In New York, conservatives across the party spectrum realized that the tenuous bipartisan coalition of 1861 was crumbling. Attempting to hold off the radical tide, Republican Thurlow Weed conspired with Democrat John Van Buren on a plan designed to elect John A. Dix as governor in 1862. Dix's resume had broad cross-party appeal. A lifelong Democrat, Dix served briefly as Buchanan's final secretary of the Treasury, where he earned national adoration with his January 29, 1861, telegram to Treasury agents in New Orleans, instructing them that "If any one attempts to haul down the American flag, shoot him on the spot." Despite his bellicosity, Dix had urged concessions during the secession crisis and demonstrated conservative credentials as a commander in the Union army through his unwillingness to interfere with slavery. This did not prevent Republicans from hailing his military record, which included overseeing the arrest of the prosecession Maryland legislature in 1861. Weed's plan was that Dix would be adopted first by the Constitutional Union Party (still just about in existence in New York) and then by a joint Union ticket composed of Republicans and Democrats. But Weed's plan soon failed when Dix narrowly lost the Constitutional Union Party nomination to Seymour, whom the Democrats immediately endorsed. The conservative wing of the Republican Party, controlled by Thurlow Weed, William Seward, and Henry Raymond, hoped now to take Dix as their candidate. To their dismay, Horace Greeley's forces secured a victory for James Wadsworth, an avowed abolitionist. Greeley lauded Wadsworth for his vocal support for emancipation and his equally public condemnation of the actions of General George Brinton McClellan.[21]

Wadsworth's radical candidacy opened up a window for Seymour to convince New York's voters that the Democratic Party now best represented a nonpartisan, conservative vision for the war. Seymour's campaign would relentlessly highlight his determination to salvage a Union war effort he depicted as collapsing under the weight of divisions within the Republican Party.

The Democratic Vision for War

Seymour's first task was to justify the renewal of political opposition. He did this on the basis that parties served national ends, a theory he practically demonstrated in the proud history of the Democratic Party. When Jeffersonians first attacked the Federalists, transgressing against the nonparty spirit of the age, they cited the need to contain the natural drift to tyranny. Party opposition became another of the institutional checks and balances that kept government serving the people. Seymour harked back to this august heritage, warning that those calling for the silencing of dissent should remember "the vigilance kept alive by party contest guards against corruption . . . and abuses of power." Underpinning this rhetoric existed a principle that Democrats repeatedly maintained during the war—that a distinction existed between the administration and the government. Patriots owed unyielding loyalty to the government but could oppose, carefully, the administration when they deemed it was acting for narrow partisan ends rather than the national interest. Seymour argued he and his colleagues could be trusted to make this delicate judgment because nobody could question the nationalist credentials of the Democratic Party.[22]

While opposition parties came and went, Democratic presidents had won the nation's wars, put down would-be secessionists at Hartford and Charleston, and expanded the boundaries of liberty. The governor had no doubt that the Democratic Party had "been so closely identified with the history and progress of our country, that its dissolution would seem like the severance of the last bond which holds our country together." Despite the Democrats' own schism, Seymour still considered them the only national party. Although Northern Democrats had been tarnished by their Southern colleagues spearheading secession, Seymour believed this stigma had now been removed by having taken up arms against their former brethren. And to achieve reunion after military victory, some kind of reconciliation would be required, and he questioned whether the Republican Party—a "thing of yesterday" that "never embraced our whole country"—could ever facilitate it. Seymour's logic spoke to the party faithful but also to conservative Republicans who fretted over their party's lack of Southern representation.[23]

Even while he lauded party, Seymour simultaneously claimed legitimacy as a leader of a nonpartisan coalition of conservatives that would defend President Lincoln against radicals. While Radical Republicans repeatedly assailed the nation's chief executive, Democrats understood that he should be "treated with deference, and spoken of in respectful terms." Quoting critiques from Republican newspapers, he assured listeners that the conservative president would welcome relief from extremists who "do not wish to restore the Union unless they can revolutionize the social system of the South." Seymour's claims did not sound implausible to his audiences.[24]

Democrats genuinely hoped, and Radical Republicans feared, that Lincoln's true sentiments were conservative. To make this case, Democrats looked to Lincoln's border-state policies, his revoking of the attempts by generals Frémont and Hunter to further emancipation, his known opposition to the Second Confiscation Act, and his consistent statements, most recently in his famous response to Horace Greeley, that his only concern was to "save the Union." John Van Buren, campaigning for Seymour, would argue that the war had to be won under Lincoln and that conservative triumph would "carry vigor to him [Lincoln] in resisting what I am sure he feels disposed to resist—the demands of the Abolitionists."

Stand by him. He is a cross of Kentucky on Illinois, and cannot be an abolitionist." The *New York Herald* welcomed the Democratic victories in 1862 for strengthening "President Lincoln's conservative war policy." Democrats worked hard to secure their own legitimacy by defending a president they claimed to be under siege from his own party.[25]

Sparing Lincoln formed part of the Democrats' more general attempt to assure voters that none of their criticism of the administration would ever lead them to accept disunion. An October 1862 memo prepared for Seymour by his fellow New Yorker and close associate Samuel Tilden made abundantly clear that leading Democrats understood their precarious predicament. Tilden urged Seymour to make a public address aimed at Confederates in which the governor should explain that "in no event can the triumph of the conservative sentiment of New York in my election, mean consent to Disunion." Rather it would constitute the restoration of the Constitution. And while Democrats would oppose the radicals, they would always maintain the government. To anyone who thought they intended "to dissolve the federal bond between these States, to dismember our country," Democrats countered, "we will not, no *never, never, never.*" Tilden resoundingly affirmed Democratic loyalty to the Union, if not the administration.[26]

Seymour's arguments for the necessity of an active Democratic Party during wartime clearly catered to the Democratic base, but not solely. Many Democrats saw parties as "nationalizing force[s]" and elections as "celebrations that began as a display of difference and ended in consent." Seymour's message found a ready audience among the thousands of voters who grew up believing that the nation and the Democrats shared a symbiotic relationship. Whigs, by contrast, had tended to believe that "parties posed a threat to the proper social order." Seymour's respect for Lincoln and the reframing of party competition as conservative and antiradical clearly was intended to court conservative former Whigs as well as recently departed Democrats uncomfortable with wartime partisanship.[27]

Democrats also believed their party had to endure in order to ensure that sectional compromise remained a valued principle of the American political system. A commitment to the legitimacy of compromise has been an underappreciated and misunderstood dimension of Democratic appeals. The prominence of peace enthusiasts in the later years of the war and their success in securing a peace plank in the 1864 platform have made it seem that compromise emerged as an opportunistic attempt to capitalize on war weariness. In fact, Democrats defended this principle throughout the war and did not see it as necessarily incompatible with continuing to wage armed conflict.

Seymour would defend compromise before and during the conflict. During the secession crisis, Seymour had indicted those, North and South, who cried "no compromise" as guilty of "senseless, unreasoning fanaticism" and of "treason to the spirit of the Constitution." He stressed that slavery was not a new issue and that "our fathers disposed of the same or similar difficulties, by compromises." At this stage, he implored people to realize that the only true choice was whether "to have compromise after the war, or compromise without war." Once the war began, espousing compromise became politically more problematic, but Seymour would not abandon what he considered "the vital principle of social existence." Other Democrats echoed him. In 1861, the New York Democratic State Committee adopted a platform that resolutely backed the war but also urged the administration to remember that "our political system was founded in compromise, and it can never be dishonourable in any Administration to seek to restore it by the same means." In his inaugural address, Seymour echoed this with his assertion that "the exertion of armed power must be accompanied by a firm and conciliatory policy" to entice the South back into the Union.[28]

A remarkable letter written by August Belmont—national Democratic Party chairman, New York financier, and Seymour ally—to Thurlow Weed demonstrated the Democratic belief that compromise and war both represented valid means of restoring the Union. In this letter, which proves the limitations of classifying Democrats as either for war or peace, Belmont proposed two options to save the Union: "The one is by an energetic and unrelenting prosecution of the war to crush the rebellion; the other would be to negotiate with the leaders of that rebellion." To achieve the first, Belmont advocated a draft for five hundred thousand men. To secure the second, he recommended sending one or two "conservative" men to Richmond (he suggested Seymour) as a prelude to a "national convention for the purpose of restructuring the Federal compact." Belmont valued restoration of the Union above all else. He would never rule out compromise as a means to achieve it, but if the "sword had to be the arbiter," then so be it. When Democrats like Belmont or Seymour entertained ideas of negotiation, it was because they thought that the absolute closing down of nonmilitary options to secure reunion constituted a blunt, one-dimensional approach to an unpredictable national crisis. Particularly at moments when the military effort seemed stalled, Democrats appraised Republicans' unwillingness to consider any but an absolute military solution as reckless and liable to scuttle what might prove to be the only achievable routes to reunion.[29]

If compromise represented "the spirit of the constitution," Seymour cared even more deeply for the concrete individual and state's rights he believed the founding document enshrined. Attacking the administration's infringements on constitutional liberty became central to Democratic indictments of the war effort. As Mark E. Neely has noted, Seymour did a great deal to initiate and sustain this trend, particularly when it came to the thousands of arbitrary arrests made by the Lincoln government. As William Blair has argued, these arrests formed part of a number of administration actions that make it indisputable that "there was much to criticize concerning abuses of liberty." Democratic arguments that the Republicans trampled on constitutional liberty touched incredibly sensitive nerves because of the still powerful historical memory of the American Revolution.[30]

The dogmas of republicanism suffused the political culture of both major parties and offered a ready set of lessons for the dangers liberty faced during times of war. The Republican lawyer and congressman Lyman Trumbull captured the concerns of many when he asked Congress in 1861, "What are we coming to if arrests may be made at the whim or caprice of a cabinet minister?" Trumbull's fears hung on the belief, espoused explicitly by Delaware Democratic congressman James Bayard Jr., that "Human nature is the same in all ages and in all countries. Power always tends to corruption." When Seymour saw the Lincoln administration carrying out military arrests distant from the battlefield, he immediately compared them to the "despotism of the Old World." Such notions underpinned the broad appeal of Democratic critiques of constitutional abuses.[31]

While many Republicans worried about growing centralization, Democrats felt their party lineage gave them a particular responsibility to form an institutional bulwark against government excess. As Joel Silbey has written, when Democrats looked across the partisan divide they believed that "at heart, Republicans, as the Whigs before them, were centralizing, overbearing, Federalist-Tories, intent on destroying the liberties of the American people through the extensive intrusion of government power." For Seymour, the danger of Republicanism lay particularly in William Henry Seward's concept of a "higher law." Seymour repeatedly returned to the idea that a "higher law" clearly lay outside the Constitution, could only be subjective, and opened the way to untethered power and tyranny.[32]

The long heritage of Democratic fears about governmental power ensured that leading spokesmen like Seymour and Stephen Douglas sounded a note of warning as soon as war broke out. In 1861, Douglas exhorted Democrats to remember that "there can be no neutrals in this war, only patriots—or traitors." But he also begged them to "say that you will sanction no war on rights . . . we were born under the constitution of the United States . . . be prepared to enforce the inalienable rights which it confers." Seymour echoed Douglas in October

1861, specifying the need to protect "freedom of conscience, the protection of our persons, the sacredness of our homes, the trial by jury, [and] the freedom from arbitrary arrests." While he withheld final judgment, Seymour fretted that the administration had already taken actions suggesting that "the Constitution should be trampled under foot."[33]

As the 1862 canvass approached, the Lincoln administration seemed to confirm the prescience of such Democratic orators. Just six weeks before the North went to vote, Lincoln suspended the writ of habeas corpus, subjecting to martial law all persons "within the United States . . . guilty of any disloyal practice." The broad language and geographic reach sent chills down the spines of those watching for the fate of civil liberties. Throughout the campaign, Democrats talked repeatedly not just about the Emancipation Proclamation but about the president's "two proclamations." Republicans invoked the doctrine of military necessity to defend their actions, but Seymour vehemently rejected this notion. Instead he argued that "in these times of trial and danger we cling more closely to the great principles of civil and religious liberty and of personal right." Straits might be dire, but anyone who claimed "that Abraham Lincoln . . . may rightfully do what George Washington would not do in the darkest days of the Revolution, does not know what Constitutional liberty is." The hugely influential *New York Herald* sung from Seymour's hymn sheet when claiming that, if elected, the Republican candidate James Wadsworth would "have his adversaries consigned to dungeons and their property seized and confiscated."[34]

Contemporaries cared more about civil liberties than historians have, and the Democratic pledge to wage the war "constitutionally" allowed for an easily articulated practical alternative. In September 1862, the *New York World*, a Democratic newspaper, pledged its willingness to support a candidate of any stripe willing to promise a war "vigorously prosecuted by strictly constitutional methods." To all those unsettled by the administration's actions, Seymour promised a clear alternative. Democrats would wage war constitutionally, never allowing the government or military arbitrarily to seize property, deny legal rights, or muzzle the press.[35]

On the fraught question of emancipation, Seymour would employ the Constitution as one of several cudgels with which to assail the Lincoln administration. Even so, Democratic hostility toward emancipation did not negate the fact that, by the eve of the Civil War, most Northern Democrats believed in the superiority of the free-labor system. Many shared the Republican view that slavery had a negative effect on Southern whites, and virtually all wanted the territories free for white laborers. Democrats like Seymour imagined that the United States would, ultimately, become all free. But questions of timing and method were critical. Democrats had no interest in forcing the issue and would wait as long as it took for Southern states to take their own decisions to free their slaves. Democrats feared immediate emancipation because they believed it would risk servile insurrection, race war, and permanent disunion. Dangerous and unconstitutional, emancipation would constitute a fundamental breakdown of law and order. A virulent racism underpinned these perspectives, but, while far more acute among Democrats, it is important to acknowledge that racial prejudice and fear of emancipation crossed party lines.[36]

Lincoln's election in 1860 demonstrated that the Republican brand of antislavery could secure an electoral majority, but this was often achieved by explicitly merging antislavery with racism. Even Republicans who abhorred slavery stressed that their constitutionalism would prevent them from interfering with the institution where it existed. This resonated with many Northern states that had taken measures in the 1850s to limit the already restricted rights of free blacks. The Ohio Republican congressman John Sherman had little doubt that while "the great mass of this country are opposed to slavery," the black race "was spurned and hated all over the country North and South." In 1860, 54 percent of New Yorkers gave their votes to Abraham Lincoln, while 64 percent of them also voted to reject a proposal for black suffrage.[37]

The purpose of outlining the depth of Northern prejudice is to make clear that when emancipation became a reality, it presented a challenge to both parties. Much Republican success with conservatives in 1860 had hinged on convincing voters that a great deal of space and substance lay between the labels "Republican" and "Abolitionist." Democrats could now use emancipation to reignite claims that the Republican Party was obsessed with race, the premise behind the "Black Republican" label. Yet they had to tread carefully. In time, Republicans would reverse this accusation, using the Democratic backlash to emancipation to argue that the Democrats were now the party who had lost sight of saving the Union over their infatuation with questions of race.

This context helps explain why emancipation featured prominently for Democrats in 1862, but generally as part of a larger indictment of Republicanism and not merely as a visceral racist backlash. On one occasion Seymour did refer to schemes of immediate emancipation and the arming of slaves as a "proposal for the butchery of women and children, for scenes of lust and rapine, and of arson and murder." This is probably the most commonly used Seymour quotation, but it represents the exception rather than the rule. Seymour made these comments in a speech before President Lincoln issued the Emancipation Proclamation, using it to characterize the desires of radicals like Thaddeus Stevens and Charles Sumner, desires that he believed the president fiercely opposed. Seymour attempted to drive a wedge between the president's approach to slavery—promoting gradual, compensated, state-led emancipation coupled with colonization—and the desire that was unfairly but commonly attributed to radicals of wanting to incite slaves to slaughter their masters. Seymour clearly held racist views, but he generally left the crasser appeals to be voiced by extremists within the Democratic base. Organs like the *New York Daybook* (which became the *Weekly Caucasian*), the *New York Daily News*, and the *New York Journal of Commerce* were much more willing to openly race-bait. At this point in the war, politicians like Seymour and newspapers like the *New York World* and the *New York Herald* held the line against these more extreme elements within the Democratic Party.[38]

The *New York World*, indeed, came closest to being Seymour's official mouthpiece, and the political trajectory of the paper and its editor, Manton Marble, illustrates how the Democrats broadened their base in 1862. The *World* began publication in the summer of 1860 and, until deep into the election campaign of 1862, maintained itself as an independent conservative periodical unaffiliated to either party. Marble himself was a conservative Republican who expended considerable energy trying to persuade Thurlow Weed to secure the paper's finances and make it his official organ in New York City. With Weed losing out to Greeley in Republican circles and Democrat Samuel Barlow providing the much-needed financial support, Marble, now sole editor, steadily moved into the Democratic camp. In private, Marble claimed to abandon Lincoln only with "profound regret" and on the basis that the only possibility for "a conservative party . . . to achieve practical success" lay with backing Seymour and the Democrats. Marble would later explain his party switch as the result of his "fixed, perhaps excessive, conservatism." While he had long opposed the Democrats, the Emancipation Proclamation now left him certain that the Republicans' general turn to radicalism would result in "accessions from conservatives of other names and creeds" that would "leaven" the undesirable elements of the Democratic Party. Once the *World* joined the Democratic camp, it quickly became, as Harold Holzer has written, "New York's loudest anti-administration voice." While paling in comparison to the circulations of over fifty thousand boasted by the *Herald* and the *Tribune*, the *World* shipped around twenty thousand copies daily.[39]

Seymour and organs like the *World* adopted a more restrained approach, one that reframed emancipation in order to speak to conservatives who placed all questions of race far below their adherence to the Union and the Constitution. As Russell McClintock has written, former Whigs "feared Republican antislavery agitation yet frowned on Democratic race-baiting." After Lincoln issued his famous document, Seymour immediately took to questioning its constitutionality. Given that the slaves of Southerners in rebellion could be freed under the terms of the Second Confiscation Act, Seymour argued that Lincoln's proclamation could apply only to "those who have been true to our Union and our flag." This may still sound strange, given that Lincoln exempted loyal Border States from the proclamation. But Seymour referred to loyal slaveholders living within the Confederacy whose personal allegiance to the Union could not be negated by the rebellion of their state. Treason could only forfeit property rights on an individual basis, and he rejected the idea that "the conduct of a disloyal majority can forfeit the property of a loyal minority." This perspective aligned perfectly with his concern for loyal Unionists within the Confederacy.[40]

Seymour, like many Republicans, worried about the consequences of emancipation for Southern Unionism. The war had to embolden the hibernating loyalists who could weaken the Confederacy and represent the future leaders of a restored South. But emancipation served to "humiliate and mortify the loyal men of the South." A conservative war policy, by contrast, would "kindle anew the fires of patriotism" among the "many thousand loyal men who only waited to hear that they could be safe within the limits of the Union." Seymour grossly overestimated the scale of Unionism within the Confederacy, but, in doing so, he embraced a core tenet of Republican beliefs about a Slave Power conspiracy. Seymour's rhetoric had cross-party appeal by tapping into the notion that a minority of slaveholders had repressed and deluded the loyal white majority of the South. Seymour argued repeatedly that the radical agenda of immediate and total emancipation would abandon exactly the Unionists whom Republicans claimed to support.[41]

Yet even while he critiqued emancipation, Seymour also left the door open to accept the measure, under the right circumstances. At this stage in the war, many conservatives began to conceive that emancipation might be necessary to save the Union. This did not prevent them from simultaneously fearing that, done too suddenly, the policy would endanger law and order and pose a threat to the Union. Seymour spoke to these concerns by acknowledging that "no man has ever doubted that the slaves of men in rebellion can be rightfully taken from them." Such a process could take place within controlled bounds and held the possibility of a perfectly gradual embrace of freedom. Charles G. Loring, a Massachusetts conservative, explained the perfect scenario. After military defeat, the slave states would return "with the political power of slavery essentially crippled or destroyed," after which the government could "provide for the termination of the system by gradual emancipation, under wise and humane laws administered by a highly civilized and powerful nation, with a just regard to the rights, welfare and interests of all." Loring captured the perspective of many conservatives trying to reconcile freedom with order to avoid anarchy.[42]

It is also significant that the November elections fell between the preliminary and final versions of the Emancipation Proclamation. The Democratic-leaning *Herald* actually endorsed the proclamation, saying that it represented merely the enforcement of the Second Confiscation Act and praising the inclusion of colonization. The *World* strongly disapproved of the document but the editors admitted their struggle to reconcile it with the president's "sagacity, his sense of justice, or his self-poise of character." If these Democrats had known that the final version would jettison colonization and embrace black military service, it is unlikely they would have exhibited as much restraint. As it was, some Democrats vainly expressed the hope that Democratic election successes would provide Lincoln the justification to rescind a document they yearned to believe he had issued only reluctantly under radical pressure.[43]

Seymour's overall approach to emancipation attempted to cater to the many Northerners who disapproved of both black people and slavery. Even more than this, he tried always to place the issue in relation to, but firmly below, Democrats' commitment to restoring the Union.

Seymour's Unionism represented the most important element of his electoral pitch. At one level, as recent studies have demonstrated, Union represented an almost universally revered concept. Union invoked the Founders and their fragile experiment in self-government that now offered an unprecedented level of religious toleration, personal and political freedom, economic opportunity, and social mobility. For a nation of European immigrants, these possibilities offered an idyll unthinkable under the autocratic, class-ridden monarchies of their past. On these points nearly all Northerners agreed, and preserving these benefits formed the most common motivation among soldiers in the Union army.[44]

Nonetheless, two strands of Unionism developed in the late antebellum years that became a clear dividing line during the war. The historian Rogan Kersh, tracing ideas about Union since the founding, distinguished between those who argued for a "sustainable" Union and those who sought a "moral" one. Those who focused on the Union's sustainability, like Seymour, believed that the Union was a "sacred trust received from our fathers," which only needed to be preserved to guarantee its blessings would spread abundantly to all parts of the country. Frederick Douglass proclaimed the alternative, moral conception of Union when he proclaimed himself a "believer in Union . . . because I believe it can be made a means of emancipation." Far more Northerners subscribed to the "sustainable" Union, and conservatives particularly fumed at the idea that Union did not represent, in and of itself, the highest moral cause.[45]

Seymour's stump speeches made powerfully clear that his conception of the Union included a prominent place for the South. Seymour had no doubt that "the whole country rallied as one man" behind the cause of restoring the Union "complete in all its parts . . . for the common good of all sections." Seymour affirmed that anyone who would "put out one glittering star from its azure field, is a traitor." A national war for Union had to be fought to free loyal Southern brethren from Confederate oligarchs. As a Tammany Hall enlistment pamphlet explained, the Union army waged war to prove that "Bunker Hill and Mount Vernon, New York and New Orleans shall never be dissevered." At one level, Seymour's encomiums seemed generic, a "bewildering set of generalities," according to one Republican paper, but they served the joint purpose of asserting loyalty and establishing a wholly national vision of Union.[46]

Democrats' determination to protect and restore the South's constitutional privileges also laid down a clear marker for the postwar years. Radicals like Charles Sumner and Thaddeus Stevens were already articulating theories that the seceded states had "committed suicide" or that the North should treat them as "conquered provinces." Both scenarios would place them under congressional control and make possible a wholesale restructuring of Southern society. If conservatives held the reins of power, there would be only a sectional reconciliation forged in shared sacrifice. Emancipation represented the biggest obstacle to realizing this outcome.

A conservative war would never equate Union and emancipation. James Oakes has recently claimed that Republicans did not distinguish between liberty and Union. The war's purpose "never had to move from Union to emancipation because the two issues—liberty and union—were never separate for them." But to conservatives of all former political affiliations, this distinction mattered greatly, and, in New York at least, conservative Republicans forcefully articulated it. Indeed, it formed the dividing line between the Weed and Greeley wings of the party. As one conservative Republican newspaper put it, radicals advocated "an unscrupulous and revolutionary radicalism, which would seize upon the rebellion as a pretext to break down the barriers of law" and unleash an "anarchy of radicalism." Democrats latched onto this to argue that emancipation demonstrated that congressional radicals controlled the White House, speaking of Union only as a cloak for emancipation and racial equality. Men like the preacher Lyman Beecher fueled Democratic fires when proclaiming that at last "the Union as it was meant to be, and not as it was, is to be our doctrine." Against such heresy Seymour maintained that only "this great conservative party" could foil the "theorists and fanatics" and "rear up the shattered columns of Union."[47]

Seymour made a powerful case to voters uncomfortable with emancipation, but he knew Democrats had to maintain their pro-war credentials to reap electoral rewards. Democrats had enlisted with ardor in 1861, and Democratic politicians and newspapers argued that they represented the party whose pro-war sentiments and plans had the best chance of success. Seymour stated that the party must "re-enforce our armies in the field" and "strengthen the hands of government" to put down rebellion. Initially, supporting the war had simply made Democrats credible; now they found ways to offer a compelling alternative to a divided Republican Party.[48]

As the fall elections approached, Democrats used unqualified support for General George B. McClellan as a key means to stress their pro-war but antiradical position. Offering Little Mac all the troops he could dream of, the *Herald* contrasted such loyalty with the "abolition radicals" in Congress who "held back reinforcements" and "interfered with the commands of our ablest and most patriotic generals." Democrats widely circulated this explanation for the failings of the Peninsula Campaign. When McClellan repelled Lee's invasion of the North at Antietam in September, Democrats lambasted men like Greeley who continued to criticize Little Mac, even in the aftermath of a battle that Democrats deemed a vital triumph. Democrats argued that radical criticism both undermined military operations and strengthened the resolve of "even the most unwilling rebels" by stressing the need for immediate emancipation.[49]

Timing is crucial to grasping the plausibility of demonstrating loyalty and commitment to the war effort by backing McClellan. In July, McClellan had written his famous letter to Lincoln from Harrison's Landing, outlining his conservative view that war should not interfere with slavery, not be fought for purposes of "subjugation," but rather be conducted according to the highest principles "known to Christian civilization." But while the general was known to be conservative, this letter did not circulate during the 1862 campaign. If it had, it might have undermined Democrats' depiction of him as an apolitical, patriotic general. As it was, McClellan remained at the head of the Army of the Potomac as the fall elections approached. Soldiers of all political allegiance continued to adore him and raged at politicians meddling in military affairs. By contrast, the Republican candidate for New York governor, Brigadier General James Wadsworth, had bitterly attacked McClellan, his commanding officer, after the Peninsula Campaign. Wadsworth claimed, correctly, that Lee had far fewer men and that no excuse justified the failure to take Richmond. But while McClellan retained command, such attacks lent credence to conservative fears that Radical Republicans represented the true threat to military success. John Van Buren readily twisted this knife, proclaiming that "when the country is at war, the bitter enemy of the Commander-in-Chief should not be placed at the head of the government of this State." At least one New York regiment expressed its support for Seymour specifically because Wadsworth had been one of the leaders of a clique within the army known to be "loud and virulent in its abuse of McClellan."[50]

The consistency and plausibility of the Democrats' pro-war position is pivotal to grasping why many conservative voters deliberately chose them in 1862. A former Whig from Kentucky wrote to Millard Fillmore, celebrating that Seymour had triumphed rather than the "Abolitionists, headed by Wadsworth." Now, the bluegrass native crowed, they would "beat the Northern Radicals, who have so bedeviled President Lincoln, at the ballot box, so we shall soon overwhelm the southern Radicals now in open secession, with the Bayonet." Numerous soldiers expressed similar opinions. The New York soldier Asa Holmes, 114th New York Infantry, wrote in January 1863 to his son Frank, instructing him that "if you here Eny man or woman talk abolition or against slavery cick his ass for me." Holmes stressed to his son that if he should die in this war, "I want you to say that I died A good cause fighting to save the Union."[51]

Democrats recognized the critical importance of Seymour's pro-war stance in securing victory in New York and across the nation in 1862. The Illinois State Supreme Court's Chief Justice John D. Caton expressed his gratitude after Seymour's victory that "the radicals among the democrats have not the control of their party as have the radicals among the Republicans . . . as it is, all conservative men are coming to us daily, thus increasing the conservative strength in our party." Judge Caton knew that the administration's great hope had been that Democrats would refuse to support the war, and he rejoiced that "this big Gun Gov Seymour has spiked effectually." A glorious future for the party seemed certain as long as no one forgot that "we must support the war." Much of the election postmortem in New York's newspapers would confirm that contemporaries saw the Democratic message not as a sign of widespread peace sentiments or defeatism but as an alternative conservative vision of the war.[52]

At the end of Election Day in November, Seymour had secured just under 51 percent of the ballots, defeating Republican James Wadsworth by a little under 11,000 votes. In the aftermath, Republican newspapers revealed the deep split in their party. Radicals offered something close to the interpretation that has trickled down through the historiography. Greeley's *Tribune* cited Republicans "absent in arms" and others who refused to vote because they were "disheartened and disgusted by the no-progress of the War." Greeley claimed that Lincoln had only to stop kowtowing to slavery and arm black men by the thousands in order to see the army overflow with recruits and march triumphantly across the South. Thurlow Weed, in his *Albany Evening Journal*, offered the conservative Republican explanation. Weed decried Wadsworth's radicalism and the foolish platform that had cemented emancipation alongside Union. These "obnoxious . . . Ultra

Figure 3 "Hon. Horatio Seymour, Governor-Elect of the State of New York." *Harper's Weekly* devoted its entire front page to Seymour's victory, noting in the accompanying article that "the great bulk of the Northern Democracy are as loyal to the Union as Mr. Lincoln himself."
Source: *Harper's Weekly*, November 22, 1862, 737–38.

Abolitionists" had abandoned the issue "upon which we were united" and "narrowed down to an Anti-Slavery War, about which the People have been and will remain divided." In appearing to modulate their Unionism, Weed believed that the Republicans had tossed away their huge majorities of 1861. This Republican infighting had clearly been of significant benefit to Seymour.[53]

Democratic newspapers, and even some Republican ones, acknowledged, joyously or grudgingly, the strengths of Seymour's message. The *New York Herald* and *New York World* both celebrated a victory for conservatives over radicals that showed New York had "thunder[ed] out her demand for a more vigorous prosecution of the war." The *Herald* added that, now that the "Jacobins" had been rebuked, "President Lincoln's administration" might be able to carry out a "vigorous prosecution of the war" and "win the glory of a Union restored." *Vanity Fair*, a weekly Democratic and conservative satire published in New York, welcomed the election of Seymour and published a cartoon showing Lincoln exclaiming that he could keep the Union train on the Constitution tracks now that he had "the right fuel," in the form of wood, marked "Dem Maj," in the engine. In private, *World* editor Manton Marble judged of the canvass that "the Democratic leaders owe the triumph to the unpledged, unbought conservatives of every former name and creed."[54]

While celebrating the Democratic victories, the Democratic press also hailed the defeat of their party's most notorious extremist, Clement Vallandigham. Despite Democrats sweeping Ohio, Vallandigham, already the most notorious antiwar voice in the nation, managed to lose his bid for reelection to Congress. The *New York World* welcomed Ohioans' recognition of his "personal unpopularity and secession sympathies"; *Vanity Fair* placed Vallandigham on the front page of their postelection issue, under the tagline "Out in the Cold." The moderate Republican Henry Raymond doubted that Seymour and his party could deliver his conservative vision, but he still acknowledged in the *Times* that the governor had pledged fealty to the Union and to a renewed zeal in the prosecution of the war.[55]

The historian Thomas E. Rodgers, in a recent review of scholarship on the Democratic Party, challenged scholars to "try to explain why Republican politicians' efforts to motivate their voters with claims of disloyal Democratic organizations had so little effect in 1862 and so great effect in 1863 and 1864."[56] Answering this question becomes much simpler when you focus on the Democrats themselves rather than only on the Republican depictions of them. Through 1861 and much of 1862, the number of Democratic candidates and state parties who could be credibly attacked as disloyal—willing to countenance disunion or failing to advocate a vigorous prosecution of the war—was tiny. In 1862, men like Horatio Seymour garnered support because they offered an alternative, seemingly feasible vision for conducting the Union war.

Seymour pledged to reinvigorate military operations by providing extra men and support for McClellan and his army. He rejected claims that "freedom of speech, personal liberty, honesty of administration, are not consistent with a vigorous prosecution of the war." Indeed, he believed such a "constitutional" war would improve Northern morale while dissolving popular support for the Confederacy. Seymour would never entertain disunion, but neither would he discount the possibility of restoring the Union through negotiation and compromise. Saving the Union meant restoring *all* states to their rightful place, and a Democratic-led war would make clear to the South that they need only lay down their weapons to see their rights returned. Southerners had to be convinced, simultaneously, of the hopelessness of their cause *and* of the bright future awaiting them within the Union.[57]

Observers at the time and historians since have understandably questioned the feasibility of Seymour's vision. While infringements on personal liberties were unfortunate, could they be avoided during war on such an unprecedented scale? Could the war be won without obliterating slavery? Did Unionism survive in the Confederacy on a scale significant enough to envisage a willing return to the colors? Republicans raised many of these objections, but these were tough questions, and both parties faced a thorny problem when it came to deciding on the appropriate means of conducting the conflict against the Confederacy. Fighting a soft, constitutional war laid Democrats open to the charge that victory would be impossible. Embracing a hard war, one that attacked the foundations of Southern society, left Republicans struggling to explain why Southerners would ever accept reunion on such terms. In 1862, many voters still hoped a limited war could be fought and won. Seymour's electoral appeals captured this while drawing on rhetoric and beliefs that resonated with conservatives within and without the Democratic Party.

Two days after Seymour's election, the *New York Times* accurately foresaw the obstacles that Seymour would face trying to implement his vision. During his term they imagined that he would be called on to "give more vigor to the war," while releasing "the people from the burdens which war involves." He must "swell the armies and prevent the draft . . . prosecute the war, and at the same time give the country all the blessings of peace." They foresaw that he would be "utterly powerless to do any of these things" unless "willing to bring the State authorities into direct and armed collision with the National Government." Seymour crashed upon these rocks during his term as governor. President Lincoln would not reverse the course of emancipation or soften other edges of an increasingly hard war. Seymour voiced increasingly shrill dissent during his tenure, but he complied with measures that strengthened the Union war effort even if they tested the Constitution. This preserved his loyalty but revealed the limits of his political power, just as the *New York Times* predicted.[58]

Despite the challenges Democrats faced in office, it was the rise of a vocal and strengthening Peace faction that constituted the primary reason why Democratic prospects faded after 1862. Men like Clement Vallandigham never actually admitted they would accept a permanent peace based on disunion, but their vituperative criticisms and determination to secure an immediate armistice made their Unionism decidedly hollow. Most believed they demanded peace and only desired Union. The popular effect of these "Copperhead" positions is demonstrated by revisiting the New York soldier Asa Holmes, who, in January 1863, had instructed his son to assault anyone who "talk[ed] abolition or against slavery." By the middle of 1863, Holmes had found a new target for his wrath, positively frothing with venom against Copperheads. These peace men "ar trators to the union" who "ourter be in prison with the Rebels or in hell." Almost every letter instructed his son to try to secure a sticky end for these despicable vermin. While Holmes might have been more emotive than most, many soldiers and civilians expressed such antiabolitionist, pro-war, and anti-Copperhead views. And Copperheads came to far outrank abolitionists in the degree of hatred they engendered from Northern civilians.[59]

Even though the antiwar minority hurt Democratic prospects, significant elements of their conservative message continued to resonate, although not always under Democratic auspices. In gubernatorial elections in 1863, administration-supporting governors in Ohio and Pennsylvania secured crucial victories, presaging Lincoln's triumph the following year. But Union candidates won these victories running on Union Party tickets, and the campaigns included parts of the conservative vision for the war. Emancipation became a reality, but one seldom embraced by candidates. Republicans infrequently made controversial "radical" measures significant features of their campaigns. When they talked of the morality inherent in the conflict, they focused predominantly on the vast merits of a reunited nation, preserving the world's bastion of democracy and liberty for white men. Many in Lincoln's army supported him not so much to free the slaves as to punish Copperheads and win the war. Northerners' eventual jubilation at the fall of the Confederacy sadly did not equate to a desire to bring anything resembling equality to the nation's slaves. The greater success in appending treason to the Democratic Party actually allowed Republican candidates to focus exclusively on the issue of continuing the war and restoring the Union—at its core, much the same message Seymour and the Democrats had put forth in 1862 and that both parties had agreed on in 1861. In 1864, the Democrats nominated George B. McClellan as their presidential candidate, attempting to unite behind a pro-war candidate who could stand on much of the same ground Seymour laid out in 1862. Although hamstrung by the inclusion of a peace plank in the national platform, McClellan still secured 45 percent of the vote.[60]

The Democrats' sweeping victories in 1862 had reflected a moment when their party could lay an equal claim to supporting a patriotic, nonpartisan, national war for Union. The failings of extremists within their party and the conservatives' misreading of the president's true agenda severely damaged their prospects thereafter. Even so, the continued resilience of the Democratic vote and the policy positions taken by Republicans during the second half of the war both suggest the durability and popularity of the conservative vision of the Union war.

The Union as It Was

*Northern Catholics'
Conservative Unionism*

William B. Kurtz

"Attachment" to the Union, more than any other factor by far, motivated loyal citizens bent on defeating the rebellion," argued the historian Gary W. Gallagher persuasively in his book *The Union War* (2011). This was true for white Northerners from the Northeast to the Midwest, of different classes, ethnicities, and religions. Preserving the Union was of paramount importance to Irish Americans and other Catholic Northerners as well. For them the Union stood for the liberties and economic opportunities they found in their new home in America, and in saving the Constitution they were protecting their rights as naturalized citizens and ability to practice their Catholic religion freely. As the New York *Irish-American* reminded its readers in the war's first year, "Our standing in this community, the freedom and equality we proudly claim ... come to us directly from the whole Union, to which our first allegiance is due, under the guarantees of the Constitution we have sworn to uphold." Not only in New York, where thousands gathered in 1861 to send the largely Irish Catholic 69th New York Regiment off to war, but across the entire North pro-Union journalists and civilians noted, appreciated, and celebrated Catholic and immigrant patriotism in the war's first months.[1]

Catholic Unionism represented a fervent desire not only to save the nation but also to further a number of other important causes as well. Irish nationalists, known as Fenians, agreed wholeheartedly with most white Northerners that Union victory would "keep aloft the banner of democracy" abroad. They hoped the North's victory and the military experience they gained during the war would aid in the creation of an independent, democratic Ireland. Many of the church's leaders also saw the war as a chance to dispel concerns about their religion and its compatibility with American democracy. For them, the symbolic act of raising the American flag above their churches as well as Catholics' bravery and sacrifice on the battlefield would not only save the Union but also signal the end of nativism as a force in American society and politics. Catholics' Unionism, in short, would lead to a better future, one with their religious rights intact and their faith better respected by their Protestant neighbors. Thus Color Sergeant Peter Welsh, an Irish Catholic in the 28th Massachusetts Regiment, defended enlisting in the war to his wife for two main reasons. First, he argued that "when we are fighting for America we are fighting in the interest of Ireland." Second, he told her he had a "duty" to save the Union because its government protected "the most important of all rights enjoyed by the citezen [sic] of a free nation [which] is the liberty of conscience."[2]

As conservatives and Democrats, however, Catholics also strongly resisted attempts to enlarge the purpose of the war, especially on the issue of emancipating Southern slaves. While "most Republicans and many Democrats eventually accepted emancipation as a useful tool to help defeat the Rebels," as Gallagher pointed out, Irish Catholic immigrants as a whole proved unwilling to go so far. As the historian Christian Samito aptly put it, many Irish Catholics had a "conservative loyalty" that "sought restoration of the Union, but only on terms as if secession had never happened."[3] Remembering the connection between antislavery politics and anti-Catholic nativism in the antebellum North, they feared Republicans' attack on slavery, an institution protected by the Constitution, would open the door for future assaults on immigrants' and religious minorities' rights. In short, although Northern Catholics rallied in large numbers to the stars and stripes in 1861, they did so to restore the Union *as it was*, not to abolish slavery.[4]

The most prominent pro-Union Catholic leaders were Archbishop John Hughes (1797–1864) of New York and the Bostonian Patrick Donahoe (1811–1901), owner and editor of the *Boston Pilot*. During the antebellum period, Hughes emerged as the foremost Catholic leader in America, having publicly defended the faith and immigrants in lectures, debates, and print. Aware of his influence and high esteem among the growing body of Catholics in America, presidents from James K. Polk to James Buchanan and finally Abraham Lincoln sought his advice and support. Although most Catholics were Democrats, Hughes enjoyed good relationships with Whigs such as William H. Seward and Winfield Scott, and in 1847 he became only the second Catholic bishop to address Congress. Meanwhile, Donahoe's *Pilot*, an implacable foe of anti-Catholic nativism, became the most widely published Catholic weekly in the nation, with fifty thousand subscribers in 1855. Read not just in Massachusetts but across the North, South, and West, so influential was Donahoe's paper that it became unofficially known "as the 'Irishman's Bible' and its owner as the 'Apostle of the Irish.'" Their combined influence was reflected in Sergeant Welsh's correspondence, for he was both a frequent reader of the *Pilot* and cited Hughes as an influence on his pro-Union views.[5]

Reflecting the widely held worldview of their fellow Catholic Americans, most of whom were foreign born or of Irish ancestry,[6] Donahoe and Hughes fought for Catholics' freedom of conscience in the public schools, denounced bigotry wherever they found it, and promoted the idea that Catholics were as fully American as their Protestant neighbors. Additionally, they were both staunch Unionists who never embraced emancipation. Although they rarely corresponded, their ideas on the war were remarkably similar, with Donahoe commending one of Hughes's patriotic letters for being "so nearly in harmony with those [views] we have from time to time expressed in our paper since the commencement of the civil war."[7] Taken together, the two men wielded more influence with Irish and other Catholics during the war than anyone else in the United States. In understanding their wartime careers, scholars can better comprehend Catholics' conservative allegiance to the *Union as it was* before the war.[8]

Concerns about Catholic immigrants' fitness to be American citizens loomed large during the antebellum years. Their poverty, lack of experience with democratic government, and adherence to a dogmatic religion led by a European monarch, the pope, made a number of Protestant American citizens uneasy with the rapid growth of the church and Irish immigrants' political influence in the Northern states of the Union. Put on the defensive, Irish and Catholic leaders sought to reaffirm their community's patriotic credentials. They did so in part by seeking to avoid affiliating with divisive political issues, particularly abolition. Thus during the 1840s, they rejected calls from the great Irish nationalist hero Daniel O'Connell to join with American abolitionists in opposing Southern slavery. Irish Catholic Northerners saw O'Connell's actions as an unwelcome foreign intrusion that threatened their hopes to be accepted as equals in American society. As one Catholic newspaper put it, they resented any foreign attempt to "shackle the opinions of Irishmen and America." Later in the 1850s, Irish Catholic laymen, almost all members of the Democratic Party, were so outspoken against abolitionists and Republicans that they would be regularly accused of being proslavery. Thus a nativist Massachusetts newspaper alleged that "Catholicism and slavery are twin sisters," while Henry Wilson, a Republican senator from that state, called Irish Democrats "the cornerstone of American slavery."[9]

Although many Catholic leaders, lay and clerical, weighed in on debates between Catholics and Protestants and immigrants and nativists, Archbishop John Hughes of New York and the layman editor Patrick Donahoe of Boston were the foremost champions of the Irish and the church during this time. Both men were born in Ireland and were always ready to promote their homeland's interests, although never at the expense of the United States. Hughes earned his fame as a defender of immigrants, the poor, and a champion of Catholic children's freedom-of-conscience rights in the early 1840s. In the wake of nativist violence in Philadelphia in 1844, he controversially defended his flock from nativist forces by threatening to turn New York City into "a second Moscow" should a single Catholic church be harmed, thus cementing his status as the primary target of anti-Catholic rage during these years. Indicative of Catholics' appreciation for his talent, oratory, and defense of the faith, Father Isaac Hecker called him "the most able bishop we have." Refuting nativist criticisms of his flock, Hughes never ceased arguing that his religion and adopted homeland were fully compatible, authoring numerous newspaper articles and giving sermons and speeches to that effect. In a speech in 1852, for example, Hughes recalled the contributions of American Catholics to victory during the Revolution as proof that they were just as patriotic as their Protestant neighbors. He further argued that the Constitution's guarantee of religious freedom was "almost literally copied from the provision of the charter and statutes of the Catholic colony of Maryland." "Let [Americans] without distinction of creed, unite, and be united, in preserving the common inheritance," Hughes urged, for the time might come "when our country shall have need of all her children."[10]

Donahoe's newspaper, the *Pilot*, was an ardent defender of Irish and Catholic interests in America, with a circulation reaching more than one hundred thousand a few years after the Civil War. Donahoe completely agreed with Hughes on the need to fight nativism head on. Rarely did a week go by in the 1850s without an article attacking the Know-Nothings, a nativist political party founded in the early part of that decade, or denouncing a new outrage they had perpetrated on Catholics or immigrants. The editor mocked the nativists' violent ways, predicting that they would so appall other Americans that "thousands of lukewarm Catholics will become faithful and practical . . . and thousands of Protestants will be converted to the Church." An ardent Democrat, Donahoe believed the best antidote to nativism was voting for that party in local, state, and national elections. Although many historians tend to see 1856 as the Know-Nothings' last hurrah, Donahoe and other Catholics had no guarantee that they would not return again. "There can be no greater mistake than to suppose that the spirit and prejudice which called the party into existence is dead," he warned in 1857. "They exist in full vigor, and are as likely to affect public affairs with the virus of illiberality as at any time within the past three years." Thus he was not surprised when Know-Nothing support of the Republican Nathaniel Banks played a significant role in electing him Massachusetts's governor later that year. Donahoe's concerns about nativism in American society would greatly influence his understanding of the Civil War.[11]

Donahoe and Hughes were also largely in agreement on slavery, being opposed to it on general principle but doing nothing directly to end it either. As a young man, Hughes had written an antislavery poem, and as bishop he went on record several times as opposing slavery's abuses and hoping for its eventual demise. Returning from a trip to Cuba, Hughes deplored slavery's existence but argued "it is not an absolute and unmitigated evil," for had the slaves been left in Africa they might never have learned the truths of Christianity. Hughes also frequently derided the abolitionist cause, suspecting them of being dangerous anti-Catholic radical reformers. Like the archbishop, most Catholics believed that abolitionists were usually hostile to the church and sound social order in America. Donahoe's *Pilot* repeatedly expressed similar sentiments, and its editor believed, like many Northern Democrats, that slavery's fate was something best left to the South to decide. "The Catholic church sets her face against slavery . . . and abolished it in all countries where her voice was respected," Donahoe claimed, "but she anathematizes the Protestant and freesoil principle that the end justifies the means." In commenting on the antislavery lectures of Ralph Waldo Emerson in 1855, Donahoe blasted him and other abolitionists for prescribing "false remedies" for the problem. "Slavery is an evil," he declared, "but the remedy for it does not fall within their premises." He further distrusted abolitionism for what he saw as its deep ties to nativism, alleging that "large numbers of antislavery and free soil men are joining the order of Know Nothings."[12]

Unlike the ostensibly apolitical archbishop, Donahoe's *Pilot* again and again publicly berated the Democrats' political foes, be they New England abolitionists, nativist Know-Nothings, or the new Republican Party. For example, he accused a mob that had freed the escaped slave Anthony Burns from jail in Boston in 1854 of having committed treason against the Constitution. "Freesoilism has begot secular and ministerial threats affecting the safety of the Union,—it has begotten riots, robbery and murder," argued Donahoe. "We are thankful to have it in our power to say that we do not know a Catholic who, throughout this freesoil agitation, has not been on the side of the Union and the Constitution." When Republicans in the state legislature amended the state's naturalization laws in 1859 to make naturalized immigrants wait an additional two years before voting, he denounced them as no better than the Know-Nothings. Campaigning strongly on behalf of Stephen A. Douglas in the 1860 presidential campaign, Donahoe's paper reminded its readers that to vote for the Republicans was to endorse the two years' amendment. "A naturalized citizen who would vote for a party who proscribes his race," he continued, "does not deserve the rights of citizenship." When his hopes were disappointed with the Republican Abraham Lincoln's election that November, Donahoe gloomily predicted that "northern aggression on the principle interest of the Southern States" would lead to secession. Nonetheless, he encouraged his readers always to "Stand by the Union; fight for the Union; die by the Union."[13]

With the firing on Fort Sumter, Catholics joined their fellow Northerners in loyally supporting the Union and putting down the treason of the Southern Confederates. Hughes declared in a public letter read aloud at a massive war rally in Union Square in New York City only a week after Sumter surrendered that he had "none but one country," thereby emphasizing his allegiance to the Union of all of the states. He also encouraged his fellow naturalized citizens to follow their consciences and do their duty to the nation. Meanwhile, no layman spoke more fiercely or unhesitatingly in favor of Irish and Catholic enlistment in the nascent federal army of volunteers than Donahoe. Now was the perfect time to show anti-Catholic and nativist Americans just how wrong they had been about Catholics' fidelity to America's democratic government. Denouncing those who claimed the Irish would be disloyal to the nation, Donahoe's *Pilot* boasted that it was the "Irish [Catholic] Bishops" who had first spoken out for the Union and that the church "always countenanced loyal submission to legitimate rule." Praising Hughes's patriotic example, Donahoe asserted that Catholics were unquestionably supporting the nation in its time of peril. America's Irish Catholic citizens had remained "true, to a man, to the Constitution." In what would be a constant theme for him, Donahoe contrasted Irish and Catholic patriotism favorably with that of the abolitionists, whom he described "as the real sources of all our troubles."[14]

Throughout the conflict, Donahoe defended his church and fellow Irish immigrants from charges of cowardice or disloyalty. On the contrary, Irishmen and other Catholics were true to the Union and brave warriors precisely because of their faith. Although brave of their own accord, having access to chaplains who could say Mass and hear their confessions before a battle made them more courageous in confronting death on the battlefield. Hughes had personally admonished the men of the 69th New York Infantry Regiment before they left for Virginia to be "brave in battle," "humane and kind after the battle is over," and to do nothing to "bring a tarnish upon their name, their country or their religion." Shortly after the First Battle of Bull Run, Donahoe argued that the Catholicism of the 69th New York's soldiers "increased their bravery" at that battle. "Catholicity is the best incentive to valor," Donahoe argued, taking pride that after the battle it was "now universally acknowledged that the terrific heroism of the 69th at Manassas had Catholicity shining brilliantly before it."[15]

The *Pilot*, like other Catholic weeklies, continued to promote the cause of the 69th New York, and later the Irish Brigade, during the war. Starting in late 1862 and through the end of the war, Donahoe published a weekly column entitled "Records of Irish American Patriotism" that highlighted the contributions of Irish regiments and Irish American Union officers to Northern victory. Donahoe was actively engaged in enlisting local Irishmen into the 9th and 28th Massachusetts Infantry Regiments, and he received further support for his efforts from his local bishop, John Fitzpatrick. Although not as prolifically patriotic as Hughes, Fitzpatrick proved to be one of the ablest pro-war voices in the Northern episcopacy and was rewarded for his patriotism with an honorary degree from Harvard. Public sendoffs for the Massachusetts Irish regiments in Boston, the end of laws forcing Catholic children to read from the Protestant King James Bible in the state's common schools, and other signs of declining anti-Catholic nativism in Massachusetts seemed to show that Donahoe was initially right in seeing the war as increasing tolerance for Irish Catholic immigrants.[16]

Donahoe went beyond merely championing Irish soldiers' bravery to defending the loyalty of the clergy as well. Having previously boasted of Archbishop Hughes's patriotism at the start of the war, in the summer and fall of 1862 the *Pilot* printed several more articles about Catholic clergymen. First, it noted that although more than one hundred thousand men in the Army were Catholic, only twelve of the four hundred priests assigned to the army were. Arguing that Irish soldiers were bravest when accompanied by a priest, the paper hoped that the government would amend its laws to allow more priests to serve. Second, in a seemingly preemptive move, Donahoe sought to portray the clergy as a whole as patriotic and loyal. "Our clergy are truly loyal, and therefore not at all the friends of the revolt." Conveniently ignoring the pro-Confederate sympathies of most Southern priests, he argued that the clergy's refusal to support the rebellion was a powerful argument against it, for "when the priests of the Catholic Church are against a movement there is *prima facie* evidence that it is profoundly bad." Given the patriotic examples of Hughes, Fitzpatrick, and Catholic chaplains, Donahoe believed that clergy's loyalty and patriotism were beyond question.[17]

For Donahoe, the Union's humiliating loss at Manassas was nonetheless an important turning point in the country's perceptions of Irishmen and Catholics. In late 1861, the war promised to be the final "Irish triumph over Know-Nothingism," the last nail in the coffin of nativism. Arguing that Irish far outnumbered nativists in the army, he reminded his readers and, he hoped, the North as a whole that Irish Catholics had proved their loyalty despite antebellum misgivings about their foreign birth or religion. "There is no doubt that the arms they have assumed will re-construct the Union. To enlist is [an Irishman's] duty," Donahoe stated, "for the country they have adopted has a claim on their blood." Anti-immigrant, anti-Catholic nativism was now "dead, disgraced, and offensive, while Irish Catholic patriotism and bravery are true to the nation and indispensable to it in every point of consideration." Donahoe persisted in these beliefs throughout the war. Almost a year later, after the Union had suffered additional defeats during the Seven Days Battles, he reiterated his argument that Irishmen had a duty to serve and that they had proven to be patriots in the country's time of need. "Historians of America will point them out to future generations as the best soldiers the Republic ever had." Believing even then in the eventual triumph of the Union, he argued that any nation with 160,000 Irishmen in its ranks "cannot be destroyed."[18]

A future with the Union destroyed was one that most Northern Catholics, including Donahoe, could not imagine. Strongly held antebellum beliefs that the Constitution safeguarded their rights as immigrants and Catholics came full circle in the Civil War when the nation and its laws were imperiled. Irish Catholics believed in American exceptionalism just as much as other Northerners, a belief evident in Donahoe's frequent depictions of the United States as "the best government that ever existed" and "the freest government in the world." For naturalized Irishmen, America was their "real country," and as he had argued before, they owed their loyalty and blood to it. Lamenting the Confederates' rebellion as threatening to "undo the great work of 1776," he warned his readers that not only would they live in a "broken-down community" if secession succeeded but that Ireland would be completely at the mercy of England if the Union failed. Obligations of "duty, and honor, and common sense" thus obligated Irish Catholics to do "everything in [their] power against the rebellion—to induce as many as possible to enlist for its suppression." Noting his own substantial role in promoting enlistment, Donahoe argued that the cause of the Union was the cause of Irishmen in America and Ireland.[19]

Not to be outdone, Archbishop Hughes quickly established a reputation as the most important Catholic episcopal supporter of the Union cause. In addition to his early pro-Union speech, he joined fellow bishops across the North in flying the flag from his cathedral, thus putting his Unionism on display for all to see. He arranged for Father Thomas Mooney, a priest of his diocese, to be chaplain to the 69th New York Infantry Regiment, and he publicly addressed and blessed the men of New York Irish regiments on several occasions throughout the war. He wrote to his friend General Winfield Scott, offering even more priests (Jesuits from Fordham) as chaplains and New York City nuns as nurses for the troops around Washington.[20] Although some of Hughes's critics, such as Horace Greeley and William Lloyd Garrison, would accuse him of not supporting the war strongly enough, Catholics in the Confederacy were dismayed by Hughes's strong support for the Union. They believed that Hughes had scandalously mixed politics with religion, with one acerbic chaplain in General Robert E. Lee's army remarking, "It was galling to hear for the first time that a Catholic Archbishop had urged a rigorous prosecution of a war waged for an unjustifiable object and conducted in a manner unworthy of a barbarous nation."[21]

Despite his Unionism, Hughes tried to stay on good terms with Southern bishops during the war. For example, after Fr. Mooney angered Maryland Catholics by blessing a Union cannon before the First Battle of Bull Run, Hughes removed him from his post in order to placate Baltimore's Archbishop Francis Kenrick. Criticized by Richard V. Whelan, the bishop of Wheeling, Virginia, for his seemingly political stand on behalf of the North, Hughes carefully assured his fellow prelate that he had not overstepped his bounds as a religious and moral shepherd of his flock. Just as Catholics in the South had flocked to the Confederacy, Hughes pointed out, so too had those in the North to the Union cause. "Public opinion . . . would not tolerate them staying at home," he argued, pointing out correctly that "the press would have sounded the report that the Catholics were disloyal, and no act of ours afterward could successfully vindicate us from the imputation." Hughes defended his decision to raise the flag above his cathedral as a moderate one compared with the "unnecessary, inexpedient, and for that matter a doubtful if not a dangerous position" taken by Southern clergymen who argued that the right of secession was based in the "principles of Catholic Theology."[22]

Hughes's most important public contribution to the Union cause in 1861 was in a public dispute with a Southern bishop. Writing privately to Hughes shortly after Bull Run, Charleston's pro-Confederate bishop Patrick N. Lynch advised Northern Catholics: "The Separation of the southern States is un fait accompli. The Federal government has no power to reverse it." Blaming "black republicans" for the conflict, Lynch advised Hughes to keep Northern Irish Catholics out of the conflict and boasted that the South could never be militarily subjugated. Hughes, who decided to publish both Lynch's letter along with his own response, strongly denied that the Southern states had acted justly in seceding. Dismissing Lynch's idea that the conflict was not one of Northern "conquest," he opined that "foreigners now naturalized, whether Catholics or not, ought to bear their relative burthen in defense of the . . . country." This firm rejection of secession and the alleged

Figure 4 "Grand Requiem Mass in St. Patrick's Cathedral, New York, Friday, January 16, for the Repose of the Souls of the Officers and Men of the Irish Brigade Killed in the War." Archbishop John Hughes celebrated this mass a month after the brigade had suffered terrible losses at the battle of Fredericksburg on December 13, 1862.
Source: Library of Congress, Prints and Photographs Division, reproduction no. LC-USZ62-119851 (reproducing an image from *Frank Leslie's Illustrated Newspaper*, February 7, 1863, 308).

merits of South Carolina's complaints, published in the *Metropolitan Record* and reprinted in Catholic and secular periodicals around the country, added considerably to Hughes's reputation as a Northern patriot. Even his longtime newspaper opponent, James Gordon Bennett of the *New York Herald*, applauded Hughes's letter, predicting he would "win as the prize for his logic the cardinal's hat."[23]

Hughes also frequently corresponded with his old friend Secretary of State William H. Seward about the war, offering advice in lengthy letters to the busy statesman. For example, only a few weeks after Fort Sumter fell, Hughes wrote Seward with thirteen propositions for how the government should conduct the war. Flattering him as the most competent of all of Lincoln's cabinet, Hughes urged him to be vigorous in recruiting soldiers so the full force of the North's numerical superiority over the South would come to bear sooner rather than later. The same reasoning led him to recommend that the next Congress appropriate $300 million in order to demonstrate Northern resolve to the Confederacy. Always expressing confidence in the Union's inevitable victory, Hughes shrugged off the defeat at Bull Run in July, calling it a "providential" setback that would make the federal government "more alert" and willing to raise more money and troops to win the war.[24]

At Seward and Lincoln's request, Hughes agreed to serve as the unofficial agent of the Lincoln administration in Europe in the winter of 1861–1862. Although this appointment did not sit well with some Catholics at home or abroad, Hughes believed his mission would promote peace as well as the best interests of both North and South. As Hughes later assured Cardinal Alesandro Barnabo, prefect of the Congregation Propaganda Fide, he had come to Europe representing "the interests of all the United States, just the same as if they had never been distracted by the present civil war." Furthermore, not to accept the government's invitation would have foolishly called into question Catholic loyalty during a time of war. Besides, the Lincoln cabinet intended the appointment both as a "great compliment" to all Catholic Americans and a firm repudiation of the Know-Nothings' attempts to deny Catholics their equal rights. Admitting that a number of Catholic bishops back home disapproved of his mission, Hughes assured Seward that the pope and leading cardinals "approved of my conduct." Nonetheless, such criticism bore down heavily on him upon his return home.[25]

Hughes wrote long dispatches to Seward during his trip, which saw him visit London, Paris, Rome, and Dublin. Writing pessimistically at first during the Trent Affair dispute with England, he became more optimistic after that crisis was averted. He argued again and again that his presence in Europe had helped dispel misconceptions there with leading secular and religious authorities, especially in France and the Papal States. In particular, he believed his personal audience with the French emperor, Louis Napoleon, had gone very well, predicting that France would stay out of the war. His personal letters attested to the good effect the Union victories in early 1862 had on tamping down pro-Confederate sympathy in Europe. Upon his return, the *New York Herald* praised Hughes's mission as evidence of his "unswerving patriotism," predicting that his recent speeches in Ireland would unite that country for the North. In performing such an important mission on behalf of the nation, Hughes had "increased [his] claims to the esteem and gratitude of the American people." There were even rumors that President Lincoln had asked the Vatican to reward Hughes's patriotism by making him the first cardinal of the American church.[26]

Nonetheless, the real impact of Hughes's trip may have been negligible, compared with the larger impact that good or bad news from the war had on Europeans' understanding of which side would win. From a friend in Rome, he received word shortly after his return to America that a prominent cardinal in the Vatican had bluntly asked "why the President recognized the Italian kingdom if the cabinet were friendly to Catholics." Nor was the Lincoln administration convinced of his mission's success. When he asked to extend his stay in Europe, Seward, despite his gratitude to Hughes, informed him that the president did not think it necessary. Even Hughes returned home pessimistic about European views of the war. In a public letter to Seward in November, Hughes admitted that "there was no love for the United States on the other side of the water." A letter from Pope Pius IX asking him to work for peace, without reference to perpetuity of the Union, further demonstrated how unconvincing his pro-Northern arguments had ultimately been in the Vatican's highest circles.[27]

Despite such pessimism about Europe, Hughes remained, as much as his poor health would allow him, a champion of the Union cause. On his return to the United States in August, he gave a rousing pro-Union sermon on August 17 that was printed in full in local papers, including the front page of the *Herald*. In it Hughes argued that from a sense of "humanity" a draft should be instituted to help put a swift "end to this draggling of human blood across the whole surface of the country." As long as the people approved of it, he argued that a draft would be more fair than volunteering and would ensure that "every man, rich or poor, will have to take his share." As a further evidence of his patriotism, Hughes parted ways with the editor John Mullaly in early 1863, no longer endorsing the outspoken antiwar *Metropolitan Record* as his official diocesan newspaper.[28]

The efforts of Hughes and Donahoe to lead a united pro-war, pro-Union Catholic front were quickly frustrated by an equally patriotic and outspoken American-born convert. Orestes A. Brownson, a Protestant newspaper editor and theologian who had become Catholic in 1844, broke with his fellow Catholics and voted Republican in 1860. A strong proponent of the federal government and the Northern cause, he irked many by denouncing most Catholic newspapers as "secession sheets . . . for we count every journal favorable to the Secessionists, that opposes the war, and clamors for peace." Brownson also doubted the patriotism of some of the clergy, pointing out that many of them were foreign born. As early as October 1861, he suggested emancipating the slaves as a possible means to win the war. Slavery, after all, was nothing but a "great moral, social, and political wrong," and the church had always worked for the peaceful and gradual abolition of the practice. He argued that slavery was the Confederacy's "weak spot" and thus that the North was bound by "common prudence and common humanity" to "strike our heaviest and deadliest blow" there to end the war as quickly as possible. In this article and others, he attempted to convince other Catholics to give up their misgivings about abolition and embrace emancipation as a wartime measure to save the Union.[29]

Such an opinion was well ahead of most Northern Catholics, whose leaders continued to denounce simultaneously abolitionism and the rebellion. In an anonymous response, Archbishop Hughes led the conservative counterattack, declaring Brownson's views "untimely and mischievous," alleging that Catholics had earned "great credit" for themselves by avoiding any such discussions of slavery. "We Catholics," the paper continued, were fighting a war for the Union and Constitution, not one to "gratify a clique of abolitionists in the North." No "true patriots" could ever advocate such a war, for an abolition war would be unconstitutional, and it would be a disgrace to the men who had fought and died for the Union to change the war to an antislavery one. Hughes denied slavery was the cause of the war, said the church had no power to end it where it already existed, and described it as an institution that had existed since "the earliest annals of the human race." Because Africa was "a country of savages," Hughes claimed, enslaved people sent to America had actually been saved by slave traders from a more wretched life under "barbarous" African leaders. Hughes played down the immorality of slave sales that led to the frequent separation of slave families by comparing slavery's problems to the "degraded condition of thousands of females in our large cities in the free States." "We have only now to say," wrote Hughes, "that we despise in the name of all Catholics the 'Idea' of making this war subservient to the philanthropic nonsense of abolitionism."[30]

Widely reprinted in other likeminded Catholic newspapers, including the *Pilot*, Hughes spoke for most Catholics who disliked abolitionism for its ties to Great Britain and sympathy with anti-Catholicism in America and Europe. Hughes's diocesan newspaper remarked that had the thousands of Catholic Union soldiers been informed before enlisting that they were fighting a war to abolish slavery, "not a single man would have crossed outwards his own threshold." James Gordon Bennett, editor of the *New York Herald*, was thrilled by the letter, for both men finally saw eye to eye on a subject after years of battling each other before the war. Applauding Hughes's "sound opinions" as substantially the same as those of the *Herald*, Bennett declared the archbishop had thoroughly "exploded" Brownson's "abolition heresies." In Hughes's letter, he continued, one would find "the true doctrine of the Catholic Church on that subject [slavery] expounded by authority."[31]

Despite Bennett's, the *Pilot*'s, and other conservatives' approval, antislavery men like Greeley sided with Brownson, and Hughes's letter was criticized by some French journals during the archbishop's European mission in 1862. Hughes felt he owed his friend Secretary Seward an explanation, writing that he had written the letter out of fear that Brownson would have confused the minds of Catholic Americans about the reasons for the war, declaring that there would be "time enough" to deal with slavery after the conflict was over. The archbishop also told Secretary of War Simon Cameron that while Catholics were willing to fight for the Union, they would "turn away in disgust" from fighting an abolition war. Although Brownson sharply rebuked Hughes in turn in early 1862, dislike of abolitionism did not hurt Catholics' reputation for loyalty at this stage of the war, before emancipation became official government policy. As the leading historian of Civil War–era religion noted, "Hughes and much of the American hierarchy had more than proved their loyalty to the Union cause by the fall of 1861."[32]

Donahoe was even more outspoken than Hughes, repeatedly criticizing abolitionist fanatics and antislavery Republicans throughout the war. Like every other Catholic editor not named Brownson, Donahoe regularly denigrated what he considered to be a group of radicals largely responsible for the war as well as anti-Irish and anti-Catholic sentiment at home and abroad. Just before South Carolina's secession, he opined that "the rabid abolitionism of the north is necessarily destructive of the union." The following June, the paper took issue with an editorial in the *New York Times* that stated, "Like Popery, Slavery is incompatible with the spirit of the age. . . . Providence seems to have doomed them to destruction by the folly of their devotees." On the contrary, Donahoe insisted, it was supposedly liberal Anglo-Saxon Protestantism that was not suited for the present—just look at what it had done to Ireland. Likening the church to slavery as did the *Times*'s editorial touched a raw nerve for Donahoe, for it was all too reminiscent of the "No Popery, No Slavery" cries of the nativist 1850s. The church was the "greatest emancipator of slaves" in history, Donahoe continued, and it was Northern editors like Henry J. Raymond and his *New York Times* whose attacks on the institution "were the main causes of the difficulties now distracting the country."[33]

Donahoe continued to denounce the fanaticism of abolition through the early years of the war, seeing it as a threat to national integrity and the successful prosecution of the war. Long after Hughes had blasted Brownson, the *Pilot* publicly denounced him as the tool of the abolitionists. Donahoe particularly took issue with a public address he gave in 1862 in support of emancipation, calling it an "insane speech" that threatened both the Union and the Constitution. "The war is not for emancipation," he reminded his readers, "nor for the overthrow of the Constitution in any way." Emancipation would subvert the nation's laws while exposing four million slaves to "certain misery and desolation." Donahoe's strong repudiation of abolitionism and consistent refusal to support emancipation throughout the war infuriated the radical editor William Lloyd Garrison, whose *Liberator* often denounced its Catholic adversary as a "vile and rabidly pro-slavery sheet."[34]

In the fall of 1862, Donahoe criticized Lincoln's Preliminary Emancipation Proclamation issued on September 22 as an act of political "tyranny" that would only strengthen Confederate resolve. Doubting that more than one in twenty slaves, who "love their masters, as dogs do," would accept emancipation, Donahoe saw the measure ultimately as the result of a "fanaticism" in the Republican Party that could be corrected in part by Democratic victories at the ballot box. Such radicalism would eventually die out altogether, he later predicted, as the population descended from the fanatical Puritans of New England decreased and the Catholic Church grew in strength throughout the country. When the final proclamation was signed on January 1, 1863, Donahoe spoke for many Catholics in lamenting that "we find ourselves, after nearly two years' fighting for the Union, as it was, and as it ought to be, engaged in an abolition war." Now, he continued, it was obvious why the Republicans rejected any kind of conciliation with the South, because, he implied, they had always wanted to attack slavery. This was a tragic turn for the country, for the notion that the North would be able to "conquer a peace under the proclamation is considered absurd by every man who knows anything about hostilities upon the vast scale now in progress." Hughes, who had also long argued and advised Lincoln and Seward against emancipation, agreed with Donahoe, seeing the final proclamation as a kind of "betrayal" of the war's original aims.[35]

As in the rest of the North, debate over emancipation continued within Catholic circles throughout the war. Despite his reputation as a proslavery man in abolitionist newspapers such as the *Liberator*, Donahoe attempted to carve out a position of being neither proslavery nor proabolition. Thus he tried to play peacemaker when a particularly unseemly intra-Catholic fight erupted between the Copperhead layman James A. McMaster of New York and the pro-Lincoln priest Fr. Edward Purcell of Cincinnati. The latter had initially joined other Catholic editors in condemning abolition, but under the influence of his brother John Purcell, Cincinnati's Irish-born archbishop, Fr. Edward used the emancipation of the Russian serfs as an opportunity to speak out against slavery. "Slavery and the Catholic Church could never get along well together," Purcell opined in an April 1863 editorial. McMaster, however, argued that the church had no right to interfere with Southern slavery and that slaves were members of a "semi-savage race" best suited for bondage. He accused his adversaries of "pandering to the infidel radicalism of the times." Purcell responded by citing church fathers and popes as authorities against the institution, insisting that the church was "no lover of slavery."[36]

Donahoe deeply regretted such Catholic infighting and begged both sides, "for the sake of decency and patriotism let them desist!" He saw both combatants as extremists, calling "Abolitionism far more than half the cause" of the rebellion on the one hand, predicting that Purcell would fail in his efforts to "taint his Irish readers" with abolitionism. On the other hand, he pleaded with McMaster to be "aware that the second cause of the rebellion is that same pro-slaveryism which he himself advocates every week." Despite his attempts to be even-handed, Donahoe blasted Father Purcell a week later as a "confirmed negrophilist" who cared little for white laborers. Archbishop Hughes's former newspaper, the *Metropolitan Record*, similarly accused the *Telegraph* of an "excess of . . . zeal in the cause of Abolitionism." "Slavery is an evil," Donahoe admitted, "but the *Greeleyizing* of our priests would be a greater evil." "May our beloved clergy never be so lost to reason as to join ranks with Greeley, Phillips, Garrison, and the Beechers!" Thus Donahoe, like Archbishop Hughes, in speaking for the majority of Catholics who were politically conservative, consistently opposed emancipation, whether its advocates were Catholic or Protestant.[37]

Donahoe wrote both of these articles in the wake of draft riots in July 1863 that took place in both Boston and New York City. Although Archbishop Hughes had previously publicly supported a draft in the fall of 1862, conscription along with emancipation were two extremely controversial issues that caused considerable unrest among Catholic immigrant communities by the summer of 1863. Like antidraft Democratic politicians such as Governor Horatio Seymour of New York, many Catholic journalists became extremely critical of the coming federal draft throughout the first half of the year. The Radical Republican Horace Greeley made matters worse by openly attacking Catholics and Archbishop Hughes over slavery just before the start of the draft in the city. Criticizing Hughes for saying Catholics had done nothing to bring on the war, Greeley argued instead that their support for Polk in 1844 and his war on Mexico had brought about the current crisis. He also criticized Hughes for not doing enough to counteract the "most unChristian, inhuman spirit of negro-hate" among his Irish followers. In short, Greeley threw a lit match into a powder keg of working-class, immigrant resentment over emancipation, the draft, and nativism.[38]

This violent anger came forth in full fury a week later. Rioters in New York attacked symbols of federal authority, the homes of Republican leaders, the offices of Greeley's newspaper, and the dwellings and charitable institutions devoted to poor African Americans. They killed many innocent blacks and raged out of control for several days in mid-July until police and Union regiments were able to halt the violence. In the end, New York City suffered widespread property destruction, and at least one hundred people died. Irish policeman and Catholic clergymen did help put down the violence, and the usually anti-Catholic *Harper's Weekly* praised them, stating "the Roman Catholic priesthood to a man used their influence on the side of the law." Irishmen were also prominent in smaller disturbances in Boston as well, but fortunately the intervention of the authorities and the Catholic clergy there under Father James Healey prevented violence on a larger scale. Certainly not every draft rioter in either city was an Irish Catholic, and many of that group remained peaceably at home. Still, many New Yorkers and other Northerners blamed the Irish for playing the leading role in the horrible violence.[39]

While a recent study has argued that the negative effect of the riots on perceptions of Catholic patriotism was relatively limited on a national scale, the large number of Irishmen in the riots predictably prompted an anti-Irish and anti-Catholic backlash in New York City and Boston. Greeley told Archbishop Hughes to stop "his people" from further rioting. Hughes replied in Bennett's *Herald*, insisting that he was not a "head constable" and that the civil authorities were the proper ones to keep the city's peace. Nevertheless, "if I can do anything, directly or otherwise, to prevent bloodshed or the destruction of property, why should I not endeavor to do so, even without any civil commission?" The archbishop wrote two public letters published throughout the city urging Catholics to refrain from violence and calling on them to visit him at his residence for a public address. On Friday, July 17, an ailing and seated Hughes gave a speech from the balcony of his home to a crowd of around five thousand men. He began by attempting to placate rather than admonish his audience, saying, "They call you rioters. I cannot see a riotous face among you." Still, he strongly urged his audience to avoid violence, to obey the laws, and finally to redress any "temporary" injustices of the government peacefully through the ballot box. This long, sometimes rambling, speech was warmly received by his audience, though not always by his critics. They recognized its good intent but accused him of making light of Catholic rioters' misdeeds. Garrison's *Liberator* was among those who found the speech "very reprehensible," and Brownson thought it showed that Hughes was afraid of the mob. "His address shows that he felt his impotence to control his people except by diverting their wrath from the draft to the English, the hated 'Anglo-Saxons.'" Nonetheless, the riots were at long last over, and Hughes had done as much as he could to quiet the unrest despite his poor health at the time.[40]

Despite his strong Unionism at the start of the war, Hughes had his limits, lamenting the war's incredible bloodshed, the adoption of emancipation as a war aim, and the nativist backlash to the draft riots. While always true to the Union, his increased prayers for peace and refusal to pay the new federal income tax were symbolic of his growing disenchantment with the war's changing nature in 1863. Suffering from Bright's disease and rheumatism since before the July riots, Archbishop Hughes remained a convalescent for the last few months of his life, finally dying on January 3, 1864. Hughes's death was widely reported in both the Catholic and secular press of the North, with only a few like Horace Greeley too petty to not make his passing front-page news. It was estimated that over one hundred thousand people turned out for his funeral Mass at St. Patrick's Cathedral, and the church was so crowded that even some local priests could not enter. Donahoe spoke for most Catholics in the country in eulogizing Hughes as the church's "ablest champion in America." "His adopted country and the Irish race [have lost] their best friend and advocate." The *New York Herald* similarly praised Hughes as the American church's "best friend" and "one of [the nation's] purest patriots." Seward expressed his and President Lincoln's condolences to the archdiocese's vicar general, Fr. William Starrs, assuring him of the government's profound respect for the recently deceased prelate who had performed a great patriotic service in his recent trip to Europe. With Hughes's passing, pro-war Catholics lost one of their leading voices and one of the few leaders of the church who had still supported the war despite emancipation.[41]

In the wake of the riots and a resurgence of anti-Catholicism, Donahoe sought to reassure his readers that the nation would always remember the "gallant Catholic chiefs" who had commanded its armies during its time of crisis and would never "tolerate any invasion of the rights of the powerful and patriotic element which they so faithfully represent." Still the draft remained controversial for Irish

Catholics, not just for the way it seemed to target the poor but also for the lack of total exemption for all clergymen. Numerous bishops and heads of religious orders lamented the fact that they had to pay to exempt their clergymen, with many writing to or meeting with President Lincoln personally seeking an exemption for their priests and other male religious. The government's refusal to pass such an exemption was an ominous sign for many and seemed a poor reward for the patriotism of Northern clergy such as Hughes. "Until the passage of the Conscription bill, America had exercised no tyranny on the Church. There can be no doubt that Heaven blessed it for such justice," wrote Donahoe. But now, "a parcel of infidels" in the US government had done something unparalleled in history, rendering it "odious to christendom." "The only satisfaction in this matter is, that there will be soon a Presidential election," Donahoe finished. The failure to exempt the Catholic clergy, while married Protestant ministers with other careers often were, was absolutely infuriating to Donahoe and other Catholic leaders. The issue, along with other incidents, such as the alleged desecration of Southern churches and the military arrest of William H. Elder, the Catholic bishop of Natchez, Mississippi, became rallying cries for those who thought many Republicans were anti-Catholic nativists at heart.[42]

Despite their strong resentment of emancipation and conscription, by early 1864 many pro-war Catholics had new reasons for optimism, especially after General Ulysses S. Grant, the victor of Vicksburg and Chattanooga, was called east to direct the war effort. Donahoe argued that "the only method by which a permanent peace may be obtained is by the overthrow of those who have made, and are still making, superhuman efforts to destroy the integrity of the Union." He wanted the war to be continued even if this meant fighting the Confederate armies "to the death." Similarly, another pro-war Catholic editor declared the Southern cause a "dead one" and opined, "In mercy to its citizens it should give up." Although Donahoe continued to criticize Lincoln's civil liberty policies and abolition, he was willing to put these issues aside to support the North's victory and with it the restoration of his beloved Union.[43]

The horrific casualties of General Grant's Overland Campaign that summer, however, put to the test pro-war Catholics' enthusiasm for continuing the struggle. Donahoe deplored the "unnecessary and frightful slaughter" and began to talk of peace and a renewed commitment to the restoration of the "old Union" under the "old Constitution," that is, a political reunion without emancipation. After three years of bloody fighting, "the time for negotiation and pacification has come." Throughout the remainder of 1864, his journal became just as much an organ of the Democratic Party as one in defense of Irish or Catholic interests in the North. Donahoe justified supporting the Democrats because Republicans were merely the successors of the anti-Catholic Know-Nothings and because peace was only possible if the constitutional rights of *all* white American citizens were respected. Other Catholic editors, from the pro-war *New York Tablet* to the antiwar *Metropolitan Record*, joined the *Pilot* in campaigning strongly on behalf of the Democrats in the 1864 elections.[44]

In the wake of the Democrats' defeat in the November elections, the *Pilot* magnanimously congratulated the Republicans and praised the Army of the Potomac for its "courage, constancy, and devotion that are not surpassed in the annals of war" despite its staggering losses since the previous May. Still, Donahoe's paper seemed to be so pessimistic about the war that it was not until a string of Union victories the following March when the editor could again see a path forward to ending the conflict and reestablishing peace. Donahoe was so cheered by news of victories at Charleston, Wilmington, and Sherman's march through the Carolinas that he declared the end of the war and its bloodshed was not far off. The surrender of General Lee's army ensured "defeat, utter defeat, and ruin" upon the Confederacy, he proclaimed, while proudly noting the important role that Irish Americans like General Philip Sheridan had played in Lee's final defeat. With the end of the war assured, Donahoe finally, and quite unexpectedly, gave up on his insistence that the North fight only for the Union and leave slavery alone. "The end of chattel slavery must be taken as an accomplished fact," he advised his readers. "It is no use to struggle against the decrees of fate, and to attempt to galvanize the lifeless body of this 'peculiar institution.'"[45]

Donahoe's unswerving loyalty to the Democratic Party and unwillingness to acquiesce in slavery's demise until the very end reflected a widely held conservative position among Catholics in the North, and this refusal to vote for Lincoln or support emancipation rankled some prominent Northerners. Predictably it was Horace Greeley who fanned the flames of anti-Irish, anti-Catholic nativism in a series of articles denigrating Catholic loyalty just after the 1864 presidential election. Throughout these articles, Greeley presented his readers with evidence that Catholic authorities in Maryland, Missouri, and Louisiana had done nothing to help local antislavery men abolish slavery from those states' constitutions. "The great body of the Roman Catholic priesthood of this country are the ardent and active partisans and upholders of Human Slavery, and do not sympathize with the Republic in the war which the Slave Power has wickedly waged against it for its overthrow," he argued. These assertions recalled longstanding accusations from before the war that Catholics were by the nature of their hierarchical religion completely beholden to their priests and were, by religious training, sympathetic to human slavery. And considering that Northerners like Greeley believed attacking slavery was essential to Union victory, Catholics' refusal to do so called into question their ultimate loyalties to the United States. "Whereas all the Catholic clergy within the rebel lines are active rebels," Greeley stated, "we know of scarcely one under the Union flag who is any more loyal than the law requires him to be." He continued: "As a body, their influence discourages enlistments in our armies, and tends to enfeeble and paralyze the prosecution of the war." Given Catholics' affinity for the antiabolitionist Democrats and their involvement in the draft riots, it is likely that many Republicans accepted Greeley's charges as accurate.[46]

Northern Catholics were understandably shocked by Greeley's accusations. Even the secular *New York Herald* accused Greely of having "commenced a crusade against the Roman Catholics." Donahoe seemed particularly sensitive on this issue, which he saw as an attack on all Catholics. Such ridiculous charges were the product of a "virulent insanity" on the part of those who were foolishly trying to alienate loyal Catholics from the war effort. In this sense, the editor of the *Pilot* proclaimed, Greeley and his ilk were the true "national foe," not Catholics. Even after Lee's surrender, Donahoe complained about the lingering "religious animosities" of many Americans toward Catholicism despite Irish Catholics' substantial wartime sacrifices. Other Catholic editors warned of a coming "Anti-Popery Crusade," with some like McMaster reminding his readers that he had always warned that the "Puritan Yankees" would come for "'Popery' next after 'Slavery.'" The *Pilot* was thus not alone in lamenting the lack of appreciation by their fellow Northerners for what Catholics had done on behalf of the Union.[47]

As the furor over Greeley's attacks died down—and since a religious war never materialized—calmer heads prevailed. In June 1865, the *Pilot* no longer feared a war on Catholics, arguing that the American people had begun to think for themselves and were no longer beholden to a "political and sectarian [Protestant] ministry." Donahoe had finally returned to his early war optimism regarding Irish Catholic military service as the death knell of nativism. He argued that the war had brought together both Catholics and Protestants as they "stood shoulder to shoulder together in defence of the country, and who, though different in faith, are brothers in love and patriotism of country, with the same baptism of precious blood upon them." The government's and people's gratitude for Irish American sacrifices during the war was to be found everywhere, he later claimed, again using the imagery of war as a bloody and fiery baptism that had united the people of the North "in a closer brotherhood in all future time." The presence of many Catholic laymen and even some priests in the North's foremost veteran's group, the Grand Army of the Republic, suggests that, at least for some former Irish and Catholic Union soldiers, Donahoe was right.[48]

Most Catholics, both immigrants and the native born, however, still faced considerable barriers to their advancement and acceptance in mainstream American society, as ethnic and religious prejudices survived the war. Most historians of Irish and German America now agree that, as a whole, the war was an alienating experience for immigrant communities. Prewar arguments between Protestants and Catholics over mandatory readings from the King James Bible in public schools or over whether parochial schools were entitled to public aid became even more heated after the war. Archbishop Purcell and his brother, despite their well-known support for the Union *and* emancipation, were excoriated by the Republican and Protestant press for their efforts to protect Catholic children's freedom-of-conscience rights. The political cartoonist Thomas Nast regularly produced images in *Harper's Weekly* warning of Catholic schemes to subvert America's common schools and democratic government, and prominent Republicans such as Rutherford B. Hayes, James G. Blaine, and even President Grant turned anti-Catholicism into a political tool to be wielded against their Democratic opponents. "If we are to have another contest in the near future of our national existence," Grant said at a veteran's reunion in Iowa in 1875, "I predict that the dividing line will not be Mason and Dixon's but between patriotism and intelligence on the one side, and superstition, ambition and ignorance on the other." In short, the long-threatened war on Catholicism seemed to some to have been revived for Republican political gain. American society had not been as united by the Civil War as Donahoe had hoped, and strong religious animosities still persisted well after Appomattox and into the twentieth century.[49]

Nonetheless, the record of patriotism and Unionism left behind by Irish Catholics such as Donahoe and Archbishop Hughes remained important to subsequent generations of Catholic Americans as evidence of their loyalty during the Union's time of greatest crisis. Both Hughes and Donahoe actively encouraged enlistments in the army and wholeheartedly gave their support to local and federal government leaders during the early years of the war. Their unflinching belief that the nation must be preserved as a united whole, however, has been overshadowed perhaps by their conservative insistence that the Union be reconstituted on its antebellum status as a nation divided, half-free, half-slave. While it is difficult to sympathize with past Americans who held such beliefs today,

Donahoe and Hughes believed that their position was the only one compatible with bringing about a swift and lasting peace. Neither man approved of slavery, but neither was willing to endorse an attack on slaveholders' rights under the Constitution that might become a precedent for nativists to restrict immigrants' or religious minorities' rights. Catholics' Democratic allegiances, combined with their fear of political nativism, ensured they would not support emancipation during the Civil War. This failure to oppose slavery certainly angered radicals like Greeley, but more importantly antiwar Catholics' prominent participation in the draft riots and strident criticism of Lincoln's government overshadowed the memory of Hughes's and Donahoe's strong, albeit conservative, Unionism of the war's early years and thus accounted for much of the lingering animosity toward the Irish and Catholic communities during and after the war.

"Certain Ill-Considered Phrases"

Edward Bates and the Disunionist Dangers of Radical Rhetoric

Jesse George-Nichol

Shortly after Abraham Lincoln's reelection in November 1864, Attorney General Edward Bates submitted his resignation to the president. "Heretofore, it has not been compatible with my ideas of duty to the public & fidelity to you, to leave my post of service for any private considerations, however urgent," he explained to Lincoln. "Then, the fate of the nation hung, in doubt & gloom. . . . Now, on the contrary, the affairs of the government display a brighter aspect; and to you, as head & leader of the government, all the honor & good fortune that we hoped for, has come. And it seems to me, under these altered circumstances, that the time has come, when I may, without dereliction of duty, ask leave to retire to private life."[1]

At seventy-one, Bates was tired. His health had deteriorated during the close to four years he had spent in office, culminating in a stroke in the spring of 1864 brought on, he thought, by "continued, unremitting mental labor." He thus faced retirement with "a sensible relief, as the lifting of a burden." But Bates's growing physical exhaustion was accompanied by a corresponding disillusionment with the government and the war effort. When Bates agreed to join Lincoln's cabinet in late 1860, he did so with the hope that he could act as a conservative force in the administration. Bates believed—and, indeed, feared—that Lincoln was susceptible to the arguments of antislavery radicals, and Bates sought to pull the president in a more pragmatic, conciliatory direction. By 1864, Bates concluded that he had failed. "He grew weary of it all, and expressed to the President his desire for retirement," Lincoln's secretaries, John Hay and John Nicolay, remembered. "The natural and unavoidable triumph of the radical party . . . seemed to him the herald of the trump of doom. . . . He said he could not work in harmony with the radicals, whom he regarded as enemies of law and order; there was no such thing as a patriotic and honest American radical."[2]

When Edward Bates joined Lincoln's cabinet in late 1860, however, the triumph of immediate emancipation and, as Bates saw it, of radicalism more broadly seemed far from inevitable.³ During the secession crisis, Bates was deeply concerned about the growing influence of antislavery radicals, but he firmly believed—and he had much reason to do so—that Lincoln was fundamentally conservative. Bates was an old Whig from Missouri, and he saw in Lincoln a kindred Western centrism emulative of their mutual idol, Henry Clay. Both Lincoln and Bates opposed the extension of slavery, but they also shared a deep respect for the laws, constitutional provisions, and legislative traditions that protected slavery in the states where it already existed. Both argued that emancipation should be gradual and—dubious about the feasibility and desirability of a biracial republic—accompanied by the colonization of freed slaves elsewhere. In practical terms, Bates considered their politics to be entirely compatible.

Yet Lincoln's intemperate language sometimes made Bates nervous. He noted with trepidation that Lincoln occasionally indulged in the rhetorical excesses that Bates associated with antislavery radicals. Most well known was Lincoln's claim that "A house divided against itself cannot stand," which seemed to echo William Henry Seward's assertion that an "irrepressible conflict" simmered between the North and South. Bates saw this as evidence of Lincoln's susceptibility to radical arguments—a weakness Bates considered quite dangerous to Lincoln's reputation and integrity. Extreme rhetoric tended to alarm Southerners, no matter what Lincoln's policy positions actually were. Bates also feared the growing influence of radicals within the Republican Party, and he suspected that the contagion of radical words might eventually infect Lincoln's politics, leading him toward more radical policy.⁴

Bates privileged a language of conciliation and compromise, which he thought was essential to the peace and stability of the Union. To some extent, this attention to language reflected Bates's legal background; his profession had taught him that "the gravest difficulties arise out of careless use of terms—sometimes a mere abuse of language." Though he occasionally tended toward pedantry, his preoccupation with conciliatory language, in particular, reflected a keen insight into the political process. He intuited what modern rhetoricians have long noted: that "the rhetoric of conciliation . . . [is] vital to conflict resolution not only because it affirms a common commitment to a process of resolving disputes but also because it reveals the bedrock of cultural assumptions that support the process of adjustment." Bates understood that conciliatory language played an essential role in the compromise tradition in American political culture—a tradition that held compromise to be a symbol of political legitimacy and a powerful force that had, since its founding, held the Union together. His preoccupation with language stemmed from his commitment to this compromise tradition, and especially from his desire to prop up this tradition in an increasingly intransigent political climate.[5]

Bates blamed this climate on the proliferation of radicals and radicalism in American politics. For him, at least, what distinguished radicals was not just their extreme politics but their questionable methods. In their policy and in their rhetoric, radicals dealt in base emotionalism rather than sober reason—exciting men's most elemental passions and undermining the influence of prudence and rationality on their behavior. Bates thus defined the term "radical" in his diary: "*Radical* n. a rooter (and, figuratively, a *scratcher* or *digger*). . . . Politically, a *Radical* is a man who is always dealing with the *root*—the origin and foundation, of society. He appeals, for every thing, great and small, to the primitive principles of man's nature." To Bates's mind, this is why radicals so often focused on slavery: It, more than any other issue, seemed to excite the "primitive" fears and passions of the American people. Pro- and antislavery radicals were political opportunists of the worst kind; they played upon these fears and passions to augment their own power, careless of the consequences for the nation. They posed a threat not just because of their dangerous political ideas but also because of their tendency to debase politics and society more broadly. Bates saw radicalism not merely as a rival political movement or set of ideas—he saw it as an existential threat to the social and political underpinnings of the American Union.[6]

Edward Bates joined Lincoln's cabinet hoping to be a bulwark against what he perceived to be the dangers of radicalism. He worked to steer the president in a conciliatory direction—one, as Bates saw it, dictated by reason rather than emotion. He thought that a more charitable, pragmatic approach was more likely to preserve (and later restore) peace and to accomplish the Republican Party's goals. Bates concluded by late 1864 that he had failed in this task, believing that the radical wing of the Republican Party had finally gained ideological and political ascendancy within the government. But nothing about this radical takeover seemed inevitable to him in 1860 and 1861. On the contrary, Bates decided to support Lincoln in 1860, to join Lincoln's cabinet, and to struggle to shape administration policy for nearly four years precisely because he believed in Lincoln's fundamental conservatism. He labored not because he thought he could change the president but because he hoped that the president would remain unchanged—unbending to the seductions of extremism and unbowed by the pressure of political radicals. Bates was never particularly close to Lincoln, nor would he be one of the more influential members of Lincoln's administration. Still, Bates's alliance with Lincoln provides a lens into the complex relationship between the president, the Republican Party, and the political conservatives who sustained them both. In 1860, rhetoric was an important marker of difference between the conservative Bates and the more moderate Lincoln, yet it was their similarities that drove Bates to support Lincoln, his party, and the war effort—all of which depended on the support of conservatives like Bates for survival. Bates's faith in the president underscores how unintelligible the future course of both the war and the Lincoln administration were in 1861—even to those at its center. The arc of Bates's career spotlights just how much had changed between his acceptance of a cabinet position in 1860 and his abandonment of it in 1864; nowhere were those changes more apparent, to Bates at least, than in Lincoln's position on slavery.

Of all of the rivals that Abraham Lincoln had to defeat to secure the Republican presidential nomination in 1860, one of the most formidable—and least well remembered—was Edward Bates of Missouri. Though Lincoln would eventually triumph as an alternative to the controversial party favorite William Henry Seward, Bates seemed the most likely challenger to Seward through late 1859 and early 1860. In February 1860, the Republican and American members of the House of Representatives endorsed Bates's candidacy, and soon thereafter the *New York Herald* reported that "Mr. Bates has the advocacy of a much larger portion of the Opposition press than any other man that has been named." That same month, Lincoln confessed to his friend Orville Browning that Bates might "be the strongest and best man we can run" and that "it is not improbable by the time the National convention meets in Chicago he may be of the opinion that the very best thing that can be done will be to nominate Mr. Bates."[7]

Bates had assiduously cultivated an image of himself—in both public and private—as a man outside of party politics. His time in elected office consisted of a single term in the US House of Representatives in the 1820s, stints in the Missouri legislature during the 1820s and 1830s, and a period as a judge in the St. Louis Land Court in the 1850s. Otherwise Bates avoided public office—most famously turning down two different positions in Millard Fillmore's cabinet in 1850. Bates explained in a public letter that effectively launched his presidential campaign in 1859 that his were "not the opinions of this or that party, ready to be abandoned or modified to suit this or that platform, but my own opinions—perhaps the more fixed and harder to be changed because deliberately formed in the retirement of private life, free from the exigencies of official responsibility and from the perturbations of party policy." And indeed, Bates was keenly aware that he owed much of his prominence and reputation to this absence from public life.

He was consistently spoken of as a candidate for high office in the 1850s because he was seen as a private man, free from the partisan ambition and prejudice that had wreaked so much havoc in American politics. "I have not now to learn (for I know it already, by experience) that a man m[a]y win quite as much reputation by refusing as holding office," he explained in 1860. "A national reputation has been forced upon me, without my having any official influence or conspicuous position."[8]

In 1860 both Bates and Lincoln capitalized on an anxiety among Republicans that Seward, though the party's favorite son, was too radical to be elected. Seward had alarmed Southerners and alienated many Northerners when he pronounced that a "higher law than the Constitution" governed the nation in the struggle against slavery and that an "irrepressible conflict" festered between the free North and slave South. Such pronouncements, together with his longtime association with political antislavery, had earned Seward a reputation as a radical "eager for the immediate destruction of slavery."[9] But though both Bates and Lincoln represented alternatives to the ostensibly radical Seward, each man embodied a distinct vision of what direction the Republican Party should take. In an editorial promoting Lincoln's nomination in March 1860, the *Chicago Tribune* claimed that Lincoln represented the "large middle body" of moderate Republicans. He was not perceived to be as radical or as closely associated with abolitionists as Seward, and Lincoln's nomination would thus signal a pivot away from the party's more radical elements and toward the more moderate center of the party. Bates, meanwhile, was considered a more "conservative" choice. His advocates hoped that he could broaden the appeal of the Republican Party and, as one explained it, "bring to our support the old Whigs in the free states, who have not yet fraternized with us, and to give some check to the ultra tendencies of the Republican party."[10]

But what exactly did this distinction between moderates and conservatives mean? For the *Tribune*, the answer lay in the two men's views about slavery. Lincoln and the great bulk of Republicans were "practical and willing to wait for [slavery's] gradual decay through moral causes." Though Lincoln made clear that he considered slavery "a moral, political, and social wrong," he did not believe that the government could legally interfere with slavery in the states where it already existed. He accepted the legal and constitutional protections for slavery in the states, even those like the Fugitive Slave Law that he found odious, and instead focused on preventing slavery's spread into the federal territories. Limited in this way, he hoped that slavery would gradually weaken and eventually die out—a process he expected to take "a hundred years at the least." "I do not wish to be misunderstood on the subject of slavery in this country," he explained in 1859, "I suppose it may long exist, and perhaps the best way for it to come to an end peaceably is for it to exist for a length of time. But I say that the spread and strengthening and perpetuation of it is an entirely different proposition. There we should in every way resist it as wrong, treating it as wrong, with the fixed idea that it must and will come to an end." This, Lincoln believed, was where things had gone awry: Proslavery apologists had destroyed the "spirit which desired the peaceful extinction of slavery," and the first step to ending slavery was to restore "the belief that it is in the course of ultimate extinction." He was convinced that this had been the position of the Founding Fathers, and he embraced it—along with the nonextension of slavery—as a return to original principles.[11]

When pressed, Edward Bates espoused similar views about the expansion of slavery into the territories. Though a former slaveholder, Bates "always thought and often said that slavery is an evil." He did not believe that it was a moral wrong "inconsistent with Christianity," but over the course of his life Bates had come to believe that slavery stunted the economic and moral growth of white society. Lincoln's insistence that slavery was a moral wrong clearly distinguished him from Bates (and, indeed, from some other moderate Republicans), but both men had drawn the same conclusion about how to address the problem of slavery: Its spread into the territories under federal control must be restricted. "I am opposed to the extension of slavery," Bates wrote in 1860, "and, in my opinion, the spirit and the policy of the government ought to be against its extension." Bates hoped that with the growth of agriculture and industry, white Southerners would come to understand the limitations of slave labor and the superiority of free labor, just as he had. Similar to Lincoln, Bates thought that this idea—that slavery would eventually give way to free labor—"ought to be constantly inculcated, and kept before the public mind, by the press" in order to "aid and accelerate" the process. Bates, too, saw this as a conservative principle, believing that the Founding Fathers had thought slavery "likely to disappear in the course of time; yet, while it continued, a misfortune to the country."[12]

Although Bates was more ambivalent about the morality of slavery than Lincoln, the *Chicago Tribune* concluded—and Bates seemed to agree—that the biggest difference between the men lay in their emphasis on the slavery question. Conservatives like Bates, in contrast to moderates like Lincoln, were "anxious to get rid of the question of slavery altogether." Bates saw slavery as more of a political threat than a moral one, and he thus condemned slavery *agitation* even as he hoped to encourage slavery's ultimate demise. "The Negro question . . . is a pestilent question," Bates thundered in a public letter in 1859, "the agitation of which has never done any good to any party, section or class, and never can do any good." He condemned both pro- and antislavery agitators as political opportunists, stirring up controversy for their own gain and at the expense of national harmony. "When I see a man, at the South or the North, of mature age and some experience, persist in urging the [slavery] question, after the sorrowful experience of the last few years," he pronounced, "I can attribute his conduct to no higher motive than personal ambition or sectional prejudice." Bates wanted to divert attention away from the divisive slavery issue and toward more constructive and pressing concerns like economic development, which he thought would strengthen ties of interest and affection between the sections. He believed that an emphasis on what united rather than divided Americans would allow them to move past their differences on slavery. "We may conquer ourselves by local strifes and sectional animosities," he explained, but

> if our government would devote all its energies to the promotion of peace and friendship with all foreign countries, the advancement of Commerce, the increase of Agriculture, the growth and stability of Manufactures, and the cheapening, quickening and securing [of] the internal trade and travel of our country . . . I think we should witness a growth and consolidation of wealth and comfort and power for good.[13]

Though he shared many of Bates's hopes for the nation's growth and development, Lincoln did not think the slavery question could or should be avoided in this way. He and other moderate Republicans believed that the crisis surrounding slavery had been precipitated by the aggressions of Southern radicals; they did not, as Bates did, hold Northern and Southern radicals equally accountable. Most Republicans feared that a Slave Power conspiracy—a collaboration between Southern slaveholders and their Democratic allies—was working to seize political power by pushing slavery into the territories. More troublingly, this Slave Power seemed willing to usurp the Constitution and American political tradition in order to accomplish its ends. Republicans saw the Kansas-Nebraska Act, the *Dred Scott* decision, and the Lecompton Constitution as clear examples of this conspiracy at work, and many feared that if the assaults of the Slave Power went unchecked, slavery would be legalized not just in the territories but everywhere. If slaveholders could extend their power by forcing slavery into the territories, then what was to stop them from doing the same in the free states? If Congress could not prohibit slavery in the territories, then could slavery be prohibited anywhere? "In my opinion," Lincoln concluded in his famous "House Divided" speech, slavery agitation

> *will* not cease, until a *crisis* shall have been reached, and passed. "A house divided against itself cannot stand." I believe this government cannot endure, permanently half *slave* and half *free*. . . . It will become *all* one thing, or *all* the other. Either the *opponents* of slavery will arrest the further spread of it . . . or its *advocates* will push it forward, till it shall become alike lawful in *all* the States, *old* as well as *new—North* as well as *South*.[14]

In the crisis over slavery, Lincoln thus saw something of Seward's "irrepressible conflict"—a challenge that demanded not evasion or compromise but resistance. The conciliation and compromise of previous decades had merely emboldened the Slave Power, and so encouraged, it now threatened the survival of the nation and its republican institutions. In order to save the Union and, more importantly, "to make, and to keep it, forever worthy of the saving," Republicans needed to take a firm stand against the aggressions of Southern slaveholders. Lincoln therefore stood overtly and unwaveringly against the extension of slavery into the territories, believing that doing so was the only way to ensure the survival of the American nation. "In resisting the spread of slavery into new territory, and with that, what appears to me to be a tendency to subvert the first principle of free government itself my whole effort has consisted," Lincoln explained. "To the best of my judgment I have labored *for*, and not *against* the Union."[15]

Bates understood the similarities between his own position and Lincoln's. He conceded that Lincoln's "doctrines, as laid down *for use*, are, in my judgment, substantially right." What Bates objected to were "certain ill-considered phrases used by him in the excitement of political debate." In his *rhetoric*, if not his *policy*, "Mr. Lincoln . . . is as fully committed as Mr. Seward is, to the extremest [*sic*] doctrines of the Republican party. He is quite as far north as Mr. Seward is," Bates concluded. Southerners had certainly noted the concurrence between Seward's and Lincoln's more extreme rhetoric, and some Republicans, too, had levied this charge to refute the claim that Lincoln was more moderate and electable than Seward. Bates clearly agreed. He worried that Lincoln's rhetorical missteps would alienate conservatives and, more ominously, alarm anxious Southerners if he were elected president. The problem was not merely one of perception, however; Bates also saw indications in Lincoln's rhetoric that he was falling prey to the influence of antislavery radicals.[16]

Two of Lincoln's arguments were particularly troubling to Bates. Lincoln framed slavery as the most urgent political problem facing the country—"the living issue of the day," as he put it—and he largely blamed proslavery militants for making it so. Bates associated both arguments with radical abolitionist "agitation." He believed that "the negro question . . . ought not to overrid[e] and subordinate all others"; it dominated politics not because it was a uniquely exigent problem but because political agitators had fixated upon it. Radicals' assertion that slavery was the nation's biggest political problem was, in other words, a self-fulfilling prophecy. "All these recent notions about [slavery in the] Territories are newfangled inventions, hatched in the feverish brains of factious partizans," Bates concluded. He found it equally alarming to heap blame for this state of affairs exclusively on proslavery agitators in the South. The Missourian found a "striking coincidence of opinion" between antislavery and proslavery radicals and concluded that they were "alike stupid & wicked." Both had labored to manufacture the crisis surrounding slavery for their own political ends—adopting equally hyperbolic and shortsighted positions in order to do so—and each side's tendency to blame the other for the crisis exacerbated tensions while leaving the aggressions of radicals unchecked.[17]

Bates considered this inclination toward rhetorical excess to be a feature of radicalism in both sections, but Lincoln's adoption of such language underscored the acute dangers of abolitionist political culture in the North. Lincoln was no hotheaded immediatist; he, like Bates, had been a longtime Whig with a profound respect for the law, the Constitution, and the Union. "All [Lincoln's] old political antecedents are, in my judgment, exactly right, being square up to the old Whig standard," Bates admitted. But Lincoln's assertions that slavery was an overarching political issue and that proslavery extremists were primarily responsible for making it so made clear—at least in Bates's mind—that he was falling prey to abolitionist pressures. Inflated rhetoric was the means by which abolitionists were infecting others, and its spread had allowed a "handful of extreme abolitionists" to exert a greatly exaggerated influence on American politics and the Republican Party.[18]

Abolitionist demagoguery was dangerous because it inspired fear in both sections of the country. Radicals' claims that slavery posed an existential threat to the free states struck terror in the hearts of both Northerners and Southerners—each believing that their way of life was under assault by the other. "A man always under the influence of fear, can hardly rise to the dignity of justice, or yield to the force of thought," Bates explained. "'The first law of Nature'—the *higher law* of self-preservation—is always present to his mind and exciting his baser passions."

Fear, in other words, was the enemy of reason and moderation, and Bates lamented the spread of abolitionist demagoguery because he believed that the fear it spread constituted a material threat to the American Union. Perhaps the greatest danger came from immediatists who explicitly denounced the Union—those like William Lloyd Garrison who wanted "No Union with Slaveholders." But Bates was also deeply troubled by Radical Republicans who sought to supersede constitutional and historical restraints in order to eradicate slavery—those like William Henry Seward, who professed to ascribe to a "higher law than the Constitution." Bates considered these "lovers of free negros" to be quite as dangerous as the disunionists because they "would destroy the Constitution & thereby destroy the world's only hope of civil liberty, because it permits slavery to exist, any where, under its jurisdiction."[19]

Bates no doubt understood the differences between abolitionists like Garrison and political radicals like Seward. Despite Seward's reputation for extremism, he was a strong nationalist and a fierce defender of the Union, and his "higher law" rhetoric fell far short of Garrison's contentions that the Constitution was "a covenant with death" and an "agreement with hell." But Bates also knew that such differences mattered little to anxious Southerners. He explained of Seward: "At the South, whether justly or unjustly, there is a bitter prejudice against him; they consider him the embodiment of all they deem odious in the Republican party." This was the real danger of radical rhetoric and its spread: It eroded Southern faith in the protections of the Constitution and the Union and reinforced Southern fears that the Republican Party posed an existential threat to their slave society. And inasmuch as it did that, extremist rhetoric obscured the differences between those who invoked it.[20]

It was for this reason that Bates was so troubled by Lincoln's "house divided" language. He worried that Lincoln—and, indeed, that many Republicans—were being taken in by abolitionist arguments, but he was also concerned that Lincoln's rhetoric itself could pose a danger to the Union. Bates feared that "enemies may draw unfavorable inferences" from Lincoln's "ill-considered phrases"; they might conclude that his assertion that "this government cannot endure, permanently half *slave* and half *free*" made him no different from the "odious" Seward and his "irrepressible conflict" doctrines. Both men described an inherent antagonism between freedom and slavery that fueled Southern fears that Republicans would interfere with their peculiar institution. And Bates worried—correctly, as it turned out—that these fears would persist in spite of Lincoln's oft-declared intention *not* to "interfere with the institution of slavery in the States where it exists."[21]

Bates believed that more conciliatory rhetoric was necessary to combat this climate of fear—a rhetoric that more closely reflected his own more equivocal relationship to slavery. He resisted the stark contrasts between North and South, slave and free, that Lincoln and Seward drew in their "house divided" and "irrepressible conflict" oratory. And he did this in no small part because he hailed from Missouri. For one thing, Missouri was culturally a Western state, and Bates claimed that the people of the West "love the country as a whole and they love all of its parts, for they are bound to them all." Missouri was also a state that, perhaps more than any other, stood at the crossroads of slavery and freedom. Though Missouri was a slave state, its shared borders with the free states of Iowa and Illinois and the western territories meant that it was a literal borderland between slavery and freedom. Conflicts over slavery there were not abstract debates; the Missouri frontier witnessed repeated clashes between pro- and antislavery forces, and Bates had a front-row seat to everything from Missouri's contentious statehood campaign in the late 1810s to the violent eruptions of Bleeding Kansas in 1854.[22] These collisions produced a strong backlash among some of slavery's most strident defenders, but they also worked to convince more moderate Missourians like Bates that slavery agitation was a dangerous threat to their society. Among the latter, Missouri's precarious position on the border—together with its social, economic, and cultural ties to the North and South—produced a deeply conservative political culture that privileged stability and pragmatism and embraced ideological and regional compromise. Bates's suspicions of radicals and of slavery agitation were shared by many Missourians and closely linked to this conservative political culture. His emphasis on a language of conciliation and compromise reflected the immediacy of such values in a state that had so often served as a battleground between slavery and freedom.[23]

Bates's personal relationship with slavery also reflected the institution's ambivalent history in Missouri. He had not always opposed slavery's extension; in fact, Bates brought slaves with him when he emigrated to Missouri in 1814, and he campaigned for the unrestricted importation of slaves into the state at its constitutional convention in 1820. He continued to own slaves into the 1850s, but his views on slavery began to change in the decades after Missouri became a state. Profoundly important to this change was the Whig Party, which Bates always claimed was "the only party I ever belonged to." Indeed, the transformation began years before the party was actually founded when, during his single term in the US House of Representatives in the late 1820s, Bates developed a strong affinity for the party's future founder and spiritual leader, Henry Clay. "That man grows upon me more & more, every time I see him," Bates wrote to his wife in 1828. "There's an intuitive perception about him, that seems to see & understand at a glance, and a winning fascination in his manner.... When I look upon his manly & bold countenance, & meet his frank & eloquent eye, I feel an emotion little short of enthusiasm in his cause." The cause that had the biggest impact on Bates was Clay's "American System"—a comprehensive program to encourage American industry, commerce, and transportation in order to achieve economic independence from Europe and social and sectional harmony at home. This plan was powerfully appealing to a young St. Louis lawyer like Bates, offering him a vision of the future that suited his ambition and his ideas about human progress. Particularly once he returned home to Missouri and took up a position in the state senate, he became convinced that government intervention to foster economic growth and development was just what his state most needed. This idea became fundamental to his understanding of the role of government in society; as he later explained it: "Protection is the great object of all government," not just for "life & property" but also for "occupation & industry ... commerce & locomotion." Bates thus helped organize the pro-Bank, anti-Jacksonian faction in the Missouri legislature that would eventually become the state's Whig Party. He would remain steadfastly loyal to the Whig Party and to Clay's American System for the rest of his life, but he gradually came to see slavery as a threat to both—an impediment to economic growth and diversification and a source of dangerous political dissension in the Whig Party and the Union at large.[24]

Bates's involvement in reform movements also played an important role in the transformation of his ideas about slavery. He was deeply religious and believed strongly in the perfectibility of man; these values fueled Bates's interest in economic reform and, starting in the 1820s, drove him to promote moral improvement through various reform causes. He was actively involved in the temperance movement and in promoting public education in Missouri. But it was Bates's close association with the American Colonization Society that had the most profound influence on his ideas about slavery. He first joined the ACS in the 1820s, and Henry Clay's prominent role in the organization likely increased Bates's enthusiasm for both Clay and the colonization cause. For a slaveholder like Bates who had always considered slavery an "evil" rather than a positive good, colonization seemed to offer a solution to the problem of emancipation. It allowed him to envision an end to slavery that would not require slaveholders to live alongside their former slaves—a prospect that he considered both undesirable and dangerous—and resolving this problem allowed Bates to look forward to the end of slavery. "I consider the emancipation of slaves in the United States, as of very doubtful advantage to the slaves themselves, and of certain evil to the community, and therefore, I am not willing to aid that cause," he wrote in 1848, "but I have high hopes for the future greatness and usefulness of the new nation in the Commonwealth of Liberia." Bates signed a contract with his last slave that year, providing that "If you will serve me & my family, as a true & faithful servant, for five years from this date . . . you shall have free & full permission to migrate to Liberia."[25] This contract modeled the course that Bates envisaged for the end of slavery in the United States; over time he embraced nonextension as a way to encourage the process of voluntary emancipation, believing that limiting slavery—while promoting its safe dismantlement through colonization—would make it more "likely to disappear in the course of time."[26]

Bates also embraced colonization as a centrist political position between the extremes of abolitionism and the defense of slavery as a positive good, and it was thus part and parcel of Bates's self-consciously centrist ideology. His philosophical commitment to centrism dated back to his first campaign for Congress in 1826, when Bates campaigned as a "neutral in politics." This position in part reflected the state of flux in both Missouri and national politics at the time as well as Bates's inherent disdain for partisanship and politicking. But this kind of antiparty centrism remained an important current in Bates's politics even after he joined the Whig Party and developed a more coherent political philosophy. Though Bates was considered the "sage of Missouri's Whig party," Missouri was an overwhelmingly Democratic state. During the 1830s and 1840s, Missouri's Whigs never came close to carrying the state in a presidential or gubernatorial contest, they never won a majority in the state legislature and thus never elected a senator, and they succeeded in sending only one man to Congress. They were so weak, in fact, that historians have typically characterized them as more of a pressure group than a party. The challenges of operating as a Whig in a Democratic fiefdom like Missouri made Bates's political centrism—including his strong ideological commitment to compromise—something of a necessity. His growing opposition to slavery and his eventual association with the Republican Party, both of which were much more unpopular than Whiggery in Missouri, made moderation and compromise even more important to Bates's political survival.[27]

Still, the most powerful source of inspiration for Bates's political philosophy was and would remain his idol, Henry Clay. This, of course, did not make Bates unique; Lincoln famously considered Clay his "beau ideal of a statesman," and in fact all four men who ultimately vied for the presidency in 1860—former Whigs and Democrats alike—claimed to carry on Clay's legacy in one form or another. But Bates most admired Clay as an "ideologue of the center," upholding compromise as his most sacred principle. This idea suited Bates's conservative sensibilities, his strong Unionism, and the political and social realities of life in Missouri.

He thus came to believe, as Clay did, that "saving the Union was a matter of continual adjustment of competing interests." And though many former Whigs, including Lincoln, moved away from this principle amid anxieties about the Slave Power conspiracy, Bates's belief in the utility and importance of compromise remained strong. For him, the "adjustment of competing interests" entailed more than the grand compromises for which Clay was so famous; Bates understood compromise to be an *attitude* as well as a formal remedy, and that attitude—one that self-consciously elevated the Union above all other concerns—was essential to the peace and harmony of the nation. Bates paid such careful attention to rhetoric because it undergirded this attitude, projecting a mutualism and conciliationism upon which sectional accommodation could be reached.[28]

Bates's centrist political philosophy meant that as he moved into the Republican orbit in 1860, he concluded that a more conciliatory posture—one more in line with Clay's centrism—would better achieve the party's ends than a more radical stance. A veteran and product of Missouri politics, Bates knew well that such an attitude was essential to making inroads among more moderate Southerners, and he firmly believed that attracting Southern support was vital to the success of the party. Though some Republicans feared that a sectional party would be too weak to win a national election, Bates was also deeply concerned that a sectional Republican Party would exacerbate tensions between the North and South.[29] As Bates understood it, these two problems were related; a purely sectional Republican Party—one that endorsed radical rhetoric—would be weaker in the free states and anathema in the slave sates. He therefore hoped that the party would "mollify its tone, in order to win a broader foundation and gather new strength, both numerical and moral, from outside."[30]

When Abraham Lincoln was named the Republican presidential nominee at the party's convention in May 1860, Bates concluded that the party had failed to "mollify its tone." He worried that Lincoln's nomination constituted an endorsement of radical rhetoric and the growing influence of abolitionists within the party. The move would alienate Southerners, exacerbating sectional mistrust and stymieing efforts to create a national political coalition. "I think they will soon be convinced, if they are not already, that they have committed a fatal blunder," Bates asserted in the aftermath. "They have denationalized their Party; weakened it in the free states, and destroyed its hopeful beginnings in the border slave states." This did not bode well for the party's elective prospects, nor was it propitious for the peace and unity of the country.[31]

Perhaps more than anything else, Bates feared that Lincoln's nomination would hamper the party's ability to achieve its own goals. Despite his fervent desire to avoid sectional conflict, Bates supported the Republican Party because he hoped that it would help put slavery on the road to gradual extinction. To his mind, these were related goals; he firmly believed that sectional conflict was an obstacle to slavery's demise, and he also believed that gradually eliminating slavery was vital to national prosperity and harmony in the long run. Bates's experience in Missouri had shown him that slaveholders who felt threatened and Southerners who felt persecuted became more rather than less aggressive in their defense of slavery. It was this anxiety that drove Missouri slaveholders to clash with antislavery settlers in Kansas in 1854. They sought to control the territory not because they ascribed to an aggressive proslavery radicalism but because they sought to protect the future of slavery in Missouri; they wanted to preserve the status quo, not expand slavery or enhance their own power. The experience had convinced Bates that direct action against slavery and overt hostility to the institution were often counterproductive. Instead, he had seen economic diversification in Missouri—the growth of "Manufactures, mining, commerce, handicraft-arts, and grain and cattle farming"—peacefully "aid and accelerate the drain of slaves from the State." He had come to believe that encouraging economic growth and development was the best way to chip away at slavery—as well as the best way to increase prosperity and encourage sectional harmony. Bates thus concluded in early 1859 that "it can hardly be necessary to incur the labor and encounter the prejudice incident in [targeting slavery] *now*, when it is plain to be seen that, by the irresistable [*sic*] force of circumstances, without any statute to help the work, slavery will soon cease to exist in Missouri, for all practical and important purposes." He feared that the Republicans' nomination of Lincoln would reverse this course, leading Southern slaveholders to dig in against the perceived threat of the party. "Here in Mo. they have utterly destroyed their friends," he lamented, "and have postponed indefinitely the making of Mo. a free State."[32]

Despite these grave reservations, Bates ultimately decided to support Lincoln and the Republican Party in the election of 1860. "But after all," he concluded, "what better can be done than support Lincoln?" This decision distinguished him from many Whigs and former Whigs in Missouri—including those who had supported Bates's candidacy for the presidency.[33] In the Missouri gubernatorial election in August 1860, less than 10 percent of the non-Democratic vote went to the Republican nominee, and in the presidential contest in November, less than one-quarter of non-Democratic votes went to Lincoln.[34] Most Whigs and former Whigs in Missouri instead supported the Constitutional Union Party. The Constitutional Unionists adopted compromise as their guiding doctrine, vowing to "recognize no political principles other than the Constitution of the country, the

Union of the States, and the enforcement of the laws." But in spite of his emphasis on conciliation and compromise, Bates refused to support the Constitutional Union Party, for two principal reasons. First, Bates's strong opposition to the extension of slavery made the Republican Party far more appealing to him than it was to most Missourians. Though he emphasized a *rhetoric* of compromise, he ultimately believed that stopping the spread of slavery was essential to the nation's political stability. Second, Bates considered the Constitutional Union Party—which primarily attracted Southern Whigs—to be a "third party" movement that would divide rather than unite the remnants of the old Whig Party. "The naked truth is, the idea of forming a new party now, and under existing circumstances is simply absurd," he wrote in April 1860. "The gentlemen in the movement—and some of them are good men and wise—must make up their minds, and that quickly, to do one of three things—support the Democratic or Republican nominee, or themselves sink into political nonentity." He put it more succinctly in a public letter in June: "To me it is plain that the approaching contest must be between the Democratic and Republican Parties; and, between them, I prefer the latter." He considered the Republican Party to be a far more powerful vehicle than the nascent Constitutional Union Party, for which he could "see no possibility of success."[35]

Constitutional Unionists' unwillingness to join forces with the more powerful Republican Party made Bates deeply suspicious of their motives. That they had nominated their own presidential candidate before the Republican Party had even chosen Lincoln indicated to Bates that the Constitutional Unionists, in spite of their conciliatory language, were unwilling to make any compromises on the slavery issue. There was a personal dimension to this for Bates. Although earlier in the spring there had been a movement "in favor of shaping the policy at [the Constitutional Union Convention in] Baltimore so as to promote a union of the Opposition on Bates," the Constitutional Unionists roundly rejected Bates at their nominating convention in May. Bates was keenly aware that this rejection had to do with his position on slavery in the territories. After clarifying his views on the issue in a public letter in March—in which he asserted that "National Government has the power to permit or forbid slavery" in the territories and that "the spirit and policy of the government ought to be against its extension"—Constitutional Unionists widely denounced him. "He is a republican, and nothing else," one newspaper concluded. "As such, of course, the Constitutional Union men will scorn to touch him. He has, by a single blow, severed every tie of confidence or sympathy which connected him with the Southern conservatives." The backlash against his letter convinced Bates that the Constitutional Unionists were, in fact, proslavery apologists without any real commitment to compromise. "Trying to play a double game—'to hold with the hare and run with the house'—they pretend utterly to ignore the negro question, and yet they begin by denouncing me for my opinions on that question," he lamented. "That is unjust to me and unwise, as the means of attaining their end." Bates thus concluded that the Constitutional Unionists were "fully identified with the disunionists" of the South and were working to divide rather than unite the country.[36]

So Bates pledged his support for Abraham Lincoln, instead. At the urging of their mutual friend Orville Browning—who hoped that Bates's support might be "influential with the Whigs and Americans in the doubtful states"—Bates wrote a letter endorsing Lincoln in June 1860. In it Bates made clear his objections to the Constitutional Union Party. "What can the third party do . . . against the two great parties which are now in actual contest for the power to rule the nation?" he asked. "The most it can do is, here and there, in particular localities, to make a diversion in favor of the Democrats." But in his endorsement, Bates also made an earnest appeal on behalf of Lincoln. He defended Lincoln's position on slavery, despite his own criticisms and reservations. Bates emphasized policy rather than rhetoric, noting the concurrence between Lincoln's opinions and his own and denouncing inferences made about Lincoln based on his more radical language. "I am aware that small partisans, in their little warfare against opposing leaders, do sometimes assail them by the trick of tearing from their contexts some particular objectionable phrases . . . and holding them up to the public as the leading doctrines of the person assailed," Bates maintained. "No public man can stand that ordeal, and, however willing men may be to see it applied to their adversaries, all flinch from the torture when applied to themselves."[37]

In addition, Bates attempted to bestow the mantle of Western conservatism on his old adversary. He stressed that Lincoln was not from the North or South but was, like Bates, from the West. Bates described the West as a borderland—an amalgam of Northern and Southern people and values. It was settled by both Northerners and Southerners, and it had social, cultural, and economic ties to both sections. The Mississippi Valley "is not a section, but conspicuously, the body of the nation," he said. This set the West outside of the sectional conflict between the North and South, and it gave Westerners an innately national worldview that Bates hoped could serve as an antidote to sectional radicalism. He framed Lincoln as an archetype of this Western conservatism. "He could not be sectional if he tried," Bates asserted. "His birth, his education, the habits of his life, and his geographical position, compel him to be national." Bates thus claimed that their shared background gave him and Lincoln a set of shared values, underscoring their similarities and reiterating that this sort of national conservatism was needed to meet the sectional crisis. He concluded: "It will be most fortunate for the nation to find the powers of government lodged in the hands of men whose habits of thought whose positions and surrounding circumstances constrain them to use those powers for general and not sectional ends."[38]

Why did Bates change his tune after so many months of privately—if not publicly—condemning Lincoln? To some extent, Bates felt that propriety demanded he do so. He was advised by many of his friends that, as a defeated candidate, "my position required me to support Mr. Lincoln." But as time went on and the sting of defeat subsided, it became clear that Bates was hopeful that the things he said about Lincoln were true. Though he worried about the influence of radicals upon Lincoln, Bates believed that Lincoln's principles were fundamentally sound. He maintained hope that Lincoln would prove this if given the chance, and if he did, the Republican Party might yet become the national political coalition that Bates had hoped it would be. Bates continued to believe that the Republican Party was the best—if not the only—locus for such an anti-Democratic coalition. "The Republican Party, made chiefly of old Whigs, and professing, in the main, Whig policies, will soon absorb all the Whigs who have not already fully identified themselves with one or the other of the Democratic factions," he reflected in October. "If the Repns. be but moderately wise . . . it will . . . become the permanent governing party." Bates thus sought to minimize the prejudice against Lincoln in order to give him the chance to prove that he was a fundamentally conservative, national Whig.[39]

Bates's hopes for Lincoln became even more urgent following Lincoln's election in November. Bates noted with alarm—if not surprise—the aggressive movement among Southern radicals to push their states to secede. Disunion rhetoric was nothing new, but for the most part such threats had been just that—rhetoric.[40] "S.C. I think, stands alone in the real wish to dissolve the Union," Bates had written in March. "Every where else in the South, the threat seems to be only a political trick, used in *terrorem*, to frighten timid people into the support of favorite southern measures." But after Lincoln's election, a growing chorus of Southerners began calling for secession in earnest, arguing that Lincoln as president would pose an existential threat to the South. "The news from *the South*, as to secession, does not improve," he recorded in late November. "The leaders of the movement, in Alabama, Georgia, and especially S. Carolina, are more urgent than ever, taking every means to get their followers pledged to extreme measures, and to draw in and commit the timid and the doubtful, without allowing time to look at the consequences and reflect upon the bottomless pit that lies before them." As ever, Bates saw the dangers of radical rhetoric at work in this movement; it now reached a pitch and intensity of passion that threatened to overwhelm the rationality of anxious Southerners.⁴¹

Bates still thought that probably only "a few demented fanatics" were true disunionists, but the proliferation of radical language signaled that the dangers it posed were growing. Talk of secession among Constitutional Unionists in the wake of the election reinforced Bates's suspicions about their motives. "It begins to be apparent that a good many of these *Union men*, par excellence, whose special vocation it is to save the nation, are apologists for disunion, and see no *injustice* in it," he observed. Still, the change in tone among supposed unionists in the South was worrying. He prayed that this was nothing more than "brag and bluster" from those "hoping thus to make a better compromise with the timid patriotism of their opponents," but even if it was, the situation seemed increasingly perilous. "In playing this dangerous game, they may go farther than they now intend, and actually commit their states to open rebellion and civil war," Bates despaired.⁴²

Though Bates had predicted that Lincoln's nomination and election would antagonize the South, he had no sympathy for the disunionists. All of Bates's arguments in favor of compromise and conciliation were aimed at preserving the Union, and he would not countenance secession under any circumstances. When Lincoln approached Bates about joining his cabinet in December—the two met in Springfield on December 15—Bates made this abundantly clear. "Mr. Bates' conversation shows him to be inflexibly opposed to secession and strongly in favor of maintaining the Government by force if necessary," Lincoln's secretary John Nicolay recorded. "He forcibly illustrates his temper by saying that he is a man of peace, and will defer fighting as long as possible; but that if forced to do so against his will, he has made it a rule *never to fire blank cartridges*." Bates made plain that his inclinations toward conciliation and compromise had limits; he would never pursue peace at the expense of the Union.⁴³

This was no doubt reassuring to Lincoln, who believed, as Bates did, that "no state can, in any way lawfully, get out of the Union . . . and that it is the duty of the President, and other government functionaries to run the machine as it is." Still, both men understood that the situation was a delicate one. Lincoln, like Bates, was inclined to think that only a small number of Southerners were true secessionists; he saw the Slave Power conspiracy at work in the secession movement. So in their December 15 meeting the two men discussed at length how the new administration ought to deal with the deteriorating situation in the South. After Bates accepted a position in the cabinet, Lincoln asked Bates to consider carefully the legal question of secession—making "himself familiar with the constitution and the laws . . . so as to be prepared to give a definite opinion upon the various aspects of the question."[44] He also asked Bates to give serious thought to the delivery of mail in the South. Lincoln lamented that "the mails in the South had been violated with impunity"—a symptom of the fear of abolitionist encroachments there—but he also "feared that Radical Republicans at the North might claim the hands of the new Administration . . . and endeavor to make the mail the means of thrusting upon the South matter which even their conservative and well-meaning men might deem inimical and dangerous." Lincoln was eager to avoid an unnecessary confrontation, and Bates quite agreed; both men understood that the new administration would have to weigh its duty to enforce the laws against the peace and harmony of the Union.[45]

Bates found his meeting with Lincoln highly encouraging, and this indubitably contributed to Bates's eagerness to accept a position in the cabinet. In their discussion of the mails, Lincoln indicated that he did not intend to be a pawn of the more radical wing of his party. This constituted one of Bates's principal anxieties about Lincoln, and he was undoubtedly heartened by the president-elect's unwillingness for the "Radical Republicans" to "claim the hands of the new Administration" in this matter. Bates was further galvanized by Lincoln's careful flattery. "He assured me that from the time of his nomination, his determination was, in case of success, to invite me into the Cabinet—and, in fact, was so complimentary as to say that my participation in the administration, he considered necessary to its complete success," Bates recorded. Bates saw this as a good sign that Lincoln's fundamental tendencies were conservative and that his inclusion of Bates signaled his intention that the new administration would steer a moderate course. Indeed, the two men agreed to leak news of Bates's acceptance of a place in the cabinet to a Missouri newspaper; Bates was the first to join the cabinet and his appointment the first to be made public, and this sent an early signal that the new president was no radical abolitionist.[46]

Still, Bates's fears were not totally assuaged. Lincoln told Bates during their meeting that he had also offered a cabinet position to William Henry Seward. Bates found some comfort in what he perceived to be reluctance on Lincoln's part to extend this offer: "He is troubled about Mr. Seward; feeling that he is under moral, or at least party, duress, to tender to Mr. S. the *first* place in the Cabinet," Bates recounted.[47] But Bates worried about the prospect of Seward joining the cabinet nonetheless. He believed that "the actual appointment of Mr. S. to be secretary of State would be dangerous" because it "would exasperate the feelings of the South, and make conciliation impossible, because they consider Mr. S. the embodiment of all that they hold odious in the Republican party." Seward's appointment, particularly to what was considered the "*first* place in the Cabinet," would seemingly endorse and practically empower Republican radicalism. Bates believed that Lincoln's administration needed to project its moderate intentions in order to quell the anxieties of Southerners. Bates hoped that his own commission would have this effect, but he worried that Seward's would send the wrong message. Bates did not want Lincoln's administration to be beholden—or seem to be beholden—to the radical wing of his party. In addition, Bates almost certainly worried about the influence Seward might exert on Lincoln as secretary of state. He considered Lincoln to be susceptible to radical arguments, and giving Seward a privileged place in his administration could only make the president more vulnerable.[48]

Given these anxieties, Bates conceived of himself as a conservative force in Lincoln's administration. He hoped that his affiliation with the government would be soothing to those who were concerned about Lincoln's radical tendencies. More importantly, Bates hoped to encourage Lincoln's fundamentally conservative instincts and to use his office to help steer the country through the present crisis. Just as he did before Lincoln's election, Bates felt that the key to avoiding catastrophe lay in rallying the nation's conservative forces together. The influence of radicals must be minimized—for these extremists, North and South, had brought on the crisis—so that the forces of reason, sobriety, and mutual affection could reassert themselves. The best chance the administration had of accomplishing this was to forge alliances with Southern moderates and conservatives. That Constitutional Unionists were talking disunion made this goal even more urgent; they must come to understand Lincoln's moderate intentions if the Union were to be held together, and Lincoln's administration, in turn, must demonstrate these intentions through action. Bates believed that, as a conservative from a Western border state, he could help reconcile Northern and Southern moderates, and he felt obligated to try to do so in order to save the Union. He said as much to Lincoln when he accepted a place in the cabinet—explaining why, after decades of avoiding public office, Bates would finally serve:

> If peace and order prevailed in the country, and the Government could now be carried on quietly, I would decline a place in the Cabinet.... But *now*, I am not at liberty to consult my own interests and wishes, and must subordinate them to my convictions of public duty, and to the necessity in which I find myself, to sustain my own personal character, by acting out, in good faith, the principles to which I stand pledged.[49]

Figure 5 "The Cabinet at Washington." Edward Bates (second from the right) appears as the most physically imposing member of Lincoln's cabinet in this *Harper's Weekly's* illustration from July 1861.
Source: *Harper's Weekly*, July 13, 1861, 437.

Within weeks of Bates's appointment to Lincoln's cabinet, however, the Union was in true crisis. South Carolina passed an ordinance of secession on December 20, 1860, and within six weeks six other Deep South states did the same. Bates believed that the "madness of the hour" was the work of "a few extremists," so he entreated Lincoln to pursue some sort of compromise with Southern moderates. John J. Crittenden of Kentucky—founder of the Constitutional Union Party and Bates's friend—had proposed a set of compromise measures; among these were provisions that would protect slavery where it already existed and extend the Missouri Compromise line into the territories, protecting the future of slavery south of that line. Though Bates staunchly opposed the expansion of slavery into the territories, he encouraged Lincoln to consider extending the Missouri Compromise line. There was little territory south of this line, and what there was was ill-suited to slavery. "The Republican party, in its strength . . . can afford to be magnanimous," he implored, "and the rather, in this instance, because the practical value of the *concession* is little or nothing, there being now, little or no territory on which it can operate." Bates made a similar argument about the amendment protecting slavery where it already existed. "If the very inception of the proposition stops seditious action, & *proving* pursuant peace, our main policy is gained," he said, "it will save the pride of those southern men (they are many) who feel they have been too hastily committed, & only desire a fair excuse for coming back to their proper places."[50]

Bates beseeched Lincoln to pursue the path of compromise and conciliation—for this, he believed, was the only chance of saving the Union without civil war. He warned Lincoln explicitly about the dangers of radicalism at such a precarious moment. "I see abundant signs . . . of a design to throw firebrands into the Republican party," he warned, "and I cannot quite divest myself of the suspicion that, even under this most grave & important matter, a trap of that sort may be concealed—a scheme to *catch you in your talk*, & embroil you with your friends." Now, more than ever, Bates sought to convey to Lincoln the importance of the president's rhetoric. If Lincoln were to be taken in by the arguments of radicals or even to employ the "ill-considered phrases" he had sometimes used in the "excitement of political debate," he could ruin any chance of a peaceful restoration of the Union. Bates thus encouraged Lincoln to pursue a conciliatory course, which would give him the chance to demonstrate his conservative intentions and subdue the hysteria in the South. "The danger is imminent, & the evil impending no less than dismemberment & civil war," Bates pleaded. "The question is not whether we can have things just as we would, but whether, in our hard circumstances, it is wisest to buy present peace upon the terms proposed, so as to put you quietly in possession of the Government, & give to your administration a fair chance to win, by its good conduct—its wisdom, justice & moderation—the confidence of the Country & the respect of mankind." This, he believed, was the key: If the Lincoln administration could buy enough time to prove that it was not the menace Southern radicals feared, cooler heads would prevail, and the Unionist majority would regain control of the South. He told a friend in February that "firmness, decision and moderation of the part of the government will soon compel submission . . . real people will rebel against the traitors, and compel a return to allegiance."[51]

Lincoln was ambivalent. He clearly hoped that he would have the chance to prove, as he had often promised, that "I have no purpose, directly or indirectly, to interfere with the institution of slavery in the States where it exists." In his inaugural address, he spoke directly about a constitutional amendment protecting slavery in these states; "holding such a provision to now be implied constitutional law," Lincoln said, "I have no objection to its being made express, and irrevocable." He was far less willing to compromise on slavery in the territories, however. Lincoln had written letters to Senator Lyman Trumbull and Congressman William Kellogg of Illinois in December, directing them to "Stand firm" on the territorial issue. "Entertain no proposition for a compromise in regard to the extension of slavery," he told Kellogg. "The instant you do, they have us under again; all our labor is lost, and sooner or later must be done over." This, as Lincoln understood it, was the principle upon which he had been elected, and to concede it now would threaten the future of his party and undermine the foundations of republican government. "We have just carried an election on principles fairly stated to the people," he wrote in January. "Now we are told in advance, the government shall be broken up, unless we surrender to those we have beaten. . . . If we surrender, it is the end of us [the Republican Party], and of the government."[52]

Still, Lincoln was not prepared to adopt an obstinate attitude toward the South when he took office. He, like Bates, believed that only a minority of Southerners supported secession, and he hoped that propitiatory overtures toward the South might lead the Unionist majority to reassert itself. The long and involved process of revising Lincoln's inaugural address demonstrated that the president-elect was focused on achieving a conciliatory tone, just as Bates had urged him in January. Unusually for Lincoln, he sought the advice of a number of friends and associates on the address; most of the changes he made—almost all of them, it would have shocked Bates to learn, at the urging of William H. Seward—moderated and softened his message. This shift found fullest expression in the conclusion of Lincoln's speech, which he adapted from Seward's notes. "We are not enemies, but friends," Lincoln declared. "We must not be enemies. Though passion may have strained, it must not break our bonds of affection. The mystic chords of memory, stretching from every battle-field, and patriot grave, to every living heart and hearthstone, all over this broad land, will yet swell the chorus of the Union, when again touched, as surely they will be, by the better angels of our nature." Lincoln made few concrete pronouncements about policy in his speech, but his conciliatory tone conveyed hope that some sort of accommodation could be reached. While Lincoln decided how to handle the delicate situation in the South, he endeavored—as Bates had beseeched him—to avoid alienating his potential allies there.[53]

The administration's policy toward the South was tested almost immediately after Lincoln took office on March 4, 1861. The day after his inauguration, Lincoln learned about the desperate situation of the garrison at Fort Sumter in Charleston harbor, which would run out of provisions within weeks. Lincoln informed his cabinet on March 9 and asked each of them to submit a written opinion about whether the government should abandon or attempt to provision the fort. Bates continued to urge caution and conciliation in the hopes of a peaceful restoration of the Union. The states of the Upper South and Border South had rejected secession in February and early March, and Bates saw this as a sign that moderation was resurgent. "I am persuaded . . . that, in several of the misguided States of the South, a large portion of the people are really lovers of the Union, and anxious to be safely back, under the protection of its flag," Bates wrote. "A reaction has already begun, and, if encouraged by wise, moderate and firm measures on the part of this government, I persuade myself that the nation will be restored to its integrity without the effusion of blood." What the administration needed was time, and Bates thus encouraged Lincoln to abandon the fort if it would avert a collision and civil war. "To avoid these evils I would make great sacrifices," he insisted, "and fort Sumter is one."[54]

When the cabinet convened to reconsider the issue in late March, Bates wavered. By then, General-in-Chief Winfield Scott's assessment of the feasibility of a resupply mission to Sumter had been called into question. In mid-March Scott argued that resupplying or reinforcing the fort before it ran out of supplies was well-nigh impossible: "It is, therefore, my opinion and advice that Major Robert Anderson be instructed to evacuate the Fort . . . immediately on procuring suitable water transportation," Scott wrote to Lincoln on March 12. But when Scott also recommended the evacuation of Fort Pickens in late March—which was not in the same vulnerable position as Sumter—Lincoln and his cabinet concluded that Scott was attempting to play politician rather than general. Bates, it seems, could not bring himself to advocate for a resupply mission that would likely bring on conflict, so instead he deferred to the president's judgment. "As to Fort Sumter," Bates told the cabinet on March 29, "I think the time is come either to evacuate or relieve it." In the end, and despite his reservations, Bates supported Lincoln's decision to resupply the fort. "Either there will be some sharp fighting, or the prestige of the government will be quietly reestablished," Bates concluded on April 8. He desperately hoped it would be the latter.[55]

Instead, South Carolina forces attacked and captured Fort Sumter before the supply mission could reach Charleston harbor. Bates was distraught at the outbreak of hostilities—he had profoundly hoped for a peaceful means of restoring the Union—but he would not condone "the violent and revolutionary proceedings of the Southern States . . . in seizing upon our ungarrisoned forts; in making war upon such as refused to surrender, in firing upon and in some instances actually degrading the flag of our country." Bates had been willing to "forbear" the tantrums of the Deep South "in the hope of a peaceful solution," even though he believed that South Carolina, by seceding, had struck the "first blow." But he could not forbear war made upon the Union. When the Union was threatened by violence—just as he had promised Lincoln in December—Bates vowed "*never to fire blank cartridges.*"[56]

After Fort Sumter, in other words, Bates concluded that the time for compromise was over. In late April, the Constitutional Unionist John Minor Botts wrote to Bates beseeching him to find some way to avoid war, even if it meant recognizing the secession of the Deep South in the short term. Bates did not mince words in his reply. Because Bates valued the Union above all else—just as Botts and his Constitutional Unionist allies had claimed to do—he could not and would not countenance disunion. To do otherwise, as Bates saw it, was nothing less than hypocrisy and cowardice. "After all that is past, it seems to me that there are but two alternatives left to this administration," he told Botts, "first, to submit implicitly to all the claims of the insurgent states, and quietly consent to the dismemberment of the nation, or, second, to do its best to restore peace, law, and order by supporting 'the Constitution and the Union, and the enforcement of the laws.'" There was no compromise between two such stark choices, and Bates made clear that he would not pursue peace at the expense of the Union. As a friend explained it, Bates "did not think compromise of our difficulties was possible because he did not think two separate governments could exist together here, & because upon secession principles no government could exist at all."[57]

And so after months and years struggling for peace and sectional harmony, Bates embraced a war to restore the Union. As Bates understood it, the war represented a continuation of his efforts on behalf of the Union—however much he lamented the necessity of violence. It also meant that Bates saw the same potential dangers in war as he did in the antebellum conflict. The goal of the war was to reunite the country, and he was determined that the government should never lose sight of that objective. For Bates, that meant that war must be waged decisively but with as little disruption to Southern society as possible. "Of course, I am for 'enforcing the laws,' with no object but to reinstate the authority of the government & restore the integrity of the nation," he told the cabinet on April 15. "And, with that object in view, I think it would be wise & humane on our part, so to conduct the war, as to generate the least occasion for social & servile war, in the extreme Southern States, & to disturb as little as possible, the accustomed occupations of the people." He rejected aggressive actions against slavery in war for the same reasons he scorned them during peace. He had seen in Kansas that violent action against slavery led Southerners to dig in against perceived threats; overtly targeting slavery in war would validate Southern fears about the Republican Party, alienate the loyal slave states, and further antagonize the seceded states—prolonging the war and derailing attempts to restore sectional harmony.[58]

Thus although Bates had abandoned his hopes for political compromise, he had not abandoned his conciliatory posture. He continued to believe that most Southerners did not support secession but were instead swept up "in a ferment, a furore, regardless of law and common sense." He hoped that fighting a limited yet decisive war would sober the seceded states and allow Unionism to reassert itself there. If the administration was judicious and proved that it fought only to restore the Union—and not in a crusade against slavery—Southern moderates might regain their senses and stop secessionist radicals. He still considered radicalism to be the great enemy in the sectional conflict in both the loyal and seceded states. Within the administration, therefore, he continued to see himself as a force for moderation and as a counterbalance to the more radical members of the Republican Party—both in the cabinet and in Congress. Bates hoped to steer the president away from such radical influences, encouraging Lincoln to act independently and according to his own inherently conservative values. He sought to ensure that the war would be and would remain a war for Union.[59]

The inauguration of the war also marked a shift in Bates's focus on rhetoric. Language remained vitally important to his work as attorney general, but his private critiques of Lincoln and his advice to the president as a member of the cabinet often focused more on Lincoln's actions than his words. Though he maintained his diary throughout the war, Bates wrote nothing in it about Lincoln's speeches during that period. He did, however, write a lot about Lincoln's failures as commander-in-chief, especially during the first year of the war. He criticized Lincoln for his lack of firmness and want of decisive action, betraying the same anxieties about Lincoln as a military leader that Bates expressed about him as a political one. Bates feared that the president lacked backbone, tending to allow those more aggressive than he to determine his course. He repeatedly told Lincoln "that it was not his *privilege* but his *duty* to command." Bates urged the president to "trust his own good judgment more, and defer less, to the opinions of his subordinates," convinced that if he did, the war effort would be "quickly and greatly changed for the better." "But I fear I spoke in vain," Bates lamented on one such occasion. "The Prest. is an excellent man, and, in the main wise; but he lacks *will* and *purpose*, and, I greatly fear he has not *the power to command*."[60]

In politics, however, Bates remained focused on the dangers of Radical Republicans, and he spent much of his tenure in office working to blunt their influence. He consistently advised Lincoln to be wary of the "schemes of the Radical leaders," urging him to stand "manfully against the unprincipled designs of the

Radicals." "My chief fear is that the President's easy good nature will enable them to commit him to too many of their extreme measures," Bates confided to his diary. As attorney general, Bates took charge of the "superintendence and direction" of the Confiscation Acts, ensuring—to the chagrin of Radical Republicans in Congress—that these measures were not vigorously implemented. He threw his support behind Lincoln's Preliminary Emancipation Proclamation, hoping that it would allow the president to wrest control of emancipation from Congress. He was sorely disappointed when the president issued the final proclamation in January 1863, lamenting that the pressure of "extremists" had resulted in the "intensifying of the Prests. proclamation."[61]

Bates was particularly upset about two differences between the preliminary and final versions of the Emancipation Proclamation. He deeply regretted that the provision of the proclamation vowing to continue the "effort to colonize persons of African descent" was absent from the final version. Because Bates could not envision a truly biracial society in the United States, he considered colonization of freed slaves to be an essential component of any emancipation scheme. He thus entreated the president to "open as many channels, and offer as many inducements for the egress of that population as possible." Bates was also intensely troubled that the final proclamation provided for freed slaves to "be received into the armed service." He believed that black men—and particularly ex-slaves—could never make good soldiers: "Once repulsed and broken, they cant be rallied; because they have no habit of *moral discipline*," he later told a young commander of United States Colored Troops. Bates's commitment to colonization and his objections to the enlistment of black soldiers reflected his deep-set prejudice and spoke to his understanding of the purpose of the war. To Bates, the war was and should always remain a war to restore the Union, and in Bates's conception the Union—America's experiment in ordered liberty—was fundamentally *white*. He thus rejected the idea that black soldiers should play a part in its restoration; it was not their Union, as he saw it, and he resented that their service should give them any claim to it. The idea of a biracial republic was both dangerous and undesirable, and he therefore hoped that war measures targeting slavery would work to preserve the Union by removing the political dangers of the institution as well as the social dangers of a racial underclass from the nation.[62]

Even when Bates found himself on the same side as Republican radicals, he worked hard to separate himself from them. In 1862, for example, Bates published an opinion affirming that African Americans could be citizens of the United States. The treatise inspired much adulation from radicals, including—as Senator Charles Sumner informed Bates at a chance meeting a few months later—the abolitionist William Lloyd Garrison. "Perhaps Mr. Garrison mistakes me for an Abolitionist," he replied, but Bates suspected that "the *Radicals . . .* would never forgive me for proving that negros had some rights by law, whereas they [the radicals] insist that all the rights of negros are derived from their [the radicals'] bounty!" He refused to believe that radicals were anything other than political opportunists; although the "negro is ever uppermost in their thoughts," he claimed, the "subject is used only as a topic (very sensitive) for electioneering—not at all for the good of the negro." As the election of 1864 approached, Bates hoped that Lincoln, too, would distance himself from the radical elements of his party. "I think Mr. Lincoln could have been elected without them and in spite of them," he wrote in September 1864. "In that event the Country might have been governed, free from their *malign influences,* and more nearly in conformity to the constitution." Instead, Lincoln's collusion left the administration beholden to its radical allies, and Bates feared that Lincoln's reelection on these terms would be "a melancholy defeat for their Country."[63]

By late 1864, Bates concluded that Lincoln had fully aligned himself with the radical wing of the Republican Party. Bates's warnings about the dangers of radicalism had gone unheeded, and he returned to the theme of rhetoric to illustrate the extent of the damage. "Respectable writers on government and constitutional law . . . say, habitually, what they do not mean," Bates lamented in October 1864. "The most popular news-writers, wantonly, abuse language, by using words in a false sense. . . . Even the dictionaries have cought [*sic*] the mania for *cant phrases,* and are doing their worst to render our language vague and indeterminate, by digging up its very *roots.*" For Bates, the widespread corrosion of language signaled the triumph of passion over reason in American society, and with that usurpation the American experiment in ordered liberty, posing the great question of whether people were fit to govern themselves, had definitively failed. This process of "stirring up of all the fiercest passions of our nature, and the loosening of all bands of society . . . [has] undermined the foundations of our Government, by destroying all respect for principles, and all obedience to law," Bates concluded. The war that began to save the Union—the war Bates had embraced as the only means of saving it—had destroyed the Union as he knew it. Having failed to protect the country from this radical onslaught and hold the administration fast to its conservative principles, Bates retired—utterly defeated.[64]

"Responsible to One Another and to God"

Why Francis Lieber Believed the Union War Must Remain a Just War

D. H. Dilbeck

Francis Lieber believed a war to save the Union had to remain a justly waged war. If the Union military effort lapsed into indiscriminate violence and barbarity, Federal armies would fail to truly preserve the Union, even if they emerged victorious from the battlefield. For Lieber, the Berlin-born jurist and intellectual who immigrated to America in 1827, the Union political and military leadership had a near-sacred obligation to guarantee their armies did not wage war against the Confederacy in a patently immoral manner. Even in times of war (perhaps *especially* in times of war), Lieber wrote, soldiers and civilians both remained "moral beings, responsible to one another and to God."[1] If Federals failed to take seriously this obligation, the Union would face a first-order existential crisis. It might cease to be the exceptional nation it had once been, Lieber feared, because an unjustly prosecuted war would belie the grand claims that the Union was a beacon of enlightened civilization marked by freedom and opportunity. For that reason, the loyal citizenry could lose their Union not only through Confederate military triumph but also through their own army's immoral conduct in war.[2]

The very fate of the Union demanded thorough and practical consideration of how to wage a just war against the Confederacy. Even before the Civil War began, as a scholar Lieber had carefully studied the laws of war, the branch of international law concerned with how belligerent nations conduct their wars. In the traditional just-war framework, the laws of war chiefly concern the demands of *jus in bello*, just conduct *in* war, a moral issue long separated from the question of *jus ad bellum*, the legitimate reasons for engaging in war. Lieber never doubted that the war to save the Union met the dictates of *jus ad bellum*; it was unquestionably just in that sense. But in April 1861 it remained unknowable whether Federal armies would also abide by the laws of war governing *jus in bello*. Would the war to save the Union that had begun a just war *remain* a just war? Lieber insisted that this was the great moral dilemma facing the Union in the Civil War.

However, recent Civil War scholarship has not adequately recognized the extent to which many loyal citizens such as Lieber carefully considered what it meant to wage a just war. Lieber was not alone in contemplating this question, even if his answers possessed a greater technical sophistication and significance compared to that of other Federals. But as Civil War historians increasingly emphasize in grim detail the war's gruesome, often remorseless, supposedly unprecedented violence, they also typically ignore just-war thinking by Lieber and others. This oversight tends to foster a distorted understanding of the nature and limits of the destruction wrought by the Civil War. But the case of Francis Lieber suggests an equally important additional point: Failing to take seriously Union just-war thinking can lead not only to a misunderstanding of the character of the Federal military effort but also to an incomplete understanding of what the Union meant to loyal citizens. To Lieber, the meaning of the Union and the meaning of a just war were inseparable.

Lieber made it his personal quest to ensure Federal armies waged war against the Confederacy in a moral manner, in keeping with the dictates of the laws of war and the even older just-war tradition.[3] Lieber thereby hoped to contribute to the task of saving the Union. Throughout the first two years of the Civil War, as an academic teaching at Columbia College in New York City, Lieber wrote on several pressing just-war issues—publicly commenting, for example, on what the laws of war instructed about guerrilla warfare or the treatment of captured enemy soldiers.[4] But in the winter of 1862 and spring of 1863, Lieber's effort to provide Federals a clear vision of just warfare reached its culmination. In these months, Lieber drafted "Instructions for the Government of Armies of the United States in the Field," issued in April 1863 by President Abraham Lincoln as General Orders No. 100, known informally thereafter as the Lieber Code. The code consisted of 157 articles, distilled from the laws of war, guiding Union soldiers and officers in how to wage war justly.[5]

Lieber's document contained a distinct moral vision of just warfare. That is, it possessed a coherent take on the nature of a justly waged war. Lieber assumed, as the code proclaimed, that the "more vigorously wars are pursued, the better it is for humanity. Sharp wars are brief."[6] This proved to be the definitive assumption shaping his vision of just warfare. Lieber thought a "vigorous" or "sharp" war, one that affected soldiers and civilians alike, might well be the most humane kind of war precisely because it would presumably end (in victory) faster than a "conciliatory" war effort. The war that ended soonest occasioned the least death and suffering. Some might take this logic to its extreme and argue that *any* action that hastened a war's end was legitimate, whatever the cost. Lieber never followed this line of argument; his code, in fact, expressly prohibited certain actions as never justifiable in war. General Orders No. 100 instead sought to set forth in careful detail the moral limits of a "vigorous, sharp" war.

The 157 articles of the Lieber Code together amounted to a compelling plea for moral warfare.[7] Lieber sought to convince the loyal citizenry of the necessity of waging war justly, even as he explained in detail how exactly to do so. Ultimately, Lieber rooted his plea in the warning that the fate of the Union hinged on how Federal armies waged war against the Confederacy. "To save the country is paramount to all other considerations," Lieber's code declared.[8] But the point of this declaration was not to justify disregarding the boundaries of moral warfare but to convince Federals to abide by them. Because, in the end, by disregarding the laws of war and the just-war tradition, the loyal citizenry would risk losing their Union by irrevocably tarnishing its character.

Lieber's moral vision of warfare and his dogged insistence that the Union war remain a just war arose over time out of his life experiences, intellectual career, and long fascination with war and the United States. Lieber was born in Berlin near the dawn of the nineteenth century and came of age during Napoleon's conquests of Europe. He remained fascinated with warfare, despite all its horrors, for the rest of his life. He certainly knew firsthand of these horrors; while fighting in the latter phase of the Napoleonic wars, Lieber was shot through the neck. Eventually, Lieber left behind the soldier's life and became a scholar of wide-ranging intellect. He received an advanced degree in mathematics in Jena, then hobnobbed briefly with leading intellectuals in London, and then, having failed to secure a teaching post, immigrated to Boston to lead a new gymnasium along the Friedrich Ludwig Jahn model.[9]

Although several wealthy Bostonians funded the gymnasium, it proved a largely unsuccessful enterprise. But Lieber remained in America and partnered with the publisher Matthew Carey to produce *Encyclopaedia Americana*, the wildly popular eight-thousand-page, multivolume work. Despite the *Encyclopaedia*'s success, Lieber did not secure the teaching appointment at Harvard he desired. The search for steady employment led Lieber finally to Columbia, South Carolina, to teach history and political economy at South Carolina College. Lieber and his family remained in the South Carolina Midlands for the next twenty years.[10]

Lieber wrote widely in these years on political philosophy and economy. But, intellectually, he always remained fascinated by the moral implications and significance of war—how it could inspire moral triumph and amoral desolation. As a grim fact of human existence, war was "not of an ethical nature, so far as the physical force goes," Lieber once wrote. But, he added, "it is not immoral on that account." After all, Lieber believed, war revived noble and virtuous qualities in soldiers just as easily as it unleashed depraved behavior. Lieber opposed the Mexican-American War, which he labeled "an unrighteous war." But he also criticized the war's pacifist opponents, like his friend Charles Sumner, the future Massachusetts senator, because they assumed war was always pure and unadulterated amorality. Lieber explained at the time, "I am no vilifier of war under all circumstances." Instead, Lieber devoted himself to explaining how a people might uphold morality in warfare and thereby channel war's power toward truly moral ends—such as virtue, civilization, and justice. War thus contained "the spark of moral electricity," Lieber wrote, making even more momentous the challenge of comprehending when and how to prosecute a war justly.[11]

In the aftermath of the Mexican-American War, as the sectional crisis intensified throughout the 1850s, Lieber's position in South Carolina proved increasingly tenuous. He was passed over for the presidency of South Carolina College in 1855. Within two years, the Liebers relocated to New York City, where Columbia College offered Francis a position as professor of history and political economy. He remained in New York the rest of his life. At the onset of the Civil War, Lieber, likely sixty-three-years old, was both an acknowledged authority on the laws and usage of war and also an ardent Union nationalist.

The immigrant Lieber found in his adopted American homeland a nation worthy of loyalty and affection. He, like Lincoln, saw American democracy as "the last best, hope of earth," a sacred compact worth preserving whatever the costs. "God has given us this great country for great purposes," Lieber wrote Attorney General Edward Bates in July 1861, and therefore the nation "must be maintained at any price under any circumstances," unless the divinely appointed mission went unfulfilled.[12]

But what were the "great purposes" of the Union, according to Lieber? It is an important question to ask because Lieber's understanding of the meaning of the Union profoundly shaped his vision of the nature and necessity of just warfare against the Confederacy. Lieber embraced thoroughly conventional notions of what the Union meant to most nineteenth-century Americans. In fact, Gary W. Gallagher's explanation in *The Union War* of what the Union meant to the overwhelming majority of loyal citizens in the Civil War era perfectly captures Lieber's views on this adopted homeland.[13] According to Gallagher, the Union chiefly represented to the loyal citizenry of the mid–nineteenth century

Figure 6 Francis Lieber.
Source: Library of Congress, Prints and Photographs Division, reproduction no. LC-DIG-cwpph-01401.

"the cherished legacy of the founding generation, a democratic republic with a constitution that guaranteed political liberty and afforded individuals a chance to better themselves economically . . . the only hope for democracy in a western world that had fallen more deeply into the stifling embrace of oligarchy."[14] For Lieber and his fellow loyal citizens, the Union embodied a flourishing democracy and the freedom and rule of law upon which it rested. As the Massachusetts senator Daniel Webster famously proclaimed in 1850, Americans possessed "a great, popular, constitutional government guarded by law and by judicature . . . they live and stand under a government popular in its form, representative in its character."[15]

The liberty upheld by the Union, though, was political and economic in character. That is, it included the freedom for social mobility and economic uplift. President Abraham Lincoln thus explained in a special message to Congress in July 1861 that the Union existed "to clear the paths of laudable pursuit for all—to afford all, an unfettered start, and a fair chance, in the race of life."[16] To loyal citizens like Lieber, the slaveholding oligarchy of the South threatened for Northerners and Southerners alike the chance to seize "an unfettered start, and a fair chance," as Lincoln promised. Secession and the formation of the Confederacy was simply the latest and most profound challenge yet from Southern slaveholders to the economic opportunity widely afforded by the Union.

Loyal citizens also typically understood the meaning and significance of the Union with some reference to its unique role as the standard bearer of democracy on the world stage, a point exceedingly important to the immigrant Lieber. He and many others believed the Union remained exceptional because it remained set apart from the prevailing political trends in Europe hostile to genuine democracy. *Harper's Weekly* warned its readers in May 1863 that the Union's war against the Confederacy had assumed international consequence as "the final decisive contest between free popular government on the one side, and government by an oligarchy or a monarch on the other." Union defeat would bring "self-government and humanity itself into merited contempt" and would vindicate the "oligarchs of Europe" who had claimed "republics are impracticable, and human self-government a delusive dream."[17]

Lieber celebrated the Union for precisely the same reasons. He adhered fully to this mainstream understanding of what the Union represented and why it had to be maintained, whatever the costs. In 1861, soon after the Civil War began, love of country proved to be an intoxicating muse for Lieber. He penned several short verses of patriotic poetry that reflected his deeply held assumptions about what the Union represented. The lines came to him after witnessing the raising of the American flag on the Columbia College campus in New York City, his home institution. He hoped, if nothing else, that his poetry would rouse the young men of Columbia to take up arms in defense of their nation against the Confederacy. "Our country is a goodly land," Lieber assured his students. "We'll love her, live for her or die; To fall for her is not to fail." To ensure that the Union fulfilled its divinely appointed "great purposes," some of its citizens may have to sacrifice their lives.

Lieber's most direct comments on the nature of the Union, though, were inspired by the colors of the American flag. "Our Flag! The Red shall mean the blood/ We gladly pledge; and let the White/ Mean purity and solemn truth,/

Unsullied justice, sacred right." The crimson-colored offering that citizens should willingly pledge to their nation stood in stark contrast to the unimpeachably pure character of the Union itself. The white stripes of the flag testified to the fact that the American nation was founded upon, and still embodied, pure and solemn truths—not least the truths of life, liberty, and the right to pursue one's own happiness, truths upheld in the Declaration of Independence and Constitution. In America, "unsullied justice"—the rule of law uncorrupted—reigned supreme. America was a land of justice unsullied because, on the whole, its legal and political systems respected the "sacred" rights enjoyed by American citizens. The flag's blue color conjured in Lieber's mind images of the ocean water that "laves the heaven-united land" of the United States' shores. The Union is not merely a human invention; it also is in some mystical sense a heavenly creation forged by a divine power for a grand purpose.[18]

Lieber remained keenly aware of the unique significance of America's experiment in democracy, particularly in a nineteenth-century Western world that had increasingly drifted toward autocracy. "Let never Emp'ror rule this land, / Nor fitful Crowd, nor senseless Pride. / *Our* Master is our self-made Law; / To *him* we bow, and none beside." The genius of the American republic, at its best, was that it avoided both authoritarianism and the mob rule of democracy run amok. The blind, chaotic passions of the "fitful crowd" equally threatened all that the Union represented. What truly governed America? Not the whims of a dictator or the democratic masses. Instead, the nation's final master was its "self-made law." The rule of law reigned supreme in America, a key reason to Lieber why the Union remained so exceptional and admirable.[19]

However, the Confederate rebellion fundamentally threatened Americans' "self-made Law." Lieber believed secession was the utter rejection of the rule of law, a hasty and foolish action driven by "senseless pride." For that reason, among others, the Confederacy was more like the autocracies of Europe than the American Union. The nation that Confederates forged was not rooted in "solemn truth, / Unsullied justice, sacred right," as was the Union. Instead, its cornerstone was the petty rejection of the rule of preexisting law. The war between America and the Confederacy was more than merely a conflict over the future of slavery; it was also a conflict over whether the rule of law, undefiled, could endure in any democratic republic.[20]

Lieber saw the Union as a beacon of truly free, democratic, enlightened civilization—a righteous land of liberty and opportunity in a world of tyranny and oppression. He preached this gospel throughout the Civil War, for the conflict tested, as President Abraham Lincoln said, whether any democracy like America could endure. Lieber set forth these ideas in a particularly powerful fashion in a pamphlet written to German immigrants in the heat of the 1864 election. The pamphlet implored its readers to support Abraham Lincoln instead of George McClellan in the presidential contest, for a Democratic Party victory would surely lead to the Confederacy's triumph in the Civil War and the dissolution of the Union.

In this pamphlet, Lieber asked, "German working men! why did you leave home, family, the friends of your youth, and seek this distant America?" The reason was simple, he replied in answer to his own question: to seize the opportunities and freedom afforded to citizens of the Union.

> It was because you had heard that in the United States you would find a country wherein you and your children would enjoy all the rights of the free citizen; where skill and industry would surely find their reward, and where your children would never find themselves debarred from any merited attainment by the privileges of others.

The Union, Lieber proclaimed, not only upheld the rule of law and natural rights. It also embodied the spirit of a true meritocracy, a land of true social mobility—where individuals who were capable of improving their lot in life had the free opportunity to do so. But if McClellan's Democratic Party triumphed at the polls and the Confederacy triumphed on the battlefield, then all the lofty promises, freedom, and opportunities offered by the Union might well disappear entirely. Instead, in its place, especially in the new Confederate nation, there would appear a "grinding tyranny far worse than any endured in the oppressed countries of Europe."

Lieber's understanding of the meaning of Union was wholly conventional for the time and place in which he lived. He never held innovative or unusual views on what the Union embodied and the promises it afforded its citizens. He embraced instead the ordinary but profoundly significant conception of Union widely shared by his fellow loyal citizens. But if the Union truly was the last, best hope of earth, then the war to save it must remain just—aligned fully with the exceptional moral character of the Union itself.

When eleven Southern states seceded and formed the Confederacy and a civil war erupted, Lieber remained fiercely loyal to the Union. His commitment to the Union war effort never wavered, even as one of his sons joined the Confederate ranks. Ambitious as always, Lieber sought some meaningful way to contribute to the war to save the Union. He soon came to believe his greatest contribution would be to provide Union armies practical, intelligible instructions for how to wage a just war. That is, in his effort to offer ordinary officers and soldiers guides to the prevailing laws and usages of war, Lieber hoped to help truly save the Union.

As the Civil War commenced, Lieber embarked on a quest to inculcate in Union officers and soldiers a correct understanding of justly waged wars. Lieber came to see successfully finishing this quest as his best possible contribution to the grand work of saving the Union. Throughout the first two years of the war especially, Lieber refined and disseminated a distinct vision of just warfare. He worked to distill an often-technical legal tradition—the laws and usage of war—into a clear set of military rules and guidelines. His effort culminated in April 1863 with the issuance of General Orders No. 100, known also as "Instructions for the Government of Armies of the United States in the Field" or, simply, the Lieber Code.

Lieber set forth in 157 pithy articles a blueprint for waging morally upright warfare—the only kind of warfare befitting the morally exceptional Union. Lieber's code expressly prohibited a wide array of practices, particularly in regard to the treatment of Southern civilians. Even so, Lieber's vision of just warfare was one not simply of restraint but also of concerted action in service of a swift victory. The core assumption behind Lieber's code justified immense carnage as necessary to restoring peace and saving the Union: "The ultimate object of all modern war is a renewed state of peace. The more vigorously wars are pursued, the better it is for humanity. Sharp wars are brief."[21] Vigorous wars presumably restored peace as rapidly as possible, thereby limiting the total suffering and destruction. Lieber worked throughout the war to explain in clear detail how to wage a just war both vigorous in its prosecution yet still mindful of certain inviolable restraints imposed by the laws of war. To Lieber, only by balancing vigor and restraint in its war effort would Federal armies successfully save a Union still worth saving.

Lieber's quest to define just warfare began almost as soon as the Civil War did. From April 1861 until the issuing of General Orders No. 100 two years later, Lieber fretted that widespread confusion reigned among Federals about the nature of the laws of war and what it demanded. Lieber believed this deadly confusion revealed itself in how Union forces handled several recurring problems early in the war—prisoner exchanges, guerrilla warfare, and paroling.

Some Federals worried that by engaging in prisoner exchanges with the Confederacy, the Union would thereby implicitly acknowledge the Confederacy as a legitimate *nation* by treating it and its soldiers according to the laws of war. But to deny the legitimacy of the Confederate nation, as President Abraham Lincoln and many other Union leaders did, raised a troubling prospect: Would that then mean that the laws of war, which governed conflicts only between legitimate belligerents, held no sway in the Union's war against the so-called Confederacy? Lieber scoffed at this sort of handwringing early in the war. In a newspaper editorial published in August 1861, he assured Union leaders that they could abide by the humanitarian restraints of the laws of war without extending de facto recognition to the Confederacy as a legitimate nation. "The exchange of prisoners involves no question of acknowledgement of right, but is a simply recognition of fact and reality," Lieber argued.[22] That many Union political and military leaders did not already understand this fact confirmed to Lieber that even a basic understanding of the laws of war was sorely lacking at the precise moment it was most desperately needed.

This conviction grew in Lieber's mind as he witnessed how Federals dealt with guerrilla warfare and paroling. Intractable problems combating guerrillas posed similar sorts of thorny questions about who counted as a legitimate soldier and why. Implicit also in these questions were uncertainties about how exactly to treat various kinds of legitimate combatants and illegitimate marauders as well as their Southern civilian abettors. Lieber tried to bring some clarity to these questions in the summer of 1862 when he drafted a six-thousand-plus-word essay, "Guerrilla Parties Considered with References to the Laws and Usages of War." Henry Halleck, then general-in-chief, had dealt firsthand with guerrillas earlier in the war as a Union commander in Missouri, and he thought so highly of Lieber's essay that he distributed five thousand copies to Union officers.[23]

To Lieber, the "fearful abuse of paroling," as he labeled it, posed an equally dire threat to efforts to conform the Civil War to the laws of war. Lieber believed that the Confederate practice of paroling captured Union soldiers was plainly illegitimate. He advised Senator Charles Sumner in August 1861 that the Federal government ought to "proclaim that no man, in arms for his country against rebellion, and having taken a solemn oath to that effect, has a right to invalidate that oath by his own parole."[24] None of these issues—prisoner exchanges, guerrilla warfare, paroling—might seem particularly significant in the wider context of the Union war effort. But together, to Lieber, they confirmed a troubling fact about the present state of the war to save the Union: Most Federal leaders, officers, and ordinary soldiers knew little about the laws and usages of war and what those required of them.

By the late autumn of 1862, then, Lieber adamantly believed Union armies needed a clear and useable guide to the laws of war. He had considered drafting such a document for some time but now decided to broach the issue formally with the Lincoln administration.[25] In November 1862, Lieber wrote to his friend General-in-Chief Henry Halleck about the matter: "Ever since the beginning of our present war it has appeared clearer and clearer to me, that the President ought to issue a set of rules and definitions providing for the most urgent issues, occurring under the law and usages of war."[26] Halleck initially thanked Lieber for his suggestion and then politely ignored it. But Lieber continued to press Halleck on the matter. Within a week, Lieber wrote again to reiterate how "the more I reflect on the matter, the more important it appears to me."[27] The back and forth continued until mid-December, at which point a committee was officially formed to draft the rules. Lieber was one of its five members.

Although Lieber's fellow committee members were all distinguished military officers, his knowledge of the laws and usage of war far exceeded theirs. He assumed responsibility for preparing the first draft of the new rules. He completed this work in Washington, DC, and New York City in late 1862 and early 1863, a demoralizing period for the Union war effort. Lieber sought out the advice of leading Northern political and military leaders as he drafted the code, and the committee edited Lieber's draft on matters of style and organization.[28] But, by and large, the code was Lieber's creation, and it bears the marks of his vision of how and why to wage a just war. On April 24, 1863, President Abraham Lincoln officially promulgated the code as General Orders No. 100. Secretary of War Edwin Stanton made plans to distribute three thousand copies to Union armies. "Our people as well as our army are very ignorant of the laws of war, and required to be educated on the subject," Henry Halleck wrote Lieber soon after the code's promulgation. "I think this is the time and mode for beginning the education."[29]

Lieber's code offered Union officers and soldiers as fine an introduction to the laws and usages of war as they could possible hope to achieve. Its 157 articles, many as brief as a sentence or two, addressed a remarkable array of topics—from martial law to retaliation to prisoners of war to private property to spies to flags of truce to irregular warfare to armistice and capitulation. Lieber wrote the articles in a declarative, normative style. He meant to establish rules for soldiers to follow, not to disregard at their own choosing. Yet General Orders No. 100 is not inflexible, inviolable law. It more closely resembles a plea for moral warfare and recommended guidelines for how to uphold morality in war.[30]

The code's articles encapsulated Lieber's distinct moral vision of warfare. The lodestar of this vision was the idea that vigorously prosecuted wars are the most humane: "The more vigorously wars are pursued, the better it is for humanity. Sharp wars are brief."[31] The surest way to reduce suffering caused by war was to end war as quickly as possible, Lieber argued; the surest way to end a war as quickly as possible was to wage it with stern, vigorous fury. Lieber scoffed at overly sentimental restraint in war because he believed mild conciliatory wars only prolonged suffering and destruction. Still, he believed that even "sharp wars" have their limits, for certain actions remained unjustifiable. Soldiers fighting to save the Union had to abide by certain moral obligations in the prosecution of their war. After all, as Lieber wrote, "Men who take up arms against one another in public war do not cease on this account to be moral beings, responsible to one another and to God."[32]

Lieber, however, also carved out a fairly wide degree of latitude for Union armies in the name of "military necessity," which the code defined as "the necessity of those measures which are indispensable for securing the ends of the war, and which are lawful according to the modern law and usages of war."[33] Lieber did not hesitate to describe what military necessity might justify. Armies could destroy all "life or limb of armed enemies, and of other persons whose destruction is incidentally unavoidable." They could demolish public and private property and essential lines of travel and communication. They could withhold "sustenance or means of life." They could appropriate from enemy countryside whatever they might need for their "subsistence and safety."[34]

Still, "the necessity of those measures which are indispensable for securing the ends of the war" did not justify *all* actions in war. Lieber established concrete limits to military necessity to protect against gross violations of the laws of war. The code did so both by reminding Federals that the "ultimate object of all modern war is a renewed state of peace" and by clearly identifying several specific actions never justified by "military necessity," even under the direst circumstances. Military necessity did not allow armies to inflict suffering "for the sake of suffering or for revenge." It did not allow the use of torture to extort confessions. It did not allow the use of poison "in any way." It forbade the "wanton devastation" of an area and disclaimed all acts of perfidy.[35] Lieber believed he had to provide soldiers with more than mere talk about moral obligations to God and the importance of restoring peace. They needed specific examples of what military necessity did not justify. According to Lieber's code, to transgress the moral limits of military necessity would mean to undermine true victory in a just war to save the Union.

Of the many topics the code addressed, its articles on slavery and the treatment of prisoners of war and enemy civilians most clearly capture Lieber's underlying moral vision of war. These articles deserve careful consideration, for they reveal what kind of military policies Lieber had in mind when he advocated for a just war both vigorous and uncompromising against soldiers and civilians but still constrained by the laws of war. In the code's articles on slavery, prisoners of war, and civilians, Lieber set forth what it would look like for Federal armies to prosecute a war both *effective* enough to defeat the confederacy and *moral* enough to not compromise the character of the Union it sought to save.

When President Lincoln issued the Lieber Code in the spring of 1863, the Emancipation Proclamation had been in effect for nearly four months. The Federal military effort, it now seemed, would directly target slavery in the Confederate states. Some interpreters of the laws and usages of war in the eighteenth and nineteenth centuries had adamantly declared that an emancipatory war could never be a civilized war. If an army liberated its enemy's slaves, a near-apocalyptic violence against former masters would result. According to this perspective, no supposedly enlightened people or its army could instigate such chaos and devastation.[36] Put simply, this line of thinking argued that a justly waged war to save the Union could not deliberately strike against slavery.

However, Lieber's code, in contrast, declared without qualification that the laws of war did not protect slavery. "The law of nature and nations has never acknowledged [slavery]," the code proclaimed, which existed only according to "municipal law or local law." Therefore, Lieber concluded, slaves who "come as a fugitive under the protection" of Union forces are thereby "immediately entitled to the rights and privileges of a freeman."[37] To Lieber, this was a settled question in the laws of war needing no elaborate explanation or justification. Lieber had earlier in the spring of 1862 argued to Edwin Stanton that Federals ought to put escaped slaves to work in Union armies—some perhaps, eventually, even in combat roles. The laws of war, Lieber wrote in his memorandum to Stanton, fully upheld the "justice of employing the slaves of the enemy, and thereby of course making freedmen of them."[38] Lieber insisted nothing in the laws of war condemned a war effort that targeted the institution of slavery. Therefore, Federals did not need to worry: If their war to save the Union also became a war to end slavery, it did not thereby also become in the eyes of the laws of war an unjust or uncivilized war. A justly waged war to preserve the Union could legitimately destroy Southern slavery.

Lieber began the code's sections on prisoners of war by defining who exactly deserved the privileges afforded to legitimate prisoners of war. He sought to ensure that no one arguably deserving the protections of the laws of war would fail to receive them. A prisoner of war, the code said, was "a public enemy armed or attached to the hostile army." This included all soldiers and many sorts of citizens usually accompanying armies, especially "sutlers, editors, or reporters of journals, or contractors," as well as the leaders of an enemy government, its diplomatic agents, and anyone else "of particular and singular use and benefit to the hostile army or its government."[39]

Belligerents must treat prisoners of war humanely, Lieber wrote. Captors must never inflict on prisoners "any suffering, or disgrace, by cruel imprisonment, want of food, by mutilation, death or any other barbarity." Confinement and imprisonment should never degenerate to "intentional suffering or indignity." In practice this meant that a captor must provide prisoners "plain and wholesome food" and could never use violence to extort sensitive information from a prisoner or even plunder a prisoner and steal cherished personal belongings.[40] Lieber did not provide a truly comprehensive list of unjustified actions toward prisoners of war. Instead, he trusted Union army officials to take the general principle he set forth—to avoid the intentional infliction of suffering or indignity—and apply it in particular circumstances.

The code declared that any army that resolved "in hatred and revenge" to give no quarter to captured enemy soldiers grossly violated the laws of war.[41] The code warned Confederates that if they systematically gave no quarter to captured Union troops, then captured Confederates would receive none, either. The code insisted that belligerents could not deny certain categories of soldiers the privileges and protections they justly deserve if captured: "No belligerent has a right to declare that enemies of a certain class, color, or condition, when properly organized as soldiers, will not be treated by him as public enemies." The chief purpose of this article was to warn Confederates that the Union would not tolerate a systematic denial of quarter to African American troops (or their white officers). Many Confederate officials and officers had threatened to treat captured black soldiers as insurrectionary slaves and their white officers as instigators of slave rebellion. Lieber sought to prevent this from occurring by sternly warning that if Confederates refused to treat captured black soldiers as normal prisoners of war, "it would be a case for the severest retaliation" against captured Confederate soldiers—in this case, death.[42]

Formal retaliation was "the sternest feature of war," the code said, but it remained an essential part of the laws of war. "Reckless enemies" often leave an opponent no other way of "securing himself against the repetition of barbarous outrages." Retaliation must occur not for "mere revenge" but "protective retribution." Even when justified, Lieber found nothing pleasant in retaliation; a nation ought to resort to it "cautiously," only after all other efforts to remedy the offense failed. Lieber remained wary of retaliation because it made a speedy and lasting return to peace more difficult. Any belligerent who embraced retaliation should remember that it "removes the belligerents far and farther from the mitigating rules of a regular war, and by rapid steps leads them nearer to the internecine wars of savages." Retaliation was sometimes necessary, but all things permissible by the laws of war were not always advisable, certainly not as a first recourse. This call for prudence aside, even though Lieber sought to ensure the humane treatment of prisoners of war he still maintained that captors, if necessary, could subject prisoners to the harsh "infliction of retaliatory measures."[43]

A similarly harrowing and humane vision of just warfare defined the code's articles on the treatment of enemy civilians. The code praised as sacrosanct the distinction between "the private individual belonging to a hostile country and the hostile country itself, with its men in arms." In other words, an army must treat enemy combatants and noncombatants differently. By way of a general principle for how civilians ought to be treated, the code proclaimed, "the unarmed citizen is to be spared in person, property, and honor as much as the exigencies of war will admit."[44]

Federal soldiers simply could not commit certain actions against civilians: "wanton violence . . . all destruction of property not commanded by the authorized officer, all robbery, all pillage or sacking, even after taking a place by main force, all rape, wounding, maiming, or killing of such inhabitants." For these and similar crimes, the code authorized severe punishment, in many instances, death. But the code also granted that not all noncombatants deserve equal treatment. As such, the code advised officers to distinguish loyal from disloyal civilians in enemy country and then separate the disloyal civilians who actively "give positive aid and comfort" to enemy armies from those who did not. Having made these distinctions, the code insisted Federals should spare loyal citizens as much as possible from "the common misfortune" of war and should instead "throw the burden of war" on disloyal citizens.[45]

Lieber's attempt to shield at least some civilians always came with an important disclaimer: "as much as the exigencies of war will admit." The real challenge remained to balance the humanitarian demand to protect civilians with the relentless demands of military necessity. While soldiers should never resort to certain actions against civilians—wanton violence, pillage, rape, or maiming—Lieber insisted military necessity sometimes compelled armies to subject civilians to hardship and suffering. This was the consequence of "the overruling demands of a vigorous war." For example, while the Union ought to "acknowledge and protect" private property, its armies could seize it "by way of military necessity, for the support or other benefit of the army."[46] Lieber's justification of subjecting civilians to war's hardships rested upon his larger vision of a moral war. The harsh treatment of civilians sometimes proved necessary in a vigorously prosecuted war intended to end war as quickly as possible, the most moral and humane thing a belligerent could do. To induce civilian suffering in war was never desirable, Lieber believed, but it might be a necessary path to the most moral of wars: stern and short.

"The more vigorously wars are pursued, the better it is for humanity. Sharp wars are brief."[47] This is the fundamental logic of Lieber's moral vision of warfare. Lieber pleaded for a "sharp war" not simply as an expert on the laws of war but also as a father of three soldiers, one who fought and died for the Confederacy in June 1862. Earlier in the year, another son was maimed at Fort Donelson, Tennessee, fighting for the Union. Lieber's call for a vigorously pursued war was not reckless bombast from a warmonger; it was closer to the cry of a father who had tasted firsthand the war's devastation and heartbreak. Although it may seem like a cruel kind of paradox, only a "vigorously waged" war could save more families from the pain and turmoil the Liebers had experienced—because, Francis believed, such a war would in theory end sooner and therefore limit the total suffering and destruction unleashed. Lieber intended for his code to offer a guide to waging precisely this sort of war—one that proved humane to the greatest number of people, did not contradict the prohibitions of the laws of war, and also cohered with the grandest moral claims American citizens made about their Union.

Lieber's moral vision of just warfare was always inextricably tied to his understanding of the meaning of the Union and the war to save it. Lieber rightly suspected that his code could have international influence, shaping how people around the world thought about warfare. Still, even so, the Lieber Code arose out of one *particular* war. It is nearly impossible to understand Lieber's code or his vision of just warfare apart from Lieber's conception of the nature and moral character of the Union itself. To Lieber, the quest to draft General Orders No. 100 and ensure soldiers adhered to it was about more than whether Federal armies waged a just war. This quest ultimately concerned whether the Union would continue to exist after the Civil War as it had always existed—as a morally exceptional nation. In that sense, an unjustly waged war threatened to destroy the Union.

Therefore, to Lieber, the war to save the Union had to remain a justly waged war. If, as Lieber said, the Union truly embodied the "unsullied justice, sacred right" of freedom in the world, it helps explain why Lieber thought the stakes were so high for waging war justly. Only by waging a just war could the Union remain an unsullied example to the world of a free, enlightened, democratic civilization. When Lieber proclaimed in his code that to "save the country is paramount to all other considerations," he undoubtedly had a very literal meaning in mind: Federals needed to endeavor earnestly to restore a unified nation.⁴⁸ Yet, there was for Lieber an even grander sense in which waging war justly was, in a way, "saving the country": A just war vindicated the Union's highest claims about itself—its supposed moral mission and uniqueness in world history. The only Union worth saving was a Union saved by a justly waged war, one waged in accordance with the highest ideals of a free and enlightened people.

Building a Union of Banks

Salmon P. Chase and the Creation of the National Banking System

Michael T. Caires

On February 25, 1863, the US Congress passed a bill that would cast a long shadow over America's economic future. The new law established a system of federally chartered and regulated banks, a system that endures to this day and that at the start of the twenty-first century holds over 12 trillion dollars in assets. No one at the time, however, could see the outlines of this future in 1863. In fact, very few financiers or politicians could understand how a reform of the banks where Americans kept and borrowed their money or the currency they used in their exchanges might have something to do with a war to preserve the Union. In truth, the policy was the longtime project of President Abraham Lincoln's secretary of the treasury, Salmon Portland Chase. An unlikely financial architect, Chase attempted to use the moment of the Civil War to solve one of the oldest problems in American policy and politics—creating a stable and uniform currency that he thought would perfect and strengthen the American Union in the decades to come.[1]

As evidenced by the essays in this volume, the drive to preserve the Union set the rhythm and pulse of politics and culture in the United States during the Civil War era. That concern for Union, however, extended far beyond the political sphere or the battlefield and into markets and the pocketbooks of millions of average Americans. Well before the Civil War, "Union" not only referred to America's democratic institutions and practices but to the economic and commercial Union forged in the 1780s that brought the country out of the economic conflict fostered by the Revolution. In the Civil War era, the citizenry of the Union still held to the idea that the Union preserved and promoted economic freedom and prosperity. In this spirit, during the Civil War the Republicans in Congress passed a score of new federal policies, including the Homestead Act, the Morrill Land Grant Act, the tariff, and funding for the transcontinental railroad. Coupled with emancipation and Reconstruction, Republicans imagined that they could remake America as a shining example of free labor in which government could help promote, support, and release the energies of its citizens. As a concept, the cry of "Union" offers insights into why soldiers fought and politicians postured and voted as they did. It also holds new perspectives on how Civil War Americans thought about their economic futures and about the place of their central government in that future.[2]

Chase saw a national banking system as the key to creating a more harmonious Union and the war as a catalyst for that end. Understanding the national banking system as an act of Union-building puts this admittedly dense and obscure law in a different light than have previous historians. Among Progressive Era historians and their modern adherents, the National Banking Act was yet another sign that Republicans meant to use the occasion of the war to empower the capitalist class in Washington. Recent historians of the Civil War lump the national banking system together with the other economic acts of the Civil War or mention it as a means of selling more war bonds. In the end, the national banking system was all these things, but none fully captures Chase's original ambition in pushing for the law. In Chase's mind, the problems he was solving with this policy dated back to the founding of the Union. While internal improvements, post offices, and telegraph wires provided the sinews of economic union before the Civil War, banks were the lifeblood and circulation of the system. Hundreds of state-chartered banks gave fluidity to exchange by offering loans and paper currency. The variety of banks and general lack of oversight created confusion, panics, and generally made commerce across the Union more difficult for over fifty years. For that same period, the clash between various political parties over how to use government to harness the power of debt, banking, and money defined two generations of American politics.[3]

Chase and his allies imagined and justified the National Banking Act of 1863 as an innovative policy that would slice through these old debates and issues. At the heart of his idea, Chase imagined national banking as a means to build a meaningful partnership between classes, regions, and peoples. National banking would avoid the errors of the past by making not one but hundreds of banks rooted in their localities and communities. Moreover, national banking would evade the failures of the Jacksonians by using federal power to reassure and ensure the value of paper money held by farmers and wageworkers rather than withdrawing that power from the commercial sphere. Lastly, Chase imagined a consensual and mutually beneficial plan of banking that would simultaneously enrich the banker, the worker, and save the Union, all while providing a reasonable rate of interest for all parties.

Rather than bypassing old divisions in American thought, Chase's notion of a mutually profitable union of federal banks reawakened old fears of centralization and compulsion. Civil War Democrats and Republicans celebrated the fact that within the Union power over banks rested closer to home, in their states. Bankers and merchants sneered at the idea that the government offered fair terms for bringing their assets under federal supervision. All critics of national banking feared that such a policy was an opening wedge to greater federal oversight and centralization of the economy as a whole. Indeed, in many ways, the critics won the first battle over this economic reconstruction of the Union. When the law passed in 1863, it was a resounding failure, with only a small number of banks opening under the law. It was only when Americans did not buy into Chase's vision and plan that he and other Republicans turned to hard forms of compulsion and state power to bind the country's finances together definitively at the end of the war. Just a few years after Appomattox, almost every commercial bank in the country was a national bank subject to supervision by a collection of new federal regulatory agencies. If this was a "Yankee Leviathan," it was the unintentional result of the clash between Chase's imagination and the realities of nineteenth-century federalism and capitalism.[4]

To understand better the significance of Chase's project, we must place the story of Civil War–era national banking in conversation with the much longer history of debates and controversies over money and banking in American history before the war. Antebellum Americans believed that financial policy, specifically as it pertained to the country's rowdy banking system, could prove disastrous to the Union as a whole. The Civil War resurrected and reanimated old debates and policy problems in American governance that had lain dormant since the rise of the slavery issue in the West. Moreover, Chase was trying to structure his banks in a way that would avoid falling into the economic, political, and social errors of the past.

On the eve of the Civil War, the financial system of the country presented a confusing series of complications for anyone who wanted to buy, sell, or travel within the American Union. Northern boosters and politicians played up the seemingly endless bounty of the free-labor North, connected by and crisscrossed with the trains, canals, and telegraph lines of the communications and transportation revolutions. Paying for anything within the United States before the Civil War, however, required a thorough knowledge of the dizzying array of banknotes, counterfeit notes, gold coin, silver coin, and, on occasion, gold dust that Americans used to lubricate the wheels of trade.[5]

Standing at the heart of this system were banks—more than a thousand of them dotting the landscape across almost every state in the Union. While these banks lent money and held deposits, in many respects these institutions did not operate like their twentieth- or twenty-first-century counterparts. Their core business was lending slips of paper, promissory notes or banknotes, which acted as the principal currency of the United States in the years between the War of 1812 and 1861. The United States, like many other of the sovereign powers of the nineteenth-century world, declared that gold and silver was the legal dollar of the American Union. With a gold coin minted and stamped by the US government, a person could pay their taxes, settle all manner of debts, and find that merchants, innkeepers, and even trading partners across the Atlantic would be happy to take their money. However, for a variety of reasons, the United States suffered from a chronic shortage of specie for much of the nineteenth century. Gold strikes in California, Colorado, and Montana might have made gold more prevalent in the West, but for Americans who lived east of the Mississippi River, an American gold eagle or double eagle coin was a rare sight.[6]

Sometime after the writing and ratification of the Constitution, bankers on the eastern seaboard hit upon a means of overcoming this problem and multiplying the power of the limited hoard of American treasure. A group of merchants or capitalists would pool their wealth to form a bank. The bank would then keep gold on reserve and make loans and payouts of paper notes that promised to pay out the amount pledged at the cashier's window of their bank. In almost every case, these banks of issue, as they were known, issued banknotes in excess of the gold they held in their vault. Banks could get away with this based on the assumption that on any given day the number of people who would show up to claim their gold would not exhaust the reserve. In the midst of a dynamic and expanding marketplace, state legislatures embraced this financial model and authorized the creation of hundreds of different banks of various sizes and locations because they promised cheap credit to feed a hungry market. There was no single way to craft a bank or banking system in antebellum America, and the various states experimented with all manner of organizations, restrictions, and regulations.[7]

Many things went wrong with these banks. The worst-case scenario involved news or rumors of a poorly managed bank that could drive the public to redeem all their notes within a short period. A run on a bank could turn into a financial panic that would spread like an infection across the banking system, attacking seemingly healthy banks, as happened in the Panic of 1837.[8]

Since so much of the value and worth of these banknotes depended on information about the bank that issued it, people in a position to leverage that intelligence did so, often to the detriment of others in the economy. A typical example of this arose when a person with a banknote from their local bank tried to use it in a distant locality or another state. In many cases, a traveler would be forced to exchange their banknotes for the notes current in that part of the country at a discount rate that depended on the bank's distance and creditworthiness. Factory owners could and did play this game to their advantage by using the more valuable notes of a reputable bank to buy a pile of cheap notes from a distant bank. When payday came to the factory, the owner would distribute these to his employees. This situation had the advantage of saving the owner on his overhead expenses while leaving his workers with a wad of bills of dubious value. The notes also could be counterfeits. A bustling underground economy of counterfeiters supplied the country with spurious notes that could be excellent facsimiles of a sound bank's notes or the notes of a bank that did not even exist.[9]

People from all walks of life hated this system. Their anger at the long-term costs, periodic panics, and power of the banks fueled a generation of activism and policy across the country. At its core, the problem of banks and money boiled down to an issue of trust and self-interest. Everyday Americans craved a reliable system of paper money that they could trust without any specialized knowledge. On the other hand, banks that issued too many notes or counterfeiters were all merely working toward turning a profit in the rough-and-tumble capitalism of the early to mid–nineteenth century. Distrust and caution spread into almost every transaction using these financial instruments and permeated and attenuated the bonds between banks, citizens, and the various regions of the Union.[10]

The origins of the problem could be found in the first federal effort to build the young republic's financial network. The country's first finance minister, Alexander Hamilton, set to work to create a system that would bind the country more tightly together. One way he would do that was with debt. His shrewd but controversial suggestion involved the US government's assuming all the state debts. This act, he argued, would bind peoples and states to the new federal government. The second involved a bank. Banks, it should be noted, were a strange and rare bird at this moment in American history. In 1790, when Hamilton wrote his report on the bank, there were only three, including the Bank of North America chartered by the Continental Congress and the Bank of New York, which Hamilton had a part in creating. Hamilton's proposed new Bank of the United States would be a giant compared to these other institutions. More importantly, it would help link the country together through a common form of paper money. His bank could unite the far-flung locations with a common currency, which would make business easier and aid in the collection of taxes. Banks in general, in Hamilton's words, would serve as a "nurseries of national wealth." Nor was Hamilton alone in this line of thought. When Robert Morris suggested the plan for the Bank of North America, he explained to John Jay that it would "unite the several States more closely together in one general money connexion . . . by the strong principle of self-love and the immediate sense of private interest."[11]

Hamilton's bank turned out to be only the first of many. After a well-publicized debate over the merits of a national bank, Congress authorized the First Bank of the United States (BUS) in 1791. At that same moment, bankers up and down the East Coast began creating smaller banks built on the model of the BUS. These new banks, chartered by the several states, also issued banknotes, just like the BUS. Unlike the BUS, they lacked the lucrative partnership with the federal government that kept BUS banknotes at a steady value everywhere in the Union. These new state banks grew exponentially. In 1800, with Thomas Jefferson's "Revolution" over the Federalists, there were twenty-four banks in the country. Within a decade, the number passed a hundred, and by the eve of the Civil War, more than 1,300 banks dotted the country. The rise of the state banks took almost everyone by surprise. In the years between 1791 and 1811, the First BUS had to adapt and take on a regulatory role in the economy through indirect and direct pressures on its smaller cousins. In 1815, Thomas Willing, president of the First BUS, called his institution the "great regulating wheel of all the Commercial Banks in the United States." In 1812, Jefferson and his allies killed the First BUS, leaving the country's financial network in the hands of the state banks.[12]

To an entire generation of Americans, these hundreds of banks issuing millions of notes represented a terrible problem that they feared could weaken or destroy the Union. The first crisis came right after the fall of the First BUS, during the War of 1812. The war put heavy financial and fiscal pressure on the United States, which then lacked a national bank. In some cases, the US government resorted to using the banknotes of local banks to pay their soldiers. Then disaster struck. In 1814, the banks of the country suspended specie payments, meaning that every person who held a banknote now held a worthless piece of paper— leaving the country with no currency. From Monticello, Jefferson had lived long enough to see the one bank he hated and destroyed replaced with a hundred. Nevertheless, Jefferson, the state's rights advocate, understood well the depth of the problem.[13]

States made the banks. Jefferson, as well as almost all judges and politicians, agreed that the states retained the rights to make corporations of all sorts, including for banking. In later years, the Supreme Court would give their sanction to the idea that while states could not directly make money, there was nothing in the Constitution to prevent them from chartering these banks. The only solution, it appeared to Jefferson, was to ask the states to give up the power via a constitutional amendment. On this point, Jefferson did not hold any hope. The self-interest of the states and the bankers would defeat any measure to bring order to the country. He wrote to John Adams that "the Mania is too strong. It has seised by its delusions & corruptions all the members of our governments, general, special, and individual."[14]

The politics and economics of the next thirty years revolved around how to best use federal power to balance growth, self-interest, and federalism in America's financial system. In the wake of the War of 1812, Madison embraced an idea he had bitterly fought to suppress earlier in his career—the creation of another Bank of the United States. The Second BUS would, like its predecessor, act as the beating heart of the nation's circulating currency by regulating the flow and volume of notes in the economy. The Second BUS's work overseeing the system became even more critical as the number of state banks expanded with the boundaries of the developing nation, jumping from low hundreds to more than three hundred when Andrew Jackson took the presidency in 1829. The Second BUS's president, Nicholas Biddle, a writer and diplomat before leading the biggest corporation in America, understood well the power of the bank to keep the country's economy humming. Conversely, it was this vast power of the bank that disturbed some in Washington. In 1832, when asked by a Senate committee if the BUS had ever oppressed the state banks, Biddle said no but indicated that it possessed the power to destroy or save any bank it wished. Biddle's answer sent a shiver down the spines of an alliance of state's rights advocates, including Andrew Jackson, who feared that the BUS held too much power over the finances of the Union.[15]

The coalition that formed around Andrew Jackson in the 1830s feared the power of the BUS and all banks. When Jackson took office in 1828, it was hard to imagine the country without some central institution that could coordinate the needs of the federal government, state governments, and citizens in the market. More to the point, the bank was popular. In the capital-poor West as well as in the East, merchants and entrepreneurs regarded the BUS as a necessary tool for growth.

Despite its popularity, when the BUS came up for an early renewal of its charter in 1832, Jackson surprised everyone and began a retreat of federal power from the financial world. His veto message laid out a dark picture of an organization controlled by wealthy elites granted unnatural powers by their association with the federal government. Jackson went so far as to say that foreign investors controlled the bank and could drain the country's gold reserves or deny the state its resources in a time of war. Here Jackson could see very little that could check or curb the self-interest of the banks. "It is easy to conceive that great evils to our country and its institutions might flow from such a concentration of power in the hands of a few men irresponsible to the people." More than that, the Second BUS enjoyed a special relationship and powers over state banks that formed "a bond of union among the banking establishments of the nation, erecting them into an interest separate from that of the people." Jackson envisioned two separate commercial spheres, one for the wealthy elites that associated with the bank and another for the "merchant, mechanic, and other private citizen." In what he said was an effort to restore equality to the law and the Union, Jackson killed the Second BUS in a protracted political battle that ended in 1836.[16]

Jackson took away the BUS and, in its place, offered a vision of a paperless world. With the Second BUS gone, the country was right back to where it was in the War of 1812, except now there were hundreds more banks issuing even more variations of currency, under varying values. The problems of paper money and the Union seemed to be getting worse, not better, under Jackson's leadership. Jackson and his advisors eventually planned out and executed a radical plan to replace every state banknote in the pockets of Americans with the jingle of gold coins—what they called the "constitutional currency" of the country. By outlawing and suppressing paper money, the Jacksonians thought government would promote a reliably stable form of currency that would unite the country.

Jackson and the Democratic Party passed a slate of measures to achieve this. The most important, proposed by Jackson and carried out by Martin Van Buren and James K. Polk, established a new rule in which the United States would no longer put its money in any bank nor take or pay out a single paper note. Jacksonians hailed this as a "divorce of bank and state." If the bank, telegraph, and steamship were the symbols of modernity in the mid–nineteenth century, critics in Jackson's day and since decried this move as a step backward. The government would keep its gold in a system of institutions called the Independent Treasury and only accept or pay out coin in the course of its business.[17]

In the midst of these swirling debates, a disaster struck the country that underlined the fears about a financial and commercial Union held together by a system of exploding banks. The Panic of 1837 and the long depression that followed ravaged the economy and left deep scars on the politics and institutions of the country. Soon after the panic hit, Congress met in special session to consider what, if anything, the federal government could do to stop the crisis. On the floor of the Senate, Thomas Hart Benton was desperate to put a stop to the power of the banks when he cried, "Are men, with pens sticking behind their ears, to be allowed to put an end to this republic." At the grassroots of the Democratic organization, voters and the press rallied around the idea of a divorce that would restore order. At a Democratic meeting on Bunker Hill held on the Fourth of July, the organizers promised to oppose "all union of the Government with Banks, State or National." Well before the Panic, the New York *Evening Post* went so far as to instruct its readers that they should write on banknotes "NO MONOPOLIES!" "NO UNION OF BANKS AND STATE!" "HARD MONEY BEFORE RAGS!" "JACKSON AND GOLD!" to make their feelings known to the banks and the public at large.[18]

The rising anti-Jackson party, the Whigs, laid the blame for every woe coming out of the panic on the president and the Democrats. Caleb Cushing, then a young Whig from Massachusetts, tried to push his colleagues to look at the problem from outside the American context. He invoked the image of a "traveller in Europe" who could expect to exchange their coins or paper money as they entered different countries. The problem was that Americans had to do the same exact thing, but America pretended to be "union of States." If every state could create money, what was to prevent them from creating their own passports and devolving into separate countries? This, he proclaimed, is "simply the old question, Union or not?" The Whigs offered the promise of a third BUS as the solution to the chaos. A new BUS would be beneficial in every respect, restraining the smaller banks of the states, providing a paper-medium good in any corner of the country, and at its highest level fostering the conditions that could raise the American economy to a new level of prosperity. To the founders and leaders of the Whigs, for example Senator Henry Clay, the proposition that you could unwind the country's financial system was preposterous. "We are all" Clay explained, "people—States—Union—banks, bound up and interwoven together, united in fortune and destiny, and all, all entitled to the protecting care of a parental Government."[19]

After a series of lost elections and missed opportunities, most Whigs gave up on the push for a third BUS. In turn, the federal government did very little to keep the American commercial Union glued together. Merchants in one part of the country were obliged to buy special credit instruments, bills of exchange, to trade with partners in another part of the country. A person traveling crosscountry would have to exchange their banknotes in the same way people did going from country to country. Jackson's dream of a paperless world never came to fruition. Gold and silver might have been the legal money of the United States, but as the New York Board of Trade pointed out in 1837, the "states represented 27 sovereignties with an indefinite power to make currency." The Board of Trade accurately summed up the status quo in America—the banks could not "control each other," and "the state governments cannot control them."[20]

The Civil War provided an unexpected opportunity to rethink not only the banking system but also the bonds of commercial Union forged in the 1780s. Almost no one, however, was thinking about banks during the election of 1860 or when the Southern slave states began to secede from the Union to form the Confederate States of America. Indeed, the California gold rush and the rising prosperity of the 1850s, temporarily interrupted by the Panic of 1857, calmed fears about banks just as the fears and anger about the future of slavery began their rise. The Democratic platform of 1860, which had contained a plank dealing with banking every four years for the last three decades, said nothing on the topic.[21]

Nevertheless, the war provided an unexpected season for a full slate of legislative measures for the young Republican Party. With the departure of so many Southern members of Congress and the Senate, Northern and Western Republicans found that they could pass long-hoped-for measures, like free homesteads in the West, federal lands to support agricultural colleges, tariffs, and federal support for the creation of a transcontinental railroad that would physically bind the Union along its east-west axis. War necessity proved a powerful catalyst for change. President Abraham Lincoln's Emancipation Proclamation is the single most powerful example of this trend, but it also showed itself in other areas. The federal government took possession of the nation's railroad system and created state-owned facilities to sew uniforms, bake hardtack, and supply horses to the army. Americans paid their first income taxes during the Civil War, as well as financially supporting their government directly through a program of direct bond sales to the public. To this list of innovations, Lincoln's secretary of the treasury, Salmon Portland Chase, wanted to add a new banking system.[22]

Nothing in Salmon P. Chase's career before 1861 gave any indication that he would become the architect and advocate of a continent-spanning national banking system. To the contrary, Chase had made a national name for himself as an antislavery lawyer and politician. The politics and business of banking only sporadically entered into his life, and the moments when it did give little indication of his future efforts. Chase, as far as anyone knew, had no secret ambitions to be the Alexander Hamilton of the nineteenth century. Moreover, his political upbringing would have seemed to push him away from creating a new national banking system. While the antislavery cause was Chase's chief concern before 1861, he was an avowed Democrat in his views on the economy. Moreover, in the few statements he did make on financial measures before 1861, Chase only showed his hostility to banks and banking. As governor of Ohio during the Panic of 1857, he went so far as to suggest a state-level independent treasury system on the model of the federal system championed by Democrats. Lincoln chose Chase for the Treasury as a means to appease former Democrats and balance the competing factions within the Republican Party.[23]

It is difficult to imagine a worse time to suggest a complete reworking of the nation's financial structure than the winter of 1861–1862, yet that is precisely what Chase did. Starting in August and again in October 1861, he negotiated fifty-million-dollar installments of a loan of 150 million dollars from the banks of New York, Philadelphia, and Boston. Tensions emerged early on between Chase and the bankers over the terms of the loan—the interest rate as well as Chase's insistence to accept payment from the banks only in gold. Then, sometime in November 1861, as Chase negotiated a third fifty-million-dollar loan from the banks, he advised the bankers of his plans to create a system of federally chartered and regulated banks across the country. George S. Coe, president of the American Exchange Bank in New York City and a critical member of the interbank committee that was negotiating the government loans, wrote Chase that after hearing the idea he was convinced of its "impolicy" and called it a "bomb shell." Coe thought it would prove impossible to attract capital and iron out the details of an entirely new system at the same moment he was negotiating with the bankers of the old state system to fund a massive civil war. Coe disliked the proposal on its merits as well. He delicately suggested to Chase that trying to fix the country's financial problems by making more banks, even if they had the sanction of the federal government, could prove destructive.[24]

Chase ignored Coe's advice and unveiled his idea to the country in his first full report to Congress on the nation's finances in December 1861. Chase went about proposing his plan in an unusual manner. Rather than couch his ideas about currency and banking in the context of war necessity, he opened with an attack on the constitutionality of a system, or "lack of system," of thirty-four states regulating 1,600 banks that provided the people of the country with a currency that was prone to "great fluctuations, and heavy losses." A recent rash of bank failures in the Midwest served as proof of this. He instructed Congress that now was the time to use its latent power to regulate the financial system. It was a peculiar introduction to the issue because reading the sections of Chase's plan dealing with currency made it sound as if there was no war going on at all.[25]

Chase offered two avenues of reform in his message. The first would require the government to print and support a currency that could replace the state notes.

While having the benefit of being simple and straightforward in its outlines and execution, Chase warned that the "inconveniences and hazards" were too great for him to consider or recommend this option. Frankly, Chase feared that "in times of great pressure and danger" the government would issue too many notes, leading right back to the problems of an unstable system. In a worst-case scenario, Chase fretted that the government would substitute the depreciated paper of the Union for the depreciated paper of the state banks.[26]

Making it clear that Congress should ignore the first option, he led them toward his second, and preferred, means of achieving financial freedom from the state banks and their notes. The core of Chase's plan was to link banks, people, and the government into one coherent and safe financial framework. The connections among these three would be the same bond Hamilton proposed in 1791—debt. The government would sell bonds to "associations," a term for corporations that Chase lifted from the New York free banking law of 1838. In return for this consideration, these associations would be allowed to issue a new government currency as well as collect the interest on the bonds. In Chase's description, everyone gained something from the bond of debt: the government a new and guaranteed market for its bonds; the banks interest on their investment as well as the value of some sort of federal backing; and the people a stable, safe, and uniform currency—good at every point of the Union. Lastly, the sum of those parts, the Union, would become stronger and safer "springing from the common interest in its preservation, created by the distribution of its stocks to associations throughout the country, as the basis of their circulation." Chase expressed confidence that his plan would make the "the safest currency which this country has ever enjoyed." As Hamiltonian as the plan sounded, in Chase's vision this proposal had the benefit of achieving stability "without risking the perils of a great money monopoly." In other words, whatever this system would become, it would not be another Bank of the United States.[27]

Chase offered Congress and the country a triumphant vision of a Union bonded by banks. He promised Congress could achieve a "great transition" from hundreds of different currencies to a single currency by means that would make it seem "almost imperceptibly accomplished." Some newspapers quickly celebrated this vision. From the far West, an editor at the San Francisco *Bulletin* lauded how the country could achieve the dream of a true national currency "unawares." The *Bulletin* took up the theme of unification and touted how under Chase's policy every coin and note would knit the country together while serving as a "pledge of the existence of the solvency of the Union." In the Midwest, a region plagued by unstable state banking systems, the *St. Louis Democrat* took up

Chase's Jacksonian themes and approved of the move away from a large national bank that would promote corruption and monopoly power. The paper explained that Chase's policies "may be aptly termed the democratic or diffusion system, the central idea being a unity of interests in the expansion and uniformity of results from centre to extremes." From this perspective, each region would capitalize and create banks that were bonded nationally while remaining rooted in their local communities.[28]

The utopian vision Chase nurtured quickly fell apart in the face of the financial facts of such an extensive plan. Chase's message offered the slimmest outlines of the structure of the new banking and currency system. Chase had stayed silent on several critical points, perhaps to placate potential critics. For example, how would he treat existing banks that owed their powers and existence to the states? Would the government charter new "associations," or would existing banks be allowed to issue notes as well? Chase left these details and more to the Ways and Means Committee to work out. Writing from the financial hub of the country, the New York papers found Chase's aspirations well meaning but unrealistic. Both the *New York Times* and the *New York Herald* thought that a policy like this would take years to achieve. Personal letters from allies to Chase echoed this same objection.[29]

At the end of December, actions of the New York banks would destroy any hope of passing a bill in 1862. In New York, a majority of the associated banks of the major cities dropped their own bombshell on Chase when they decided to suspend all specie payments at a meeting on December 28, 1861. Just like in the War of 1812, almost every bank in the Union would now refuse to honor their notes. For Chase, this meant that the major banks of the country would cease loaning money to the government and that the government would have to stop paying out gold. At the December meeting, James Gallatin, the son of Thomas Jefferson's secretary of the treasury, Albert Gallatin, put some blame for the decision on Chase's proposed banking system. Gallatin and his colleagues only heard about the plan by "rumors from the street." Gallatin claimed he had confronted Chase and explained that there was not enough money in the country to absorb the existing loans plus millions in new loans to form the foundations of the new federal banks. Gallatin thought so low of the banking plan that he told his colleagues that Chase must not understand "the nature of financial affairs" or that he was "controlled" by advocates of issuing massive amounts of paper money. In this conspiratorial view, suspension by the major banks was an act of security and safety to protect the country's gold from a dangerous and unpredictable finance minister.[30]

The effect of the bank suspension was to kill the national banking plan and force the government down the road of issuing paper money directly. In January 1862, Congress began drafting and debating a bill that would authorize the Treasury to issue 150 million dollars in notes. In a way, this bill was worse than the nightmare Chase had dreamed up in his annual message. Because the banks and the federal government could not pay out specie, Congress made their new notes a legal tender for all debts public and private—effectively declaring coin and paper to have the same legal value. Congress passed the Legal Tender Act on February 25, 1862. The notes, called "greenbacks" by the public for their unique color, made their way into the channels of Union commerce and provided many Americans with a new link to their national government. Chase reluctantly supported the greenbacks and kept his distaste for the policy mostly to himself and his inner circle. It was only when a group of well-placed Republicans began to worry about the economic destruction created by the greenbacks that the national banking idea received a second airing.[31]

The prospect of financing the war for another year brought a host of challenges for the federal government. General George B. McClellan's failure in the Peninsula Campaign between April and early July, along with Lincoln's call for three hundred thousand new troops later in the summer, signaled that it would be a more protracted and more expensive war than anyone had guessed in 1862. From the perspective of the Treasury, Chase could not keep up with the cost of the war after raising more than 114 million dollars through loans, along with the 300 million in greenbacks authorized by Congress. By November 1862, Chase could not meet the demands and requisitions on the Treasury, with over 48 million dollars in unpaid warrants. As Congress prepared to pass new funding measures to sustain the next year of fighting, Chase began to press his national banking "scheme" as the only possible means of salvation.[32]

On Capitol Hill, Republicans chafed at Chase's banking plan. Several members of the critical Ways and Means Committee in the House, including its chair, Thaddeus Stevens, remained opposed to Chase's complicated and obtuse measure. The committee proposed to inject 300 million dollars in greenbacks into the economy, doubling the amount already in circulation. This proposal, Chase believed, would compound another financial problem that was quickly growing out of control—inflation. As the greenbacks made their way into the economy, the torrent of new cash would start to push up the prices of the most basic staples in the economy, as well as people's rent, not to mention the supplies needed by the Union army. In late 1862, inflation was starting to become a creeping concern for farmers, city dwellers, and the government alike. The best measure at the time of inflation was the price of greenbacks in gold. In December, when Chase gave his message, 100 dollars of greenbacks was worth around 75 dollars in gold coin, a reduction in value of 25 percent. When the news of the 300 million in greenbacks made it to Wall Street, the price of the paper notes dropped again on January 8, 1863. Moreover, bankers, members of Congress, and Chase were aware that banks were taking greenbacks, holding them, and using them to issue millions more in their state notes. In other words, every dollar the government printed might give birth to more state bank notes. From Chase's perspective in the Treasury, doubling the number of greenbacks in America could lead to a deluge of paper that would swamp the Union.[33]

In his second annual message, Chase described the national banking proposal as "a firm anchorage" for the entire financial system of the Union. Greenbacks depended on the command and promise of the nation for their value. In a war for the survival of the Union, some took the promise and command printed on the greenbacks as a symbol of their patriotism and commitment to victory. Americans of every walk of life also feared that the government would print too many notes or fail to redeem them for gold at the end of the fighting. Merchants and capitalists would buy and trade gold, bonds, or stocks out of fear that their greenbacks would not hold their value. Chase's new national banking plan and the notes it would provide would harness that power of the market by turning it to their advantage. He would do this not by forcing Americans to use greenbacks or a single national bank but by giving all classes a fair value for their investment in his system.[34]

Chase thought every note issued by one of his banks would be linked to Union debt. While that debt was also a type of promise, it was a promise that paid interest in regular installments. Rather than raise the faint possibility that the government would one day redeem their greenbacks for gold, Chase told Congress in his annual message that "every individual . . . every merchant, every manufacturer, every farmer, every mechanic" could rest assured that the money in their hands had both the backing of the country's debt as well as the firm regulation of the government. Chase, perhaps realizing the awkwardness of a former Democrat espousing Hamiltonian notions, confessed that he did not indulge in the "phantasy" that "debt is a benefit." Rather "it is the duty of public men to extract good for evil whenever possible." The war, he pointed out, had created an ocean of debt. He only wanted to manage and redirect that debt in a way that could link every citizen in the Union and guarantee a safe and productive financial future.[35]

When pressure grew for Congress to act quickly to solve the Union's money problem in early 1863, the House and Senate passed a joint resolution authorizing another 100 million dollars in greenbacks on January 17. This measure bought time to craft a long-term solution, but the politics of the situation became more complicated when Lincoln sent a note to Congress with his approval of the joint resolution. Lincoln had already publicly endorsed Chase's national banking plan in his annual message the previous December. In his special message to Congress, written the same day Congress passed the joint resolution, Lincoln took the position that more greenbacks in conjunction with the problems of the old state bank system were driving inflation and "augmenting the cost of living to the injury of labor, and the cost of supplies to the injury of the whole country." Because there were "actual financial embarrassments of the Government and the greater embarrassments sure to come," Lincoln felt compelled to give his opinion that Congress should stop creating more greenbacks and consider the plan to supply a currency "by banking associations, organized under a general act of Congress, as suggested in my message at the beginning of the present session."[36]

Within a matter of weeks, the push to pass the bill gained momentum. Some prominent Republicans joined Chase and Lincoln in advocating for the bill. John Sherman, a Republican senator from Ohio, had already started 1863 with a fiery speech on the need to restrain the state banks. Sherman agreed to introduce a new national banking bill, drafted by Chase and his staff, on the floor of the Senate. Chase managed to get Horace Greeley to support the idea of the bill in the pages of one of the country's most widely read newspapers, the *New York Tribune*. To push wayward members of Congress who thought the plan foolish or poorly timed, Chase enlisted the help of Jay and Henry Cooke, Philadelphia bankers he had entrusted with the sale of US bonds to the public, who put all of their lobbying efforts into helping the bill make its way through the House and Senate. Behind all of this was Chase, who wrote and cajoled editors of newspapers, bankers, and members of Congress to build pressure for the bill in and outside of Congress.[37]

In the ensuing public discussion, several Republicans began to explore what it might mean to the country to reunify and rebuild the Union through a system of banks. One surprising source of support was that of Robert J. Walker. In February 1863, the month in which the bill began to pick up speed in the Senate, Walker published a widely read defense of Chase's banking system in the *Continental Monthly*. Walker was an unlikely proponent of a union of banks because, in his younger days, he had been the architect of the divorce of bank and state that Chase sought to resurrect. Walker, born in Pennsylvania and for a time a slaveholder and senator from the state of Mississippi, had served as secretary of the treasury under Polk and drafted the bill that became the Independent Treasury

System. Walker admitted to his readers that it was he who "made the divorce complete," but now he would "make the union complete, so far as proposed by the Secretary" and support a "reunion" of bank and state because within Chase's plan he could see a real means of bringing together the various regions of the nation and their people into an unbreakable and productive relationship.[38]

Sherman agreed that the national banking system could unite various classes of people on a common footing. Writing under the pen name "S" in the pages of the *New York Times*, he emphasized the theme of unification. Whereas the old BUS had settled authority on a single board of directors, the national banking plan would contain hundreds of boards, each rooted in their community, each based on the debt of the United States—the people's debt. It was by this means that Sherman could argue that the national banking bill would take labor, capital, government, and people and "for the first time" make them "inseparably united and consolidated." Only weeks after the "S" letters appeared in the *Times*, Sherman reiterated how this plan could finally "harmonize" the various classes and regions of the Union into a coherent whole and assist the Union in its time of need.[39]

The national banking bill as a war measure was also a prominent theme in the writings and speeches given by Sherman and Walker, complete with military references and metaphors. One way Chase tried to sell the national banking plan to Congress was by pointing out how it would create a captive market for selling US bonds. In the proposed bill, every bank that wanted to issue the new national currency notes would have to buy an equal value of US bonds to back those notes. Chase imagined that in the clamor to get the new notes, bankers would gladly buy more bonds at par value, thus providing the country with a currency more stable than the greenbacks and a needed injection of capital for the government of about 250 million dollars. Walker, who had managed the financing of the Mexican-American War, agreed with Chase on this point, adding that readers needed to remember that war was "much more a financial than a military question" and that Chase was the "generalissimo" in this regard. Sherman, in one of his "S" letters, was much more direct in the way that he described the role of the banks in the new bill. Each bank, he declared, would be a "powerful auxiliary for the overthrow of rebellion, and would feel constrained to lend its every exertion to that end."[40]

The defenders of Chase's plan seized on the lessons of secessionism as the reason for passing the bill. Reacting to and anticipating the state's rights reactions prompted by the idea of a national banking system, Walker and Chase equated bankers and legislators that clung to their state systems with the secessionists who started the war. Walker criticized the complaints of New Yorkers that a new national system would destroy the value of their bonds as "the State first, the Union afterward," which was only a breath away from the language of rebellion and "the echo of South Carolina treason." In the *Times*, Sherman called the idea that states had a right to control their banking systems "the accursed heresy of State Sovereignty." In his speech introducing the national banking plan in the Senate, Sherman took a more measured tone, actively appealing to the self-interest of the "moneyed men and holder of property" who would lose everything if the Union should fall. In closing his speech, he ended on a note that gave an imperial cast to the project of national banking. "The policy of this country ought to be to make everything national as far as possible; to nationalize our country, so that we shall love our country." A true national currency, declared Sherman, would foster "a broader and a more generous nationality."[41] Years later, Silas M. Stilwell, who claimed to having assisted Chase in actually drafting the national bank bill in the 1860s, reiterated his impression that Unionism helped drive the creation of the system. In his recollection, Chase and Congress were channeling the Unionist feelings of the 1860s into a plan of unification through a banking union. It was that "feeling," Stillwell said, that "thrilled through the free states" to "to bind up the States more strongly together, and break up at once and forever the arrogance of secession and independent State action."[42]

Walker offered one last benefit of the system: that it would be a useful tool of Reconstruction of the Union in the South. In a public letter, Walker told Sherman that he knew of several people in New Orleans ready to form national banks under the new law. This, he told Sherman, would represent "a most important step towards restoring the allegiance of Louisiana and the whole Southwest." He predicted banks would organize across the South wherever Union armies put a garrison. He rattled off the names of potential sites, including Memphis, Nashville, Alexandria, Norfolk, and Newbern. In Walker's imagination, national banks would march right behind Union forces and "operate as an immense reinforcement to our armies, in restoring the supremacy of the Union." Despite his glowing rhetoric, Walker did not explain how Southerners, in the midst of their own failing financial system, would find fresh capital to build the new banks.[43]

Chase, Sherman, and Walker made the proposed national banking system sound like it was an opportunity without costs. Their idea of Union increasingly meant standardization under the federal government's aegis. Creating one system of banking would better integrate and share the benefits of Union compared to the selfish interests of those who would favor the local over the national. Nevertheless, such a dramatic policy change produced skepticism and outright hostility among financial elites, Democrats, and even members of the Republican Party. To all these critics, Chase's system would quash existing state banks that the citizens of each state had tailored to their own unique needs. Union not only connected a state like Iowa to Vermont through a common bond and values but also allowed for and protected a variety of laws and institutions that sometimes made one state drastically different than its neighbor. Chase's vision of banking disregarded this variety for a level of federal control that was unheard of in their lifetimes.

One example of these critics was H. H. Van Dyck. Van Dyck held the post of superintendent of the Banking Department of the state of New York, a perch from which he could beam with pride while managing one of the very best banking systems in the country, not to mention the very center of finance in all of the Americas—New York City. New York's free banking system, passed in 1838, provided the model from which Chase borrowed in constructing his plan. In the wake of 1837, New York pioneered a policy of general incorporation of banks policed by state regulators and backed by state bonds. Chase admitted the intellectual debt, but Van Dyck was not flattered by the imitation. From Van Dyck's reading of the national banking bill, the federal government was coming to take away their state banks and transfer to Washington control over the financial system of New York.[44]

Van Dyck felt both indignation and fear over the idea of federal consolidation over the banks of the country. He pointed out that the only reason Chase and Congress were seriously entertaining this plan was because banks and state governments outside the state of New York had failed to make their banks safe and secure. New York banks were safe because their banknotes rested on the securities of New York State, whose value and credit was unmatched within the Union and "garnered up through long years by unfaltering payment of her obligations." It was not New York's duty to sacrifice its financial standing because of the negligence of other states. Van Dyck's fears grew when he began to contemplate what the federal government might do with this power. He spoke about how the federal government could "plant within the State" national banks "independent of control by its legislature." This notion of the central state within the economies of the several states prompted related concerns about the unique nature of each state's economy.[45]

This idea that the federal government could flatten the regional diversity and varying markets of the country with a single banking system struck some members of Congress as blind to the real conditions within their home states. Jacob Collamer, an old Whig and senator from Vermont, voiced this fear on the floor of the Senate when he accused the bill's supporters of not understanding the delicate place of a bank within its local community. Collamer could not understand how Congress, composed of representatives born in different communities and who did not understand the "the minute business relations of other distant sections," could create a bank that would meet the needs of every part of the country. In his native Vermont, banks provided important links between mechanics, farmers, and bankers, links built on local knowledge. "The connections of the banks enter into all the filaments of our business; it is the warp and woof of it." Collamer warned that if the government tried to "burst these connections," they would "carry distress up the sides of all our mountains, and to the homes of all our farmers . . . you destroy all our young mechanics."

Moreover, the idea that federal paper could be superior to that of every state was simply wrong. Both members of the Kentucky delegation in the Senate pointed out that the notes of their state banks traded at a 3 percent premium to government greenbacks. Garrett Davis, the Unionist senator from Kentucky, added that the government debt Chase proposed to build this system also traded at below its par value: "If that is not introducing at once the most extravagant and gigantic system of banking upon the most spurious principles, I have no idea what is. But everything now is gigantic."[46]

Lastly, Van Dyck did not trust yoking New York banks to national banks in far-flung spots of the country. He asked how the federal government could make a single banknote of equal value in every part of the country "regardless of distance." The *Chicago Tribune*'s special reporter to Washington, DC, a paper hostile to state banks and banknotes in the Midwest, attacked the idea of uniformity as well. The *Tribune* held that a national bank note from a bank on Wall Street would always trade higher than "a national bank note signed by the President and Cashier of a bank in Nebraska." Uniformity, explained the *Tribune*, was an illusion that only existed in the text of the bill.[47]

For many Democrats, Chase's scheme was a conspiracy to grab power from the states. In the pages of *The Old Guard*, Chase's proposal became the means by which the government would empower bankers and capital to the loss of the rest of the country. A Democratic satire of 1863, "The Lincoln Catechism of Abraham Africanus I," instructed readers that the task of the secretary of the Treasury under this bill would be to "destroy State banks, and fill the pockets of the people with irredeemable, United States shinplasters." Collamer, on the floor of the Senate, agreed with the Democratic diagnosis when he predicted that a national banking system directed by the Treasury would be worse than anything feared under the BUS. He speculated on how the proposed system would work to make

Chase president. This law will, he prophesied, would make "the Secretary of the Treasury a very dangerous person, or a very powerful person."[48]

Among all these groups, none was more wary and hesitant of Chase's scheme than the bankers of the country. In his speech introducing the national banking bill to the Senate in February 1863, Sherman said that many bankers initially opposed the idea but that most had a change of heart within a few months. An anonymous Philadelphian, who only called himself a "practical banker," agreed that the deal offered by Congress could provide several important policies for the banks of the country, as long as the terms were right. This banker cut through Chase's, Walker's, and Sherman's flowery rhetoric by arguing that Congress must create a system with "some prospect of profit for the banker," which he found "entirely overlooked in the preparation of bills now before the Congress." According to the author's calculations, the bill before Congress would yield a bank 1.5 percent profit on issuing banknotes. He suggested that Congress alter the bill to get that number up to 3 percent, which would make the national banking system on par with other state systems. Aside from this modification, the unnamed banker held that there was very little to pull existing banks into the national system. Banks who specialized in only taking deposits or investing would have no reason to apply for a federal charter. In a letter to the *New York Times*, one writer agreed that if the major incentive of the law was buying bonds, there was very little to stop the banks from doing that without Chase's system. E. N. Sill, president of the Summit County State Bank in Ohio, explained to Sherman, "it is as unreasonable as it is idyllic to expect of Moneyed Capitalists a greater than an average patriotism. And that they will volunteer or be compelled to withdraw their capital from tried and satisfactory investments." The message from the financial community seemed clear—patriotism alone would be a weak force at best.[49]

Back in Washington, Chase and Sherman pushed ahead despite these concerns. Although relatively long and complicated by the standards of the nineteenth century, the bill offering Chase's scheme became law in a matter of months. Although Chase had begun his drive to pass the bill in December, Sherman would not introduce it on the floor of the Senate until February 9, 1863. By sheer chance, Lincoln signed "An Act to provide a National Currency, secured by a Pledge of United States Stocks," popularly known as the "National Banking Act," on February 25, 1863, exactly one year after signing the greenbacks into law. The final version of the law contained some interesting amendments, including one specifying that banks with existing state charters would not have to convert to the new system and could apply to issue notes under the new law. The law contained other inducements to join the system, including a modification

Figure 7 One-dollar paper note issued by the First National Bank of Lebanon, Indiana, in 1872. Its design combines allusions to nation, state, and locality and assures users: "This Note Is Secured By Bonds Of The United States Deposited With The U.S. Treasr. At Washington."
Source: Wikimedia.

of the Independent Treasury that allowed member banks to hold government funds. Perhaps most important, and for all of Sherman and Walker's talk of wartime necessity, the law contained no tax or any other form of compulsion that would force an existing bank into the federal government's plan. In fact, the new notes of the system would try to negotiate federal and local identities by carrying both the name of the federal government and the name of the local bank on the same note.

Congress's speed in passing the National Banking Act did not make it any more popular in the Union. The law passed by the razor-thin margin of 23 to 21 in the Senate and 78 to 64 in the House. Bankers, especially those in large Northeast cities, exercised their power by not converting to the new system. At the end of 1864, there were only 467 national banks versus 1,089 state banks. Banks in the major Northeast cities did not need the right to issue a national currency, as they conducted their business by check, unlike banks in the interior of the country.

In this regard, the pseudonymous "Practical Banker" turned out to be correct—there was very little to attract the most powerful of the banks into Chase's new system.

The bankers of New York City could see immense value in a national system that reaffirmed and strengthened their position at the center of the country's financial system. The National Banking Act already had one provision that aroused the attention of New York's banking elite—the ability to hold government funds on account. However, that was not enough. The critical measure these bankers wanted was a new redemption system that would funnel the deposits and reserves of hundreds of banks around the country into New York City. Before the Civil War, banks that served agricultural communities often sent their excess reserves to a major city bank during the seasons when farmers would not need their cash. In the cities, especially New York, the country bank's "correspondent" bank could loan those funds at a higher interest rate to merchants and stockbrokers. While this practice was common, it was not a national imperative. To attract more conversions to the system, Congress passed the National Banking Act of 1864 in June of that year. Under the terms of the law, Congress lowered the reserve requirement of the national banks and created a new pyramid reserve system. According to the law, country banks could keep up to three-fifths of their reserves in one of eighteen named redemption cities. The redemption cities, in turn, could keep 25 percent of their reserves in New York, making it by law the center of the country's financial flows. The new law encouraged a rash of conversions, putting the national banks ahead of state banks for the first time in 1865, 1,294 to 349. The state banks would not die, however, and by the end of the war, the tripartite currency system of greenbacks, national banknotes, and state banknotes seemed like too much. The American union would have to move toward centralization or suffer under growing inflation.[50]

The mood in Washington around 1865 favored a future without the state banks. Comptroller of the Currency Hugh McCulloch thought that the state banks were "unfitted for a commercial nation as well as a Union of States." Sherman and others in Congress changed their rhetoric about the banking act, saying it was "intended to supersede the state banks. Both cannot exist together." Former opponents, such as Henry Laurens Dawes in the House, accepted the National banking plan as a necessary means "to cure an existing and acknowledged evil." After an extended debate in 1865, in which some senators darkly predicted "a centralization of power . . . strong enough to wield an empire," Congress approved a 10 percent tax on state notes that effectively drove any state bank of issue out of existence.[51]

The union of banks and state created by Chase and the Republicans not only attested to the Unionist impulse of the war but also helped contribute to the tone and tenor of the postwar Union in several ways. One important outcome was the early establishment of national banks and the rise of the manufacturing belt of the Midwest and Mid-Atlantic. Towns and counties that acquired a national bank in the early to late 1860s saw a rise of available funds that banks could loan to businesses to purchase such things as the steam engines that fed growth. The national banking system also contributed to industrialization in the Gilded Age by a more roundabout means. The pyramid reserve system of the National Banking Act of 1864 poured millions of dollars, belonging to depositors across the country, into New York City. By 1870, 24 percent of banking capital could be found in New York City, and 84 percent of that was in national banks. Once there, banks made loans to Wall Street operators and brokers who in turn bought the railroad stocks on Wall Street that financed the railroad corporations of the Gilded Age and, along with them, postbellum economic development.[52]

For all its successes, Chase's banking system failed to bring wealth and commerce to every part of the Union. The first, most significant barrier was the high entry requirements to establish a national bank. As it stood, a group of would-be bankers needed to raise the enormous sum of $50,000 to start a bank in a town with a population fewer than six thousand, $100,000 in cities of six thousand to fifty thousand people, and $200,000 in cities with more than fifty thousand people. This meant that outside the cities one national bank usually could exercise near-monopolistic power over the market in a given area. Also, there were limitations on the kinds of business the banks could conduct. The National Bank Act of 1864 included a critical limitation on mortgages; this essentially shut out the farmers of the Midwest from the system's benefits.[53]

The South and West suffered from imbalances in the system as well. The reformation of the South on the basis of a free-labor economy was a central tenet of Republican policy during Reconstruction. But while Republicans attempted to use the law to alter the political economy of the South, they did very little to link the South to the capital flows of the North. Immediately after the war, Northern capitalists established a few Southern national banks, especially in Virginia. After 1865, the South suffered alongside the West in being denied their designated share of national banks and circulation. In 1870, Alabama had two national banks in operation, with an operating capital of $400,000, compared to sixty-nine banks in Indiana, with $13.3 million, and New York with 292 banks and $113.5 million. To keep exchanges going, Southerners used railroad tickets, notes issued by merchants, general-store credit, and barter.[54]

Lastly, the lack of elasticity in the system created a penchant for panics. The Treasury, with a reserve of gold and greenbacks, could sometimes inject liquidity into the market during a crisis. Without a central bank, banks did not have a lender of last resort in an emergency or one that could act more nimbly than Congress. Structurally, the flow to and from New York City proved incapable of handling the seasonal demand for money during the planting and harvest seasons in the country's interior. Money would rush into the city, which would heat up the stock market and create credit bubbles, or rush out and create stringency in the market, fostering panics, as it did in 1873, 1893, and 1907. To make matters worse, a statutory reserve requirement for national banks prevented each bank from dipping below a certain point. On the farmer's side, the flow of cash was not always sufficient, and farmers took to the practice of keeping enough money on hand for the next year's crops in case their local national bank failed to make good on deposits.[55]

At the end of the nineteenth century, Chase's image of a consensual Union bounded by banks began to fade in the face of industrialization and class conflict. The antimonopoly movements of the late nineteenth century universally disparaged the national banking system as the primary means by which the federal government handed power over money and wealth in America to the bankers of the Northeast. The federal debt that each bank held as part of the system, which Chase thought would be a powerful bond, represented the unfair advantage of bankers to profit on the national debt. One anonymous antimonopolist wrote of the national banks: "Never before was so great a concentration of wealth organized on earth or conceived by mortal man."

The bankers were also unhappy with the system, especially in the 1890s, albeit for different reasons. By that time, financial elites around the country considered the structure of the national system ill-suited to meet the demands of corporate finance and industrial development. In other words, many Americans saw the national banking system as exacerbating the very sectional and class issues it had sought to avoid.[56]

Chase died in 1873 and thus did not see these problems come to maturity at the end of the century. In his last years, he took extraordinary pride in the creation of the national banking system. His speeches and letters held up this policy as something that improved the lives of everyday workers and merchants. The story of the origins and development of the system is a powerful reminder that the massive change in the relationship between the central state and the economy during the Civil War was not always the intention of the architects of wartime policy. In many ways, Chase's views of a consensual union of wage workers, farmers, merchants, and bankers bounded by banks recalled the ideals of an American past in which government, as one scholar put it, could help Americans through the "release of private energy and the increase of private options." But as many in the Republican Party began to learn as early as 1864, such success also would require a stronger state. The tax on state banknotes that forced conversion into the new system was but one example. The federal government also organized departments and hired employees to create, oversee, and police these new institutions. Changes in the nature of technology, society, and the economy, unknowable in the 1860s, would require new debates and ideas about the nature of Union at the turn of the century.

The story of the National Banking Act is ultimately one of irony. In trying to build consensus, Chase's banking system divided Americans in new ways. In trying to fashion financial uniformity, Chase's national banking system created new fissures and inequalities in American capitalism. It is also a story that reaffirms a more significant point about the idea of Union that can help us understand the connections between the antebellum, wartime, and postbellum years. By considering how notions of Union guided the countless decisions that Americans made during the Civil War, including the creation of the National Banking System, we can better appreciate how a generation's push to protect the Union promoted drastic change. Republicans like Salmon P. Chase discovered that in fighting a war for the preservation and perfection of the Union, they could not help but start a process that would forever change that Union.[57]

"To Transmit and Perpetuate the Fruits of This Victory"

Union Regimental Histories and the Great Rebellion in Immediate Retrospect

Peter C. Luebke

Union Civil War veterans wrote some fifty regimental histories in the years 1865 and 1866. These books made clear the camaraderie soldiers had created during their service in the war, tied their service in the field to their communities at home, and gave an explicit statement on what they thought the war had been about from the perspective of immediate retrospective. These works provide a discrete, valuable body of testimony written immediately after the war at a time when soldiers no longer wrote letters home. While individual regimental histories varied widely in the geographical theaters they represented, the kinds of regiments, and overall quality, the fifty published after the war but before the start of Reconstruction demonstrate a consensus that the Civil War had been a conflict to preserve the Union, though that necessitated destroying slavery. The views of soldiers at the conclusion of the war but before the struggles of Reconstruction demonstrate how many Northerners evaluated the war in the wake of the Confederate surrender. The views expressed in regimental histories undercut common notions of racial accommodation in 1865 and should be considered when discussing the development of Civil War memory.

Many have dismissed regimental histories. Typifying such a sentiment, James M. McPherson claimed they suffered "from a critical defect: they were written for publication." For McPherson, letters and diaries provided a better sense of what soldiers thought because they gave "the immediacy of experience" more "than anything soldiers wrote for publication then or later." The historian Aaron Sheehan-Dean dubbed regimental histories "simultaneously antiquarian and heroic" and thought that "the narrow focus and celebratory tone" rendered them poor sources through which to study how Civil War soldiers interpreted the war.[1]

Yet the same aspects that McPherson and Sheehan-Dean use to indict regimental histories—that authors kept a narrow focus and wrote them for publication—reveal their broader importance. While individual authors put their names on the title pages, they often engaged in a collaborative process, seeking input from other members of the regiment. They aimed to write books that would appeal to all the members of the regiment and their families and that could serve as a source for future historians. Because of these factors, a regimental history presented noncontroversial consensus opinions; these books sought to inform rather than argue.

A surprising number of regimental histories appeared immediately after the war; between 1865 and 1866 Union soldiers produced more than fifty regimental histories, ranging in length from fifty pages to several hundred.[2] This scale of output would be unrivaled; even at the height of Civil War commemoration in the 1880s, any given year saw the appearance, on average, of about ten volumes. The boom years of regimental histories in 1865 and 1866 suggest that the soldiers themselves found the works deeply important and that they wanted to tell their stories immediately after the war.[3] These works presented more than simply the views of individuals.

Veterans sought to write accurate and authoritative works both for themselves and their communities at home. During the Civil War, states organized companies, usually from the same general geographical area, into regiments. The historian Gerald J. Prokopowicz has argued that "the soldiers' loyalty centered on the smallest units to which they belonged . . . especially the regiment." He explained that "the regiment, more than any other unit, was a self-aware community, held together by bonds based on common geographic, social, cultural, or economic identities, strengthened by months of training and campaigning as a unit."[4] Prokopowicz might have also extended his claim to embrace the home communities from which these units hailed.[5]

The authors of regimental histories believed that their stories also encompassed those at home. With their narratives, they looked both toward posterity as well as those who had not shouldered a musket in the war. W. H. Chamberlin of the 81st Ohio Infantry Regiment told his readers that

> the design of producing this little work originated in the belief that such a record, in permanent form, would be acceptable to the living as a memento of their suffering and services in the War of the Rebellion, and that it might also serve as a slight tribute to the memory of those gallant and heroic members of our Regiment who have laid their lives upon the Country's altar.[6]

Henry Davidson, likewise, avowed

> no desire to gather laurels as an author. If the narrative is sufficiently readable to preserve fresh memories of each other in the bosoms of my comrades in arms,—memories of the struggles, hardships, and dangers to which they were exposed in defence of the glorious flag of our united country,—my feeble efforts will have been amply rewarded.[7]

While Chamberlin and Davidson told how regimental histories looked inward to the members of the regiment, other authors pointed out how their works served to tie regiments back to the communities from which they had come. William H. Rogers of the 189th New York Infantry Regiment "hoped that any member of the command will find each historical sentence a text from which he may entertain his children and grand-children with stories of his soldier-deeds and sufferings which may otherwise have fallen into oblivion."[8] James Clark of the 115th New York Infantry Regiment dedicated his volume "to the widows, children, fathers, mothers, brothers, sisters, friends, and surviving comrades of the brave men who left the pleasures and comforts of home, enlisted in the 115th Regiment, and have gone down to untimely graves while serving their country."[9] Joshua H. Horton and Solomon Teverbaugh, the writers of a history of the 11th Ohio Infantry Regiment, included "several pages of good paper, neatly ruled" at the back of their book. They did so because the "book [was] intended as a 'keepsake' in the families of the members of the regiment" and had the extra pages bound in "in order that a fuller record" of each member's service could be penned. They asked that "whenever possible, this should be done by the hand of him who was a soldier, thus preserving the record in the handwriting of the soldier himself. It will be but a few years at best until all who took part in putting down the late gigantic rebellion will have passed away."[10]

Although most regimental histories bore the names of individuals as authors, the works emerged as collaborations among soldiers. Rather than giving individual viewpoints, the works aspired to present a small-scale history of the war rooted in the authority of personal experiences.[11] But because the regiment extended beyond the observation and experiences of any individual, authors took steps in order to tell the collective story.

Often, recognizing the momentous events they were participating in, regimental historians began to compile material for their histories before the war ended. Colonel W. W. H. Davis, who penned the history of the 104th Pennsylvania Infantry Regiment, told his readers of how "when I reentered military ser-

"To Transmit and Perpetuate the Fruits of This Victory" 189

Figure 8 Regimental histories underscored the importance of Union and the liberties it conveyed to citizens, as did this *Harper's Weekly* illustration titled "The Great Uprising of the North—An Anniversary Picture—April 12, 1862." The artist, Charles Parsons, depicted men from the various states coming together to save the nation.
Source: *Harper's Weekly*, April 19, 1862, 228–49.

vice, in the fall of 1861, I became possessed of two hobbies; one, that of writing the history of my regiment, and the other, to have a monument erected to the memory of those who might fall in action, or die of wounds or disease."[12] Here, Davis linked both of his "hobbies" to the commemoration of the service of the regiment; one would mark its service in the written record of the nation, and the other would mark its service on the physical landscape.

Writers engaged in the same process as other historians; they gathered primary-source material, weighed it, and assembled it into a greater whole. Harris Beecher of the 114th New York Infantry Regiment used "extensive journals and memoranda kept by the author throughout his service" as well as "the journals and memoranda of others, which in the main have been corroborative of each other, or at least have enabled him to arrive at more correct results." Beecher also used the files of soldier correspondence that had been published in local newspapers over the course of the war.[13] Others, such as Henry Davidson of the 1st Ohio Light Artillery, used headquarters records and other official reports.[14] Similarly,

Lyman Pierce of the 2nd Iowa Cavalry Regiment explained that he consulted personal "notes taken upon the march, at the time the incidents recorded transpired" and compared them with notes "taken by others, and the *official* reports."[15] These soldiers all exhibited a dedication to relating accurate histories of their respective regiments, based on a broad range of primary sources.

In several instances, authors circulated their manuscripts in a kind of peer review, seeking to have other soldiers look over the materials, detect errors, and vet the work. John Kinnear of the 86th Illinois Infantry Regiment met with his colonel, Allen Fahnestock, in order to discuss his narrative. He also notified readers that "General [David] Magee, Major [J. F.] Thomas, Dr. [I. J.] Guth, Captain [S. L.] Zinser, and others at Peoria ... examined [the manuscript] before publication."[16] Pierce of the 2nd Iowa Cavalry noted that his volume had been inspected "by Gen. [Edward] Hatch ... and the field officers of the Second Iowa cavalry, all who have attested to its correctness; hence we claim for our book a degree of anthenticity [sic] which no historian, not a participant in the events he records, can attain."[17] W. W. H. Davis averred that his book "has been written without passion or prejudice, and with a sincere desire to do justice to all."[18] These authors, in seeking out other authorities and their approval, aimed to produce an accurate and factually correct account.

As with most other books and print media during the Civil War era, regimental histories circulated almost entirely on local networks.[19] A typical regimental history appeared in a limited, local print run, reflecting the expected audience. Evidence suggests that only several hundred copies, at most, existed for any given regimental history. Henry Davidson's history had a small edition of 250 copies, while Horton and Teverbaugh "printed but a limited number" of their volume, expecting it would be of "little interest to any but the members of and immediate friends of the regiment."[20] Chaplain Louis N. Beaudry of the 5th New York Cavalry Regiment took up a subscription for his history in camp and recorded in his diary "subscriptions for 388 books."[21]

Despite this primary focus on the parochial audience, soldiers also wrote with posterity in mind. They often sought to function as historians, writing an accurate account based in source materials that might serve the purposes of future historians. As Eileen Ka-May Cheng has perceptively pointed out, writers before the Civil War began to write what could be considered modern histories. She noted that antebellum historians such as George Bancroft and William Prescott "were responsible for developing the very ideals—impartiality and originality—that was used to marginalize them, as the 'scientific' historians at the turn of the century sought to demonstrate their own commitment to these ideals."[22] Soldiers read these popular historians, such as Bancroft, Prescott, and Francis Parkman, and sought to emulate them.[23]

Chaplain F. T. Brown, in his preface to George L. Wood's history of the 7th Ohio Infantry Regiment, demonstrated familiarity with nineteenth-century historians and tied their work to the importance of the regimental history. Even in 1865, Brown questioned the need for another book on the Civil War. He mentioned Merle d'Aubigne's history of the Reformation and observed that d'Aubigne had sought the advice of Guizot, who told him to "Give us facts, incidents, details." Brown thought that "the result was a history that, though it discusses doctrines and themes commonly held to be dry and uninteresting, has . . . all the charm of romance." Brown thought that the histories of Macaulay proved lively because of the "facts, incidents, details." Crucially, Civil War soldiers had to write their own books, so that future historians would have those facts, incidents, and details at hand. He averred that "to transmit and perpetuate the fruits of this victory we must have records of the war—many records, made from many different points of view, and of many kinds, great and small." Explicitly linking the regimental history at hand to large narratives by prominent historians, Brown observed that regimental histories would "be invaluable to the Bancroft, who fifty years hence, shall write the history of the war." Thus, Brown concluded that "there is a demand, therefore, for another book, for many other books, on the war."[24]

Northern veterans wrote their regimental histories in order to explain why they had fought the Civil War and what it had meant to them. The contents of regimental histories provide a snapshot of what Northern soldiers thought of the Civil War while memories were still fresh and before the struggles of Reconstruction had taken place. The corporate nature of the works, as well as the desire to write for posterity, meant that regimental histories gave the consensus view of the soldiers. Because Northern regimental histories appeared in such numbers immediately after the end of the war, they give a window into the immediate postwar period. Regimental historians saw the Civil War as a contest to preserve the Union against the machinations of a domestic aristocracy.[25] These views suggest that Northern soldiers, in 1865 and 1866, viewed the war as a success because the aristocracy had been wiped away. The testimony of regimental historians pointed toward this kind of consensus.

Regimental historians cast the contest for Union as a struggle between republicanism and aristocracy. Chaplain Moses Gage of the 12th Indiana Infantry Regiment thought that "the important lesson inculcated by a careful review of the conflict is the permanency of republican institutions and the self-preserving power of a free people." Gage saw that the war had ratified the destiny of the

United States; as he wrote, "the monarchs of Europe may no longer hope to see the republican form of government set aside as impracticable. The capacity of a representative democracy to resist and suppress insurrection and rebellion against the constituted authority of the people has been fully tested and triumphantly established."[26] He continued this parallel, remarking that while George Washington had been the father of the country, "so is Lincoln her Saviour."[27] Gage proceeded to list and detail the nefarious actions of "the foul conspiracy." The actions of secessionists "fired the masses with an unalterable determination to preserve national integrity."[28] Just as the American Revolution had resulted in Americans humbling an aristocracy and securing democracy for themselves, the Civil War had saved the American experiment.

Gage, like many other writers, saw the survival of the Union and republican democracy in global-historical as well as religious terms. The triumph of the Union "cast down the idolaters' Dagon before the ark of the covenant, in which were deposited the sacred rights of man."[29] With this allusion, Gage cast the South as the Philistines who had taken the Ark of the Covenant; in biblical passages, the image of Dagon falls down before the Ark. Subsequently, God visited afflictions upon the Philistines (1 Samuel 5:2–7). Thus, in Gage's telling, the victory of the Union demonstrated the righteousness of the North's devotion to the democracy and natural law, while the South's idol fell to pieces and led its worshippers to ruin. Gage also thought that war had been "for the maintenance of civil and religious liberty in our land, and for its extension throughout the world."[30] Union, fathered by George Washington, had lit the flame of democracy on the world stage. Democracy represented a God-given directive, like the Ark of the Covenant, which held the Ten Commandments. Southerners' leaders and their Northern allies worshipped a false idol, which led them to rise up against the Union and the sacred rights of man. For Gage and his readers, the Civil War had been a democratic uprising against aristocracy. In both of these examples, Gage emphasized a chain of continuity from the faith of the Hebrews to the democracy of the United States.

Slavery played a distinctly secondary role in Gage's analysis. In his discussion of the causes of the Civil War, he mentioned it only in connection with the assassination of Abraham Lincoln. Lincoln "had performed no miracles, but he had struck the chains of slavery from the necks of four millions of bondmen." In repayment of this, "he was upbraided by the blind devotees of the Baal of African slavery. He fell by the hand of one of those base idolators, at the very zenith of his fame."[31] For Gage, emancipation had arisen along the way to protect the Union.

Other authors provided narratives similar to Gage's; they pointed to emancipation as a wartime measure that supported the preservation of the Union. Writing of the end of slavery, Wales Wood pointed out that "it was claimed by some people, and there are probably those who still adhere to the opinion, that the war against secession was carried on by the Government from the beginning with the prominent idea on the part of the Administration of abolishing slavery."[32] Wood denied that this had been the case and pointed to the incremental series of orders that had led to emancipation. He stated that emancipation "was proclaimed only as a *war measure* to hurt traitors and kill rebellion."[33] He pointed out that "the policy of the Federal Administration was necessarily changed to more vigorous measures against the rebellion, and its handmaid, slavery, as demanded by the stern necessities of the times."[34] The Emancipation Proclamation "str[uck] a death blow at the head and front of the rebellion itself."[35]

Another author, J. A. Mowris, in his history of the 117th New York Infantry Regiment, tied the Civil War to the American Revolution. He wrote of how the soldiers looked upon the US Capitol and "regarded it as having been, both by the blood of our revolutionary fathers, and by the bond of the constitution, consecrated to the holy cause of human freedom." It had almost been destroyed by "the *horrid* plot of secession, which was itself, designed as the handmaid and champion of a galling social despotism."[36] Mowris, as with most authors, suggested that Southern leaders had exercised their despotism against other white people in the South.

As with Gage and Wood, Mowris identified slavery as a poison in America. He declared that "Slavery, like a deadly Upas, had been planted beside the tree of Liberty."[37] For Mowris, though, slavery became an ill because it enabled the creation of a domestic aristocracy bent on destroying the Union. Mowris placed the blame for the Civil War on the Southern aristocracy. He averred that "Political economy does not regard the rebellion as a freak of human nature, but the unavoidable effect of an obvious cause." He identified that cause as "the acknowledged and practical supremacy of the few, excited in them a growing desire to rule. . . . How clear, that if they could effect a separation, they, the aristocracy, could rule absolute."[38]

Other writers indicted Southern leaders. George L. Wood, of the 7th Ohio Infantry Regiment, blamed a Southern aristocracy for the war. He recounted that "there had existed in the minds of the Southern people a desire for an independent government, which would give the aristocracy a firmer footing. In other words, the Federal Government was too democratic."[39] A. W. M. Petty of the 3rd Missouri Cavalry Regiment indicted the institution of slavery not because it had deprived African Americans of liberty but because it had created "that insatiable and ungovernable spirit of aristocracy which has for so many years been so prominently manifested by the lords of southern soil."[40]

The idea that conspiratorial leaders had led the South into rebellion suffused regimental histories. Soldiers expressed vehement hatred of Confederate leaders. James Clark of the 115th New York Infantry Regiment wrote of how Union soldiers would mock captured Confederate generals; soldiers would "sing out . . . 'They're the chaps who keep up the war; if he was a private we'd have sympathy for him, but he is a leader.'"[41] Osceola Lewis of the 138th Pennsylvania Infantry Regiment refused to call General Robert E. Lee by name in his book, instead choosing to identify him as "the wicked idol of a deluded people."[42] Edwin Houghton informed his readers of Confederate general William Barksdale's humble grave: "Such is the reward of lawless ambition! A United States representative turned traitor to the country, whose laws he had sworn to uphold, and paying the penalty of treason by death at the hands of United States soldiers, buried in a blanket, with a pasteboard monument erected to his memory!"[43] Wales Wood called Confederate leaders "original and persistent traitors."[44]

Regimental histories by Union soldiers excoriated Confederate leaders, but these works evinced no such hostility toward the Confederate rank and file. Seeing them as deluded and misguided, they could forgive them. Samuel Hurst mournfully wrote of dead Confederate soldiers: "It was so sad . . . even though they were enemies; for we knew that many had persuaded themselves that they were dying in a noble cause . . . driven on by reckless and conscienceless leaders."[45] George Powers of the 38th Massachusetts Infantry Regiment wrote that "Perfect good feeling existed between the late belligerents."[46] Wales Wood noted that surrendered Confederates seemed

> perfectly satisfied with the result of the war, and claimed that they had never been in favor of it from the beginning. Many of these soldiers were honest in such assertions, and had been forced into the ranks by that reign of terror which the leading traitors had instituted and carried out to advance their base schemes and sustain their rotten Confederacy.[47]

The sympathy of regimental historians for the average Confederate soldier extended to the white Southern agricultural class as a whole. Soldiers wrote of what they perceived as the degraded conditions of Southern whites and laid the blame for this state of affairs on Southern leaders. Samuel Hurst of the 73rd Ohio Infantry Regiment wrote of "abundant 'white trash.' . . . They were such wretched, sallow, squalid, ragged and unclean starvelings as only a land of 'chivalry' could produce."[48] James Mowris, in a similar vein, remarked that "a practical Democracy engenders no distinct class of 'poor white trash' groveling in hopeless ignorance over beyond the impassable gulf of social caste."[49] John Kinnear found white Southerners "sluggish, indolent, and careless in their habits and works" and acidly judged a farmer as "a poor ignorant being, who like a parrot, can talk and palaver with simple unmeaningness."[50]

Union regimental historians also blamed what they saw as Southern ignorance for the generally poor agricultural conditions in the South. Louis Beaudry avowed that he was "particularly impressed with the vastness of the forests" in Virginia. It differed "from the impressions we had formed of Virginia when reading of its early settlement, and its agricultural advantages." Thus it came as a surprise to him that instead of cultivation he found so much productive land unused below the trees. He argued that "the system of labor" created "this backwardness in agricultural pursuits." Beaudry, of course, meant that the masses of Southern whites remained ignorant and indolent; he reasoned that if the Southern people could "realize the true dignity of labor," then "the almost interminable forests disappear, and in their places the industrious yeoman will behold his rich fields of waving grain." The yeoman, in turn, would call forth the "factory and the mill, whose fabrics bring wealth and prosperity to the nation."[51] Warren Cudworth, of the 1st Massachusetts Infantry Regiment, found the environs of Virginia's Middle Peninsula "remarkable alike for its beauty and fertility, and in [the] proper hands might be a paradise." But he thought that "a new race was evidently needed to save the land from sinking into a wilderness."[52] All of these examples demonstrated that many Union soldiers saw the aristocracy as leading to ignorance in several areas of Southern life. The baleful effects of this misrule had undermined politics, the economy, and the nation. Because the ruling class had been humbled—through the end of slavery—Northern historians believed that the South could rejoin the Union and prosper. The impediments to progress had been wiped away.

In contrast, although Northern regimental historians expressed consensus on what they thought had led to poor conditions in the South, they expressed a range of opinions about the enslaved African Americans whom they encountered. Soldiers sometimes expressed sympathy, but they never fully integrated slavery and emancipation into their narratives. Authors tended to regard African Americans as yet another interesting characteristic of the South. That African Americans appear in regimental histories yet never in a central role suggests that regimental histories did not see their freedom as the primary goal of the Civil

War. This neglect of African Americans by writers, coupled with the view that the war had been fought to preserve republicanism against a native aristocracy, undermines notions that the end of the Civil War presented a moment for racial accommodation.

While regimental histories generally agreed that a slaveholding plutocracy had engineered the war, there was much less consistency among the narratives regarding the enslaved African Americans themselves. On one extreme lay Chaplain Warren Cudworth's *History of the First Regiment Massachusetts Infantry*. As might be expected of a chaplain from Boston, Cudworth took a remarkably tolerant and understanding view of African American culture. He noted that the enslaved individuals "greeted our coming among them with almost unconcealed delight, and were of the greatest possible service." He enthusiastically welcomed the "Proclamation of Emancipation" because he thought its "influence in deciding the doom of the Rebellion . . . potent and irresistible. It was better than many victories gained by gunpowder and battalions; being a declaration for justice and righteousness."[53] Another chaplain, Moses Gage, admonished: "Let none say that the bondmen do not love their liberty, when such cheerfulness is manifested in the midst of trials attendant upon the pursuit of that object."[54] The chaplain of the 6th Massachusetts Infantry Regiment, John Hanson, wrote of "the long files of dusky pilgrims [who] came in . . . dragging the household penates," much as Aeneas rescued the household gods from Troy in order to found Rome. Though these escaped enslaved presented a ragged appearance, Hanson "found them intelligent as, and every way the equals, and in ability to take care of themselves the superiors of, the white people left in our neighborhood."[55] Hanson also "was very much interested in the fact that [black] worshippers would pray with great fervor for our soldiers. One eloquent petition referred to them as dashing through the 'roar of the cannon, the smoke of battle, and the flash of the rifle' and supplicated the Divine protection for them, in terms that would have done honor to any prayer." In another instance, Hanson preached alongside a black minister. He recalled: "With an audience of white and black, of ministers and laity, and of many denominations, we, a Universalist and Methodist preacher, administered the communion. It seemed a foregleam of the millennium, as we all worshipped together; for, though speaking many sectarian dialects, we were united in one spirit."[56]

Though regimental historians who served as chaplains most often exhibited this tolerance, others expressed sympathy for the plight of the slaves as well. Lyman Pierce of the 2nd Iowa Cavalry exclaimed,

What a comment upon the institution of slavery, that it crushes even *poor whites*, with whom it comes in contact, until every spark of manhood becomes extinct. Who, after such a sight, will brand the black race unfit for freedom, and assign as a reason for the course the fact that they lack the snap usually seen in the free Anglo-Saxon of the North? Can we expect the negro to withstand the direct influence of an institution, the indirect contact of which has so degraded our race?[57]

Major George Wood, of the 7th Ohio Infantry Regiment, from the abolitionist hotbed of the Western Reserve, wrote the most understanding account of slavery. Wood felt "confident that the slaves of the South, were just as well informed with regard to their relation to their masters, as we were." Wood continued, "it is well enough to talk of the deep devotion of slaves to their masters; but the latter have found ere this, I trust, that this devotion of which they have relied, has not prevented them from cutting their throats, when it was in the line of their duty, and by means of which they could gain their freedom." Wood also wrote of how enslaved African Americans "obtain[ed] scraps of newspapers and parts of books, and thus gain[ed] a great deal of information entirely unobserved." He greeted emancipation with joy:

What a glorious thought! thousands of oppressed fighting for the redemption from slavery of a race which has ever worn the chain. When it is remembered that by this strife questions are to be settled which have ever disturbed the harmony of this country, and not only that, but questions which, when settled, will release millions of our fellow-men and women from the power of the oppressor, ought we not to be thankful that we are permitted to make great sacrifices in so good a cause?[58]

On the other hand, some regimental historians expressed less empathy for the enslaved and typically viewed blacks as amusing distractions. Robert Eden recalled "darkies 'Hurrahing and Hallelujahing' around us, accompanying their expressions of delight with a grotesque exhibition of antics and grimaces, and '*Bressing* de Lord and the Yankees.'"[59] Stephen Fleharty found it strange that "the only class of people that seemed contented amid so much misery was the colored community." He disapproved of "one or two sleek, sable lasses who were accustomed to dance on the pavement with every manifestation of ecstatic delight" and lamented, "Poor creatures, they scarcely realized their own wretchedness."[60]

Harris Beecher thought "it will take many years of education, and the enlightening effects of freedom, to bring [blacks] up to the proper standard of intelligence." He recalled that "one of the chief sources of amusement, among the soldiers, was in visiting negro dances and prayer meetings. These last are the most singular and impressive sights imaginable, consisting of weird songs, incoherent shouts, mingled with violent contortion, wails and moans, quaint prayers and response." While initially amusing, Beecher complained that once the novelty wore off, "the night was made hideous by their dances and prayers meetings," which "disturb[ed] the sleep of the men."[61] W. W. H. Davis of the 104th Pennsylvania Infantry also viewed African American religious ceremonies unfavorably; they were "evidently a heathen ceremony handed down from their African ancestors, somewhat modified by their Christian training." Samuel Hurst found that "many were ignorant and degraded as brutes almost; but some were intelligent."[62]

Northern regimental historians expressed ambivalence regarding the future of enslaved African Americans. While on the whole they applauded emancipation as an important tool to save the Union, they spent little space speculating on what would occur in the future. Robert Eden of the 37th Wisconsin Infantry Regiment described a gathering of freed slaves: "Africa, of all shades, from the genuine sable 'mungo,' with skin like polished ebony, and showing between his extended gums a formidable array of ivory, to the graceful quadroon, hardly a shade darker, and very often a great deal handsomer than her late mistress . . . rejoicing in their new found freedom." He informed his readers, "what their future may be, we know not."[63] Samuel Merrill of the 1st Maine Cavalry Regiment fretted that "freedom you can give at once" but "the right to make contracts, the obligations of which are equally binding on both parties . . . you cannot so readily confer." He feared "the most dreadful of all wars, a war of the races."[64]

As all of these examples demonstrate, regimental historians saw the Civil War as a primarily struggle for the Union. They told their readers at home of the perfidy of the white Southern elites, the degraded state of common Southern whites, and the baleful influence of slavery. They stressed that the war had been fought for the preservation of the Union and that emancipation had been a necessary measure to achieve that end. Insofar as they saw emancipation as a humanitarian measure, they did so based on how the institution of slavery hurt whites in the South and the nation.

Thus, a consensus existed among Union soldiers at the end of the war. The war had been fought for the preservation of the Union, a bond soldiers saw as one of global-historical importance because it kept the light of republican democracy alive in the world. The war had been instigated by a homegrown aristocracy that worked its machinations to destroy democracy solely for its own aggrandizement. Soldiers thought that the institution of slavery had allowed these Southern elites to oppress other white men in the South, leading to degradation and ignorance, which in turn undermined independence and allowed the elite conspiracy to proceed unchallenged in the South. Union soldiers, therefore, broadly supported the end of slavery, on the grounds that attacking slavery served as the best way to sweep away the aristocracy. With aristocracy dethroned and slavery removed, the Union could continue to serve as a beacon of liberty and democracy.

The implications of these views extended far beyond the individual soldiers who penned regimental histories. As concrete evidence of a soldier's service, the regimental history provided a memento to his friends and family. The volumes tied the soldier's service at the front to the community from whence he had come. The narratives of the war contained in them, once shared with the home community, enshrined these ties in a narrative of shared sacrifice. The veteran also wrote with authority and codified the meanings of the Civil War for parochial audiences. These narratives, much like the nature of the Union itself, inscribed intensely parochial stories in a broader framework of shared sacrifice to save democracy.

The regimental histories of Union soldiers also call into question some of the findings of David Blight and others who have argued that over the course of Reconstruction and the second half of the nineteenth century white Northerners abandoned African Americans in the South. According to Blight, narratives of the Civil War as an emancipationist struggle fell out favor as time wore on; anodyne tales of shared sacrifice and generals arguing endlessly over the minutiae of individual battles supplanted any high-minded narrative of the Civil War. The authors of regimental histories, however, saw emancipation as a tool with which to destroy the aristocracy. They saw the war as the story of themselves and their communities, a story of soldiers who sprang to the defense of republicanism for the sake of the world. Freedom for enslaved African Americans arose as a tertiary outcome of the war, and soldiers supported it as a war measure rather than on explicitly humanitarian grounds. Regimental histories, when examined closely, therefore suggest that a reconciliationist narrative emerged in 1865 and 1866. Union soldiers had done their duty of humbling aristocracy and saving the Union. With treachery excoriated, the Union could continue on its proper trajectory. What that trajectory would entail, however, remained an open question.

Notes

Introduction

1. William T. Sherman, *Sherman's Civil War: Selected Correspondence of William T. Sherman, 1860–1865*, ed. Brooks D. Simpson and Jean V. Berlin (Chapel Hill: University of North Carolina Press, 1999), 708.

2. Edward Bates, *The Diary of Edward Bates, 1859–1866*, ed. Howard K. Beale (Washington, DC: Government Printing Office, 1933), 413.

3. On the nineteenth-century importance and meanings of Union, see Gary W. Gallagher, *The Union War* (Cambridge, MA: Harvard University Press, 2011).

4. Abraham Lincoln, *The Collected Works of Abraham Lincoln*, ed. Roy P. Basler (New Brunswick, NJ: Rutgers University Press, 1953–1955), 4:264–65; Frederick Douglass, "Our Work Is Not Done," speech delivered at the annual meeting of the American Anti-Slavery Society, held at Philadelphia, December 3–4, 1863, http://rbscp.lib.rochester.edu/4403.

5. Edwards, as quoted in Gallagher, *Union War*, 107. On the meanings of disunion, see Elizabeth R. Varon, *Disunion! The Coming of the American Civil War, 1789–1859* (Chapel Hill: University of North Carolina Press, 2008).

6. On these debates, see William B. Kurtz, *Excommunicated from the Union: How the Civil War Created a Separate Catholic America* (New York: Fordham University Press, 2015); J. Matthew Gallman, *Defining Duty in the Civil War: Personal Choice, Popular Culture, and the Union Home Front* (Chapel Hill: University of North Carolina Press, 2015); and Stephen Kantrowitz, *More Than Freedom: Fighting for Black Citizenship in a White Republic, 1829–1889* (New York: Penguin, 2012).

Waiting for the Perfect Moment

1. Wendell Phillips Garrison and Francis Jackson Garrison, *William Lloyd Garrison, 1805–1879: The Story of His Life* (Boston, MA: Houghton, Mifflin, and Company, 1885), 3:412. For more on Garrison, see Henry Mayer, *All on Fire: William Lloyd Garrison and the Abolition of Slavery* (New York: St. Martin's, 1998).

2. *Liberator*, July 12, 1861.

3. Studies in the first, inevitability school include Chandra Manning, *What This Cruel War Was Over: Soldiers, Slavery, and the Civil War* (New York: Knopf, 2007); James Oakes, *Freedom National: The Destruction of Slavery in the United States, 1861–1865* (New York: Norton, 2013); James Oakes, *The Scorpion's Sting: Antislavery and the Coming of the Civil War* (New York: Norton, 2014); and Adam Goodheart, *1861: The Civil War Awakening* (New York: Knopf, 2011). Studies in the second, contingency school include Gary W. Gallagher, *The Union War* (Cambridge, MA: Harvard University Press, 2012);

and Daniel W. Crofts, *Lincoln and the Politics of Slavery: The Other Thirteenth Amendment and the Struggle to Save the Union* (Chapel Hill: University of North Carolina Press, 2016).

4. *Liberator*, June 28, 1861, June 20, 1862. A number of recent studies of Lincoln have presented a balanced portrayal of the president, acknowledging that, while he personally detested slavery, he put his constitutional duty of preserving the Union at all costs first. Such studies include Richard Carwardine, *Lincoln: A Life of Purpose and Power* (Edinburgh: Pearson Education, 2003); Eric Foner, *The Fiery Trial: Abraham Lincoln and American Slavery* (New York: Norton, 2010); and Crofts, *Lincoln and the Politics of Slavery*.

5. *Liberator*, March 8, 1861; *Weekly Anglo-African*, September 28, 1861. For more on abolitionists and nationalism, see Rogan Kersh, *Dreams of a More Perfect Union* (Ithaca, NY: Cornell University Press, 2001); Melinda Lawson, *Patriot Fires: Forging a New American Nationalism in the Civil War North* (Lawrence: University of Kansas Press, 2002); W. Caleb McDaniel, *The Problem of Democracy in the Age of Slavery: Garrisonian Abolitionists and Transatlantic Reform* (Baton Rouge: Louisiana State University Press, 2013); and A. J. Aiseirithe and Donald Yacovone, eds., *Wendell Phillips: Social Justice and the Power of the Past* (Baton Rouge: Louisiana State University Press, 2016). For the definition of immediatist abolitionism, see James M. McPherson, *The Struggle for Equality: Abolitionists and the Negro in the Civil War and Reconstruction* (1964; Princeton, NJ: Princeton University Press, 2014), 3.

6. The only dedicated study of the Fosters is Dorothy Sterling, *Ahead of Her Time: Abby Kelley and the Politics of Antislavery* (New York: Norton, 1991). Other works that discuss the pair include McPherson, *The Struggle for Equality*; Margaret Hope Bacon, *I Speak for My Slave Sister: The Life of Abby Kelley Foster* (New York: T. Y. Crowell Co., 1974); Stacey Robertson, *Parker Pillsbury: Radical Abolitionist, Male Feminist* (Ithaca, NY: Cornell University Press, 2000); and A. J. Aiseirithe, "Piloting the Car of Human Freedom: Abolitionism, Woman Suffrage, and the Problem of Radical Reform, 1860–1870," PhD diss., University of Chicago, 2007. None of these works, however, discusses the Fosters with reference to their overarching moral nationalism.

7. Abby Kelley Foster to Alla Foster, October 1883, series 1, box 1, Kelley-Foster Papers, Worcester Historical Museum, Worcester, MA.

8. See Sterling, *Ahead of Her Time*, 214–27.

9. For the Fosters and nonresistance, see Sterling, *Ahead of Her Time*, 74.

10. For more on abolitionist doctrines and antebellum factions, see James Brewer Stewart, *Holy Warriors: The Abolitionists and American Slavery* (1976; New York: Hill and Wang, 1997).

11. *Liberator*, May 10, 1861; Henry Grew, "To the Friends of Righteousness," October 23, 1861, folder 1, Abolitionist Movement Collection, Special Collections Research Center, Swem Library, College of William and Mary, Williamsburg, VA.

12. Abby Kelley Foster to Sydney Howard Gay, April 19, 1850, box 13, Sydney Howard Gay Papers, Butler Rare Book and Manuscript Library, Columbia University, New York, NY (collection hereafter cited as SHG); Abby Kelley Foster to Wendell Phillips, June 26, 1859, item 556, Crawford Blagden Collection of Wendell Phillips Papers,

Houghton Library, Harvard University, Cambridge, MA (collection hereafter cited as HOU).

13. Abby Kelley Foster to Wendell Phillips, March 29, 185[6?], item 556, HOU; *Liberator*, February 4, 1859.

14. Abby Kelley Foster to Wendell Phillips, March 29 and October 185[6?], item 556, HOU.

15. *Liberator*, 6 June 1856.

16. Abby Kelley Foster to Wendell Phillips, March 29, 185[6?], item 556, HOU; Abby Kelley Foster to Stephen Symonds Foster, n.d. [1857?], box 2, Abby Kelley Foster Papers, American Antiquarian Society, Worcester, MA (collection hereafter cited as AAS); *Liberator*, February 4, 1859.

17. *Liberator*, February 4, 1859; Maria Weston Chapman to Sydney Howard Gay, n.d. [1858–1859], box 7, SHG; Maria Weston Chapman to Samuel May Jr., March 17, 185[7?], Ms.B.1.6 v.6, 53, Anti-Slavery Collection, Boston Public Library, Boston (collection hereafter cited as BPL); Maria Weston Chapman to Wendell Phillips, n.d. [1859?], item 394, HOU.

18. Abby Kelley Foster to Samuel May Jr., June 9, 1859, item 881, HOU; William Lloyd Garrison to Abby Kelley Foster, July 22, 1859, Ms.A.1.1 v.5, 96, BPL; Abby Kelley Foster to William Lloyd Garrison, July 22, 1859, item 10, Alma Lutz Collection, Schlesinger Library, Radcliffe Institute, Harvard University, Cambridge, MA.

19. William Lloyd Garrison to Abby Kelley Foster, July 25, 1859, Ms.A.1.1 v.5, 97, BPL; William Lloyd Garrison to Abby Kelley Foster, September 8, 1859, Ms.A.1.1 v.5, 98, BPL; Samuel May Jr. to Wendell Phillips, August 6, 1859, item 881, HOU.

20. Stephen Symonds Foster to Lysander Spooner, January 8, 1859, BPL; Stephen Symonds Foster to Wendell Phillips, n.d. [late 1850s], item 559, HOU. For more on Stephen's political exploits, see Jane Pease and William H. Pease, "Confrontation and Abolition in the 1850s," in *Abolitionism and American Reform*, ed. John R. McKivigan (New York: Garland, 1999), 293–307.

21. Samuel May Jr. to Richard Davis Webb, August 7, 1859, Ms.B.1.6 v.7, 58, BPL; Stephen Symonds Foster to Wendell Phillips, n.d. [late 1850s], item 559, HOU; Abby Kelley Foster to Wendell Phillips, July 21, 1857, item 556, HOU; *Liberator*, September 7, 28, 1860.

22. Abby Kelley Foster to Gerrit Smith, October 30, 1860, box 18, Gerrit Smith Papers, Special Collections Research Center, Syracuse University, Syracuse, NY; Abby Kelley Foster to Wendell Phillips, December 9, 1860, item 556, HOU. For a pro-Lincoln abolitionist's argument, see *Douglass' Monthly*, November 1860.

23. Abby Kelley Foster to Wendell Phillips, December 9, 1860, item 556, HOU.

24. *Liberator*, February 1, March 8, 1861. For contingency and compromise during the secession winter, see Robert J. Cook, William L. Barney, and Elizabeth R. Varon, *Secession Winter: When the Union Fell Apart* (Baltimore, MD: Johns Hopkins University Press, 2011); and Crofts, *Lincoln and the Politics of Slavery*. For disunion, see Stewart, *Holy Warriors*.

25. *Anti-Slavery Bugle*, November 17, 1860; *Worcester Spy*, February 11, 1861; Wendell Phillips, "Disunion," January 20, 1861, in *Speeches, Lectures, and Letters by Wendell Phillips*, ed. James Redpath (Boston: James Redpath, 1863), 370.

26. For the Fosters and disunionism, see Pease and Pease, "Confrontation and Abolition."

27. *Proceedings of the Yearly Meeting of Congregational Friends (Waterloo Meeting)* (Cortland, NY: Van Slyck and Ford's, 1861), 24; William Lloyd Garrison to Wendell Phillips, April 19, 1861, item 590, HOU; Wendell Phillips, "Under the Flag," April 21, 1861, in Redpath, *Speeches*, 396; *Liberator*, April 26, 1861. For the Northern rally to war, see Russell McClintock, *Lincoln and the Decision for War* (Chapel Hill: University of North Carolina Press, 2008).

28. *Liberator*, February 22, 1861, June 6, 1862; *Anti-Slavery Bugle*, April 27, 1861.

29. *Liberator*, June 7, 1861.

30. Parker Pillsbury to Wendell Phillips, May 1, 1861, item 1001, HOU.

31. *Anti-Slavery Bugle*, April 27, May 4, 1861; George Bassett, *A Discourse on the Wickedness and Folly of the Present War* (Ottawa, IL: n.p., 1861), 14.

32. *Liberator*, August 16, 1861; *Anti-Slavery Bugle*, May 4, 1861.

33. *Liberator*, May 24, August 16, 1861; Bassett, *Discourse*, 17.

34. *Liberator*, May 31, July 12, 1861.

35. *Liberator*, July 12, 1861.

36. William Lloyd Garrison Jr. to Abby Kelley Foster, August 7, 1861, box 2, AAS; Abby Kelley Foster to William Lloyd Garrison Jr., August 14, 1861, box 2, AAS.

37. Stephen Symonds Foster to Wendell Phillips, November 8, 1861, item 559, HOU.

38. *Liberator*, January 10, 1862.

39. *Liberator*, January 31, 1862. Manning, *Cruel War*, and Goodheart, *1861*, especially, argue that a popular mandate for emancipation existed.

40. *Liberator*, January 31, 1862.

41. Stephen Symonds Foster to George Thompson, March 16, 1862, box 2, AAS. For more on British abolitionists during the war, see Richard Blackett, *Divided Hearts: Britain and the American Civil War* (Baton Rouge: Louisiana State University Press, 2001).

42. *Liberator*, May 16, June 6, 1862.

43. *Liberator*, June 6, 1862.

44. *Liberator*, June 5, 1863. For more on Douglass and the Union war, see David W. Blight, *Frederick Douglass' Civil War: Keeping Faith in Jubilee* (Baton Rouge: Louisiana State University Press, 1989).

45. *Liberator*, June 5, 1863.

46. *Liberator*, June 5, 1863; William Lloyd Garrison to James Miller McKim, November 14, 1863, Ms.A.1.1 v.6, 66, BPL.

47. Sarah Pugh to Elizabeth Gay, December 31, 1863, box 57, SHG; *Liberator*, January 8, 1864.

48. *Liberator*, January 15, 1864.

49. *Liberator*, January 15, 22, 1864.

50. *Liberator*, February 5, July 1, 1864.

51. "*Liberator*, February 5, 1864. For more on Lincoln and black rights, see Foner, *Fiery Trial*.

52. Stephen Symonds Foster to Wendell Phillips, February 1, 1864, item 559, HOU; Abby Kelley Foster to Wendell Phillips, February 1, 1864, item 556, HOU.

53. *Liberator*, May 20, June 3, 1864.
54. *New York Times*, May 6, 1864.
55. *Liberator*, July 8, 1864; *New York Times*, June 1, 1864; *New York Independent*, printed in the *Liberator*, July 1, 1864.
56. William Lloyd Garrison to Helen Garrison, April 7, 1865, Ms.A.1.1 v.6, 100, BPL; *Liberator*, January 27, February 3, 1865.
57. *Liberator*, May 26, June 2, 1865.
58. *Liberator*, June 2, July 8, 1865; Mary Estlin to Caroline Weston, February 23, 1865, Ms.A.9.2 v.32, 32, BPL; Oliver Johnson to Maria Weston Chapman, May 4, 1865, Ms.A.9.2 v.32, 37, BPL; Abby Kelley Foster to Gerrit Smith, January 13, 1869, box 18, Special Collections Research Center, Syracuse University, Syracuse, NY.

Elizabeth Keckly's Union War

1. For commentary on popular depictions of Elizabeth Keckly, see Kate Masur, "In Spielberg's 'Lincoln,' Passive Black Characters," *New York Times*, November 12, 2012; and John Williams, "A Strong Thread in a Torn Union," *New York Times*, January 9, 2013. Various versions of the spelling of Keckly's name appear in the literature (Keckley, Keckly). "Keckly" will be used throughout this essay, following the lead of the historian Jennifer Fleischner, who found a signature with this particular spelling.

2. Kate Masur, "Introduction," in *They Knew Lincoln* (New York: Oxford University Press, 2018), xxxvi.

3. Masur, "Introduction," xxxix.

4. Stephen Kantrowitz, *More Than Freedom: Fighting for Black Citizenship in a White Republic, 1829–1889* (New York: Penguin, 2012), 40.

5. Chris Myers Asch and George Derek Musgrove, *Chocolate City: A History of Race and Democracy in the Nation's Capital* (Chapel Hill: University of North Carolina Press, 2017), 116, 124. The Social, Civil, and Statistical Association (SCSA) was a civic organization composed of well-educated black men in Washington, DC.

6. Kate Masur, *An Example for All the Land: Emancipation and the Struggle over Equality in Washington, D.C.* (Chapel Hill: University of North Carolina Press, 2010), 7.

7. Jennifer Fleischner, *Mrs. Lincoln and Mrs. Keckly: The Remarkable Story of Friendship between First Lady and Former Slave* (New York: Broadway Books, 2003), focuses on the relationship between Keckly and Lincoln with alternating biographical elements in each chapter. Francis Smith Foster, in "Autobiography after Emancipation: The Example of Elizabeth Keckley," introduction to *Behind the Scenes: Formerly a Slave, but More Recently Modiste, and Friend to Mrs. Lincoln; or Thirty Years a Slave, and Four Years in the White House* (1868; Champaign: University of Illinois Press, 2002), explores the African American biography, offering insight into nineteenth-century reactions to the biography and the literary qualities of her memoir. Santamarina Xiomara, *Belabored Professions: Narratives of African American Working Womanhood* (Chapel Hill: University of Chapel Hill Press, 2005), examines the social meanings and the relational process behind Keckly's work as a dressmaker. Additional scholars included in this essay offer brief analyses that contribute to these three themes, but the strongest evidence comes from Keckly's memoir.

8. Elizabeth Keckley, *Behind the Scenes: or Thirty Years a Slave and Four Years in the White House* (1868; New York: Penguin, 2005), 4–5.
9. Keckley, *Behind the Scenes*, 14–15.
10. Keckley, *Behind the Scenes*, 3.
11. Keckley, *Behind the Scenes*, 16.
12. Keckley, *Behind the Scenes*, 16–17.
13. Darlene Clark Hine, "Rape and the Inner Lives of Black Women in the Middle West," *Signs* 14 (Summer 1989): 912.
14. Keckley, *Behind the Scenes*, 133.
15. Keckley, *Behind the Scenes*, 28.
16. Wilberforce University was founded in 1856 in Xenia, Ohio, as the nation's oldest private, historically black college. Keckly's son, George Keckly, would attend Wilberforce University before serving as a soldier in the Civil War, and Keckly would serve as an instructor at the university in 1892.
17. Keckley, *Behind the Scenes*, 29.
18. Keckley, *Behind the Scenes*, 31.
19. Keckley, *Behind the Scenes*, 31.
20. Treva B. Lindsey, *Colored No More: Reinventing Black Womanhood in Washington, D.C.* (Urbana: University of Illinois Press, 2017), 15.
21. Janaka B. Lewis, "Elizabeth Keckley and Freedom's Labor," *African American Review* 49 (Spring 2016): 14.
22. Keckley, *Behind the Scenes*, 33.
23. Martha S. Jones, *All Bound Up Together: The Woman Questions in African American Public Culture, 1830–1900* (Chapel Hill: University of North Carolina Press, 2007), 6; Elsa Barkley Brown, "Negotiating and Transforming the Public Sphere: African American Political Life in the Transition from Slavery to Freedom," *Public Culture* 7 (Fall 1994): 16.
24. Brown, "Negotiating and Transforming the Public Sphere," 125.
25. Evelyn Brooks Higginbotham, *Righteous Discontent: The Women's Movement in the Black Baptist Church, 1880–1920* (Cambridge, MA: Harvard University Press, 1993), 14.
26. Erica L. Ball, *To Live an Antislavery Life: Personal Politics and the Antebellum Middle Class* (Athens: University of Georgia Press, 2012), 132; Bettye Collier-Thomas, *Jesus, Jobs, and Justice: African American Women and Religion* (New York: Knopf, 2010), 44; Michele Mitchell, *Righteous Propagation: African Americans and the Politics of Racial Destiny* (Chapel Hill: University of North Carolina Press, 2004), 85.
27. Brittney C. Cooper, *Beyond Respectability: The Intellectual Thought of Race Women* (Urbana: University of Illinois Press, 2017); Lindsey, *Colored No More*, 17.
28. Masur, *An Example for All the Land*, 55.
29. Keckley, *Behind the Scenes*, 62.
30. Keckley, *Behind the Scenes*, 8.
31. Chandra Manning, *Troubled Refuge: Struggling for Freedom in the Civil War* (New York: Knopf, 2016), 32. For more on the term "contraband," see also Chandra Manning, "Working for Citizenship in Civil War Contraband Camps," *Journal of the Civil War Era*

4 (June 2014): 172–204; and Kate Masur, "'A Rare Phenomenon of Philological Vegetation': The Word 'Contraband' and the Meanings of Emancipation in the United States," *Journal of American History* 93 (March 2007): 1050–84.

32. "Societies in DC for the Benefit of Contraband," *Christian Recorder*, November 1, 1892.

33. Masur, *An Example for All the Land*, 87.

34. *Christian Recorder*, March 14, 1863.

35. *Christian Recorder*, March 14, 1863.

36. *Christian Recorder*, August 22, 1863.

37. *Christian Recorder*, August 22, 1863.

38. Frederick Douglass, "Men of Color, to Arms!" March 3, 1863, manuscript/mixed material, https://www.loc.gov/item/mfd.22005/.

39. Douglass, "Men of Color, to Arms!"

40. Douglass, "Men of Color, to Arms!"

41. Douglass, "Men of Color, to Arms!"

42. Keckley, *Behind the Scenes*, 47.

43. Frederick Douglass, "Emancipation, Racism, and the Work before Us: An Address Delivered in Philadelphia, Pennsylvania, on 4 December 1863," in *Frederick Douglass Papers*, series 1: *Speeches, Debates, and Interviews*, vol. 3: *1855–1863* (New Haven, CT: Yale University Press, 1979), 606–7.

44. *Christian Recorder*, August 22, 1863.

45. *Christian Recorder*, August 22, 1863.

46. Kantrowitz, *More Than Freedom*, 349.

47. Kantrowitz, *More Than Freedom*, 349; *Evening Star* (Washington, DC), September 8, 1862.

48. Margaret Leech, *Reveille in Washington, 1860–1865* (New York: Harper & Brothers,1941), 253; *Evening Star*, August 5, 1864.

49. "Outrages on the Colored People," *National Republican*, July 3, 1862.

50. "Arrival of Contrabands," *National Republican* (Washington, DC), June 4, 1863.

51. Joint Resolution by the Washington, DC, City Council, April 1862, 37A-J4, Senate Committee on the District of Columbia, Petitions & Memorials, ser. 547, 37th Congress, US Senate, Record Group 46, National Archives, K. Richards signed as president of the Board of Common Council, W. T. Dove as president of the Board of Aldermen. Mayor Richard Wallach endorsed the resolution "Approved." The resolution was presented on the floor of the US Senate on April 2, 1862.

52. Joint Resolution by the Washington, DC, City Council, April 1862.

53. An Act of April 16, 1862 [For the Release of Certain Persons Held to Service or Labor in the District of Columbia], Record Group 11, National Archives; US Congress, *Congressional Globe*, 39th Congress, 1st Session, 1507–8; "An Inquest," *Daily National Republican* (Washington, DC), March 12, 1863.

54. Susan Zaeske, *Signatures of Citizenship: Petitioning, Antislavery, and Women's Political Identity* (Chapel Hill: University of North Carolina Press, 2003), 42–43.

55. Rosalyn Terborg-Penn, *African American Women in the Struggle for the Vote, 1850–1920* (Bloomington: Indiana University Press, 1998), 87–94, 162; John Francis

Cook et al. to the Honorable Senators and Members of the House of Representatives in Congress Assembled [December 1865], 39A-H4, Committee on the District of Columbia, Petitions & Memorials, ser. 582, 39th Congress, US Senate, Record Group 46, National Archives. Approximately 2,500 names appear on the petition, each apparently in the handwriting of the signer.

56. "Societies in Washington, DC, for the Benefit of the Contraband," *Christian Recorder*, November 1, 1862; *Christian Recorder*, August 29, 1863; Keckley, *Behind the Scenes*, 113–14; Harriet Jacobs, *Incidents in the Life of a Slave Girl* (Boston: published by the author, 1861); Jean Fagan Yellin, *Harriet Jacobs: A Life* (New York: Basic Books, 2004), 162.

57. Keckley, *Behind the Scenes*, 63.

58. Keckley, *Behind the Scenes*, 63.

59. Yellin, *Harriet Jacobs*, 184.

60. "Louisa Managed to Finish 'Jacob's School,'" Harriet Jacobs, Alexandria, January 13, 1865," *Freedmen's Record*, March 1865, 41.

61. Cook et al. to the Honorable Senators and Members of the House of Representatives in Congress Assembled.

62. Cook et al. to the Honorable Senators and Members of the House of Representatives in Congress Assembled.

63. Constance Green, *Secret City: A History of Race Relations in the Nation's Capital* (Princeton, NJ: Princeton University Press, 1967), 95, 101–3.

64. *Evening Star*, January 17, 1861; *Washington Chronicle*, June, 28, 1868; Kenneth Alfers, *Law and Order in the Capital City: A History of the Washington Police, 1800–1886* (Washington, DC: George Washington University Press, 1976), 22.

65. Robert Harrison, *Washington during Civil War and Reconstruction: Race and Radicalism* (New York: Cambridge University Press, 2011), 41–43.

66. Frederick Douglass, "The Mission of the War: An Address Delivered in New York, New York, on 13 January 1864," in *Frederick Douglass Papers*, 4:24.

67. Henry Highland Garnet, "Let the Monster Perish," in *A Memorial Discourse Delivered in the Hall of the House of Representatives, Washington, D.C. on Sabbath, February 12, 1865, with an Introduction by James McCune Smith* (Philadelphia: Joseph M. Wilson, 1865), 69–91.

68. Kantrowitz, *More Than Freedom*, 273, 280–81.

69. Asch and Musgrove, *Chocolate City*, 115–16.

To Save the Union "in Behalf of Conservative Men"

1. Allen C. Guelzo, *Lincoln's Emancipation Proclamation: The End of Slavery in America* (New York: Simon & Schuster, 2006), 187–90; George Templeton Strong, quoted in William D. Mallam, "Lincoln and the Conservatives," *Journal of Southern History* 28, no. 1 (February 1962): 42. Few historians have considered the elections as a deliberate endorsement of the Democratic Party. Edward K. Spann has written that "the November elections were basically a referendum on the Lincoln administration, emancipation, and freedom for black Americans." James McPherson has echoed Lincoln's claim that absentee soldier ballots explain the result, questioning the many historians who see the results

as a repudiation of the Emancipation Proclamation. Eric Foner and Philip Paludan both view the elections as primarily a referendum on emancipation. Paludan argued that the results hinged on war fatigue and frustration at the lack of military progress, concluding that "Democrats had won because Republicans stayed home." William Blair has recently highlighted the reality and importance of political arrests, but like all of these studies, he frames this in terms of reasons to vote *against* Republicans rather than *for* a larger Democratic vision. Edward K. Spann, *Gotham at War: New York City, 1860–1865* (Wilmington, DE: Rowman & Littlefield, 2002), 90; James McPherson, *Battle Cry of Freedom: The Civil War Era* (New York: Oxford University Press, 1988), 561–62; Eric Foner, *The Fiery Trial: Abraham Lincoln and American Slavery* (New York: Norton, 2010), 234; William A. Blair, *With Malice Toward Some: Treason and Loyalty in the Civil War Era* (Chapel Hill: University of North Carolina Press, 2014), 166–75; Philip Shaw Paludan, *A People's Contest: The Union and Civil War, 1861–1865* (Lawrence: University Press of Kansas, 1988), 98–102.

2. Jerome Mushkat, *The Reconstruction of the New York Democracy, 1861–1874* (Rutherford, NJ: Fairleigh Dickinson University Press, 1981), 9; Jean H. Baker, *Affairs of Party: The Political Culture of Northern Democrats in the Mid-Nineteenth Century* (New York: Fordham University Press, 1998); Joel H. Silbey, *A Respectable Minority: The Democratic Party in the Civil War Era, 1860–1868* (New York: Norton, 1977); Jennifer L. Weber, *Copperheads: The Rise and Fall of Lincoln's Opponents in the North* (New York: Oxford University Press, 2008); Michael Todd Landis, *Northern Men with Southern Loyalties: The Democratic Party and the Sectional Crisis* (Ithaca, NY: Cornell University Press, 2014); Robert Sandow, "Damnable Treason or Party Organs? Democratic Secret Societies in Pennsylvania," in *This Distracted and Anarchical People: New Answers for Old Questions about the Civil War–Era North*, ed. Andrew L. Slap and Michael Thomas Smith (New York: Fordham University Press, 2013), 42.

3. The claims made here are only extensively substantiated for New York, but the mix of priorities, beliefs, and policies articulated by Seymour applied and resonated well beyond the confines of the Empire State. For evidence of similar dynamics in other states as part of a larger examination of the role of conservative swing voters in the wartime North, see Jack Furniss, "States of the Union: The Rise and Fall of the Political Center in the Civil War North," PhD diss., University of Virginia, 2018.

4. Horatio Seymour, *Public Record: Including Speeches, Messages, Proclamations, Official Correspondence, and Other Public Utterances of Horatio Seymour*, ed. Thomas M. Cook and Thomas W. Knox (New York: I. W. England, 1868), 52, 74. This chapter touches only briefly on the knots that the Democratic Party tied themselves in during the last two years of the war. For the party's descent into factionalism, see Weber, *Copperheads*, 103–204; Frank L. Clement, *The Limits of Dissent: Clement Vallandigham and the Civil War* (Lexington: University Press of Kentucky, 1970); and William Frank Zornow, "McClellan and Seymour in the Chicago Convention of 1864," *Journal of the Illinois State Historical Society* 43, no. 4 (Winter 1950): 282–95.

5. Ethan Sepp Rafuse, *McClellan's War: The Failure of Moderation in the Struggle for Union* (Bloomington: Indiana University Press, 2005).

6. For an extended analysis of conservatives in the Civil War era, see Adam I. P. Smith, *The Stormy Present: Conservatism and the Problem of Slavery in Northern Politics, 1846–1865* (Chapel Hill: University of North Carolina Press, 2017). For an archetypal

conservative, see Matthew Mason, *Apostle of Union: A Political Biography of Edward Everett* (Chapel Hill: University of North Carolina Press, 2016).

7. William E. Gienapp, "Who Voted for Lincoln?" in *Abraham Lincoln and the American Political Tradition*, ed. John L. Thomas (Amherst: University of Massachusetts Press, 1986), 77; Chase, quoted in William C. Harris, "Conservative Unionists and the Presidential Election of 1864," *Civil War History* 38 (December 1992): 302.

8. Eric Foner, *Free Soil, Free Labor, Free Men: The Ideology of the Republican Party before the Civil War* (New York: Oxford University Press, 1970), 187. Former Democrats who had bolted the party in frustration at the controlling influence of Southern colleagues tended to be the most anti-Southern in their sentiments (149–85).

9. Sarah Bischoff Paulus, "America's Long Eulogy for Compromise: Henry Clay and American Politics, 1864–58," *Journal of the Civil War Era* 4 (March 2014): 41; R. J. Stevens to R. B. Connolly, January 20, 1863, box 7, Horatio Seymour Papers, SC7008, New York State Library, Albany, New York (collection hereafter cited as Seymour Papers, NYSL). For the heritage of compromise, rooted in Whig ideas about social harmony, see Peter B. Knupfer, *The Union as It Was: Constitutional Unionism and Sectional Compromise, 1787–1861* (Chapel Hill: University of North Carolina Press, 1991); and Daniel Walker Howe, *The Political Culture of the American Whigs* (Chicago: University of Chicago Press, 1979), 23–43. For early manifestations of Democratic-Whig common ground on questions of compromise, see Michael F. Holt, *The Rise and Fall of the American Whig Party: Jacksonian Politics and the Onset of the Civil War* (New York: Oxford University Press, 1999), 607–15.

10. John White Geary to Mary Church Henderson, October 24, 1864, quoted in John White Geary, *A Politician Goes to War: The Civil War Letters of John White Geary*, ed. William A. Blair (University Park: Pennsylvania State University Press, 1995), 211.

11. Richard F. Bensel, *The American Ballot Box in the Mid-Nineteenth Century* (New York: Cambridge University Press, 2004), ix; Baker, *Affairs of Party*, 322, 317. Bensel shares with others like Glen Altschuler and Stuart Blumin the belief that, crudely put, politics was conducted mostly by an uninformed populace and had more to do with entertainment than policy preference. Baker views the nineteenth-century electorate as educated and informed. Undoubtedly, there is an element of truth to both interpretations. The fact that voters were plied with alcohol does not preclude their having made informed and considered decisions. Glenn C. Altschuler and Stuart M. Blumin, *Rude Republic: Americans and Their Politics in the Nineteenth Century* (Princeton, NJ: Princeton University Press, 2000).

12. Adam I. P. Smith, *No Party Now: Politics in the Civil War North* (New York: Oxford University Press, 2006), 6; Mark E. Neely Jr., *The Union Divided: Party Conflict in the Civil War North* (Cambridge, MA: Harvard University Press, 2002); Michael Fitzgibbon Holt, "A Moving Target: President Lincoln Confronts a Two-Party System Still in the Making," paper delivered to the Annual Symposium of the Abraham Lincoln Association (February 2004), 2. A counterexample on wartime politics would be Joel Silbey's generally superb study of the Democratic Party, which hits a sour note when claiming that "by 1860 the electorate had become locked in" and "voting behavior became entirely predictable." Silbey, *A Respectable Minority*, 157.

13. George E. Marcus, Russell W. Neuman, and Michael Mackuen, *The Affect Effect: Dynamics of Emotion in Political Thinking and Behavior* (Chicago: University of Chicago Press, 2007).

14. For discussion of this era of Democratic politics and Seymour's positions within it, see James A. Frost, Harold C. Syrett, Harry J. Carman, and David M. Ellis, *A History of New York State*, rev. ed. (Ithaca, NY: Cornell University Press, 1967); Stewart Mitchell, *Horatio Seymour of New York* (Cambridge, MA: Harvard University Press, 1938); and DeAlva Stanwood Alexander, *A Political History of the State of New York* (New York: H. Holt & Co., 1906).

15. Yonatan Eyal, *The Young America Movement and the Transformation of the Democratic Party, 1828–61* (New York: Cambridge University Press, 2007), 186. Seymour embodies some elements of what Eyal sees as the "Young America" or "New Democrat" agenda. Eyal does not identify him as such, but he was aligned with figures such as August Belmont and Stephen Douglas and shared some of their vision for a future characterized by modern economic growth and national development, believing that such projects could lessen sectional tensions. For the Seymour-Barney relationship, see Seymour correspondence in the Hiram Barney Papers, Huntington Library, San Marino, California.

16. Mitchell, *Horatio Seymour*, 206–7; Seymour, *Public Record*, 18, 13–16, 23–31.

17. Russell McClintock, *Lincoln and the Decision for War: The Northern Response to Secession* (Chapel Hill: University of North Carolina Press, 2008), 30.

18. "Crittenden Resolution | Teaching American History," http://teachingamericanhistory.org/library/document/crittenden-resolution/.

19. Alexander, *A Political History of the State of New York*, 26; election returns in *The Tribune Almanac and Political Register, 1862* (New York: The Tribune Association, 1862), 57. Other states saw similar outcomes. In Ohio, the new Union Party ran David Tod, a Douglas Democrat, for governor on a platform endorsing the Crittenden Resolution. Ohioans elected Tod by a majority of 55,000 in 1861, increasing Lincoln's majority by 35,000 votes. "The formation of the Union Party had thus transferred the political control of the state from the radical element of the old Republican Party to a combination of the conservative elements of both old parties." George H. Porter, *Ohio Politics during the Civil War Period* (New York: Columbia University, Longmans, Green & Co, 1911), 100.

20. *New York Daily Tribune*, November 19, 1861; election analysis from *The Tribune Almanac, 1862*, 57–58.

21. Ernest A. McKay, *The Civil War and New York City* (Syracuse, NY: Syracuse University Press, 1990), 28; *New York Daily Tribune*, February 8, 1861; John A. Dix to Edwin Morgan, December 24, 1860, box 4, folder 10, Incoming Correspondence, Edwin D. Morgan Papers, Collection GK11818, Manuscripts and Special Collections, New York State Library (collection hereafter cited as Morgan Papers, NYSL); John Syrett, *The Civil War Confiscation Acts: Failing to Reconstruct the South* (New York: Fordham University Press, 2005), 12, 74; Alexander, *A Political History of the State of New York*, 37–39; Gideon Welles, *Diary of Gideon Welles: Secretary of the Navy under Lincoln and Johnson* (New York: Houghton Mifflin Company, 1911), 1:154; Smith, *No Party Now*, 60.

22. Seymour, *Public Record*, 231–33, 50. A search of newspaper databases and the secondary literature suggests this distinction between "the administration" and "the

government" had not been widely invoked before the war. During the war, Democrats consistently placed it at the heart of their political appeals.

23. Seymour, *Public Record*, 50, 41.

24. Seymour, *Public Record*, 73–74.

25. *Atlas & Argus* (Albany), October 16, 1862; *New York Herald*, October 20, 1862. This approach offers an interesting parallel to Adam I. P. Smith's exploration of the means by which Republicans used nonpartisan messages and methods to advance their partisan goals. The Democratic attempt to uphold Lincoln's constitutional authority and bemoan radicals who attacked him clearly exhibits the same pattern. This tactic was not limited to New York. It also served as the basis for the People's Party (an amalgam made up of Democrats and a minority of disgruntled Republican conservatives) campaign against Republican governor John A. Andrew in Massachusetts in 1862. Smith, *No Party Now*; Furniss, "States of the Union," chap. 3.

26. Seymour, *Public Record*, 58; Samuel Tilden, "A note prepared for Mr Seymour of the 'authoritative statement of the Democratic position,'" October, 1862, box 72, folder 15, series 10, Writings and Speeches, Samuel Tilden Papers, New York Public Library.

27. Seymour, *Public Record*, 42, 50. Significant historical debate surrounds the question of whether Civil War–era voters viewed party politics as a good or an evil for the virtue of society and whether it in fact was beneficial. For an overview of these debates, see Smith, *No Party Now*; Howe, *The Political Culture of the American Whigs*, 52; and Baker, *Affairs of Party*, 316. For the roots of Whig antipartyism, see also Holt, *The Rise and Fall*, 30–32.

28. Seymour, *Public Record*, 23, 31, 24, 101; Mitchell, *Horatio Seymour*, 228; Seymour, *Public Record*, 83; Alexander, *A Political History of the State of New York*, 16. For the long history of sectional compromise, see Knupfer, *The Union as It Is*.

29. August Belmont, *Letters, Speeches, and Addresses of August Belmont* (privately printed, 1890), 79–82.

30. Mark E. Neely Jr., *The Fate of Liberty: Abraham Lincoln and Civil Liberties* (New York: Oxford University Press, 1991), 200–9; Weber, *Copperheads*, 6; William A. Blair, *With Malice toward Some: Treason and Loyalty in the Civil War Era* (Chapel Hill: University of North Carolina Press, 2014), 10, 160–90.

31. Alexander, *A Political History of the State of New York*, 19; Allan Nevins, *The War for the Union: War Becomes Revolution, 1862–1863* (New York: Scribner, 1959), 310; Baker, *Affairs of Party*, 149; Seymour, *Public Record*, 34. In a recent review of scholarship on the Democratic Party, Thomas E. Rodgers has argued that "republicanism and republican virtue may also provide a framework for sorting out the divisions of the Democratic Party during the Civil War." Jean Baker did discuss this theme, in a chapter entitled "The Revival of Republicanism," but Rodgers is right that it has fallen out of many recent discussions. Thomas E. Rodgers, "Copperheads or a Respectable Minority: Current Approaches to the Study of Civil War–Era Democrats," *Indiana Magazine of History* 31 (June 2013): 130, 137; Baker, *Affairs of Party*, 143–76.

32. Silbey, *A Respectable Minority*, 25; Seymour, *Public Record*, 41, 51–52, 59, 72, 77–78, 84.

33. Mark Hubbard, ed., *Illinois's War: The Civil War in Documents* (Athens: Ohio University Press, 2013), 63; Seymour, *Public Record*, 34–35. For Douglas's attitudes in the

secession crisis, see Robert W. Johannsen, "The Douglas Democracy and the Crisis of Disunion," *Civil War History* 9, no. 3 (September, 1963): 229–47; and Martin H. Quitt, *Stephen A. Douglas and Antebellum Democracy* (New York: Cambridge University Press, 2012): 169–85.

34. James A. Dueholm, "Lincoln's Suspension of the Writ of Habeas Corpus: An Historical and Constitutional Analysis," *Journal of the Abraham Lincoln Association* 29 (Summer 2008): 51; Seymour, *Public Record*, 57, 255; *New York Herald*, October 4, 1862.

35. *New York World*, September 18, 1862.

36. For recent elaborations of this point, see Jonathan Earle, *Jacksonian Antislavery and the Politics of Free Soil, 1824–1854* (Chapel Hill: University of North Carolina Press, 2004); and Smith, *The Stormy Present*.

37. Jacque V. Voegeli, *Free but Not Equal: The Midwest and the Negro during the Civil War* (Chicago: University of Chicago Press, 1967), 28; *Tribune Almanac, 1861*, 41. For further discussion on the ubiquity of Northern race prejudice, see Gary W. Gallagher, *The Union War* (Cambridge, MA: Harvard University Press, 2011), 42–46.

38. Seymour, *Public Record*, 54.

39. George T. McJimsey, *Genteel Partisan: Manton Marble, 1834–1917* (Ames: Iowa State University Press, 1971), 58, 40–41; Harold Holzer, *Lincoln and the Power of the Press: The War for Public Opinion* (New York: Simon and Schuster, 2014), 521; James L. Crouthamel, "The Newspaper Revolution in New York, 1830–1860," *New York History* 45, no. 2 (April 1964): 103; James L. Crouthamel, *Bennett's* New York Herald *and the Rise of the Popular Press* (Syracuse, NY: Syracuse University Press, 1989), 54. The *Herald* was more independent than the *World*. It attacked Radical Republicans but backed the war effort. It offered praise only to Democrats who supported a strong prosecution of the war.

40. McClintock, *Lincoln and the Decision for War*, 36; Seymour, *Public Record*, 54, 69.

41. Seymour, *Public Record*, 43, 74, 47, 364.

42. Charles G. Loring's speech at an enlistment-drive meeting at Faneuil Hall, reported in *Boston Advertiser*, July 14, 1862.

43. *New York Herald*, September 24, 1862; *New York World*, September 26, 1862.

44. For the resonance and substance of the concepts of "Union" and "disunion" in this era, see Elizabeth R. Varon, *Disunion! The Coming of the Civil War, 1789–1859* (Chapel Hill: University of North Carolina Press, 2008); and Gallagher, *The Union War*.

45. Rogan Kersh, *Dreams of a More Perfect Union* (Ithaca, NY: Cornell University Press, 2001), 165.

46. Seymour, *Public Record*, 47, 104; pamphlet issued by the Democratic Republican General Committee from Tammany Hall, folder 4, box 24, Horatio Seymour Papers, NYSL; Buffalo *Morning Express*, September 17, 1862.

47. James Oakes, *Freedom National: The Destruction of Slavery in the United States, 1861–1865* (New York: Norton, 2013), xxiii; *Buffalo Commercial Advertiser*, September 23, 1862; Seymour, *Public Record*, 104, 84, 73; Varon, *Disunion!*, 345; *New York Herald*, September 30, 1862.

48. Seymour, *Public Record*, 58.

49. *New York Herald*, September 11, 1862.

50. McClellan letter, in Stephen W. Sears, ed., *The Civil War: The Second Year by Those Who Lived It* (New York: Library of America, 2012), 306–9; Van Buren, quoted in *Atlas & Argus*, October 16, 1862; letter of William Chittenden Lusk, quoted in Jonathan W. White, *Emancipation, the Union Army, and the Reelection of Abraham Lincoln* (Baton Rouge: Louisiana State University Press, 2014), 188.

51. Leslie Gormly to Millard Fillmore, October 30, 1862, roll 50, Millard Fillmore Papers on Microfilm, Alderman Library, University of Virginia, Charlottesville; Asa Holmes to Frank Holmes, January 22, 1863, item DL0526.7, and July 3, 1863, item DL0526.49, box 45, John L. Nau III Civil War Collection, Houston, Texas (collection hereafter cited as JLNC).

52. T. Churchill to Horatio Seymour (including letter from Judge Caton), January 28, 1863, box 7, Horatio Seymour Papers, NYSL.

53. *Albany Evening Journal*, November 8, December 9, and December 13, 1862; *New York Tribune*, November 10 and December 12, 1862.

54. Silbey, *A Respectable Minority*, 144; *New York World*, November 7, 1862; *New York Herald*, November 5, 6, 1862; *Vanity Fair*, November 8, 1862; McJimsey, *Genteel Partisan*, 43.

55. McJimsey, *Genteel Partisan*, 43; *Vanity Fair*, November 8, 1862; *New York Times*, November 6, 1862.

56. Rodgers, "Copperheads or a Respectable Minority," 145.

57. Seymour, *Public Record*, 65.

58. *New York Times*, November 6, 1862.

59. Asa Holmes to Frank Holmes, January 22, 1863, item DL0526.7, April 24, 1863, item DL0526.37, July 3, 1863, item DL0526.49, all document box 45, JLNC.

60. In 1863 and 1864, Republicans consistently attacked antiwar Democrats while classing their own measures as conservative by wrapping them firmly in the banner of Union. For discussion, see Smith, *No Party Now*, 101–65; White, *Emancipation, the Union Army, and the Reelection of Abraham Lincoln*; and John J. Hennessy, "Evangelizing for Union, 1863: The Army of the Potomac, Its Enemies at Home, and a New Solidarity," *Journal of the Civil War Era* 4 (December 2014): 533–58.

The Union as It Was

1. Gary W. Gallagher, *The Union War* (Cambridge, MA: Harvard University Press, 2011), 53; *Irish-American* (New York), quoted in Christian G. Samito, *Becoming American under Fire: Irish Americans, African Americans, and the Politics of Citizenship during the Civil War Era* (Ithaca, NY: Cornell University Press, 2009), 27–29; Susannah Ural Bruce, *The Harp and the Eagle: Irish-American Volunteers and the Union Army, 1861–1865* (New York: NYU Press, 2006), 62–64; Ryan W. Keating, *Shades of Green: Irish Regiments, American Soldiers, and Local Communities in the Civil War Era* (New York: Fordham University Press, 2017), 26, 49–50, 74–77.

2. Gallagher, *The Union War*, 34–35; Bruce, *The Harp and the Eagle*, 51–60; Randall M. Miller, "Catholic Religion, Irish Ethnicity, and the Civil War," in *Religion and the American Civil War*, ed. Randall M. Miller, Harry S. Stout, and Charles Reagan Wilson (New York: Oxford University Press, 1998), 263–64, 273–75; Lawrence F. Kohl, ed., *Irish Green*

and Union Blue: The Civil War Letters of Peter Welsh, Color Sergeant, 28th Regiment Massachusetts Volunteers (New York: Fordham University Press, 1986), 67, 102.

3. Gallagher, *Union War*, 34; Samito, *Becoming American under Fire*, 28–29. Certainly some Catholics such as the Irish-born Archbishop John Purcell of Cincinnati, the editor Orestes A. Brownson, and Maj. Gen. William S. Rosecrans saw emancipation as crucial to Union victory, but their voices were not as influential as those discussed in this essay.

4. On Catholics' conservatism on slavery and their belief in nativism's ties to antislavery politics in the North, see Michael Hochgeschwender, *Wahrheit, Einheit, Ordnung: Die Sklavenfrage und der amerikanische Katholizismus, 1835–1870* (Paderborn: Ferdinand Schöningen, 2006); John T. McGreevy, *Catholicism and American Freedom: A History* (New York: Norton, 2003), 56–65; and Tyler N. Anbinder, *Nativism and Slavery: The Northern Know Nothings and the Politics of the 1850s* (New York: Oxford University Press, 1992), 44–47.

5. John Loughery, *Dagger John: Archbishop John Hughes and the Making of Irish America* (Ithaca, NY: Cornell University Press, 2018), 1–7, 190–92; Francis R. Walsh, "The Boston *Pilot* Reports the Civil War," *Historical Journal of Massachusetts* 9 (June 1981): 5. For publication statistics of major Catholic papers during the Civil War era, see "Appendix A" in William B. Kurtz, *Excommunicated from the Union: How the Civil War Created a Separate Catholic America* (New York: Fordham University Press, 2016), 167; and Kohl, *Irish Green and Union Blue*, 28, 30, 37, 55, 65.

6. A number of important ethnic studies by Susannah Ural, Christian Samito, and Ryan Keating examine Irish American's Unionism during the war and how their support for the war and opposition to Lincoln's government shaped popular perceptions of the Irish and their place in postwar society. These studies, however, focus on ethnic factors, often relegating their subjects' Catholicism to a minor role. While Hughes's and Donahoe's Irish birth played an important role in their similar conceptions of Unionism, this essay takes their religious convictions just as seriously as their ethnic backgrounds.

7. *Pilot* (Boston), September 14, 1861. There is no record of any correspondence between the two in Archbishop John Hughes's papers microfilmed at the Catholic History Research Center and University Archives of the Catholic University of America. Unfortunately, Donahoe's personal papers were probably destroyed in a series of fires his newspaper's offices sustained after the Civil War. Sr. Mary Alphonsine Frawley, "Patrick Donahoe," PhD diss., Catholic University of America, 1946, vii–viii, 206–14.

8. While often absent from general histories of the war, both Donahoe and Archbishop Hughes have been better studied by historians of ethnicity and American Catholicism. On Donahoe and the *Pilot*, see Frawley, "Patrick Donahoe"; Walsh, "The Boston *Pilot* Reports the Civil War," 5–16; and Francis R. Walsh, "Who Spoke for Boston's Irish? The Boston *Pilot* in the Nineteenth Century," *Journal of Ethnic Studies* 10, no. 3 (Fall 1982): 21–36. For scholarship on Hughes relevant to this study, see John R. G. Hassard, *Life of the Most Reverend John Hughes, D. D.* (New York: D. Appleton and Co., 1866); Thomas F. Meehan, "Archbishop Hughes and the Draft Riots," in United States Catholic Historical Society, *Historical Records and Studies*, vol. 1, part 2 (January 1900), 171–90; Rena Mazyck Andrews, "Archbishop John Hughes and the Civil War," PhD diss., University of Chicago, 1935; Walter G. Sharrow, "John Hughes and a Catholic Response to Slavery in Antebellum America," *Journal of Negro History* 57, no. 3 (July 1972): 254–69;

Richard Shaw, *Dagger John: The Unquiet Life and Times of Archbishop John Hughes of New York* (New York: Paulist Press, 1977); Martin L. Meenagh, "Archbishop John Hughes and the New York Schools Controversy of 1840–43," *American Nineteenth Century History* 5, no. 1 (Spring 2004): 34–65; Mary C. Kelly, "A 'Sentinel of Our Liberties': Archbishop John Hughes and Irish-American Intellectual Negotiation in the Civil War Era," *Irish Studies Review* 18, no. 2 (May 2010): 155–72; Mary E. Brown, "John Joseph Hughes (1797–1864): Definitions of 'Assimilation,'" in *The Making of Modern Immigration: An Encyclopedia of People and Ideas*, ed. Patrick J. Hayes (Santa Barbara, CA: ABC-CLIO, 2012), 1:273–86; and Loughery, *Dagger John*.

9. Angela F. Murphy, *American Slavery, Irish Freedom: Abolition, Immigrant Citizenship, and the Transatlantic Movement for Irish Repeal* (Baton Rouge: Louisiana State University Press, 2010), 1–14, 75–84; Anbinder, *Nativism and Slavery*, 45–46. The *Bee* and Senator Henry Wilson quoted in Frawley, "Patrick Donahoe," 166. For a recent study of the transatlantic nature of Irish antiabolitionism, see Ian Delahanty, "The Transatlantic Roots of Irish-American Anti-Abolitionism, 1843–1859," *Journal of the Civil War Era* 6, no. 2 (June 2016): 164–92.

10. Lawrence Kehoe, ed., *Complete Works of the Most Rev. John Hughes, Archbishop of New York: Comprising His Sermons, Letters, Lectures, Speeches, Etc.* (New York: Lawrence Kehoe, 1866), 2:107–9, 114, 121; Shaw, *Dagger John*, 1–2, 139–75, 196–202; Loughery, *Dagger John*, 166.

11. *Pilot*, July 8, 22, 1854, May 16, November 14, 1857; Frawley, "Patrick Donahoe," vii–x.

12. Kehoe, *Complete Works of John Hughes*, 2:222; Sharrow, "John Hughes and Slavery," 258–64; *Pilot*, July 22, November 11, 1854, February 3, 1855. Donahoe frequently linked Protestantism to abolitionism before and during the war, and many other Catholic journalists would join him from 1860 through 1865 in blaming Protestantism as the cause of sectional discord and ultimately the war. Mark A. Noll, "The Catholic Press, the Bible, and Protestant Responsibility for the Civil War," *Journal of the Civil War Era* 7, no. 3 (September 2017): 355–76.

13. *Pilot*, July 8, 22, 1854, November 3, December 1, 1860; Frawley, "Patrick Donahoe," 166–67, 172–77; Walsh, "Boston *Pilot* Reports the Civil War," 6–7.

14. *New York Herald*, April 21, 1861; *Pilot*, April 27, 1861.

15. *Pilot*, September 7, 1861; Shaw, *Dagger John*, 340.

16. Thomas H. O'Connor, *Civil War Boston: Home Front and Battlefield* (Boston: Northeastern University Press, 1997), 72–79.

17. *Pilot*, July 5, August 2, 1862.

18. *Pilot*, October 19, 1861, July 19, 1862.

19. *Pilot*, July 19, August 30, 1862.

20. Loughery, *Dagger John*, 296–302, 312. Hughes's offer was declined by Scott, who, seemingly under the impression that the war would be short, assured him that they had enough priests on hand for chaplain duty. Unfortunately for all concerned, the result of this exchange was that Hughes, as he told a fellow archbishop, lost interest in sending more of his priests or nuns to look after Catholic soldiers' spiritual welfare. Hughes to Gen. Winfield Scott, May 7, 1861; Scott to Hughes, May 13, 1861; Hughes to Abp. Francis P. Kenrick,

October 21, 1861, John Hughes Papers, American Catholic History Research Center and University Archives, Catholic University of America, Washington, DC (hereafter CUA).

21. Patrick J. Hayes, ed., *The Civil War Diary of Father James Sheeran: Confederate Chaplain and Redemptorist* (Washington, DC: Catholic University of America Press, 2016), 77.

22. Hughes to Kenrick, July 3, 1861; Bp. Richard Whelan to Hughes, May 3, 1861; Hughes to Whelan, May 7, 1861, Hughes Papers, CUA; Shaw, *Dagger John*, 339–42.

23. *Metropolitan Record* (New York), September 7, 1861; *Pilot*, September 14, 1861; *Catholic Telegraph* (Cincinnati), September 14, 1861; *New York Herald*, September 4, 1861.

24. Hughes to William H. Seward, April 28, June 1, July 22, 1861, William Henry Seward Papers, University of Rochester, Rochester, NY (hereafter Seward Papers).

25. Hughes to Card. Alesandro Barnabo (English translation), February 13, 1862, Hughes Papers, CUA; Hughes to Seward, March 1, 1862, Seward Papers; Shaw, *Dagger John*, 345–46, 355–56.

26. Hughes to Seward, December 5, 27, 1861, February 21, March 15, April 25, June 12, 1862, Seward Papers; *New York Herald*, August 14, 1862; Loughery, *Dagger John*, 19–20.

27. Seward to Hughes, January 9, 1862, Seward Papers; Bernard Smith to Hughes, September 27, 1862, Hughes Papers, CUA; Hughes to Seward, November 1, 1862, published in *New York Herald*, November 12, 1862; Pope Pius IX to Hughes, October 18, 1862, Hughes Papers, CUA.

28. *New York Herald*, August 18, 1862; Shaw, *Dagger John*, 360. In March 1863, Mullaly's paper dropped the claim to be Hughes's "Official Organ" from the heading of its editorial section, instead calling itself merely "A Catholic Family Paper." *Metropolitan Record*, March 21, 1863.

29. Patrick W. Carey, *Orestes A. Brownson: American Religious Weathervane* (Grand Rapids, MI: Eerdmans, 2004), 268–72; *Brownson's Quarterly Review*, October 1861.

30. *Metropolitan Record*, October 12, 1861.

31. *Pilot*, October 19, 1861; *Metropolitan Record*, October 19, 1861; *New York Herald*, October 8, 1861.

32. *New York Tribune*, October 9, 12, 1861; Hughes to Seward, October 10, 1861, Seward Papers; Hennesey, *American Catholics*, 149; Shaw, *Dagger John*, 343–44, 350; *Brownson's Quarterly Review*, January 1862; George C. Rable, *God's Almost Chosen Peoples: A Religious History of the American Civil War* (Chapel Hill: University of North Carolina Press, 2010), 85–87.

33. *Pilot*, December 1, 1860, June 8, 1861.

34. *Pilot*, September 13, 1862; *Liberator* (Boston), April 11, 1862, April 24, September 25, 1863.

35. *Pilot*, October 4, November 1, 1862, January 10, 1863; Loughery, *Dagger John*, 325.

36. *Telegraph*, March 25, April 8, 22, 1863; *New York Freeman's Journal*, April 4, 1863.

37. *Pilot*, July 25, August 1, 1863; *Metropolitan Record*, July 11, 1863.

38. *New York Tribune*, July 9, 1863; Loughery, *Dagger John*, 318–21, 326; Hennesey, *American Catholics*, 150.

39. *Harper's Weekly*, August 1, 1863; Hennesey, *American Catholics*, 150–51; O'Connor, *Civil War Boston*, 139–41. "It is a fact, patent to everyone who has seen anything of the

mob, that it is composed almost exclusively of Irishmen and boys." *New York Times*, July 16, 1863.

40. Keating, *Shades of Green*, 132–54; *New York Tribune*, July 16, 1863; *New York Herald*, July 18, 1863; *Liberator*, July 31, 1863; *Brownson's Quarterly Review*, October 1863; Shaw, *Dagger John*, 366–69.

41. *Pilot*, January 9, 1864; *New York Herald*, January 4, 7, 8, 1864; Shaw, *Dagger John*, 369–72; Seward's letters to Starrs are printed in Kehoe, *Complete Works of John Hughes*, 1:24; Loughery, *Dagger John*, 317, 334–41.

42. *Pilot*, August 1, 8, 1863, September 17, 1864; *New York Freeman's Journal*, May 23, 1863, August 20, 1864; Kurtz, *Excommunicated from the Union*, 116, 122.

43. *Pilot*, March 5, May 7, 1864; *Catholic Herald* (Philadelphia), January 9, 1864.

44. *Pilot*, July 9, 23, October 29, 1864; *New York Tablet*, September 24, 1864; *Metropolitan Record*, October 15, November 5, 1864.

45. *Pilot*, November 12, 1864, March 4, April 8, 15, 1865; Walsh, "The Boston *Pilot* Reports the Civil War," 12.

46. *New York Tribune*, November 10, 19, December 20, 1864.

47. *New York Herald*, January 1, 1865; *Pilot*, December 10, 1864, February 25, April 22, 1865; *New York Tablet*, January 7, 21, 1865; *New York Freeman's Journal*, December 31, 1864.

48. *Pilot*, June 3, August 26, 1865; Kurtz, *Excommunicated from the Union*, 146, 150–52.

49. Christian B. Keller, "New Perspectives in Civil War Ethnic History and Their Implications for Twenty-First-Century Scholarship," in *This Distracted and Anarchical People: New Answers for Old Questions about the Civil War-Era North*, ed. Andrew L. Slap and Michael Thomas Smith (New York: Fordham University Press, 2013), 123–41; Margaret C. DePalma, *Dialogue on the Frontier: Catholic and Protestant Relations, 1793–1883* (Kent, OH: Kent State University Press, 2004), 130–39; Kurtz, *Excommunicated from the Union*, 136–43; McGreevy, *Catholicism and American Freedom*, 91–118.

"Certain Ill-Considered Phrases"

1. Edward Bates to Abraham Lincoln, November 24, 1864, Abraham Lincoln Papers, Library of Congress, Washington, DC (collection hereafter cited as Lincoln Papers, LC).

2. Edward Bates, *The Diary of Edward Bates: 1859–1866*, ed. Howard K. Beale (Washington, DC: Government Printing Office, 1933), 363, 427; John G. Nicolay and John Hay, *Abraham Lincoln: A History*, 10 vols. (New York: The Century Co., 1917), 9:344.

3. The historian James Oakes has claimed that "by the time Lincoln was inaugurated, virtually all Republicans believed that secession meant war and war meant immediate emancipation." Edward Bates would have taken umbrage at Oakes's assessment. Bates worked tirelessly to prevent both eventualities; he struggled to find a peaceful solution to the secession crisis and dedicated much of his tenure as attorney general to thwarting the emancipationist agenda of the radical wing of the Republican Party. What is more, Bates would never have joined the Lincoln administration or supported the Republican Party in 1860 if he thought that either was committed to immediate emancipation. On the contrary, Bates labored in the Lincoln administration until 1864—fueled by the conviction that he had Lincoln's "*personal* confidence, but [Lincoln] is under constant

pressure of extreme factions"—precisely because he believed that immediate emancipation and especially the incorporation of freed slaves into the body politic were neither desirable nor inevitable. Bates was just one man—sometimes criticized as out of touch and not particularly influential in Lincoln's cabinet—but his politics were representative of the great body of conservative Old Line Whigs who threw their support to the Republicans in 1860. It was these conservatives who, like Bates, had not supported Frémont in 1856 that elected Lincoln president in 1860. Bates's career provides a glimpse into the minds of these conservatives. His support for the Republican Party in 1860 and his subsequent tenure in the Lincoln administration underscore Lincoln's more moderate stance on slavery in 1860 and 1861, and Bates's growing dissatisfaction with Lincoln and his policies highlights how that stance changed over the course of the war. James Oakes, *Freedom National: The Destruction of Slavery in the United States, 1861–1865* (New York: Norton, 2013), 50; *Bates Diary: 1859–1866*, 280. For more on Oakes's argument, see also Daniel Crofts, *Lincoln and the Politics of Slavery: The Other Thirteenth Amendment and the Struggle to Save the Union* (Chapel Hill: University of North Carolina Press, 2016), 276–78. For more on Republican conservatives, see also Eric Foner, *Free Soil, Free Labor, Free Men: The Ideology of the Republican Party before the Civil War* (New York: Oxford University Press, 1970), 186–93.

4. Abraham Lincoln, "House Divided Speech at Springfield, Illinois, June 16, 1858," in *Abraham Lincoln: Speeches and Writings, 1832–1858*, 2 vols., ed. Roy P. Basler (New York: Library of America, 1989), 1:426; William H. Seward, "Freedom in the New Territories, March 11, 1850," in *The Senate 1789–1989: Classic Speeches*, 4 vols., ed. Robert C. Byrd and Wendy Wolff (Washington, DC: US Government Printing Office, 1995), 3:308.

5. Edward Bates to Francis Lieber, August 23, 1861, box 2, Francis Lieber Papers, Huntington Library, San Marino, California; Peter B. Knupfer, *The Union as It Is: Constitutional Unionism and Sectional Compromise, 1787–1861* (Chapel Hill: University of North Carolina Press, 1991), 6.

6. *Bates Diary: 1859–1866*, 431–32.

7. *New York Herald*, March 7, 1860; Orville Hickman Browning, *The Diary of Orville Hickman Browning, 1850–1864*, 2 vols., ed. Theodore Calvin Pease and James G. Randall (Springfield: Illinois State Historical Library, 1825), 1:395. *New York Times*, February 10, 1860; *Civilian & Telegraph* (Cumberland, MD), March 8, 1860; Michael F. Holt, *The Election of 1860: "A Campaign Fraught with Consequences"* (Lawrence: University Press of Kansas, 2017), 98.

8. Historians have offered different explanations for why Bates held public office only a handful of times during his life. According to Doris Kearns Goodwin, Bates's absence from public office was a symptom of his unusually happy home life; accordingly, "the enticements of public office gradually diminished in his contented eyes." Bates's biographer Marvin Cain paints a slightly more nuanced picture, in which Bates's own missteps and the struggles of the Whig Party in Missouri—which was always in the minority—played a significant role in his limited public experience. Bates also indicated that financial concerns limited the appeal of elected office. He had an extremely large family (he and his wife had seventeen children, eight of which survived to adulthood), and he consistently worried about his ability to support them. Amid speculation that Zachary Taylor would appoint Bates to his cabinet in 1848, Bates confessed that "I could not *afford* to accept

any office that would involve an abandonment of my profession." He reiterated in 1860: "My pecuniary circumstances (barely competent) ... make it very undesirable for me to be in high office with low pay." Doris Kearns Goodwin, *Team of Rivals: The Political Genius of Abraham Lincoln* (New York: Simon & Schuster, 2005), 63; Diary of Edward Bates 1846–1852, January 1, 1850, box 8, Bates Family Papers, Missouri History Museum, St. Louis, Missouri (collection hereafter cited as Bates Papers, MHM); *Bates Diary: 1859–1866*, 1:153; Marvin R. Cain, *Lincoln's Attorney General: Edward Bates of Missouri* (Columbia: University of Missouri Press, 1965), 26–79.

9. As many scholars have noted, Seward's reputation as a radical was, for the most part, undeserved. "His devotion to the Union had always been far deeper than that of the radicals with whom he had been associated in the 1850s," Eric Foner explains. "He was never comfortable in the doctrinaire circles of [Joshua] Giddings, [Salmon] Chase, and [Owen] Lovejoy, and his perception of the slavery controversy was always more political than theirs." Seward would distinguish himself from such hardliners during the secession crisis, when he became one of the most vocal advocates of conciliation and compromise in the Lincoln administration. But as Michael Holt has argued, "Perceptions often matter more than reality in motivating historical actors ... and Seward was most certainly perceived as radical, [and] as the Republican presidential possibility most favored by genuine abolitionists." Foner, *Free Soil*, 222; Eric Foner, *The Fiery Trial: Abraham Lincoln and American Slavery* (New York: Norton, 2010), 86–87; Holt, *Election of 1860*, 89–91; *Bates Diary: 1859–1866*, 164–65, 171–72.

10. William H. Seward, "Freedom in the New Territories, March 11, 1850," in Byrd and Wolff, *Senate Speeches*, 3:308; *Chicago Tribune*, quoted in *Emporia News* (Emporia, Kansas), March 10, 1860; *Browning Diary*, 1:407.

11. *Chicago Tribune*, quoted in *Emporia News*, March 10, 1860; "Fourth Lincoln-Douglas Debate: Lincoln's Rejoinder, Charleston, Illinois, September 18, 1858," in Basler, *Lincoln Speeches and Writings, 1832–1858*, 1:677; Abraham Lincoln to George Robertson, August 15, 1855, in Basler, *Lincoln Speeches and Writings, 1832–1858*, 1:359; Abraham Lincoln, "Speech at Springfield, Illinois, July 17, 1858," in Basler, *Lincoln Speeches and Writings, 1832–1858*, 1:470; Abraham Lincoln, "Speech at Chicago, Illinois, March 1, 1859," in Basler, *Lincoln Speeches and Writings, 1859–1865*, 2:16–17; Crofts, *Lincoln and the Politics of Slavery*, 68–73; Foner, *The Fiery Trial*, 84–88.

12. *Bates Diary: 1859–1866*, 12, 63, 112; Crofts, *Lincoln and the Politics of Slavery*, 68–73; Foner, *The Fiery Trial*, 84–88; Holt, *Election of 1860*, 92–97.

13. *Bates Diary: 1859–1866*, 2, 6; Foner, *The Fiery Trial*, 84–91.

14. Abraham Lincoln, "House Divided Speech at Springfield, Illinois, June 16, 1858," in Basler, *Lincoln Speeches and Writings, 1832–1858*, 1:426; Foner, *The Fiery Trial*, 99–102.

15. Abraham Lincoln, "Speech on the Kansas-Nebraska Act at Peoria, Illinois, October 16, 1854," in Basler, *Lincoln Speeches and Writings, 1832–1858*, 1:340; Foner, *The Fiery Trial*, 102–3.

16. *Bates Diary: 1859–1866*, 129, 131.

17. Abraham Lincoln to Thomas Corwin, October 9, 1859, in Harold Holzer, *Lincoln at Cooper Union: The Speech That Made Abraham Lincoln President* (New York: Simon & Schuster, 2005), xix; *Bates Diary: 1859–1866*, 1, 76, 131; Bates Diary 1846–1852, January 1, 1850, Bates Papers, MHM.

18. Edward Bates to Orville Browning, June 11, 1860, in *New York Times*, June 23, 1860; *Bates Diary: 1859–1866*, 129, 131.

19. Not all Radical Republicans were abolitionists who campaigned for the immediate eradication of slavery. Eric Foner concludes that what united Radical Republicans was their "persistent refusal to compromise with the South on any question involving slavery" and their "determination to keep the moral side of the slavery issue from being obscured by any other aspect." But Bates made little distinction between immediatists and more pragmatic radicals; in his eyes, what made them particularly dangerous is that they shared an eagerness for the destruction of slavery and a seeming willingness to take steps that Bates considered impolitic and unconstitutional. Foner, *Free Soil*, 104, 110; *Bates Diary: 1859–1866*, 67, 129; William Lloyd Garrison, "The United States Constitution," in *Selections from the Writings and Speeches of William Lloyd Garrison*, ed. R. F. Walcutt (Boston: J. B. Yerrinton & Son, 1852), 314; Bates Diary 1846–1852, January 1, 1850, Bates Papers, MHM.

20. William Lloyd Garrison to Samuel J. May, March 6, 1858, in Louis Ruchames, ed., *The Letters of William Lloyd Garrison: From Disunionism to the Brink of War*, 6 vols. (Cambridge, MA: Belknap Press of Harvard University Press, 1975), 4:517; *Bates Diary: 1859–1866*, 171. For more on Seward's radicalism, see Foner, *Free Soil*, 222–23.

21. *Bates Diary: 1859–1866*, 131; Abraham Lincoln, "First Lincoln-Douglas Debate, Ottawa, Illinois: Lincoln's Reply, August 21, 1858," in Basler, *Lincoln Speeches and Writings, 1832–1858*, 1:512.

22. Bleeding Kansas was not merely an extension of debates about slavery in the halls of Congress. Instead, it represented the escalation of a protracted struggle along the border of slavery and freedom—a struggle involving runaway slaves, slave catchers, and increasingly aggrieved populations on both sides of the border who felt that their own society was threatened. Stanley Harrold, *Border War: Fighting over Slavery before the Civil War* (Chapel Hill: University of North Carolina Press, 2010), 164.

23. Edward Bates to Orville Browning, June 11, 1860, in *New York Times*, June 23, 1860; Christopher Phillips, *The Rivers Ran Backward: The Civil War and the Remaking of the American Middle Border* (New York: Oxford University Press, 2016), 1–20; Harold, *Border War*, 1–12; Aaron Astor, *Rebels on the Border: Civil War, Emancipation, and the Reconstruction of Kentucky and Missouri* (Baton Rouge: Louisiana State University Press, 2012), 8–9, 15, 33–50.

24. *Bates Diary, 1859–1866*, 8; Edward Bates to Julia Bates, February 25, 1828, box 1, folder 1, Edward Bates Papers, Virginia Historical Society, Richmond, Virginia (collection hereafter cited as Bates Papers, VHS); Henry Clay, "'On American Industry,' in the House of Representatives, March 30 and 31, 1824," in *The Works of Henry Clay: Comprising His Life, Correspondence, and Speeches*, 10 vols., ed. Calvin Colton (New York: G. P. Putnam's Sons, 1904), 6:292; Edward Bates, speech to the Whig Convention in Rock Island, Illinois, September 11, 1852, Edward Bates Papers, VHS; Cain, *Lincoln's Attorney General*, 9–40; John Vollmer Mering, *The Whig Party in Missouri* (Columbia: University of Missouri Press, 1967), 11–27; Daniel Walker Howe, *What Hath God Wrought: The Transformation of America, 1815–1848* (New York: Oxford University Press, 2007), 270–71.

25. Bates's biographer Cain (*Lincoln's Attorney General*, 59) claims that Bates sold his last slave in 1846. This was clearly not the case, as Bates drew up this contract with his

last slave, Adam White, in 1848. If White met the terms of the contract, he would have been freed in 1853—though there is no surviving record of White's fate after this 1848 contract. Bates Diary 1846–1852, January 30, 1848, Bates Papers, MHM.

26. *Bates Diary: 1859–1866*, 12, 63, 67–68, 111–13; Bates Diary 1846–1852, January 30, 1848, Bates Papers, MHM; Cain, *Lincoln's Attorney General*, 10, 43–46; Howe, *What Hath God Wrought*, 260–64.

27. Mering, *Whig Party in Missouri*, 11; Howe, *What Hath God Wrought*, 264; Holt, *Whig Party*, 561.

28. Abraham Lincoln, "First Lincoln-Douglas Debate, Ottawa, Illinois, August 21, 1858: Lincoln's Reply," in Basler, *Lincoln Speeches and Writings, 1832–1858*, 1:526; Howe, *Political Culture*, 123, 125, 123–49; A. James Fuller, "The Last True Whig: John Bell and the Politics of Compromise in 1860," in *The Election of 1860 Reconsidered*, ed. A. James Fuller (Kent, OH: Kent State University Press, 2013), 104–5.

29. Horace Greeley, the Radical Republican editor of the *New York Tribune*, supported Bates's candidacy in the election of 1860 because he believed that a sectional Republican Party—one based solely on some form of opposition to slavery—could not win a national election. "I lack faith that the anti-slavery men of this country have either the numbers or the sagacity required to make a President," he explained. Bates, meanwhile, had always been suspicious of sectional parties—particularly those focused on the slavery issue. He eschewed the Free Soil Party in 1848 for this reason, even though Bates opposed the extension of slavery. "I would not join a sectional, geographical party," he contended. "The principle of the free soil men is true in itself, but it is not a principle of which a national party can be exclusively formed, either with dignity to the partizans or safety to the country." Bates had similar fears about the Republican Party in 1860, and he thus strove to ensure that the Republican Party was not a sectional one focused exclusively on nonextension. Horace Greeley to George E. Baker, April 28, 1859, in Thurlow Weed, *Life of Thurlow Weed, Including His Autobiography and a Memoir*, 2 vols. (Boston: Houghton, Mifflin and Company, 1884), 2:255; Bates Diary 1846–1852, August 5, 1848, Bates Papers, MHM.

30. *Bates Diary: 1859–1866*, 128, 131.

31. *Bates Diary: 1859–1866*, 131.

32. *Bates Diary: 1859–1866*, 12, 132; Harrold, *Border War*, 164.

33. Early in 1860, Bates enjoyed wide support among former Whigs in Missouri. In December 1859, the Whig and American members of the Missouri legislature endorsed Bates's candidacy, and in February 1860 the Missouri Opposition Convention—composed of "Republicans, Free[-Soil] Democrats, Americans and Whigs"—unanimously nominated Bates for the presidency. These Whigs and former Whigs hoped that Bates might be able to unite a national coalition of anti-Democratic forces. Bates's popularity waned in the late spring, however, when he composed a public letter explicating his views on slavery in the territories. In that letter, Bates made clear that he believed that the "National Government has the power to permit or forbid slavery" in the territories and that he felt "the spirit and policy of the government ought to be against [slavery's] extension." Many Missourians who had been attracted to his rhetoric of moderation and compromise could not accept Bates's views on slavery extension, and his support across

the state and the rest of the South dropped precipitately in the weeks after his letter was published. *Bates Diary: 1859-1866*, 106-7, 112, 106-27; *St. Louis Evening News*, quoted in *Bangor Whig and Courier* (Bangor, Maine), March 5, 1860.

34. In both the gubernatorial and presidential elections of 1860, Missourians showed a decided preference for the more moderate (and ostensibly national) Constitutional Union and Democratic candidates over the Republican and Southern Democratic ones. As Aaron Astor argues, Missourians "marked the acceptable boundaries of political expression, just as they celebrated their cultural values" in their centrist propensities. Astor, *Rebels on the Border*, 39; William E. Parrish, *A History of Missouri*, 6 vols. (Columbia: University of Missouri Press, 1973), 3:2-3.

35. *Bates Diary: 1859-1866*, 119, 131, 155; "Constitutional Union Party Platform," in *National Political Parties with Their Platforms*, ed. Walter W. Spooner and Ray B. Smith (Syracuse, NY: Syracuse Press, 1922), 201; Edward Bates to Orville Browning, June 11, 1860, in *New York Times*, June 23, 1860.

36. *New York Times*, April 16, 1860; *Bates Diary: 1859-1866*, 106-7, 135; *Louisville Journal*, quoted in the *Evening Virginia Sentinel* (Alexandria, Virginia), March 28 1860.

37. *Bates Diary: 1859-1866*, 132; Edward Bates to Orville Browning, June 11, 1860, in *New York Times*, June 23, 1860.

38. Edward Bates to Orville Browning, June 11, 1860, in *New York Times*, June 23, 1860.

39. *Bates Diary: 1859-1866*, 132, 152.

40. As Elizabeth Varon has argued, "disunion" was "the most provocative and potent word in the political vocabulary" of antebellum Americans. Disunion signaled the dissolution of the American republic, but it also carried with it cataclysmic implications. "This one word contained, and stimulated, their fears of extreme political factionalism, tyranny, regionalism, economic decline, foreign intervention, class conflict, gender disorder, racial strife, widespread violence and anarchy, and civil war, all of which could be interpreted as God's retributions for America's moral failings." "Disunion," in other words, constituted the zenith of radical rhetoric in antebellum America, and Edward Bates thus considered the explosion of disunion rhetoric in the aftermath of Lincoln's election to be incredibly dangerous. Bates drew conclusions similar to those of Varon— that "disunion rhetoric shaped and limited Americans' political and moral imagination, ultimately discouraging a politics of compromise and lending an aura of inexorability to the cataclysmic confrontation of North and South." This was why Bates set so much store by language and worked so hard to combat radical rhetoric with a more reasoned rhetoric of compromise. Elizabeth R. Varon, *Disunion! The Coming of the Civil War, 1789-1859* (Chapel Hill: University of North Carolina Press, 2008), 1-2.

41. *Bates Diary: 1859-1866*, 109-10, 157.

42. *Bates Diary: 1859-1866*, 156-57.

43. John G. Nicolay, "Memorandum, Springfield, 15 December 1860," in *With Lincoln in the White House: Letters, Memoranda, and Other Writings of John G. Nicolay, 1860-1865*, ed. Michael Burlingame (Carbondale: Southern Illinois University Press, 2000), 19.

44. Lincoln tentatively offered Bates the attorney generalship at their meeting on December 15, but Lincoln gave some indication that he would offer Bates the position of

secretary of state if William Henry Seward turned it down. In John Nicolay's account of the meeting, it was not clear that Lincoln intended to offer Bates the secretary of stateship if Seward declined. In Bates's account, however, this impression was so pronounced that Bates left the meeting somewhat regretful that he might be offered the State Department, though "as a matter personal to myself, and in regard to my private affairs, the Att.y. Genl.'s place is most desirable." Lincoln allegedly declared that if Seward refused the secretary of stateship, "he would at once offer me the *State Department*—but, failing that, he would offer me the Att.y. generalship." At another point Lincoln apparently said that Bates "must be either Sec.y. of State or Att.y. Genl." Bates left the meeting unsure about which cabinet position he would assume, and when Lincoln agreed to leak news of Bates's appointment to the press a few days later, the announcement Lincoln drafted specified: "It is not yet definitely settled which Department will be assigned to Mr. Bates." Nicolay, "Memorandum, Springfield, 15 December 1860," 18; *Bates Diary: 1859–1866*, 165; Abraham Lincoln to Edward Bates, December 18, 1860, Lincoln Papers, LC.

45. Abraham Lincoln to Thurlow Weed, December 17, 1860, in Basler, *Lincoln Speeches and Writings, 1859–1865*, 2:192; John G. Nicolay, "Memorandum, Springfield, 15 December 1860," 18–19.

46. Lincoln offered William Henry Seward the State Department in a letter on December 8, 1860—one week *before* he approached Bates about joining the cabinet. Seward, however, did not accept the position until December 28. Meanwhile, Lincoln asked Bates to join the cabinet during their meeting on December 15, and Bates accepted on the spot. The two discussed making the appointment public at that meeting, and three days later—on December 18—Lincoln composed a "little editorial [to] appear in the Missouri Democrat" announcing that Bates would assume "a place in the new Cabinet." Abraham Lincoln to Edward Bates, December 18, 1860, Lincoln Papers, LC; William Henry Seward to Abraham Lincoln, December 8, 1860, Lincoln Papers, LC; William Henry Seward to Abraham Lincoln, December 28, 1860, Lincoln Papers, LC; *Bates Diary: 1859–1860*, 164–66.

47. Bates's perception that Lincoln expressed great reluctance to offer Seward a position in the cabinet does not match John Nicolay's account of their meeting. Nicolay remembered that Lincoln invited Seward to join the cabinet "in view of his ability, his integrity, and his commanding influence, and fitness for the place. He did this as a matter of duty to the party, and to Mr. Sewards many and strong friends, while at the same time it accorded perfectly with his own personal inclinations—notwithstanding some opposition on the part of sincere and warm friends." Bates's dislike of Seward likely predisposed him to interpret Lincoln's references to Seward's "many and strong friends" and to the opposition among Lincoln's "sincere and warm friends" as a sign that the president offered had Seward a position only grudgingly. Indeed, after cataloging the dangers of Seward joining the cabinet, Bates admitted that "these particular arguments, as set down, are my own, but they were all glanced at in the conversation [with Lincoln]." Bates's idea that Lincoln offered Seward a cabinet position only out of a sense of duty was no doubt reinforced by Lincoln's adept flattery of Bates during their conversation: "He assured me . . . that I am the only man that he desired in the Cabinet," Bates recorded. John G. Nicolay, "Memorandum, Springfield, 15 December 1860," 18; *Bates Diary: 1859–1866*, 165.

48. *Bates Diary: 1859–1866*, 164–65; John G. Nicolay, "Memorandum, Springfield, 15 December 1860," 18.
49. *Bates Diary: 1859–1866*, 165.
50. Cain argues in *Lincoln's Attorney General* that "Bates had little use for the compromise plans that had been proffered" by Southern unionists in the winter of 1860–1861, including Crittenden's plan. In a rough draft of suggestions he planned to make to Lincoln in January 1861, however, Bates encouraged Lincoln to concede "the substance of Crittenden's amendment"—or, at least, to give "an intimation to your friends at Washington to the effect that, if Congress should choose to adopt that course, as a compromise, & the South accept it, & cease the secession movements, you & yours will throw no obstacle in its way." Bates made clear in this memo that he considered both the extension of the Missouri Compromise line and the amendment protecting slavery where it already existed to be acceptable concessions if they would halt the tide of secession and ensure peace. Cain, *Lincoln's Attorney General*, 170; "Rough Draft of Suggestions to Mr. Lincoln," January 1861, box 1, Edward Bates Papers, LC (collection hereafter cited as Bates Papers, LC). For more on Bates's relationship with Crittenden, see also *Bates Diary: 1859–1866*, 154–56.
51. "Rough Draft of Suggestions to Mr. Lincoln," January 1861, box 1, Bates Papers, LC; *Browning Diary*, 1:457.
52. Abraham Lincoln, "First Inaugural Address, March 4, 1861," in Basler, *Lincoln Speeches and Writings, 1859–1865*, 2:215, 222; Abraham Lincoln to Lyman Trumbull, December 10, 1860, in *Lincoln Speeches and Writings, 1859–1865*, 2:190; Abraham Lincoln to William Kellogg, December 11, 1860, in *Lincoln Speeches and Writings, 1859–1865*, 2:190; Abraham Lincoln to James T. Hale, January 11, 1861, in *Lincoln Speeches and Writings, 1859–1865*, 2:196; Crofts, *Lincoln and the Politics of Slavery*, 5–6, 235–37.
53. Abraham Lincoln, "First Inaugural Address, March 4, 1861" in Basler, *Lincoln Speeches and Writings, 1859–1865*, 2:218, 224; Ronald C. White Jr., *The Eloquent President: A Portrait of Lincoln through His Words* (New York: Random House, 2005), 69–79; Crofts, *Lincoln and the Politics of Slavery*, 5–6, 235–37. For more on Lincoln's belief that only a minority of Southerners supported secession, see also Abraham Lincoln, "Message to Congress in Special Session, July 4, 1861," in Basler, *Lincoln Speeches and Writings, 1859–1865*, 2:258.
54. "Edward Bates' Notes from Cabinet Meeting on Fort Sumter," March 29, 1861, Lincoln Papers, LC. The same memo appears in *Bates Diary: 1859–1866*, 180–81. See Russell McClintock, *Lincoln and the Decision for War: The Northern Response to Secession* (Chapel Hill: University of North Carolina Press, 2008), 200–15.
55. Winfield Scott to Abraham Lincoln, March 12, 1861, Lincoln Papers, LC; "Edward Bates' Notes from Cabinet Meeting on Fort Sumter," March 29, 1861; *Bates Diary: 1859–1866*, 181; McClintock, *Decision for War*, 212–32.
56. Edward Bates to John Minor Botts, April 29, 1861, in John Minor Botts, *The Great Rebellion: Its Secret History, Rise, Progress, and Disastrous Failure* (New York: Harper & Brothers, 1866), 266; *Bates Diary: 1859–1866*, 179, 167.
57. Edward Bates to John Minor Botts, April 29, 1861, in Botts, *Great Rebellion*, 266; *Browning Diary*, 492.

58. "Memos in Cabinet Council," April 15, 1861, box 1, Bates Papers, LC.

59. *Bates Diary: 1859–1866*, 185.

60. *Bates Diary: 1859–1866*, 220, 224, 185–86, 198–99, 217–19, 229.

61. *Bates Diary: 1859–1866*, 271, 333–34; Abraham Lincoln, "Order Concerning the Confiscation Act, November 13, 1862," in *Abraham Lincoln Complete Works: Comprising His Speeches, Letters, State Papers, and Miscellaneous Writings*, 8 vols., ed. John G. Nicolay and John Hay (New York: The Century Co., 1920), 2:253; John Syrett, *The Civil War Confiscation Acts: Failing to Reconstruct the South* (New York: Fordham University Press, 2005), xi–xii, 13–16, 54–72.

62. Abraham Lincoln, "Preliminary Emancipation Proclamation, September 22, 1862," in Nicolay and Hay, *Lincoln Complete Works*, 1:237; Bates Diary 1846–1852, January 30, 1848, box 1, Bates Papers, MHM; *Bates Diary: 1859–1866*, 263, 393; Abraham Lincoln, "Final Emancipation Proclamation, January 1, 1863," in Nicolay and Hay, *Lincoln Complete Works*, 1:287–88.

63. *Bates Diary: 1859–1866*, 371, 383, 413; Edward Bates, *Opinion of Attorney General Bates on Citizenship* (Washington, DC: Government Printing Office, 1862), 3–27.

64. *Bates Diary: 1859–1866*, 272, 422.

"Responsible to One Another and to God"

1. "Instructions for the Government of Armies of the United States in the Field," US War Department, *The War of the Rebellion: A Compilation of the Official Records of the Union and Confederate Armies*, 127 vols. index and atlas (Washington, DC: GPO, 1880–1901), ser. 3, vol. 3, 150. Hereafter cited as *OR*.

2. For an introduction to the life and thought of Francis Lieber, see Frank Freidel, *Francis Lieber, Nineteenth-Century Liberal* (Baton Rouge: Louisiana State University Press, 1947); Richard Shelly Hartigan, *Lieber's Code and the Law of War* (Precedent: Chicago, 1983); John Fabian Witt, *Lincoln's Code* (New York: Free Press, 2012), 139–324; Matthew J. Mancini, "Francis Lieber, Slavery, and the 'Genesis' of the Laws of War," *Journal of Southern History* 77, no. 2 (May 2011): 325–48; Burrus M. Carnahan, "Lincoln, Lieber, and the Laws of War: The Origins and Limits of the Principle of Military Necessity," *American Journal of International Law* 92, no. 2 (April 1998): 213–31; James F. Childress, "Francis Lieber's Interpretation of the Laws of War: General Orders no. 100 in the Context of His Life and Thought," *American Journal of Jurisprudence* 34 (1976): 34–70.

3. For a thorough survey of this legal tradition, see Stephen C. Neff, *War and the Law of Nations: A General History* (Cambridge: Cambridge University Press, 2005).

4. "Guerrilla Parties Considered with References to the Laws and Usages of War," in *OR*, ser. 3, vol. 2, 301–9; "The Disposal of Prisoners: Would the Exchange of Prisoners Amount to a Partial Acknowledgement of the Insurgents as Belligerents, According to International Law?" *New York Times*, August 19, 1861.

5. The full text of "Instructions for the Government of Armies of the United States in the Field," General Orders no. 100, appears in *OR*, ser. 3, vol. 3, 148–64. The citations from the code that follow will for clarity's sake reference only the article from which a quote is taken.

6. "Instructions for the Government of Armies of the United States in the Field," article 29.

7. Friedel notes this important point about the code's form and calls it one of the code's "greatest merits." Friedel, *Francis Lieber*, 335.

8. "Instructions for the Government of Armies of the United States in the Field," article 5.

9. The biographical material presented is indebted to Freidel, *Francis Lieber*.

10. Freidel, *Francis Lieber*, 80–81; Michael O'Brien has offered this insightful reflection on the effects of Lieber's time in South Carolina on his intellectual outlook: "On the whole, experiencing slavery seems to have strengthened the streak of antimillennial, empirical skepticism in Lieber—the same effect slavery had on many southerners. Lieber departed his life as a southern slaveholder in 1857 with a somewhat darker view of humanity, perhaps even of himself, than when he arrived in Columbia in 1835." Michael O'Brien, "The Stranger in the South," in *Francis Lieber and the Culture of the Mind*, ed. Charles R. Mack and Henry H. Lesesne (Columbia: University of South Carolina, 2005), 34.

11. Francis Lieber, "Law and Usages of War," October 29, 1861, box 2, folder 16, Papers of Francis Lieber, Milton S. Eisenhower Library, Special Collections, Johns Hopkins University (repository hereafter cited as JHU); Francis Lieber to Samuel B. Ruggles, April 23, 1847, box 39, Papers of Francis Lieber, Huntington Library, San Marino, California (repository hereafter cited as HL); Francis Lieber to George Hillard, April 18, 1854, box 31, Papers of Francis Lieber, HL; Francis Lieber, *Manual of Political Ethics* (Boston: Charles Little and James Brown, 1839), 2:632–33.

12. Francis Lieber to Edward Bates, July 23, 1861, box 23, Papers of Francis Lieber, HL.

13. Gary W. Gallagher, *The Union War* (Cambridge, MA: Harvard University Press, 2011).

14. Gallagher, *The Union War*, 2.

15. Daniel Webster, "The Constitution and the Union," in *The Senate, 1789–1989*, vol. 3, *Classic Speeches, 1830–1993*, ed. Robert C. Byrd (Washington, DC: Government Printing Office, 1994).

16. Abraham Lincoln, "Message to Congress in Special Session, July 4, 1861," in *The Portable Abraham Lincoln*, ed. Andrew Delbanco (New York: Penguin, 2009), 253.

17. Quoted in Gallagher, *The Union War*, 72–73.

18. Francis Lieber, "A Song on Our Country and Her Flag," container 1, Francis Lieber Papers, Manuscript Division, Library of Congress, Washington, DC.

19. Lieber, "A Song on Our Country and Her Flag."

20. Lieber, "A Song on Our Country and Her Flag."

21. Instructions for the Government of Armies of the United States in the Field," article 29.

22. "The Disposal of Prisoners: Would the Exchange of Prisoners Amount to a Partial Acknowledgement of the Insurgents as Belligerents, According to International Law?" *New York Times*, August 19, 1861.

23. *OR*, ser. 3, vol. 2, 301–9; Henry Halleck to Francis Lieber, August 20, 1862, box 9, Papers of Francis Lieber, HL.

24. Francis Lieber to Charles Sumner, August 20, 1861, box 42, Papers of Francis Lieber, HL. Paroled Union soldiers, Lieber said, had abandoned their solemn oath to defend the Union, an oath they had no right to invalidate after their capture. Lieber did not object to the exchange of prisoners, but he vehemently opposed paroling.

25. In mid-August 1861, Lieber confessed to a longtime correspondent, "I should much like to write a book of some 200 pages . . . on the Laws and Usage of War affecting the combatants, and I think I could write an acceptable book for every intelligent soldier." Francis Lieber to S. Austin Allibone, August 19, 1861, box 22, Papers of Francis Lieber, HL.

26. Francis Lieber to Henry Halleck, November 13, 1862, box 27, Papers of Francis Lieber, HL.

27. Lieber to Halleck, November 20, 1862, box 9, Papers of Francis Lieber, HL; Halleck to Lieber, November 23, 1862, box 27, Papers of Francis Lieber, HL.

28. Lieber wrote to Halleck, Stanton, and the code's committee and sought out the opinions of Charles Sumner and former New York governor and US senator Hamilton Fish, among other Union leaders.

29. Henry Halleck to Francis Lieber, May 25, 1863, box 9, Papers of Francis Lieber, HL.

30. Freidel, *Francis Lieber*, 335.

31. "Instructions for the Government of Armies of the United States in the Field," article 29.

32. "Instructions for the Government of Armies of the United States in the Field," article 14.

33. "Instructions for the Government of Armies of the United States in the Field," article 16.

34. "Instructions for the Government of Armies of the United States in the Field," articles 15, 20.

35. "Instructions for the Government of Armies of the United States in the Field," articles 29, 16.

36. Witt offers a compelling survey of this legal perspective in *Lincoln's Code*, 197–219.

37. "Instructions for the Government of Armies of the United States in the Field," articles 42–43.

38. Francis Lieber, "A Memoir on the Military Use of Coloured Persons, free or slave, that come to our armies for support or protection," in Francis Lieber to Henry Halleck, August 9, 1862, box 27, Papers of Francis Lieber, HL.

39. "Instructions for the Government of Armies of the United States in the Field," articles 49–50.

40. "Instructions for the Government of Armies of the United States in the Field," articles 56, 75, 76, 80, 72.

41. "Instructions for the Government of Armies of the United States in the Field," articles 60–63. Lieber did include one possible exception to the prohibition on no quarter, if it saved the lives of one's own soldiers: "A commander is permitted to direct his troops to give no quarter, in great straits, when his own salvation makes it *impossible* to cumber himself with prisoners."

42. "Instructions for the Government of Armies of the United States in the Field," articles 57; Francis Lieber, "A Memoir on the Military Use of Coloured Persons"; "Instructions for the Government of Armies of the United States in the Field," article 58.

43. "Instructions for the Government of Armies of the United States in the Field," articles 27–28, 59; Childress, "Francis Lieber's Interpretation of the Laws of War," 66–68.

44. "Instructions for the Government of Armies of the United States in the Field," articles 22–25.

45. "Instructions for the Government of Armies of the United States in the Field," articles 43–44. Henry Halleck had in early March 1863 advised Major General William S. Rosencrans, and by extension all Union commanders in the West, to show precisely this same sort of discretion in treating civilians differently according to their loyalties. "The people of the country in which you are likely to operate may be divided into three classes," Halleck advised: the truly loyal, the quietly disloyal who take no active part in aiding Confederate armies, and the disloyal who remain "openly and obviously hostile to the occupying army." Well aware of the rules soon to be issued in the impending Lieber Code, Halleck, like Lieber, advised a harsher treatment for the aggressively disloyal. *OR*, ser. 1, vol. 23, pt. 2, 107–9. Mark Grimsley charted this same spirit of "directed severity" throughout the entire Union war effort, yet he ultimately reached grim conclusions about the Lieber Code's articles on the treatment of enemy civilians. "It erected few strong barriers against severe treatment," he suggested, and in fact it served to guarantee "that protection to enemy civilians was the exception, not rule." Mark Grimsley, *Hard Hand of War: Union Policy toward Southern Civilians, 1861–1865* (Cambridge: Cambridge University Press, 1995), 150.

46. "Instructions for the Government of Armies of the United States in the Field," articles 23, 37.

47. "Instructions for the Government of Armies of the United States in the Field," article 29.

48. Francis Lieber, "A Song on Our Country and Her Flag"; "Instructions for the Government of Armies of the United States in the Field," article 5.

Building a Union of Banks

1. "Conditions of the Federal Banking System," Office of the Comptroller of the Currency, US Department of the Treasury, https://www.occ.gov/annual-report/condition-of-the-federal-banking-system/index-condition-of-the-federal-banking-system.html.

2. Gary W. Gallagher, *The Union War* (Cambridge, MA: Harvard University Press, 2012). For a consideration of the creation of the Constitution as an act of economic union, see Cathy D. Matson and Peter S. Onuf, *A Union of Interests: Political and Economic Thought in Revolutionary America* (Lawrence: University of Kansas Press, 1990); Heather Cox Richardson, *The Greatest Nation of the Earth: Republican Economic Policies during the Civil War* (Cambridge, MA: Harvard University Press, 1997); Eric Foner, *Reconstruction: America's Unfinished Revolution, 1863–1877* (New York: HarperCollins, 1988); and Leonard Curry, *Blueprint for Modern America: Non-Military Legislation of the First Civil War Congress* (Nashville, TN: Vanderbilt University Press, 1968).

3. Charles A. Beard, *An Economic Interpretation of the Constitution of the United States* (New York: MacMillan, 1913); Charles A. Beard and Mary R. Beard, *The Rise of American Civilization*, vol. 2, *The Industrial Era* (New York: The MacMillan Company, 1927), 52–121. See, generally, Philip Shaw Paludan, "What Did the Winners Win? The Social and Economic History of the North during the Civil War," in *Writing the Civil War: The Quest to Understand*, ed. James M. McPherson and William J. Cooper Jr. (Columbia: University of South Carolina Press, 1998), 174–200; James M. McPherson, *Battle Cry of Freedom: The Civil War Era* (Oxford: Oxford University Press, 1988), 452; Richard Franklin Bensel, *Yankee Leviathan: The Origins of Central State Authority in America, 1859–1877* (Cambridge: Cambridge University Press, 1990); Daniel Walker Howe, *What Hath God Wrought: The Transformation of America, 1815–1848* (New York: Oxford University Press, 2007); and Bray Hammond, *Banks and Politics in America: From the Revolution to the Civil War* (Princeton, NJ: Princeton University Press, 1957).

4. Bensel, *Yankee Leviathan*. For debates about the concept of a "Yankee Leviathan" in nineteenth-century America, see Gregory P. Downs and Kate Masur, eds., *The World the Civil War Made* (Chapel Hill: University of North Carolina Press, 2015), 6–7; Gary Gerstle, "The Civil War and State-Building: A Reconsideration," *Journal of the Civil War Era* forums, https://journalofthecivilwarera.org/forum-the-future-of-reconstruction-studies/the-civil-war-and-state-building/; Brian Balogh, *A Government out of Sight: The Mystery of National Authority in Nineteenth-Century America* (New York: Cambridge University Press, 2009); and Richard White, *The Republic for Which It Stands: The United States during the Reconstruction and the Gilded Age, 1865–1896* (New York: Oxford University Press, 2017).

5. Howe, *What Hath God Wrought*, 561; Stephen Mihm, *A Nation of Counterfeiters: Capitalists, Con Men, and the Making of the United States* (Cambridge, MA: Harvard University Press, 2007); Joshua R. Greenberg, "The Era of Shinplasters: Making Sense of Unregulated Paper Money," in *Capitalism by Gaslight: Illuminating the Economy of Nineteenth-Century America*, ed. Brian P. Luskey and Wendy A. Woloson (Philadelphia: University of Pennsylvania Press, 2015), 51–75; Hammond, *Banks and Politics in America*, 172–96.

6. David A. Martin, "US Gold Production Prior to the California Gold Rush," *Explorations in Economic History* 13 (1976): 437–49; Mihm, *A Nation of Counterfeiters*, 3–19; Milton Friedman and Anna Jacobson Schwartz, *A Monetary History of the United States, 1867–1960* (Princeton, NJ: Princeton University Press), 25–29; James C. Wall, "Gold Dust and Greenbacks," *Montana: The Magazine of Western History* 7 (1957): 24–31.

7. Sharon Ann Murphy, *Other People's Money: How Banking Worked in the Early American Republic* (Baltimore, MD: Johns Hopkins University Press, 2017); Hammond, *Banks and Politics in America*, 144–71; Leonard Clinton Helderman, *National and State Banks: A Study of Their Origins* (New York: Houghton Mifflin, 1931).

8. Jessica M. Lepler, *The Many Panics of 1837: People, Politics, and the Creation of a Transatlantic Financial Crisis* (New York: Cambridge University Press, 2013), 123–56; Scott Reynolds Nelson, *A Nation of Deadbeats: An Uncommon History of America's Financial Disasters* (New York: Knopf, 2012), 120–25.

9. Jeffrey Sklansky, "William Leggett and the Melodrama of the Market," in *Capitalism Takes Command: The Social Transformation of Nineteenth-Century America*, ed.

Michael Zakim and Gary J. Kornblith (Chicago: University of Chicago Press, 2012), 216–21; Mihm, *A Nation of Counterfeiters*.

10. Hammond, *Banks and Politics in America*; William G. Shade, *Banks or No Banks: The Money Issue in Western Politics, 1832–1865* (Detroit, MI: Wayne State University Press, 1972).

11. "Second Report on Further Provision Necessary for Establishing Public Credit (Report on a National Bank)," in *The Papers of Alexander Hamilton Digital Edition*, ed. Harold C. Syrett (Charlottesville: University of Virginia, Rotunda, 2011), http://rotunda.upress.virginia.edu/founders/ARHN-01-07-02-0229. Morris quoted in E. James Ferguson, *The Power of the Purse: A History of American Public Finance, 1776–1790* (Chapel Hill: University of North Carolina Press, 1961), 123.

12. Bray Hammond, *Banks and Politics*, 144–71; Howard Bodenhorn, *State Banking in Early America: A New Economic History* (New York: Oxford University Press, 2003), 11–43; Warren E. Weber, "Early State Banks in the United States: How Many Were There and When Did They Exist?" *Journal of Economic History* 66, no. 6 (June 2006): 449–50; David Jack Cowen, "The Origins and Economic Impact of the First Bank of the United States, 1791–1797," PhD diss., New York University, 1999, 156.

13. Henry Adams, *History of the United States during the Second Administration of James Madison* (New York: C. Scribner's Sons, 1891), 239.

14. *Briscoe v. Bank of Kentucky* 36 U.S. 257 (1837); Thomas Jefferson to John Adams, January 24, 1814, in *The Papers of Thomas Jefferson, Retirement Series*, ed. J. Jefferson Looney (Princeton, NJ: Princeton University Press, 2010), 6:224.

15. Weber, "Early State Banks in the United States," 450; Hammond, *Banks and Politics*, 227–50, 286–450; Worden Pope to Andrew Jackson, June 19, 1831, in *The Papers of Andrew Jackson, Digital Edition*, ed. Daniel Feller (Charlottesville: University of Virginia Press, 2015–), http://rotunda.upress.virginia.edu/founders/JKSN-01-09-02-0231.

16. Andrew Jackson, "Veto Message," July 10, 1832, in *A Compilation of the Messages and Papers of the President, 1789–1908*, ed. James D. Richardson (Washington, DC: Bureau of National Literature and Art), 3:580–81, 579.

17. Hammond, *Banks and Politics in America*, 490–99, 542–45; John M McFaul, *The Politics of Jacksonian Finance* (Ithaca, NY: Cornell University Press, 1972), 178–209; Michael F. Holt, *The Rise of and Fall of the American Whig Party*, 67–68; Sean Wilentz, *The Rise of American Democracy: Jefferson to Lincoln* (New York: Norton, 2005), 456–65.

18. *Register of Debates*, 25th Congress, 1st sess., 194; *Boston Post*, July 4, 1837; *Evening Post* (New York City), August 11, 1834.

19. *Register of Debates*, 25th Congress, 1st sess., 873, 260.

20. Helderman, *National and State Banks*, 25–29, 41–46, 91–100, 101–32; Shade, *Banks or No Banks*; James Roger Sharp, *Jacksonians versus the Banks: Politics in the States after the Panic of 1837* (New York: Columbia University Press, 1970); "Memorial of the Board of Trade of the City of New York," *Niles Weekly Register* 1, fifth ser., 22 (January 28, 1837): 343.

21. "Democratic Party Platform," June 18, 1860, from the Avalon Project, Documents in Law, History, and Diplomacy, Lillian Goldman Law Library, Yale Law School, http://avalon.law.yale.edu/19th_century/dem1860.asp.

22. Bensel, *Yankee Leviathan*, 303–48; Balogh, *A Government out of Sight*, 285–91, 303–8; Leonard Curry, *Blueprint for Modern America: Non-Military Legislation of the*

First Civil War Congress (Nashville, TN: Vanderbilt University Press, 1968); Richardson, *The Greatest Nation of the Earth*; William G. Thomas, *The Iron Way: Railroads, the Civil War, and the Making of Modern America* (New Haven, CT: Yale University Press, 2011); Mark R. Wilson, *The Business of Civil War: Military Mobilization and the State, 1861–1865* (Baltimore, MD: Johns Hopkins University Press, 2006); David G. Thomson, "'Like a Cord Through the Whole Country': Union Bonds and Financial Mobilization for Victory," *Journal of the Civil War Era* 6 (September 2016): 347–75.

23. Michael T. Caires, "The Greenback Union: The Politics and Law of American Money in the Civil War Era," PhD diss., University of Virginia, 2014, 26–34.

24. Bray Hammond, *Sovereignty and an Empty Purse: Banks and Politics in the Civil War Era* (Princeton, NJ: Princeton University Press, 1970), 71–105; George S. Coe to Salmon P. Chase, November 11, 1861, in *The Papers of Salmon P. Chase*, ed. John Niven (Frederick, MD: University Publications of America, 1987), text-fiche, reel 18 (hereafter cited as Chase Papers).

25. *Report of the Secretary of the Treasury, on the State of the Finances, for the Year Ending June 30, 1861* (Washington, DC: GPO, 1861), 17.

26. *Report of the Secretary of the Treasury, 1861*, 18.

27. Hammond, *Banks and Politics*, 583; *Report of the Secretary of the Treasury, 1861*, 19.

28. *Report of the Secretary of the Treasury, 1861*, 20; *Daily Evening Bulletin* (San Francisco), January 7, 1862; *St. Louis Republican*, December 16, 1861.

29. E. G. Spaulding, *A Resource of War—The Credit of the Government Made Immediately Available: History of the Legal Tender Money* . . . (Buffalo, NY: Express Printing Company, 1869), 12. E. G. Spaulding served on Ways and Means during the Civil War and recounted how Chase provided no draft to the committee, which Spaulding worked on sometime around December 24, 1861. *New York Herald*, December 28, 1861; *New York Times*, December 31, 1861.

30. Hammond, *Sovereignty and an Empty Purse*, 150–159; James Gallatin, "Gallatin on the Currency," *Bankers Magazine* 11 (February 1862): 627.

31. Salmon P. Chase to William P. Fessenden, January 7, 1862, Chase Papers, reel 18; Spaulding, *History of the Legal Tender Paper Money* (1875), 18–22; *New York Daily Tribune*, January 13, 1862; Chase, "Memorandum on Financial Measures," January 15, 1862, Chase Papers, reel 42. This is an original draft of the joint message from the bankers and Chase. A reprint of the final draft submitted to the Associated Press can be found in Spaulding, *History of the Legal Tender Paper Money* (1875), 21–22. Jay Cooke to Chase, January 18, 1862, Chase to John A. Stevens, January 17, 1862, Chase Papers, reel 19.

32. Wesley Clair Mitchell, *A History of the Greenbacks: With a Special Reference to the Economic Consequences of Their Issue* (Chicago: University of Chicago Press, 1903), 100–5.

33. Chase to Thaddeus Stevens, December 23, 1862, Chase Papers, reel 24; Mitchell, *A History of the Greenbacks*, 425; Timothy W. Guinnane, Harvey S. Rosen, and Kristin L. Willard, "Messages from 'the Den of Wild Beasts': Greenback Prices as Commentary on the Union's Prospects," *Civil War History* 41 (December 1995): 323.

34. *Report of the Secretary of the Treasury on the State of the Finances for the Year Ending June 30, 1862* (Washington, DC: GPO, 1863), 20; "Lines Written on a Greenback,"

Daily Cleveland Herald, September 8, 1864; James Knowles Medbery, *Men and Mysteries of Wall Street* (Boston: Fields, Osgood, & Co., 1870), 244.

35. *Report of the Secretary of the Treasury, 1862*, 20.
36. Richardson, ed., *Messages and Papers of the Presidents*, 6:130, 149–50.
37. *Cong. Globe*, 37th Cong., 3d. Sess., Appendix, 47–52; John Sherman to Salmon P. Chase, February 7, 1863, Chase Papers, reel 25; Salmon P. Chase to Horace Greely, January 28, 1863, Chase Papers, reel 24; Henry Cooke to Jay Cooke, January 10, 1863, Jay Cooke papers, box 7, folder 4, Historical Society of Pennsylvania, Philadelphia; Salmon P. Chase to Jay Cooke, February 2, 1863, Chase Papers, reel 25; Chase to Abraham Lincoln, February 19, 1863, Chase Papers, reel 25.
38. Robert J. Walker, "Our National Finances," *Continental Monthly* 3 (February 1863): 136.
39. "The National Banking Project," *New York Times*, February 2, 1863; *Cong. Globe*, 37th Cong., 3d. Sess., 844.
40. *Report of the Secretary of the Treasury, 1862*, 17–18; Walker, "Our National Finances," 140; "The National Banking Project," *New York Times*, February 2, 1863.
41. Walker, "Our National Finances," 143; "The National Banking Project," *New York Times*, February 2, 1863; *Cong. Globe*, 37th Cong., 3d. Sess., 843.
42. Silas Moore Stilwell, *Private History of the Origin and Purpose of the National Banking Law and System of Organized Credits for the United States* (New York: Trow's Printing and Bookbinding Co., 1879), 12.
43. Robert J. Walker to John Sherman, January 31, 1863, box 55, John Sherman Papers, Library of Congress, Washington, DC; *New York Times*, February 2, 1863.
44. H. H. Van Dyck, "Banking in the State of New-York: Annual Report of the Superintendent of the Banking Department of the State of New-York, December 31, 1862," *Banker's Magazine* 12 (April 1862): 749–50.
45. Van Dyck, "Banking in the State of New-York," 749.
46. *Cong. Globe*, 37th Cong., 3d. Sess., 871, 846, 870, 879.
47. Van Dyck, "Banking in the State of New-York," 750; *Chicago Tribune*, February 11, 1863.
48. "National Notes vs. Labor," *Old Guard* 2 (January 1864): 12; "Omnium: The Lincoln Catechism," *Old Guard* 1 (March 1863): 69; *Cong. Globe*, 37th Cong., 3d. Sess., 871.
49. *A National Currency: What Is Needed. Suggestions by a Practical Banker* (Philadelphia, 1863), 11, 14, 16; *New York Times*, February 15, 1863; E. N. Sill to John Sherman, January 28, 1863, box 55, John Sherman Papers, Library of Congress, Washington, DC.
50. David M. Gische, "The New York City Banks and the Development of the National Banking System, 1860–1870," *American Journal of Legal History* 23, no. 1 (1979): 49–55; Joseph Edwards Hedges, "Commercial Banking and the Stock Market before 1863," PhD diss., Johns Hopkins University, 1938; Jerome W. Sheridan, "Financing Industrial Growth: The Transformation of Bank Investments from Antebellum State Banking to the National Banks of the United States, 1840–1890," PhD diss., American University, 1990; "An Act to Provide a National Currency," Ch. 106, 13 *Stat.* 99 (1864); Richard S. Grossman, "US Banking History, Civil War to World War II," *EH.Net Encyclopedia*, http://eh.net/encyclopedia/article/grossman.banking.history.us.civil.war.wwii#_ftn2.

51. Quoted in Hammond, *Sovereignty and an Empty Purse*, 346; *Cong. Globe*, 38th Cong., 2nd Sess., 1139, 833, 1197; Act of March 3, 1865, Ch. 13, 13 *Stat.* 484 (1865).

52. Matthew Jaremski, "National Banking's Role in US Industrialization," *Journal of Economic History* 74, no. 1 (2014): 109–40; Harry N. Scheiber, "Economic Change in the Civil War Era: An Analysis of Recent Studies," *Civil War History* 11 (1965): 409; Sheridan, "Financing Industrial Growth," 367–97.

53. Act of June 3, 1864, Ch. 106, 13 *Stat.* 99 at 101 § 7; Richard Sylla, "Federal Policy, Banking Market Structure, and Capital Mobilization in the United States, 1863–1913," *Journal of Economic History* 29 (1969): 659–60; John A. James, *Money and Capital Markets in Postbellum America* (Princeton, NJ: Princeton University Press, 1976), 28–29.

54. *Report of the Comptroller of the Currency to the Third Session of the Forty-First Congress* (Washington, DC: GPO, 1870), xvi; George L. Anderson, "The National Banking System, 1865–1875: Sectional Institution," PhD diss., University of Illinois, 1933, 145–86; Larry Schweikart, *Banking in the American South: From the Age of Jackson to Reconstruction* (Baton Rouge: Louisiana State University Press, 1987), 310–11; James L. Sellers, "The Economic Incidence of the Civil War in the South," in *The Economic Impact of the American Civil War*, ed. Ralph Andreano (Cambridge, MA: Schenkman, 1967), 98–108.

55. Fritz Redlich, *The Molding of American Banking: Men and Ideas* (New York: Johnson Reprint Corp., 1968), 2:119; Jeffery A. Miron, "Financial Panics, the Seasonality of Nominal Interest Rate, and the Founding of the Fed," *American Economic Review* 76 (1986): 125–38; Elmus Wicker, *Banking Panics of the Gilded Age* (New York: Cambridge University Press, 2000), xiii–xiv, 146.

56. Gretchen Ritter, *Goldbugs and Greenbacks: The Antimonopoly Tradition and the Politics of Finance in America* (New York: Cambridge University Press, 1997), 90–96; *The National Banks. Down with the Banks, Greenbacks Forever* (c. 1868), 10, Indiana Historical Society, Indianapolis; Gabriel Kolko, *The Triumph of Conservatism: A Reinterpretation of American History, 1900–1916* (New York: The Free Press, 1963), 139–58. James Livingston, *Origins of the Federal Reserve System: Money, Class, and Corporate Capitalism, 1890–1913* (Ithaca, NY: Cornell University Press, 1986), 17–29.

57. Salmon P. Chase to James Shepard Pike, December 24, 1869, Chase Papers, reel 38; James Willard Hurst, *Law and Conditions of Freedom in the Nineteenth-Century United States* (Madison: University of Wisconsin Press, 1956), 10.

"To Transmit and Perpetuate the Fruits of This Victory"

Thanks to Gary W. Gallagher, Katherine Shively, Elizabeth R. Varon, and two anonymous readers, all of whom provided incisive comments that improved this essay. Thanks, as well, to those others who helped.

1. James M. McPherson, *For Cause and Comrades: Why Men Fought in the Civil War* (New York: Oxford University Press, 1997), 11; Aaron Sheehan-Dean, "The Blue and Gray in Black and White: Assessing the Scholarship on Civil War Soldiers," in *The View from the Ground: Experiences of Civil War Soldiers*, ed. Aaron Sheehan-Dean (Lexington: University of Kentucky Press, 2007), 10.

2. The historians Gerald Linderman and David Blight have examined the efflorescence in the 1880s of literature on the Civil War but have missed this earlier surge of books. The historian Stephen Z. Starr has published a short survey of the genre of regimental histories, but the lack of a comprehensive bibliography at the time resulted in provisional conclusions. Only recently have scholars such as Gary W. Gallagher begun to look at regimental histories from 1865 and 1866. Gerald Linderman, *Embattled Courage: The Experience of Combat in the American Civil War* (New York: Free Press, 1987), 268–69; David W. Blight, *Race and Reunion: The Civil War in American Memory* (Cambridge, MA: Belknap Press of Harvard University Press, 2001), 211–99; Stephen Z. Starr, "The Grand Old Regiment," *Wisconsin Magazine of History* 48 (Autumn 1964): 22; Gary W. Gallagher, *The Union War* (Cambridge, MA: Harvard University Press, 2011), 65–70. Others have begun to look at regimental histories in general: Peter S. Carmichael, "We Respect a *Good* Soldier, No Matter What Flag He Fought Under: The 15th New Jersey Remembers Spotsylvania," in *The Spotsylvania Campaign*, ed. Gary W. Gallagher (Chapel Hill: University of North Carolina Press, 1998); Lesley J. Gordon, "All Who Went into That Battle Were Heroes: Remembering the 16th Regiment Connecticut Volunteers at Antietam," in *The Antietam Campaign*, ed. Gary W. Gallagher (Chapel Hill: University of North Carolina Press, 1999); Robert Hunt, *The Good Men Who Won the War: Army of the Cumberland Veterans and Emancipation Memory* (Tuscaloosa: University of Alabama Press, 2010).

3. This tabulation has been compiled from Charles Dornbusch, *Military Bibliography of the Civil War*, 3 vols. (New York: New York Public Library, 1961–1972); and Silas Felton, *Military Bibliography of the Civil War*, vol. 4, rev. ed. (Dayton, OH: Morningside, 2003). See also Peter C. Luebke, "'To Transmit and Perpetuate the Fruits of This Victory:' Union Regimental Histories, 1865–1866, and the Meaning of the Great Rebellion," MA thesis, University of Virginia, 2007, 16–17, 53.

4. Gerald J. Prokopowicz, *All for the Regiment: The Army of the Ohio, 1861–1862* (Chapel Hill: University of North Carolina Press, 2001), 4–5.

5. For the classic account of how writing contributes to community formation, see Benedict Anderson, *Imagined Communities: Reflections on the Origin and Spread of Nationalism*, rev. ed. (New York: Verso, 2006). For an account of imagined nationalism, regional differences, and print culture in the antebellum United States, see Trish Loughran, *The Republic in Print: Print Culture in the Age of US Nation Building, 1770–1870* (New York: Columbia University Press, 2007).

6. William H. Chamberlin, *History of the Eighty-First Regiment Ohio Infantry Volunteers, during the War of the Rebellion* (Cincinnati: Gazette Steam-Printing House, 1865), 3.

7. Henry M. Davidson, *History of Battery A, First Regiment Ohio Vol. Light Artillery* (Milwaukee: Daily Wisconsin Print House, 1865), iii.

8. William H. Rogers, *History of the One Hundred and Eighty-Ninth Regiment of New-York Volunteers* (New York: John A. Gray & Green, 1865), 5.

9. James H. Clark, *The Iron Hearted Regiment: Being an Account of the Battles, Marches and Gallant Deeds Performed by the 115th Regiment N.Y. Vols., Also a List of the Dead and Wounded, an Account of Hundreds of Brave Men Shot on a Score of Hard*

Fought Fields of Strife, A Complete Statement of Harper's Ferry Surrender, Sketches of the Officers, a History of the Flags and Those Who Bore Them, Together with Touching Incidents, Thrilling Adventures, Amusing Scenes, etc., etc., etc. (Albany, NY: J. Munsell, 1865), iii.

10. Joshua H. Horton and Solomon Teverbaugh, *History of the Eleventh Regiment (Ohio Volunteer Infantry), Containing the Military Record, So Far as It Is Possible to Obtain It, of Each Officer and Enlisted Man in the Command, a List of Deaths, an Account of the Veterans, Incidents of Field and Camp, Names of Three Months' Volunteers, Compiled from the Official Records* (Dayton, OH: W. J. Shuey, 1866), 121.

11. For a discussion of how nineteenth-century Americans saw personal experience as the measure of literary authority, see Ann Fabian, *The Unvarnished Truth: Personal Narratives in Nineteenth-Century America* (Berkeley: University of California Press, 2000).

12. William W. H. Davis, *History of the 104th Pennsylvania Regiment, from August 22nd, 1861, to September 30th, 1864* (Philadelphia: Jas. B. Rodgers, 1866), viii.

13. Harris Beecher, *History of the 114th Regiment, N.Y.S.V. Where It Went, What It Saw, and What It Did* (Norwich: J. F. Hubbard Jr., 1866), i–ii. Other regimental historians made use of contemporary newspaper correspondence from soldiers in the field. See Stephen Fleharty, *Our Regiment, a History of the 102d Illinois Infantry Volunteers, with Sketches of the Atlanta Campaign, the Georgia Raid, and the Campaign of the Carolinas* (Chicago: Brewster & Hanscom, 1865), 5; William L. Hyde, *History of the One Hundred and Twelfth Regiment N.Y. Volunteers* (Fredonia, NY: W. McKinstry & Co., 1866), vi; and Amos Judson, *History of the Eighty-Third Regiment Pennsylvania Volunteers*, ed. James A. Trulock and Alice Rains Trulock (1865; Arlington: Stonewall House, 1985), unpaginated introduction.

14. Davidson, *History of Battery A*, iii.

15. Emphasis in the original. Lyman B. Pierce, *History of the Second Iowa Cavalry, Containing a Detailed Account of Its Organization, Marches, and Battles in Which It Has Participated; Also, a Complete Roster of Each Company* (Burlington, IA: Hawk-Eye Printing Establishment, 1865), iii.

16. John R. Kinnear, *History of the Eighty-Sixth Regiment Illinois Volunteer Infantry, During Its Term of Service* (Chicago: Tribune Company's Book and Job Printing Office, 1866), v.

17. Pierce, *History of the Second Iowa Cavalry*, v.

18. Davis, *History of the 104th Pennsylvania Regiment*, viii.

19. Until the 1880s, the book trade functioned largely through local and interlocking networks of print and trade. Book production and bookselling in America only underwent a consolidation from the local to the national in the 1880s, after the introduction of new printing technology, the creation of larger distribution networks, new methods of distribution, and the establishment of national market. See Michael Winship, *A History of the Book in America*, vol. 3: *The Industrial Book, 1840–1880*, ed. Scott E. Casper, Jeffrey D. Groves, and Michael Winship (Chapel Hill: University of North Carolina Press, 2007), 40–69, 117–30.

20. Davidson, *History of Battery A*, 3; Horton and Teverbaugh, *History of the Eleventh Regiment*, xv.

21. Louis N. Beaudry, *War Journals of Louis N. Beaudry, Fifth New York Cavalry: The Diary of a Union Chaplain, Commencing February 16, 1863*, ed. Richard E. Beaudry (Jefferson, NC: McFarland, 1996), 232. Beaudry's initial print run remained small, but evidently he kept the plates and issued subsequent editions with extra material in 1865, 1868, and 1874. See Louis N. Beaudry, *Historic Records of the Fifth New York Cavalry, First Ira Harris Guard, Its Organization, Marches, Raids, Scouts, Engagements, and General Services During the Rebellion of 1861–1865, with Observations of the Author by the Way, Giving Sketches of the Armies of the Potomac and of the Shenandoah. Also, Interesting Accounts of Prison Life and of the Secret Service. Complete Lists of Its Officers and Men* (Albany, NY: S. R. Gray, 1865); *Historic Records of the Fifth New York Cavalry* . . . 2nd ed. (Albany, NY: S. R. Gray, 1865); *Historic Records of the Fifth New York Cavalry* . . . 3rd ed., enlarged (Albany, NY: J. Munsell, 1868); and *Historic Records of the Fifth New York Cavalry* . . . 4th ed., enlarged (Albany, NY: J. Munsell, 1874).

22. Eileen Ka-May Cheng, *The Plain and Noble Garb of Truth: Nationalism and Impartiality in American Historical Writing, 1784–1860* (Athens: University of Georgia Press, 2008), 255.

23. David Kaser, in his summary of reading among soldier camps, found that Union troops read works of history as well as biographies of historical figures. David Kaser, *Books and Libraries in Camp and Battle: The Civil War Experience* (Westport, CT: Greenwood, 1984), 17, 52, 59.

24. George L. Wood, *The Seventh Regiment* [Ohio Volunteer Infantry], *a Record* (New York: James Miller, 1865), 5–8.

25. For discussions of the idea of the "Slave Power conspiracy," see Chauncey Boucher, "*In Re* That Aggressive Slaveocracy," *Mississippi Valley Historical Review* 8, no. 1/2 (June–September 1921); David Brion Davis, *The Slave Power Conspiracy and the Paranoid Style* (Baton Rouge: Louisiana State University Press, 1969); Leonard L. Richards, *The Slave Power: The Free North and Southern Domination, 1780–1860* (Baton Rouge: Louisiana State University Press, 2000); and Andre M. Fleche, *The Revolution of 1861: The American Civil War in the Era of Nationalist Conflict* (Chapel Hill: University of North Carolina Press, 2012), 119–26.

26. M. D. Gage, *From Vicksburg to Raleigh; or, A Complete History of the Twelfth Regiment Indiana Volunteer Infantry, and the Campaigns of Grant and Sherman, with an Outline of the Great Rebellion* (Chicago: Clarke & Co., 1865), ix.

27. Gage, *From Vicksburg to Raleigh*, xii.
28. Gage, *From Vicksburg to Raleigh*, x.
29. Gage, *From Vicksburg to Raleigh*, xi.
30. Gage, *From Vicksburg to Raleigh*, xii.
31. Gage, *From Vicksburg to Raleigh*, xii.
32. Wales W. Wood, *A History of the Ninety-Fifth Regiment Illinois Infantry Volunteers, from Its Organization in the Fall of 1862, Until Its Final Discharge from the United States Service, in 1865* (Chicago: Tribune Company's Book and Job Printing Office, 1865), 62–63.
33. Wood, *A History of the Ninety-Fifth Regiment Illinois Infantry Volunteers*, 63.
34. Wood, *A History of the Ninety-Fifth Regiment Illinois Infantry Volunteers*, 64.
35. Wood, *A History of the Ninety-Fifth Regiment Illinois Infantry Volunteers*, 68.

36. J. A. Mowris, *A History of the One Hundred and Seventeenth Regiment, N.Y. Volunteers, (Fourth Oneida), from Its Date of Organization, August, 1862, Till That of Its Muster Out, June, 1865* (Hartford, CT: Case, Lockwood and Company, 1866), 36.

37. Mowris, *A History of the One Hundred and Seventeenth Regiment, N.Y. Volunteers*, 40.

38. Mowris, *A History of the One Hundred and Seventeenth Regiment, N.Y. Volunteers*, 205.

39. Wood, *The Seventh Regiment*, 16.

40. A. W. M. Petty, *History of the Third Missouri Cavalry from Its Organization in Palmyra, Missouri, 1861, up to November Sixth, 1864, with an Appendix and Recapitulation* (Little Rock, AR: J. Wm. Denby, 1865), 40.

41. Clark, *The Iron Hearted Regiment*, 123.

42. Osceola Lewis, *History of the One Hundred and Thirty-Eighth Regiment, Pennsylvania Volunteer Infantry* (Norristown: Wills, Iredell & Jenkins, 1866), 159–60.

43. Edwin B. Houghton, *The Campaigns of the Seventeenth Maine* (Portland, ME: Short & Loring, 1865), 96.

44. Wood, *A History of the Ninety-Fifth Regiment Illinois Infantry Volunteers*, 186.

45. Samuel Hurst, *Journal-History of the Seventy-Third Ohio Volunteer Infantry* (Chillicothe, OH: n.p., 1866), 144–45.

46. George W. Powers, *The Story of the Thirty-Eighth Regiment of Massachusetts Volunteers* (Cambridge, MA: Dakin and Metcalf, 1866), 206.

47. Wood, *A History of the Ninety-Fifth Regiment Illinois Infantry Volunteers*, 199.

48. Samuel Hurst, *Journal-History of the Seventy-Third Ohio Volunteer Infantry*, 144–45.

49. Mowris, *A History of the One Hundred and Seventeenth Regiment, N.Y. Volunteers*, 170.

50. Kinnear, *History of the Eighty-Sixth Regiment Illinois Volunteer Infantry*, 135–36.

51. Beaudry, *Historic Records of the Fifth New York Cavalry*, 135.

52. Warren H. Cudworth, *History of the First Regiment (Massachusetts Infantry), from the 25th of May, 1861, to the 25th of May, 1864, Including Brief References to the Operations of the Army of the Potomac* (Boston: Walker, Fuller, and Company, 1866), 184.

53. Cudworth, *History of the First Regiment (Massachusetts Infantry)*, 90, 336.

54. Gage, *From Vicksburg to Raleigh*, 293.

55. John W. Hanson, *Historical Sketch of the Old Sixth Regiment of Massachusetts Volunteers During Its Three Campaigns, in 1861, 1862, 1863, and 1864: Containing the History of the Several Companies Previous to 1861, and the Names and Military Record of Each Man Connected with the Regiment during the War* (Boston: Lee and Shepard, 1866), 161.

56. Hanson, *Historical Sketch of the Old Sixth Regiment of Massachusetts Volunteers*, 169–70.

57. Pierce, *History of the Second Iowa Cavalry*, 120.

58. Wood, *The Seventh Regiment*, 77–78, 81–82.

59. Robert C. Eden, *The Sword and the Gun: A History of the 37th Wis. Volunteer Infantry, from Its First Organization to Its Final Muster Out* (Madison, WI: Atwood & Rublee, 1865), 51. Emphasis in the original.

60. Fleharty, *Our Regiment, a History of the 102d Illinois Infantry Volunteers*, 29, 125.
61. Beecher, *History of the 114th Regiment, N.Y.S.V.*, 80, 114–15, 264.
62. Hurst, *Journal-History of the Seventy-Third Ohio Volunteer Infantry*, 155–56.
63. Eden, *The Sword and the Gun*, 40.
64. Samuel Merrill, *The Campaigns of the First Maine and District of Columbia Cavalry* (Portland, ME: Baily and Noyes, 1866), 369.

Bibliographical Note

The essays in this volume respond to, and extend, a good deal of scholarship that has appeared during the past fifteen years. That scholarship, in turn, plays off important earlier titles. Although an exhaustive list of works pertinent to all the essays is both unnecessary and impracticable, some attention to exemplary or representative books is in order. These titles, many of which also appear in notes to the various essays, will guide readers interested in delving more deeply into the development of a number of themes and arguments.

Several books help establish the importance of the concept of Union and the existence of fears among loyal citizens for its survival amid increasing sectional tensions in the pre–Civil War decades. Gary W. Gallagher's *The Union War* (2011) asserts that, first to last, the loyal citizenry preeminently waged a war to restore a Union they considered exceptional within the Western world, while Elizabeth R. Varon's *Disunion! The Coming of the American Civil War, 1789–1859* (2008) explains how the specter of threats to the work of the founding generation made "disunion" one of the most fraught words in the nation's political vocabulary. Matthew Mason's *Apostle of Union: A Political Biography of Edward Everett* (2016) and Michael E. Woods's *Emotional and Sectional Conflict in the Antebellum United States* (2014) echo Lincoln's first inaugural address in emphasizing the prevalence, across the political spectrum, of the idea that bonds of affection among the nation's citizens had made the Union great—and that its future greatness depended on the strengthening of such bonds. Other perceptive general studies include Susan-Mary Grant's *North over South: Northern Nationalism and American Identity in the Antebellum Era* (2000), Rogan Kersh's *Dreams of a More Perfect Union* (2001), and Melinda Lawson's *Patriot Fires: Forging a New American Nationalism in the Civil War North* (2002). Daniel W. Crofts's *Lincoln and the Politics of Slavery: The Other Thirteenth Amendment and the Struggle to Save the Union* (2016) offers a powerful case for the ascendance of Union as a motivating force among loyal citizens.

Frank Cirillo's and Tamika Nunley's essays contribute to large literatures on abolitionists and their activities, the process of wartime emancipation, and the ways in which freed men and women navigated the often perilous shoals separating slavery and freedom. A few titles provide avenues into this scholarship. James Brewer Stewart's *Holy Warriors: The Abolitionists and American Slavery* (1976) introduces an important group of actors, and W. Caleb McDaniel's *The Problem of Democracy in the Age of Slavery: Garrisonian Abolitionists and Transatlantic Reform* (2013) situates American antislavery efforts within a spacious geographical framework. Kate Masur's *An Example for All the Land: Emancipation and the Struggle over Equality in Washington, D.C.* (2010) deals directly with Elizabeth Keckly's world in the national capital. Erica L. Ball's *To Live an Antislavery Life: Personal Politics and the Antebellum Middle Class* (2012) illuminates how black reformers urged free African Americans to meet behavioral standards that would simultaneously bring credit to themselves as individuals while also advancing the abolitionist cause. Martha S. Jones's *All Bound up Together: The Woman Question in African American Public Culture, 1830–1900* (2007) highlights how black women functioned as effective activists. Manisha Sinha's *The Slave's Cause: A History of Abolition* (2016) offers a comprehensive overview of the antislavery movement.

A number of studies explore the political sentiments and party activities pertinent to the essays by Jack Furniss, Will Kurtz, and Jesse George-Nichol. Two excellent overviews are Mark E. Neely Jr.'s *The Union Divided: Party Conflict in the Civil War North* (2002) and Adam I. P. Smith's *No Party Now: Politics in the Civil War North* (2006). Smith's *The Stormy Present: Conservatism and the Problem of Slavery in Northern Politics, 1846–1865* (2017) takes in a broader chronological sweep, with a focus on the great middle swath of the voting populace. Joel H. Silbey's *A Respectable Minority: The Democratic Party in the Civil War Era, 1860–1868* (1977) and Jean H. Baker's *Affairs of Party: The Political Culture of Northern Democrats in the Mid-Nineteenth Century* (1983) remain useful introductions to the Democrats. Mark E. Neely Jr.'s *Lincoln and the Democrats: The Politics off Opposition in the Civil War* (2017) brings the author's sharp analytical flair to bear on the topic. Probing the far ends of the political arc are James Oakes's *Freedom National: The Destruction of Slavery in the United States, 1861–1865* (2013) and Jennifer L. Weber's *Copperheads: The Rise and Fall of Lincoln's Opponents in the North* (2006), which examine Radical Republicans and antiwar Democrats, respectively.

Border areas have received increasing attention from scholars working with different geographical limits, some more expansive than the four slaveholding Border States that remained loyal to the Union. Five titles convey a sense of the richness of this developing literature. Stanley Harrold's *Border War: Fighting over Slavery before the Civil War* (2010) looks at the antebellum rhetorical and physical violence characteristic of a long border from Delaware to beyond the Mississippi River, with emphasis on regions along the Ohio River. Thomas M. Baker's *The Sacred Cause of Union: Iowa in the Civil War* (2016), Bridget Ford's *Bonds of Union: Religion, Race, and Politics in a Civil War Borderland* (2016), and Aaron Astor's *Rebels on the Borders: Civil War, Emancipation, and the Reconstruction of Kentucky and Missouri* (2012) illuminate attitudes in parts of the trans-Mississippi region and along both sides of the Ohio River. Christopher Phillips's *The Rivers Ran Backward: The Civil War and the Remaking of the American Middle Border* (2016) argues that political, social, and military conflict in Kentucky and Missouri radiated northward into the Midwest and played a major role in shaping the Civil War.

Questions of ethnicity and politics central to Will Kurtz's essay also have spawned a growing body of scholarship. Angela F. Murphy's *American Slavery, Irish Freedom: Abolition, Immigrant Citizenship, and the Transatlantic Movement for Irish Repeal* (2010), Susannah J. Ural's *Civil War Citizens: Race, Ethnicity, and Identity in America's Bloodiest Conflict* (2010), and Christian G. Samito's *Becoming American under Fire: Irish Americans, African Americans, and the Politics of Citizenship during the Civil War Era* (2009) discuss the ways in which ethnicity and race intersected in debates about citizenship. Alison Clark Efford's *German Immigrants, Race, and Citizenship in the Civil War Era* (2013) examines the largest ethnic group in the United States.

On religion, also of interest to Kurtz, the number of books is much smaller. George C. Rable's *God's Almost Chosen Peoples: A Religious History of the American Civil War* (2010) is the best overview, and Mark A. Noll's *The Civil War as a Theological Crisis* (2006) supplies a good brief introduction. Timothy L. Wesley's *The Politics of Faith during the Civil War* (2013), which assesses the role of the clergy, and William B. Kurtz's *Excommunicated from the Union: How the Civil War Created a Separate Catholic America* (2015) also merit attention.

Five books introduce contrasting interpretations about the loyal citizenry's debates about how best to fight the war. Mark Grimsley's influential *The Hard Hand of War: Union Military Policy toward Southern Civilians, 1861–1865* (1995) pushes back against the popular notion that the United States fought a "total war" by 1864, arguing instead for a policy of "directed severity" that fit comfortably within European traditions. Harry S. Stout's *Upon the Altar of the Nation: A Moral History of the Civil War* (2006) offers a much darker view of a conflict that raged beyond control as patriotic jingoism on each side promoted brutality and caused unimaginable suffering. More specifically considering Francis Lieber's role, John Fabian Witt's *Lincoln's Code: The Laws of War in American History* (2012) and D. H. Dilbeck's *A More Civil War: How the Union Waged a Just War* (2016) stress the degree to which the United States sought to avoid unbridled ferocity and the blurring of lines between civilians and soldiers. Stephen C. Neff's *Justice in Blue and Gray: A Legal History of the Civil War* (2010) also accords significant attention to debates and laws regarding the conduct of war. A pair of titles get at how popular culture shaped expectations and choices among loyal citizens: J. Matthew Gallman's *Defining Duty in the Civil War: Personal Choice, Popular Culture, and the Union Home Front* (2015) and Alice C. Fahs's *The Imagined Civil War: Popular Literature of the North and South, 1861–1865* (2001).

Michael Caires's essay, in dealing with the interrelated growth and reach of the federal government and implementation of the Republican financial program, intersects with different parts of the scholarly literature. On central expansion, Richard Franklin Bensel's *Yankee Leviathan: The Origins of Central State Authority in America, 1859–1877* (1990) continues to be essential, while Brian Balogh's *A Government out of Sight: The Mystery of National Authority in Nineteenth-Century America* (2009) counters the idea that the pre-twentieth-century US government remained tiny. Regarding financial affairs, Stephen Mihm's *A Nation of Counterfeiters: Capitalists, Con Men, and the Making of the United States* (2007) presents a lively account of paper currency during the prewar years. Bray Hammond's foundational *Sovereignty and an Empty Purse: Banks and Politics in the Civil War* (1970) and John Niven's impressive *Salmon P. Chase: A Biography* (1995) remain invaluable.

Scholarship devoted to common soldiers has grown exponentially. Anyone following Peter Luebke in training a lens on the Union side should still start with Bell I. Wiley's pioneering *The Life of Billy Yank: The Common Soldier of the Union* (1952), then move on to Reid Mitchell's *The Vacant Chair: The Northern Soldier Leaves Home* (1993) and James M. McPherson's *For Cause and Comrades: Why Men Fought in the Civil War* (1997). Also rewarding are Earl J. Hess's *The Union Soldier in Battle: Enduring the Ordeal of Combat* (1997) and, for a revealing treatment of the centrality of the regiment in forming a soldier's identity, Gerald J. Prokopowicz's *All for the Regiment: The Army of the Ohio, 1861–1862*

(2001). Chandra Manning focuses on attitudes toward slavery, emancipation, and race in *What This Cruel War Is Over: Soldiers, Slavery, and the Civil War* (2007), finding more antislavery sentiment—and finding it earlier in the war—than most other studies, where concern for the Union emerges as most important for the large majority of US soldiers. On African Americans in blue, a fine general study is Joseph T. Glatthaar's *Forged in Battle: The Civil War Alliance of Black Soldiers and White Officers* (1990), while Douglas R. Egerton's *Thunder at the Gates: The Black Civil War Regiments That Redeemed America* (2016) takes a focused look at the famed 54th Massachusetts. For the development of memory traditions that often centered on armies and soldiers, readers should consult David W. Blight's *Race and Reunion: The Civil War in American Memory* (2001) and Caroline E. Janney's *Remembering the Civil War: Reunion and the Limits of Reconciliation* (2013).

Contributors

Michael T. Caires, a research associate at the John L. Nau III Center for Civil War History at the University of Virginia, is the author of *The Greenback Union: The Transformation of Money, Capitalism, and the State in the American Civil War* (forthcoming, Harvard University Press).

Frank J. Cirillo earned his doctorate in the Corcoran Department of History at the University of Virginia and holds a Bradley Foundation Postdoctoral Fellowship at the Nau Center and J. Franklin Jameson Fellowship from the American Historical Association.

D. H. Dilbeck, a historian living in New Haven, Connecticut, is the author of *A More Civil War: How the Union Waged a Just War* (University of North Carolina Press, 2016) and *Frederick Douglass: America's Prophet* (University of North Carolina Press, 2018).

Jack Furniss earned his doctorate in the Corcoran Department of History at the University of Virginia and holds a Bradley Foundation Postdoctoral Fellowship at the Nau Center and a Postdoctoral Visiting Fellow appointment at the Rothermere American Institute at Oxford.

Gary W. Gallagher is John L. Nau III Professor in the History of the American Civil War Emeritus at the University of Virginia.

Jesse George-Nichol is a graduate student in the Corcoran Department of History at the University of Virginia.

William B. Kurtz is managing director of the John L. Nau III Center for Civil War History at the University of Virginia and author of *Excommunicated from the Union: How the Civil War Created a Separate Catholic America* (Fordham University Press, 2015).

Peter C. Luebke is a historian at the Naval History and Heritage Command and editor of *The Story of a Thousand: Being a History of the 105th Ohio Volunteer Infantry in the War for the Union, from August 21, 1862, to June 6, 1865* (Kent State University Press, 2011).

Tamika Y. Nunley is an assistant professor of History at Oberlin College.

Elizabeth R. Varon is Langbourne M. Williams Professor of History at the University of Virginia.

Index

abolitionists, 2–4, 7, 9–38, 41, 44, 55, 60–61, 67, 70, 73–75, 79, 84–85, 87, 89, 93, 95–96, 103–6, 109, 111, 122–23, 126–27, 133, 142, 197; and advocacy of disunion, 21–22; and antislavery consensus, 10; attitudes toward Union war, 33; colonization, 29, 61, 80, 82, 115, 125–26, 141; contrasted with Irish Americans, 93, 95–96, 103, 104; immediatists, 10; in Massachusetts, 9; and moral suasion, 14–19, 21–22, 26, 35; political, 15; and radical abolition, 122–23; and rejection of Constitution, 14; women as, 13

Adams, John, 166

Aeneid, 196

African Americans, 2, 6, 7, 28–29, 31, 33, 39–41, 44, 46–47, 51, 56–57, 59–62, 107, 141, 156, 195–98; abandoned by white Northerners, 199; and citizenship, 15, 49, 141; and clubwoman's movement, 45; and collective autonomy, 47; as contraband of war, 48–49, 55, 157; and education, 49; and political activism, 40; in regimental histories, view of, 194–98; women as activists, 40, 47, 50, 57, 59

African American troops (USCT), 34, 52–54, 59, 82, 141, 155; denial of quarter to, 156; in noncombat roles, 155

Agnes (mother of Elizabeth Keckly), 42

American Anti-Slavery Society, 9, 11, 13–14, 19, 26, 29, 31–34, 36–37; Declaration of Sentiments of, 37

American Colonization Society, 125

American Party, 66–68. *See also* Republican Party

American Revolution, 52, 77, 94, 98, 192, 193

American System, 125

Anderson, Robert, 138

Anthony, Susan B., 22

Anti-Catholicism, 103, 108, 112

Anti-Slavery Bugle, 14, 21–24

Antietam, Md.: battle of, 84

Appomattox Court House, Va., 61, 110–11, 162

Ark of the Covenant, 192

Arlington, Va.: Freedmen's Village at, 55; image, 56

Army of Northern Virginia, 84–85, 99, 110–11

Army of the Potomac, 84, 110

Baker, Frank, 49

Baker, Jean H., 63, 68

Ball, Erica, 47

Baltimore, Md., 44, 99, 129

Bancroft, George, 190–91

Bank of New York, 164

Bank of North America, 164–65

Bank of the United States, 164–65, 179; First BUS, 165; Second BUS, 166–67, 176

banking systems, 163–64

Banks, Nathaniel P., 94

Barksdale, William, 194

Barlow, Samuel, 80

Barnabo, Alesandro, 101

Barney, Hiram, 70, 211n15

Bassett, George, 24–25

Bates, Edward, 114–42, 146; advocates compromise, 136; and American Colonization Society, 125–26, 141; anti-Jacksonian views, 125; as Conservative Republican, 134; criticizes Lincoln, 140; encourages abandonment of Fort

Bates, Edward (*continued*)
  Sumter, 138; image of, 135; joins Lincoln cabinet, 132; political career of, 117, 126; and rhetoric of conciliation, 115, 123–24, 129, 132, 136; supports Lincoln, 128; views on expansion of slavery, 119, 124
Bayard, James, Jr., 77
Beaudry, Louis N., 190, 195
Beecher, Harris, 189, 198
Beecher, Henry Ward, 106
Beecher, Lyman, 83
Belmont, August, 76, 211n15
Bennett, James Gordon, 100, 103–4, 107
Bensel, Richard Franklin, 68, 162, 243
Benton, Thomas Hart, 168
Berret, James, 59
Biddle, Nicholas, 166
Black Republicans; *see* Radical Republicans
Blaine, James G., 112
Blair, Montgomery, image of, 135
Blair, William A., 77, 209n1
Bleeding Kansas, 124, 128, 139
Blight, David W., 199
Bonaparte, Louis Napoleon, 101
Border States, 3, 4, 34, 81, 138, 242
Botts, John Minor, 139
Bowser, D. B., 52
Breckinridge, John Cabell, 68
Brown, Benjamin Gratz, 35
Brown, Elsa Barkley, 47
Brown, F. T., 191
Brown, John, 52
Brown, Sayles J., 60
Browning, Orville, 117, 130
Brownson, Orestes A., 102–5, 108, 215n3
Buchanan, James, 73, 92
Burns, Anthony, 95
Burwell, Armistead, 42–43
Burwell, Robert, 42
Butler, Benjamin F., 49, 67

California, 163; gold rush in, 169
Cameron, Simon, 104; image of, 135
Camp Barker (Washington, D.C.), 58
Carleton, G. W., 41
Carey, Matthew, 145
Caruthers, Calvin C., 60
Catholic Americans, 94; and arguments about Union war aims, 106; and Democratic allegiance, 112–13; and intervention of clergy in draft riots, 107–8; and loyalty of Catholic clergy to Union, 97; and newspapers accused of secessionists views, 102–3; in the North, 91; and resistance of emancipation as a war aim, 92–93; as Union soldiers, 96–98, 111; voting of, 110
Catholic Church, 93, 95, 97, 104–6
Caton, John D., 85
Chamberlain, W. H., 187–88
Chapman, Maria Weston, 17–18
Charleston, S.C., 52, 74, 99, 137–38; battle of, 110
Chase, Salmon Portland, 66–67, 160–62, 169–85; and Democratic views of American economy, 169–70, 174; as governor of Ohio, 170; image of, 135; links bank proposal to Union war effort, 177; proposes banking system, 171, 174
Chattanooga, Tenn.: battle of, 109
Cheng, Eileen Ka-May, 190
Civil War, 187; alienating for immigrant communities, 112; conscription during, 108–9; and dark turn historiography, 144; as emancipationist struggle, 199; greenbacks, 173–75; international consequences of, 148, 198; nurses in, 99; and practice of paroling, 152; regimental histories of, 186–99; as sectional conflict, 130; soldier loyalty in, 187; treatment of civilians, 154–55, 157; views of common soldiers, 2; voting during, 69, 72; war bonds, 161, 171; war weariness during, 75
Clark, James, 188, 194
Clay, Henry, 4, 66–67, 115, 124–26, 168
Cleveland Movement, 12, 35

Cochrane, John C., 35
Coe, George S., 170
Collamer, Jacob, 178–80
Colorado, 163
Columbia College, 144–46, 148
communications revolution, 162
compromise, as American political tradition, 115–16
Compromise of 1850, 70
Confederate States of America, 5, 22, 30, 45, 81, 88–89, 99, 101, 103, 110, 143–46, 148–52, 155, 169, 194; as legitimate nation, 151–52; and policy of paroles, 156
Confiscation Acts, 48, 72, 81–82, 141
Congregationalism, 13–14
Congress (US), 56, 77, 117, 124, 160,168, 170–71, 177–78, 182; and control over slavery in the territories, 120–21; House Ways and Means Committee in, 172–73
conscription, 72
Constitution (US), 4, 9, 15–17, 19, 24, 33, 59–61, 65, 67, 71, 75–78, 80, 87, 89, 91–92, 95–96, 98, 103, 105, 109, 113, 118, 120, 122–23, 128, 133, 139, 142, 147, 149, 163, 166, 193; rejected Thirteenth Amendment to (1860), 20, 135–36; Thirteenth Amendment to, 36, 38, 61
Constitutional Union Party, 66, 68, 73, 128–30, 134–35, 139, 223n34
Continental Congress, 164
Contraband Relief Association, 45, 47, 49–52, 57; interracial support for, 51
Conway, Moncure, 11
Cook, John F., 40
Cooke, Henry, 175
Cooke, J. F., 52–53
Cooke, Jay, 175
Cooper, Brittney, 48
Crittenden Compromise, 70, 225n50
Crittenden, John J., 70–71, 135
Crittenden-Johnson Resolution (War Aims Resolution), 71–72
Cudworth, Warren, 195–96

culture of dissemblance, 43
currency, 5, 161, 163–67, 168–72, 175–77, 180–82; gold coinage, 162–63, 168; greenbacks, 173–75; image of, 181; paper money, 167; silver coinage, 162–63, 168. *See also* Legal Tender Act
Cushing, Caleb, 168

d'Aubigne, Merle, 191
Dartmouth College, 14
Davidson, Henry, 188–90
Davis, Garrett, 179
Davis, Jefferson, 29–31, 36, 44–45
Davis, Varina, 44–45
Davis, W. W. H., 188–90, 198
Dawes, Henry Laurens, 182
Declaration of Independence, 14–15, 149
Deep South, 135, 138–39
Democratic Party, 2, 3, 7, 16–17, 20–21, 30, 35, 48, 56, 63–80, 84–90, 92–93, 95, 105, 110–11, 129–30, 150, 162, 167–68, 170, 178–79, 209n1, 210n8, 211–12n22, 213n39, 214n60; 1860 platform of, 169; as centrists, 66–67; Copperheads, 2, 89, 106; Douglas Democrats, 211n19; emancipation, response to, 80–81; Hardshell and Hunker factions in, 68–70; and idea of Union war, 76, 88; internal schism in, 74; in New York, 69; and opposition to Lincoln administration, 74; Peace Democrats, 64; and relationship with Irish Americans, 95; Southern Democrats, 59; and support of Lincoln administration, 72; War Democrats, 64
Dickinson, Daniel S., 68, 71
disunion, 7, 11, 15, 20–22, 65, 75, 79, 87–88, 131–32, 134, 139, 201n5, 223n40, 241
Dix, John A., 73
Donahoe, Patrick, 4, 92–113; *Boston Pilot*, editor of, 92, 104; denounces abolition, 105, 109; denounces conscription, 109
Douglas, Stephen, 66, 68, 70, 72, 77, 95, 211n15; support for Irish voters, 95
Douglass, Charles, 53

Douglass, Frederick, 6, 11, 15, 30, 42, 52–53, 60, 82. *See also* abolitionists
Douglass, Lewis, 53
Downing, George T., 54
Draft riots (1863), 106–8, 11, 113
Dred Scott decision, the, 34, 120

economic crises. *See* Panic of 1837; Panic of 1857
Eden, Robert, 197
Elder, William H., 109
Elections: of 1800, 165; of 1860, 19, 79, 118, 128; of 1861, 72; of 1862, 63, 65, 69, 78, 90; of 1864, 12, 69, 90, 114, 150
Emancipation, 1, 10–12, 15, 22–24, 27, 29, 89, 160, 192–93; as instrument of war, 22, 192–93, 198; and the loyal South, 81; military policy and, 26, 28, 32; as process, 12
Emancipation Proclamation, 12, 30, 38, 54, 78–82,105, 141, 155, 169, 193, 196, 198 208–9n1; as betrayal of Union war aims, 105; preliminary proclamation, 63, 65, 72, 82, 105, 141
Emerson, Ralph Waldo, 95
Encyclopedia Americana, 145
Estlin, Mary, 37

Fahnestock, Allen, 190
federalism, 162, 166
Federalist Party, 68, 73, 77
Fenians, 91
Ferree, James J., 53
Fillmore, Millard, 67, 85, 117
Fish, Hamilton, 228n28
Fitzpatrick, John, 97
Fleharty, Stephen, 197
Foner, Eric, 67
Fort Donelson, Tenn., 158
Fort Monroe, Va., 49
Fort Pickens, Fla., 138
Fort Sumter, S.C., 22, 46, 71, 96, 100–1, 137–39
Fort Wagner, S.C.: battle of, 53

Foster, Abby Kelley, 2, 9–38; antiwar abolitionism of, 31–38; childhood and youth, 12–13; defends husband, 19; dissents from Garrisonian position, 18–19; as fundraiser, 14, 18; image of, 13; as moral suasionist, 14–15. *See also* moral nationalism
Foster, Stephen Symonds, 2, 9–38; antiwar abolitionism of, 31–38; attempts to form political party, 19; dissents from Garrisonian position, 18–19; as moral suasionist, 14–15; youth and educations of, 13–14. *See also* moral nationalism
Fox and Wisconsin Improvement Company, 70
Fredericksburg, Va.: battle of, 100
Free Soil Party, 16, 66, 70
Freedmen's Village (Alexandria, Va.), 58; Jacob's School, 58
Frémont, John C., 12, 26, 35, 74, 219n3; and emancipation, 26
Fugitive Slave Act (1850), 54, 118
Fugitive Slave laws, 21, 30

Gage, Moses, 191–93, 196
Gallagher, Gary W., 91–92, 146; *The Union War*, 91, 146
Gallatin, Albert, 172
Gallatin, James, 172; opposes Salmon P. Chase's banking system, 172
Garland, Hugh, 43
Garnet, Henry Highland, Rev., 61
Garrison, William Lloyd, 2, 9–23, 25–37, 99, 105–6, 108, 123, 137–38, 142, 177. *See also* moral suasion
Garrison, William Lloyd, Jr., 26
Geary, John White, 68
General Orders No. 100. *See* Lieber Code
German immigrants, 150
Gienapp, William E., 67
Gilded Age, 183
Grant, Ulysses S., 54, 109, 112
Greeley, Horace, 66, 72–74, 80, 83–86, 99, 104, 106–8, 113, 222n29; anti-

Catholicism of, 110–11; stokes draft riots, 107; supports Chase bank bill, 175
Green, Shields, 52
Grew, Henry, 16
guerrilla warfare, 144, 151–52
Guizot, François, 191
Guth, I. J., 190

Habeas Corpus: suspended, 65, 72, 77–78
Halleck, Henry, 152–53, 229n45
Hamilton, Alexander, 164–65, 169, 171, 174; and the national bank, 165
Hanson, John, 196
Harrison, Robert, 60
Hartford Convention, 74
Harvard University, 145
Hatch, Edward, 190
Hay, John, 114
Hayes, Rutherford B., 112
Healey, James, 107
Hecker, Isaac, 94
Higginbotham, Evelyn Brooks, 47–48
Hine, Darlene Clark, 43
Holmes, Asa, 85, 89
Holt, Michael F., 69
Holzer, Harold, 80
Homestead Act, 67, 160, 169
Horton, Joshua H., 188, 190
Houghton, Edward, 194
Hughes, John, 3, 92–108, 112–13; advises Seward, 100–1; death of, 108; rejects secession, 99; represents Lincoln Administration in Europe, 101–2; views on slavery, 95
Hunter, David, 74
Hurst, Samuel, 194–95, 198

Illinois military units: 86th Infantry, 190
Independent Treasury System, 167, 170, 175–76, 181
Indiana military units: 12th Infantry, 191
Iowa, 112, 124, 178, 190, 196
Iowa military units: 2nd Cavalry, 190, 196
Ireland, 91–93, 98, 101, 104; Dublin, 101
Irish-Americans, 91

Irish Brigade, 97, 100
Israel Bethel AME (Washington, D.C.), 40, 57

Jackson, Andrew, 65–66, 166–67; Constitution, interpretation of, 65, 72; vetoes Second Bank of the United States, 166–67
Jacksonians, 161
Jacobs, Harriet, 43, 46, 58–58, 61; *Incidents in the Life of a Slave Girl*, 43
Jahn, Friedrich Ludwig, 145
Jay, John, 165
Jefferson, Thomas, 165–66, 172
Jeffersonian Party, 73
Johnson, Andrew, 37, 59, 71
Johnson, Oliver, 32, 37
Joint Committee on the Conduct of the War, 72
Jones, Benjamin, 14, 23–25
Jones, Martha S., 46
jus ad bellum, 143
jus in bello, 143

Kansas, 128, 139
Kansas-Nebraska Act, 70, 120
Kantrowitz, Stephen, 39–40
Keckly, Elizabeth, 2, 3, 39–62; *Behind the Scenes: or Thirty Years a Slave and Four Years in the White House*, 39; dressmaking of, 43; experiences slavery, 42
Kellogg, William, 137
Kenrick, Francis, 99
Kentucky, 75, 85, 135, 179
Kersh, Roger, 82
Kinnear, John, 190, 195
Kirkland, Alexander M., 42
Kirkland, George, 42, 44, 53; death at Wilson's Creek, 53
Know-Nothings, 67, 94–95, 97, 101, 110. *See also* nativism

Landis, Michael, 64
laws of war, 5, 143–45, 151–55, 157–58
Lecompton Constitution, 120

Lee, Mary Anna Custis, 44
Lee, Robert E., 44, 84, 99, 110, 194
Legal Tender Act, 173
Lewis, Janaka B., 46
Lewis, Osceola, 194
Liberator, 10, 18, 22, 25, 33, 35, 105, 108
Liberia, 126
Liberty Party, 16
Lieber, Francis, 143–59; image of, 147; sons in the Civil War, 150, 158; as teacher 145–46; as Union nationalist, 146; views of Union as representative, 150. *See also* Lieber Code
Lieber Code, 144–45, 151; and brief wars, 144, 151, 154, 158; and private property, destruction of, 154; and retaliation, 156–57
Lincoln (2012 film), 39
Lincoln Administration, 1, 4, 7, 26–27, 29, 34, 36, 63, 65, 68, 70–72, 74–78, 80, 85, 87–89, 101–2, 114, 116–17, 132–42, 153, 193, 208n1, 211n22, 218–19n3, 220n9; arrests made by, 77
Lincoln household, 39, 41
Lincoln, Abraham, 1–4, 6–7, 10–12, 19–20, 22, 24–25, 27–36, 38–39, 41, 45, 61, 63, 65–66, 68–72, 74–75, 77–87, 89, 92, 96, 101–2, 105–6, 108–10, 113–24, 126–42, 144, 146, 148–53, 155, 160, 169–70, 173, 175, 179–80, 192; 1861 special message to Congress, 148; as abolitionist, 10; antislavery rhetoric, 121, 123; call for three hundred thousand troops, 173; and Catholic leaders, 92; First Inaugural Address, 137; House Divided speech, 121, 123; image of, 135; limited war, articulation of, 68, 71, 75; as military leader, 140; nomination and election of, 96, 127–28; and nonextension of slavery, 70, 115, 119, 123, 136; Radical association, avoiding, 133; reelection of, 114, 150; relationship with Republican Party, 117; as Western conservative, 130
Lincoln, Mary Todd, 40–41, 45
Lindsey, Treva, 48

Loring, Charles G., 81–82
Louisiana, 110, 177
Love, Alfred, 15, 23
Lynch, Patrick N., 99
Lynn Anti-Slavery Society (Massachusetts), 13

Macaulay, Thomas Babington, 191
Madison, James, 166
Magee, David, 190
mail delivery: in the South, 133
Maine military units: 1st Cavalry, 198
Mallory, Charles, 49
Mallory, Shepard, 49
Manassas, Va.: first battle of, 71, 96–97, 99, 101
Marble, Manton, 80, 87
Maryland, 73, 99, 110; as Catholic colony, 94
Massachusetts, 9, 12, 22, 27, 31, 33–34, 36, 52–53, 92–94, 97, 146–47, 168, 194–96
Massachusetts Anti-Slavery Society, 27, 33, 36
Massachusetts military units: 1st Infantry, 195; 6th Infantry, 196; 9th Infantry, 97; 28th Infantry, 92, 97; 38th Infantry, 194; 54th Infantry, 31, 52–53
Mason, Matthew, 66
Masur, Kate, 39–40, 50
May, Samuel, Jr., 19
McClellan, George Brinton, 66, 73; 84–85, 88, 90, 150, 173; as Democrat with Whig tendencies, 66; Harrison's Landing letter, 84; presidential nomination of, 90
McClintock, Russell, 71, 80
McCulloch, Hugh, 182
McLean, Margaret, 44
McMaster, James A., 106, 111
McPherson, James M., 186–87
Merrill, Samuel, 198
Mexican-American War, 107, 146, 176
Milliken's Bend, La.: battle of, 53
Mississippi, 109, 175
Mississippi River, 70, 163

Missouri, 4, 26, 35, 110, 115, 117, 122, 124–29, 133, 135, 152, 193; Whig Party in, 126, 219n8
Missouri Compromise, 135
Missouri military units: 3rd Cavalry, 193
Mitchell, Stewart, 70
Montana, 163
Monticello (Charlottesville, Va.), 165
Mooney, Thomas, 98–99
moral nationalism (abolitionist position), 10–11, 15, 21, 23–24
moral suasion. *See* abolitionists
Morgan, Edwin, 71
Morrill Land Grant Act, 160, 169
Morris, Robert, 165
Mowris, J. A., 193, 195
Mullaly, John, 102

Napoleon, 145
Napoleonic wars, 145
Nast, Thomas, 112
Nat Turner's Rebellion, 46
National Banking Act of 1863, 161, 180–82, 185; postbellum dissatisfaction with, 184–85
National Banking Act of 1864, 182–83; pyramid reserve system, 183
National Union Party, 68–69, 73, 89, 128–30, 135, 211n57
nativism, 3, 91, 94, 97, 104, 110–11, 113
Neely, Mark E., 69, 77
New England Anti-Slavery Convention, 17, 29–30, 34
New Hampshire, 13–14, 27, 29, 33
New Hampshire Anti-Slavery Society, 14
New Orleans, La., 73, 83, 177
New York Board of Trade, 169
New York City, 41, 80, 94, 96, 99, 106–7, 144, 146, 148, 153, 170, 178, 182–84; American Exchange Bank, 170; St. Patrick's Cathedral, 100, 108
New York military units: 5th Cavalry, 190; 69th Infantry, 91, 96, 98; 114th Infantry, 85, 189; 115th Infantry, 188, 194; 189th Infantry, 188

New York State, 72–73; Banking Department of, 178; Civil War voting in, 72, 79; New York Democratic States Committee of, 76; newspapers in, 80, 87; People's Convention in, 71; and Tammany Hall, 83
Nicolay, John G., 114, 132
Northup, Solomon, 42
Nullification Crisis (S.C.), 74

O'Connell, Daniel, 93
Oakes, James, 83, 218n3
Ohio, 14, 20, 22, 63, 79, 87, 89, 170, 175, 187–89, 191, 193–94, 197, 206n16, 211n19; Summit County State Bank in, 180
Ohio military units: 1st Light Artillery, 189; 7th Infantry, 191, 193; 11th Infantry, 188; 73rd Infantry, 194; 81st Infantry, 187
Overland Campaign, Va., 109

Panic of 1837, 163, 167
Panic of 1857, 169–70
Parkman, Francis, 191
Parsons, Charles, 189
Peninsula Campaign (1862), 84, 173, 195
Pennsylvania, 63, 68, 89, 175, 194, 198
Pennsylvania military units: 104th Infantry, 188, 198; 138th Infantry, 194
Peoria, Ill., 190
Petty, A. W. M., 193–94
Philadelphia, Pa., 13, 50, 52, 94, 170, 175, 180
Phillips, Wendell, 9–12, 16–22, 26, 34–37, 66, 106
Pierce, Lyman, 190, 196–97
Pillsbury, Parker, 14, 17–18, 23, 25, 35
Pius IX (pope), 102
Political Anti-Slavery Convention (1860), 19
politics of respectability, 47–48
Polk, James Knox, 92, 107, 167, 175
popular sovereignty, 70
Port Hudson, La.: battle of, 53

Powers, George, 194
Prescott, William, 190–91
prisoners of war, 144, 154–56; prisoner exchanges, 151–52
Progressive Era, 161
Prokopowicz, Gerald J., 187
public schools: freedom of conscience in, 93–94, 97
Pugh, Sarah, 31
Purcell, Edward, 106

Quakers, 12–13

racial uplift, 42, 57
Radical Republicans, 17, 19, 35, 72, 74, 79, 83, 106, 116, 123, 133, 140; blamed for the Civil War, 99; control the Republican Party, 72; influence on Lincoln, 114; oppose limited war, 71
Rafuse, Ethan S., 66
Raymond, Henry, 73, 87, 104
Reconstruction, 34, 38, 60, 160, 183, 186, 191; usefulness of banking system to, 177
reform, 15, 25
Refugees, 39, 51
regimental histories, 186; composition of, 187; as consensus opinions, 187; circulation of, 190; deal with slavery, 192–93; discuss Southern aristocracy, 194–95; as memorials, 187–88; use of official records in preparing, 189; used as models by historians, 191
Republican Party, 3, 4, 7, 11, 16–20, 23–24, 26–27, 29, 37, 44, 46, 54–55, 60–61, 63–68, 70–74, 77–81, 83–85, 87, 90, 93–96, 102, 105–7, 112, 115–18, 121–23, 126–29, 131, 134–37, 139–42, 160, 162, 169–70, 175, 178, 183, 185, 191–92, 198–99, 212n25, 218n3; attempts to form political coalitions, 67, 131; national vision, 160–61; relationship with Constitution Union party, 129; as sectional party, 127; and slavery nonextension, 79; views of Democratic Party, 64; Whig lineage, 77
Richmond, Va., 47, 76, 85
Rodgers, Thomas E., 87
Rogers, William H., 188

Samito, Christian G., 92
Scott, Winfield, 92, 98–99, 138
secession, 20–21, 99, 131, 138–39, 169, 176; illegality of, 132–33; as rejection of rule of law, 149
Secession crisis, 11, 20, 76
Seven Days Battles, 98
Seward, William Henry, 71, 73, 77, 92, 100–2, 104–5, 108, 115, 117–18, 121, 123–24, 133–34, 137, 220n9, 224n44, 224nn46–47; as defender of Union, 123; image of, 135; and irrepressible conflict, 115
Seymour, Horatio, 63–90, 106; articulates support for Union, 83–84; career overview, 69–70; elected governor of New York, 85; image, 86
Shaw, Robert Gould, 31
Sheehan-Dean, Aaron, 186–87
Sheridan, Philip H., 110
Sherman, John, 79, 175–77, 180–81
Sherman, William T., 1; March to the Sea, 110
Silbey, Joel H., 64, 77, 210n12
Sill, E. N., 180
Slave Power conspiracy, 1, 6, 22, 28, 65, 81, 110, 120–21, 127, 132, 193, 237n25; blamed for condition of poor Southern whites, 194–95; defeat of by Union soldiers, 191
slavery: extension of, 16, 70, 118, 124, 129; abolished in Federal territories, 72; brutality of, 42; effect on poor Southern whites, 195–98; legal and constitutional protections for, 118; in the Lieber Code, 154–55; as political threat, 119, 193; and radicalism, 116; Southern justifications for, 44

Smith, Adam I. P., 66, 69
Smith, Caleb B.: image of, 135
Social, Civil, and Statistical Association, 40
South Carolina, 21, 100, 104, 135, 138, 145–46, 177; leads secession movement, 131
South Carolina College, 145–46
Spielberg, Steven, 39
St. Louis, Mo., 43, 117, 125, 171
Stanton, Edwin, 153, 155, 228n28
Starrs, William, 108
Stevens, Thaddeus, 80, 83, 173
Stilwell, Silas M., 177
Strong, George Templeton, 63
Sumner, Charles, 17, 66, 80, 83, 141, 146, 152
Supplemental Act, 55
Supreme Court of the United States, 166

tariffs, 160, 169
telegraph, 161
temperance, 125
Teverbaugh, Solomon, 188, 190
Thomas, J. F., 190
Thompson, George, 28
Tilden, Samuel, 75
Tillman, Charles C., 60
Townsend, James, 49
transcontinental railroad, 160, 169
transportation revolution, 162
Treasury of the United States, 173–74
Trent Affair, 101
Trumball, Lyman, 77, 136
Turner, Henry McNeal, 40, 57
Turner, Nathaniel, 52

Union, 1–7, 9, 122; as abolition war, 42; and abolitionist support for, 11; African American conceptions of, 41, 52; as amoral, 28–29; Catholic Unionism, 91–93, 103, 105; and Civil War memory, 187–88; as conservative war of restoration, 2, 64–65, 74, 78, 115, 139, 141; Democrat Party ideology of, 64, 73, 88; and democratic uprising against aristocracy, 192; distinction with liberty, 83–84; economic and commercial, 160; feasibility of Democratic vision of war, 88; as hard war, 89; and just war, 143–44, 153, 158; and legacy of American Revolution, 83; as limited war, 68, 71, 88, 92, 103, 105; as opportunity for racial equality, 60–62; opposition to Union war, 10, 12, 23; overview of, 1–7; place of African Americans in, 141; radicalism as threat to, 116; as sacrosanct, 149, 158–59; Southern threats to, 20; Southern Unionism, 140. *See also* National Union Party
Unionists (southern), 65, 81, 140
Upper South, 138

Vallandigham, Clement L., 87, 89
Van Buren, John, 72, 74, 85
Van Buren, Martin, 68, 70, 167
Van Dyck, H. H., 178; opposes Chase's banking system, 178–79
Vatican, 102
Vermont, 178–79
Vesey, Denmark, 52
Vicksburg, Miss.: siege of, 109
Virginia, 195
voting, 68–69, 72, 110

Wadsworth, James, 73, 78, 84–86; radicalism of, 86
Walker, Robert J., 175–77, 180–81
War of 1812, 163, 165–66, 172
Washington, D.C., 39–41, 45, 48, 54–55, 153, 179, 181; Board of Aldermen in, 55; emancipation in, 49, 55, 72; Fifteenth Street Presbyterian Church in, 57, 61; opposition to emancipation in, 55–57; refugees in, 51
Washington, D.C., military units: First District Regiment of Colored Volunteers, 52

Washington, George, 78; as father of the Union, 192
Weber, Jennifer, 64
Webster, Daniel, 67, 147
Weed, Thurlow, 71–73, 76, 83, 86
Welles, Gideon: image of, 135
Welsh, Peter, 92
Western Anti-Slavery Society, 14, 20
Whelan, Richard V., 99
Whig Party, 4, 66–68, 75, 80, 85, 115, 118, 122, 124–26, 129, 131, 168, 178, 210n9; conservative wing of, 67; Old Whigs faction, 131, 178; and proposal for Third Bank of the United States, 168; Southern wing of, 129
White House, 39, 83
Wilberforce University, 44, 206n16
Willing, Thomas, 165
Wilmington, N.C.: battle of, 110
Wilson, Henry, 93
Wilson's Creek, Mo.: battle of, 53
Wisconsin military units: 37th Infantry, 198
Wood, George L., 191, 197
Wood, Wales, 193–94
Worcester County Anti-Slavery Society, 21, 25, 27
Wright, B. G., 25–26

Zinser, J. L., 190

The North's Civil War
Andrew L. Slap, series editor

Anita Palladino, ed., *Diary of a Yankee Engineer: The Civil War Story of John H. Westervelt, Engineer, 1st New York Volunteer Engineer Corps.*

Herman Belz, *Abraham Lincoln, Constitutionalism, and Equal Rights in the Civil War Era.*

Earl J. Hess, *Liberty, Virtue, and Progress: Northerners and Their War for the Union.* Second revised edition, with a new Introduction by the author.

William L. Burton, *Melting Pot Soldiers: The Union's Ethnic Regiments.*

Hans L. Trefousse, *Carl Schurz: A Biography.*

Stephen W. Sears, ed., *Mr. Dunn Browne's Experiences in the Army: The Civil War Letters of Samuel W. Fiske.*

Jean H. Baker, *Affairs of Party: The Political Culture of Northern Democrats in the Mid-Nineteenth Century.*

Frank L. Klement, *The Limits of Dissent: Clement L. Vallandigham and the Civil War.* With a new introduction by Steven K. Rogstad.

Lawrence N. Powell, *New Masters: Northern Planters during the Civil War and Reconstruction.*

John A. Carpenter, *Sword and Olive Branch: Oliver Otis Howard.*

Thomas F. Schwartz, ed., *"For a Vast Future Also": Essays from the* Journal of the Abraham Lincoln Association.

Mark De Wolfe Howe, ed., *Touched with Fire: Civil War Letters and Diary of Oliver Wendell Holmes, Jr.* With a new introduction by David Burton.

Harold Adams Small, ed., *The Road to Richmond: The Civil War Letters of Major Abner R. Small of the 16th Maine Volunteers.* With a new introduction by Earl J. Hess.

Eric A. Campbell, ed., *"A Grand Terrible Dramma": From Gettysburg to Petersburg: The Civil War Letters of Charles Wellington Reed.* Illustrated by Reed's Civil War sketches.

Herbert Mitgang, ed., *Abraham Lincoln: A Press Portrait.*

Harold Holzer, ed., *Prang's Civil War Pictures: The Complete Battle Chromos of Louis Prang.*

Harold Holzer, ed., *State of the Union: New York and the Civil War.*

Paul A. Cimbala and Randall M. Miller, eds., *Union Soldiers and the Northern Home Front: Wartime Experiences, Postwar Adjustments.*

Mark A. Snell, *From First to Last: The Life of Major General William B. Franklin.*

Paul A. Cimbala and Randall M. Miller, eds., *An Uncommon Time: The Civil War and the Northern Home Front.*

John Y. Simon and Harold Holzer, eds., *The Lincoln Forum: Rediscovering Abraham Lincoln.*

Thomas F. Curran, *Soldiers of Peace: Civil War Pacifism and the Postwar Radical Peace Movement.*

Kyle S. Sinisi, *Sacred Debts: State Civil War Claims and American Federalism, 1861–1880.*

Russell L. Johnson, *Warriors into Workers: The Civil War and the Formation of Urban-Industrial Society in a Northern City.*

Peter J. Parish, *The North and the Nation in the Era of the Civil War.* Edited by Adam I. P. Smith and Susan-Mary Grant.

Patricia Richard, *Busy Hands: Images of the Family in the Northern Civil War Effort.*

Michael S. Green, *Freedom, Union, and Power: The Mind of the Republican Party During the Civil War*.

Christian G. Samito, ed., *Fear Was Not In Him: The Civil War Letters of Major General Francis S. Barlow, U.S.A.*

John S. Collier and Bonnie B. Collier, eds., *Yours for the Union: The Civil War Letters of John W. Chase, First Massachusetts Light Artillery*.

Grace Palladino, *Another Civil War: Labor, Capital, and the State in the Anthracite Regions of Pennsylvania, 1840–1868*.

Christian B. Keller, *Chancellorsville and the Germans: Nativism, Ethnicity, and Civil War Memory*.

Sidney George Fisher, *A Philadelphia Perspective: The Civil War Diary of Sidney George Fisher*. Edited and with a new Introduction by Jonathan W. White.

Robert M. Sandow, *Deserter Country: Civil War Opposition in the Pennsylvania Appalachians*.

Craig L. Symonds, ed., *Union Combined Operations in the Civil War*.

Harold Holzer, Craig L. Symonds, and Frank L. Williams, eds., *The Lincoln Assassination: Crime and Punishment, Myth and Memory*. A Lincoln Forum Book.

Earl F. Mulderink III, *New Bedford's Civil War*.

David G. Smith, *On the Edge of Freedom: The Fugitive Slave Issue in South Central Pennsylvania, 1820–1870*.

George Washington Williams, *A History of the Negro Troops in the War of the Rebellion, 1861–1865*. Introduction by John David Smith.

Randall M. Miller, ed., *Lincoln and Leadership: Military, Political, and Religious Decision Making*.

Andrew L. Slap and Michael Thomas Smith, eds., *This Distracted and Anarchical People: New Answers for Old Questions about the Civil War–Era North*.

Paul D. Moreno and Johnathan O'Neill, eds., *Constitutionalism in the Approach and Aftermath of the Civil War.*

Steve Longenecker, *Gettysburg Religion: Refinement, Diversity, and Race in the Antebellum and Civil War Border North.*

Harold Holzer, Craig L. Symonds, and Frank L. Williams, eds., *Exploring Lincoln: Great Historians Reappraise Our Greatest President.* A Lincoln Forum Book.

Lorien Foote and Kanisorn Wongsrichanalai, eds., *So Conceived and So Dedicated: Intellectual Life in the Civil War–Era North.*

William B. Kurtz, *Excommunicated from the Union: How the Civil War Created a Separate Catholic America.*

Kanisorn Wongsrichanalai, *Northern Character: College-Educated New Englanders, Honor, Nationalism, and Leadership in the Civil War Era.*

Ryan W. Keating, *Shades of Green: Irish Regiments, American Soldiers, and Local Communities in the Civil War Era.*

Robert M. Sandow, ed., *Contested Loyalty: Debates over Patriotism in the Civil War North.*

Grant R. Brodrecht, *Our Country: Northern Evangelicals and the Union During the Civil War Era.*

James G. Mendez, *A Great Sacrifice: Northern Black Soldiers, Their Families, and the Experience of Civil War.*

Gary W. Gallagher and Elizabeth R. Varon, eds., *New Perspectives on the Union War.*

www.ingramcontent.com/pod-product-compliance
Lightning Source LLC
Chambersburg PA
CBHW030437300426
44112CB00009B/1045